MUSADDIQ
AND THE STRUGGLE FOR
POWER IN IRAN

MUSADDIQ
AND THE STRUGGLE FOR
POWER IN IRAN

Homa Katouzian

I.B.Tauris & Co Ltd
Publishers
London • New York

Published in 1990 by
I.B.Tauris & Co Ltd
110 Gloucester Avenue
London NW1 8JA

175 Fifth Avenue
New York NY10010

In the United States and Canada distributed by
St Martin's Press
175 Fifth Avenue
New York NY10010

British Library Cataloguing in Publication Data
Katouzian, Homa
    Musaddiq and the struggle for power in Iran.
    1. Iran.   Mossadegh, Mohammad, 1882–1967
    I. Title
    955.05092

    ISBN 1–85043–210–4

Set by Columns Design and Production Services Ltd, Reading
Printed in Great Britain by
Redwood Press Limited, Melksham, Wiltshire

To the memory of my parents
in honour of their morality

Contents

Preface

The Popular Movement of Iran is a long-term socio-economic trend in modern Iranian history which began in the late nineteenth century, and has been developing ever since. This book is both a political biography of Musaddiq and a history of that Movement from the time he became its leader and symbol until the suppression of the Third National Front which almost coincided with his death in 1967.

The list of those to whom acknowledgement is due is embarrassingly long. But it would be dishonest not to acknowledge those who have been most helpful. Mehdi Bazargan, Kazim Hasibi, Ghulamhusain Sadiqi and Karim Sanjaby – who themselves have played important roles in the Popular Movement – replied to my enquiries in an open and generous spirit. So did Jalil Buzurgmehr, Ghulamreza Nijati and Ghulamreza Musavvar-Rahmani who, in their time, sacrificed a good deal of their private interests for the defence and promotion of the Movement. Abbas Amanat, Fakhr al-Din Azimi, Frances Bostock, Abdollah Borhan, Houshang Chehabi, Houshang Kishavarz Sadr and Habib Ladjevardi put useful source materials and research papers at my disposal. Houshang and Sherie Sayyahpour, and Manuchehr and Shirin Rassa gave me peace and comfort at their homes when routine pressures in Oxford were threatening to halt progress for an indefinite period.

My debt to Amir Pichdad cannot be acknowledged here in full. He supplied me with many important and inaccessible sources, including unpublished letters and documents. John Gurney played his usual role of the meticulous critic, by reading the whole of the manuscript and suggesting useful improvements. An anonymous donor made a generous contribution towards the typing and photocopying costs, and Greta Ilott typed and prepared the material with efficiency and good humour. They all share in the credit, if any, but none in the blame.

Like everyone else, I, too, have personal and social values. One of these is never to suppress or bend the truth for reasons of fear, favour, expediency, personal prejudice or private profit. Others include freedom, democracy, social justice and economic development for Iran.

H.K.
Oxford
September 1989

1

From Mirza Mohammad to Dr Musaddiq al-Saltaneh (1882–1914)

Early days

In 1897, a chronicler who thought Musaddiq was then aged twenty-five wrote:

> Mirza Mohammad Khan Musaddiq al-Saltaneh is at present — insofar as employment is concerned — the chief tax officer and auditor of Khurasan. But the class, the family relations, the talent, the intelligence, and the expertise of this newborn babe who treads a hundred-year path are greater even than the chief tax officer of all the provinces and districts. Any able and worthy person with some expertise in fiscal matters can make a tax officer and provincial auditor. But he has other qualities which add to his greatness ... Such an impressive young man is bound to become one of the great ones.[1]

This was written a year after Musaddiq had become the *mustawfi* (chief tax officer) of Khurasan at the age of fourteen.

Musaddiq was born in 1882 into a wealthy and influential *divani*[2] family. His father was Mirza Hedayatullah Vazir Daftar, cousin of Mirza Yusif Mustawfi al-Mamalik, at one time *Sadr-i A'azam* (chief minister) of Iran. Vazir Daftar was a direct descendant of Aqa Muhsin Ashtiyani, founder of the Ashtiyani 'clan', which throughout the nineteenth and twentieth centuries produced men of exceptional talent in politics, public administration and scholarship.[3]

Musaddiq's mother was Malik-Taj Khanum, Najm al-Saltaneh, great grand-daughter on her father's side of Fath'ali Shah, sister of

Abdulhusain Mirza Farmanfarma, and cousin of Nasir al-Din Shah, the reigning Qajar monarch at the time of Musaddiq's birth and youth. Her brother Farmanfarma – the founder of the Farmanfarm'iyan and Firuz families – was a rich and powerful politician in his own right, both before and after the Constitutional Revolution of 1905. Decades later, Musaddiq was to recall his childhood playmate, Salar al-Saltaneh, Nasir al-Din Shah's son, in an attack in a Majlis debate on Sadr al-Ashraf, Salar's erstwhile private tutor who was prime minister at the time.[4]

He always remembered his father, who died when he was ten, with affection as well as respect.[5] But his mother's influence on him was deep and lasting. She was a woman of strong will as well as exceptional public spirit, and Musaddiq frequently used to quote from her wisdom – even in public debates and speeches. Indeed, her advice to him in a moment of despair, in 1914, at an unjust public rumour about him – 'The weight of individuals in society is determined by the amount of hardship they endure for the sake of the people' – became his life-long guide in adversity.[6] Until her death in 1933, she was behind all his major decisions both public and private. She married twice more after the death of Vazir Daftar,[7] and had other famous children.

At the age of nineteen, Musaddiq married Zia al-Saltaneh, daughter of Sayyed Zain al-Abidin, sister of Sayyed Abulqasim and Sayyed Mohammad, and aunt of Sayyed Hasan (Dr Imami), all of them *Imam Jum'eh* (semi-official chief religious dignataries) of Tehran from the late nineteenth century until 1979. She was a beautiful and graceful woman, and an extremely loyal wife. At the time of her death, less than two years before his own, Musaddiq was to cherish her memory as the most influential person in his life after his mother, and the loyal companion who had 'put up with everything I did' (see chapter 17). The couple were blessed with five children, Zia Ashraf, Ahmad (now deceased), Dr Gholam-Hossein, Mansureh (now deceased) and Khadijeh (the youngest daughter, who has lived in various Swiss psychiatric hospitals since the age of twenty).

It was after his father's death that Nasir al-Din Shah gave Mirza Mohammad the title of Musaddiq al-Saltaneh, and shortly after the shah's assassination in 1896 he was made the *mustawfi* of Khurasan.[8] Little is known about his time as a senior civil servant in that province, except the account quoted from Afzal al-Mulk above and Mohammad Reza Shah's allegation in 1960 that Musaddiq had nearly had his hand cut off on a charge of misappropriation of public property[9] – an allegation for which there is no evidence.

Musaddiq grew up during a time when there was growing hostility, first among the educated administrative elite, and later among a much wider political public, against Nasir al-Din Shah's policy of granting trade concessions to European powers, and it is against this background that his later political programme can be fully understood. He was still a child when the Tobacco-Régie movement (1890–1) led to the first major retreat on the part of the Qajar system of absolute and arbitrary power (*istibdad*) in the context of a public struggle against a foreign trade concession. He was always opposed to *any* foreign concession (of the type granted in the nineteenth century) to *any* foreign power – whether in the case of shipping rights in Lake Urmiyyeh (see chapter 2), the proposed concession of North Iran's oil to the Soviet Union (see chapter 5), the 1933 oil concession to the Anglo-Iranian Oil Company (see chapter 7), or the concession of Caspian fishing rights to a Russian company (see chapter 10).

The frustrated deputy

The Tobacco-Régie protest against the grant of a tobacco monopoly to a foreign company became a rallying point for all the actual and potential forces opposed to the traditional arbitrary government and to the growing threat of the country's domination by European powers. Its success was an achievement without precedent in Iran's history. There had been palace murders, assassinations and coups; there had also been violent change through tribal and military revolts. But this was the first time that an organized (and orderly) *popular* movement had succeeded in defeating the arbitrary state on a major issue.

The movement's success cleared the way for more generalized campaigns for the abolition of arbitrary rule and the establishment of a legal constitutional government, which were the beginning of the Popular Movement of Iran. It took almost two decades for the Movement to articulate its aims into a clear demand for modern democratic government along West European lines, but it was clear from the start that it was opposed to arbitrary rule (*istibdad*, or *hukumat-i zur*), and in favour of a system based on the 'rule of law' (*hukumat-i qanun*) (see chapter 18). Nasir al-Din Shah's assassination in 1896 – by a disciple of Sayyed Jamal al-Din Asad-Abadi (Afghani) – was one of the more drastic actions during the period between the Tobacco-Régie protest and the Constitutional Revolution. In 1905, the campaign for the establishment of a Court of Justice was publicly launched in reaction to the arbitrary flogging of a much-respected sugar merchant accused of speculative activities. The ranks began to close between the pro-*istibdad* and pro-rule of law leaders of urban society. The state's attempt to break up the students' *bast* ('sit-in') in Masjid-i Jum'eh, in the Tehran bazaar, led to bloodshed. As is usual in Iranian popular campaigns, the movement now had both a slogan and a 'martyr'. The body of the dead student – a certain Sayyed Abdulhamid – was immediately carried round the bazaar, with the marchers chanting:

> Once again, Husain was martyred by Yazid,
> Abdulhamid was killed by Abdulmajid.[10]

Some of Musaddiq's close relatives – notably, his uncle, Farmanfarma, and his brother-in-law, Sayyed Abulqasim Imam Jum'eh – were among the movement's leaders, though the latter quickly defected to the other side after a private deal with Ain al-Dawleh, the chief minister.[11]

Upon Muzaffar al-Din Shah's consent to constitutional government in 1905, an assembly of popular leaders drafted the procedure for elections to a National Consultative Assembly, the First Majlis. This procedure (which was to be changed into universal male suffrage from the Second Majlis onwards) was based on 'class' lines.[12] Musaddiq was returned for the 'class' of *A'yan va Ashraf* – i.e. notables and higher *divanis* – but was unable to take his seat because he did not meet the minimum age qualification (of thirty) for becoming a Majlis deputy.

By this time he had become a member of a progressive society, *Adamiyyat*, which apparently had Freemasonry connections. The Freemasonry movement had made some Iranian contacts around the mid-nineteenth century,[13] and became an effective channel for the transfer of European social and political values in the latter half of the century. The Freemasons' attitude towards the Persian revolution resembled their stand in the French Revolution a century before: many leading radical revolutionaries were affiliates. For example, Sayyed Jamal al-Din Asad-Abadi (Afghani) had been a leading Freemason in his time, and Sayyed Hasan Taqizadeh was a Freemason during the revolution and afterwards. But, for both genuine and trumped-up reasons, Freemasonry became a dirty word in Iranian politics from the 1940s onwards, and Musaddiq's detractors, on discovering his membership of the Adamiyyat Society a year after his death (in 1967), were quick to pounce on this as evidence that he had been a British agent all along.[14] In any event, he remained in that society only for a couple of weeks, and later joined the *Insaniyyat* society, of which Ali-Akbar

Dehkhuda ('Dakhaw', the famous satirical columnist of the *Sur-i Israfil* newspaper, later to become a renowned scholar) was also an active member.[15] This society was a radical revolutionary organization, with thirty voluntary musketeers to its credit. But the young Constitutionalist was soon to be disillusioned in his association with them.[16]

The movement for constitutional government neither stopped all bad habits overnight nor wiped out traditional political methods and relations in the short run. The nobility, the *ulama* (senior religious authorities) and the merchants kept up their usual political and financial contacts and interests. For example, Sayyed Abdullah Bihbahani – who, together with his more learned rival, Shaikh Fazlullah Nuri, were the most important *ulama* of Tehran – spent much time improving his financial position. And Sayyed Mohammad Tabataba'i's son, Sayyed Mohammad Sadiq (later Chairman of the Iranian Senate), used his enhanced political power to provide favours in return for money.[17]

Musaddiq was also busy on behalf of his uncle, Farmanfarma, who was governor-general of Azerbaijan during the First Majlis and had been one of his close mentors after his father's death. Letters in Musaddiq's own hand, as well as those from another correspondent, from Tehran to Tabriz are principally concerned with politics, or rather, politicking.[18] They show that Farmanfarma wanted to return to Tehran to a higher post – the war ministry at least – and that his two correspondents in Tehran were trying to gauge the mood of the Majlis, the shah, the chief minister, the court minister, and the minister of the interior, and advise him on his choice of tactics. The shah was not happy with Farmanfarma, they wrote, because of his moderately pro-Constitutionalist stance in Azerbaijan. The Majlis deputies for that province, on the other hand, (Taqizadeh, Mustashar al-Dawleh and Haj Mirza Ibrahim Aqa) thought him too moderate. The interior minister, Nizam al-Saltaneh, was also not enthusiastic about Farmanfarma, because of the shah's displeasure with him, in addition to their personal rivalry. Musaddiq's emphatic advice – though given in the most respectful terms – was that his uncle should hold on to his governorship in Azerbaijan, and await his turn with patience and dignity. In one of the letters in his own hand he wrote:

> But if your highness definitely resigned, then the very first people who would prepare the ground for your return to [a higher post in] Tehran would be those who at present oppose the idea. Therefore, now that your blessed person is so much in demand, you should act in such a way as to make them bring your

highness in[-to the cabinet] by going down on their knees. Not [as at present] resigning once a month, and each time deciding to remain in Azerbaijan once again. For the deputies would then say that his [sole] intention is to become minister of war: he occasionally resigns [his governorship], but when he realizes there is no other post for him, he is left with no choice but to stick to the same post in Azerbaijan.

If, however, Farmanfarma was genuinely unhappy about the state of affairs in Azerbaijan, he should definitely resign his post, go to Tehran and stay there for a couple of months, out of office, until (Musaddiq was sure) everyone concerned, including the shah himself, installed him in a new post 'with pomp and dignity'.

The theme comes up fairly regularly in all the letters and everywhere Musaddiq's advice was the same. In another letter written by himself, he quoted the interior minister as telling him that not all the deputies and ministers were in favour of Farmanfarma, and added in brackets: 'friend, you speak with our tongue'. Apart from its historical interest, the correspondence shows Musaddiq's concern (even in the case of his uncle) for dignified behaviour vis-à-vis high political office, the kind of freedom and self-assurance with which he was to regard worldly prestige and power throughout his political career.

The first doctor of law

In March 1909, less than a year after Mohammad Ali Shah's anti-Constitutionalist coup, Musaddiq decided to continue his studies in France. Throughout his life he was prepared to risk everything he had in politics if he thought it was of any use, and to beat a complete retreat if he regarded the situation as hopeless. Knowing his Constitutionalist connections, the shah had once asked for his help to bring Bihbahani over to his side. He answered plainly – and this, too, was an enduring characteristic – that Bihbahani's influence came from the fact that he was selling a product called Constitutionalism. If the shah himself did the same he would have no need of Bihbahani's support. 'It is clear that you, too, are hot-headed', the shah had replied, although Bihbahani later agreed that Musaddiq's analysis had been correct.[19] When he decided to go to France therefore he was seriously concerned that he might be refused a passport, but things worked out all right in the end.[20]

In Paris, he registered for a course in public finance. The

psychological pressures facing a young married Iranian, with a classical Persian education, an important state office, and involvement in a revolutionary campaign, mixing in a completely alien culture with appreciably younger students in the same classroom must be left to the imagination. But he was keen – perhaps too keen – to succeed, and this may have contributed to the onset of a nervous disease which he himself was always reluctant to mention in public by its real name.[21] The tendency towards the illness must have existed already (it might even have been, at least partly, genetic), for it would not otherwise have reappeared in a severe form at difficult times throughout the rest of his life,[22] resulting in fits and breakdowns in public on a few occasions. These incidents were unfairly used against him – when he was prime minister, and afterwards – by his Iranian and foreign detractors. In any event the illness caused him to give up his studies and rest in the care of a French nurse.

He returned to Iran in the hope of a full recovery. Meanwhile the Constitutionalists had defeated Mohammad Ali Shah's *coup d'état* by capturing Tehran and driving him into exile, and this must have made it easier (at least psychologically) for Musaddiq to stay at home. He returned to Europe once he had regained his health and strength, this time to Switzerland and in the company of his mother, his wife and their three children. His mother was suffering from cataract, which was her reason for making a difficult journey to a strange land: she insisted on maintaining the *hijab*, and sartorial techniques had to be devised to meet the obligation without her actually wearing the usual veil. His wife, on the other hand, had no such inhibitions and removed the veil while in Europe.[23]

Having put the children into school in Neuchâtel, Musaddiq returned to Paris to pursue his old public finance course, but soon gave up the idea and became a law student in Neuchâtel. After obtaining his *licence*, he spent some time in a law firm while working on a doctoral dissertation on the law of last will and testament in Islam. He was about to apply for Swiss citizenship – for which he then qualified – in order to practise in Switzerland, when he decided to seek supervision for his thesis from expert Islamic jurisprudents in Iran – especially Shaikh Mohammad Ali Kashani, 'my master'.[24] He succeeded in obtaining his doctorate and, leaving his two oldest children at school in Neuchâtel, he returned to Tehran on the eve of the First World War. He was now called Dr Mohammad Khan Musaddiq al-Saltaneh, a form he retained until the Qajar titles were abolished and he became universally known as Dr Mohammad Musaddiq.

2

Academic, administrator
and politician

The School of Law and Political Science

Musaddiq was obviously proud of his new (and, at the time, unique) title and status, which gave him an important advantage over his peers. However, these were difficult times for Iran. The country had declared itself neutral on the outbreak of war but was virtually under Russo-British domination, while the nationalists and radicals of all political shades were pro-German. Germany was extremely popular throughout the Middle East at the time, largely because, unlike Britain and Russia, it was not an imperial power in that part of the world. The fact that the Germans were allied to the (Muslim) Ottoman Turks, and that they achieved a few dashing victories, was an added attraction. German agents – chief among them the romanticized figure of Wassmuss – were busy organizing Iranian nationalists, especially in the western, central and southern provinces of the country. Even poets wrote romantic descriptions of German victories and praised the Kaiser, much in the style of the eleventh-century poems in praise of Mahmud of Ghazneh and his conquests. The Kaiser was honoured with the title of Defender of Muslims (*Islam-panah*), and rumours were rife that he had converted to Islam.[1]

There was considerable pressure for Iran's formal entry into the war on the side of the Central Powers. The conservatives – such as Vusuq al-Dawleh, a distant relative of Musaddiq – were opposed to the idea. The popular democrats – best represented by Mirza Hasan Mustawfi al-Mamalik, Musaddiq's second cousin – were sympathetic, but thought it unwise. Certain radical nationalists and democrats – led by Nizam al-Saltaneh, Mirza Mohammad Ali Khan (later, Farzin), Sulaiman Mirza (later, Iskandari), and Sayyed Hasan Mudarris –

ultimately lost patience and set up a rival ('provisional') government in the west, linking up with the Turkish troops who, following the Russians and the British, had violated the country's formal neutrality. They were known as the *muhjarin* ('migrants') on account of their move from Tehran to Kirmanshah which became the capital of their provisional government.

At the same time, a considerable number of prominent radical nationalists and democrats, including Sayyed Mohammad Reza Musavat, Mirza Mohammad Khan Qazvini, Kazimzadeh Iranshahr, Sayyed Mohammad Ali Jamalzadeh, and other noted writers and intellectuals, gathered around Sayyed Hasan Taqizadeh (the most influential of the younger intellectuals of the Constitutional Revolution), and set up the *Kumite-yi Melliyun*, a kind of democratic national liberation committee, in Berlin. They published an anti-Allies (but especially anti-Russian) newspaper, *Kaveh*, which became the provisional government's mouthpiece in Europe, and supplied it with advice as well as manpower when they could.[2] The provisional government collapsed shortly after the fall of Mesopotamia to British troops.

Musaddiq made no such moves, but later joined the radical (*zidd-itashkili*) wing of the Democratic Party, many of whose leaders, notably Sulaiman Mirza, were in the provisional government. In the meantime, he eagerly accepted Mohammad Ali (Zuka' al-Mulk) Furughi's invitation to join the academic staff of the School of Law and Political Science. The School had been founded with the principal aim of training modern diplomatic staff for the foreign ministry, but since the constitutional revolution had been turned into a full-scale academic institution. Musaddiq himself has recalled his joy at being invited to teach at a school where he had always wanted to be a student in his youth.[3] He went to work with a zeal rare even among beginners, spending hours, days and months preparing his lecture notes. At the same time, he began to write and publish on law and politics.

In 1914 he published an article on the uses of statutory limitations in certain litigation and a short book on the principle of 'capitulation agreements', or the right of foreign residents in Iran to be tried by their own courts. The idea of the article 'Invalidation of Litigation' was based on European judicial procedures, though this is nowhere mentioned. It put forward many reasons why such a practice of limitation would be in the interest of all parties and argued that it would be consistent with both the spirit and the letter of Islamic jurisprudence.[4] The article was well written and presented, and the material was original for Iran at the time.

But his *Kapitulasion va Iran* (Iran and the Capitulation Agreements) – which he published at his own expense and distributed gratis in 1914 – is, in many ways, of quite a different order. The argument is mostly in legal language, but its political purpose and implications are perhaps even more evident because of their relative subtlety. For instance, chapter 1 contains the usual (European) classification of national law into public and private law. Public law 'governs the relationship between the state and the citizen', and is divided into two categories: *Droit Politique*, and *Droit Pénale*, themselves categorized as *Droit Constitutionelle*, *Publique*, and *Administrative*, and *Droit Pénale* and *Principes des Procès Penales*.[5] To illustrate the use of these classifications, Musaddiq gives two examples, the first of which combines daring with some subtlety. According to article 15 of the Iranian constitution. 'no proprietor can be deprived of his property except by *Shari'a* Law . . .' Would this mean that if the state deemed the compulsory purchase of a property to be in the public interest it should seek a *fatva* (religious edict) from the *shari'a* courts, he asks. 'No,' he answers: there should be a law *not inconsistent with the shari'a*, which would be generally applicable without the need to refer to *Shari'a* courts in each and every case.[6] The example was not randomly chosen, and it provides the background for his argument in favour of the abolition of the nineteenth-century capitulation agreements, which were justified at the time on the ground that European Christians should not be subject to the Islamic penal code which was the source of *Shari'a* court rulings. A modern penal code could therefore on the grounds of this agreement be created for criminal cases involving European offenders in Iran, thus removing the apparent basis for the continuation of the capitulation agreement. As we shall see further below, this was precisely how Musaddiq proposed to solve the problem when (in 1923) he became foreign minister.

Chapters 2 and 3 discuss in some detail the history, meaning and implications of such agreements between the Ottoman Empire and Iran, on the one hand, and the European powers – mainly Britain, France and Russia – on the other, and in particular the importance of precedent. Not all precedents are sacred Musaddiq argued and cited that in fact Turkey had abolished its own capitulation agreements.

Chapter 4, *Reform*, contains Musaddiq's main argument: that it is an affront to a people as well as to their religion for foreign residents in their country to be immune from their laws; on the other hand, the abolition of the agreements would require a reform of the existing laws (so that the European powers would agree to their citizens being subjected to Iranian law). This is an argument not against but for

Islam, because non-Muslims would not have extra-territorial rights in Muslim countries 'of which only two [Iran and Turkey] still barely survive' and because the *Shari'a* is flexible and adjustable in cases where fundamental principles are involved. The chapter includes many references to legal reforms carried out by other traditional states, ranging from Turkey and Tunisia to Japan and Bulgaria, and a couple of European names are cited, including that of Edmund Burke.[7]

The last chapter of Musaddiq's book concludes the argument. 'Islam is in danger and is getting weaker day by day. If we had respected the Islamic rules, and observed the true intentions of the Law-giver, Islamic countries would not have been in their present state, subjugated as they are by Christian powers.' Insistence on non-basic rules is forbidden (*haram*) in Islam: 'necessities remove impediments'.[8] Therefore, both public and private law must be reformed to suit the needs of the times, and thereby bring about the abolition of the capitulation agreements.[9]

In terms of methodology, and style of presentation, this small book was almost unique for its time. The author was well aware of the provocative nature of his argument, and in several places displayed modesty in phrases such as 'We stated what we believe to be useful, but do not claim that they are [necessarily] right'.[10] However, the closing paragraph sums up his position in a nutshell. In presenting this argument, he says, we face two sets of opponents (though he uses the more diplomatic term 'rivals'):

the internal rivals [i.e. the *ulama*] might regard these views as being in the interest of European countries, thinking that, as we have studied in Europe, we must wish to import their laws into our own country as well; the external rivals [i.e. the European powers] would regard our views as being good for the independence as well as the survival of Iran and Islam. Hence, we are caught in between these two rivals, and would beg our compatriots to study and discuss our views fairly and dispassionately.

With hindsight, the book's significance lies in showing the early formation of Musaddiq's views on an Iranian approach to social progress and modernization: his belief in the creation of a synthesis between Iranian and European ideas, values and techniques – much as has since been achieved in Japan – such that the country would neither remain backward nor lose what it had even if it achieved no lasting gain from pure aping and emulation. This vision was to remain with him for the rest of his life, and to turn him into an outsider among the pseudo-modernists of Right and Left, as well as the reactionary diehards. It came up time and again, now against this and now against that tendency throughout his life (see chapter 3).

In October 1915, during the premiership of Mustawfi al-Mamalik, Musaddiq was elected to the five-man Committee for the Co-ordination of Budgetary Allocations in the Ministry of Finance, when Vusuq al-Dawleh was Minister of Finance. The Committee members were chosen by the Majlis, their task being to check and assess the expenditure allocations made to various government departments, and, in particular, to make sure that the allocations were paid from existing Treasury funds so that the overall budget balanced at the end of the year – a predictably difficult task in a country suffering from chronic shortages of funds. While he was there, his uncle Farmanfarma became prime minister, and tried without success to persuade him directly (as well as through his sister, Musaddiq's mother) to accept the finance portfolio. Musaddiq refused. He felt he could not serve in a cabinet led by a kinsman, but his uncle misinterpreted his motives and broke off relations with him until the fall of his cabinet.

How not to catch thieves

Musaddiq was still a member of the Co-ordination Committee when he was operated on for appendicitis in 1917, in a Baku hospital.[11] While convalescing in Tiflis he was urgently summoned to Tehran to become Qavam al-Saltaneh's deputy at the ministry of finance, in the cabinet of Vusuq, Qavam's brother. He accepted the post under pressure from his mother as well as Qavam who was a paternal relation and a one-time friend. He found Qavam lazy, pleasure-seeking, and inattentive towards his duties.

The hardest lesson he learned as deputy minister of finance was in his attempt to 'catch thieves' in the department. By chance he discovered a network of swindlers among the ministry's senior civil servants, and managed to persuade a reluctant Mustawfi, now again prime minister, to let him proceed with a formal inquiry. The matter dragged on for months, and various unscrupulous methods – including 'excommunication' – were used to dissuade him from his relentless pursuit of the wrongdoers.[12] He refused to budge, and finally managed to have two directors and two departmental heads convicted by a government commission of inquiry. But he did not manage to get away with it unscathed: the defendants brought a charge of administrative misconduct on a procedural point and he ended up with a fine. When a member of the commission was asked why Musaddiq himself had also been fined he answered: 'because he managed to catch thieves'.[13] The story has further significance for the historian, however: it is the first important public evidence of the stubbornness with which Musaddiq stuck to matters of principle. He eventually lost his post over the issue.

Emigré-cum-Governor

By now it was 1919. The country was in greater chaos than ever before; the Majlis was in a long recess; the shah was forced to dismiss Samsam al-Saltaneh's cabinet by unconstitutional means; and Vusuq formed a new government, bringing in martial law against his opponents. It was believed, at least with hindsight, that the whole process had been engineered by the British government via their legation in Tehran. Musaddiq was put forward to head the department of tax assessment, but he did not wish to co-operate with Vusuq's new cabinet, and had to apologise to the shah himself for his refusal, explaining that he was missing his son and daughter at school in Switzerland.

He had not been back in Neuchâtel long when the Agreement of 9 August 1919 was concluded between Vusuq and the British government. Its most important provisions handed over the direct supervision of both the Iranian army and the Iranian financial system to British advisers. This event – which almost every enlightened radical politician described as 'the agreement for turning Iran into a protectorate' (to use Musaddiq's own words) – threw him into a state of frenzy. He talked and corresponded with other prominent Iranians in Europe, published leaflets, and wrote to the League of Nations protesting against the agreement. He even travelled to Berne for the sole purpose of having a rubber stamp made for the *Comité de Résistance des Nations* in whose name the anti-agreement statements were issued. Anger, frustration and loneliness must have taken their toll on his nerves, for it is unlikely that, as he suspected, he was being watched by British agents – one of them in the shape of the '*chic*, pretty and bouncy' woman next door who called from her balcony, 'Est-ce que vous voulez fumer ce soir?' and was disappointed when Musaddiq answered, 'Pardon, madame. Je suis malade. Je suis très occupé. Je suis fatigué. Excusez-moi. Je n'ai pas le temps.'[14]

Anger gradually gave way to depression when Musaddiq saw his country as being lost for good, and he decided to become a Swiss citizen and practise law in that country for the rest of his life. This is another example of two dialectical forces – at once opposite and united – in his nature: to fight fearlessly and with boundless energy when he thought there was still hope; and to go through an equally forceful reversal of mood, beating a full retreat, when he felt that all was lost. It was to happen again several times at critical points in his career.

He was not destined to become a Swiss lawyer, however. He had already toyed with the idea of acquiring Swiss citizenship in 1914; but that was solely to obtain a licence to practise in that country, and he did not pursue the matter further. Now that he was serious, Swiss immigration laws had been greatly tightened in view of the large inflow of war refugees and Musaddiq no longer qualified for quick naturalization. He therefore decided to become a permanent resident in Switzerland and set up an import-export business. The new plan made it necessary for him to return to Iran to wind up his financial and other affairs. He travelled as far as the Caucasus but had to return to Europe because civil war in Russia had closed that route. He then applied for a transit visa for India to the British embassies in Switzerland and Italy, to be able to travel from Marseilles to Bombay, and thence to Iran. But his applications were turned down.

In the meantime, a massive campaign in Tehran against Vusuq's government had led to its fall, and Mushir al-Dawleh (a politician of a similar mould to Musaddiq) had formed a new cabinet, naming Musaddiq as minister of justice. He himself has said in several places that he accepted the post only because it would enable him to obtain the visa for India, implying that he was still determined to emigrate. Even if this was so at first, a few days' reflection must have modified his plans. True, the 1919 Agreement was still standing (or, rather, sagging), but the danger of the country becoming a 'British protectorate' had largely abated; the figure of Mushir at the helm was living proof of this. At any rate, on his way through Paris he promised Furughi to keep him as President of the Supreme Court.

Sailing from Marseilles, together with his children, Musaddiq came face to face with Sir Percy Cox – the architect of the dreaded Agreement – on the same boat. Their exchanges were cordial, and Cox was kind enough to enquire at Aden and discover that Musaddiq could not return to Iran via the Baghdad-Basra railway because it had been cut. But a tacit hint by Cox that he did not regard Bushire as an Iranian port stuck in the Iranian patriot's memory at least until the mid-1950s when he was writing his early memoirs in jail.[15]

The new minister of justice who had yet to attend a cabinet meeting bought a motor car and hired a chauffeur in Bombay, and sailed to

Bushire. After spending a few days in Bushire, he drove straight through Kazirun to Shiraz. As it happened, his uncle Farmanfarma had recently relinquished the governorship of the Fars province, and the post was still vacant. The provincial magnates united, as they seldom did, to keep Musaddiq in Shiraz as the new governor. They contacted the prime minister and obtained his agreement to the exchange of Musaddiq's portfolio for the governorship of Fars (which, at the time, was in fact a more important post) if Musaddiq was himself agreeable.

They then offered Musaddiq an extra 68,000 tumans a year from their own pockets to entice him to stay. He turned down their financial inducement and said that if, instead, they agreed to co-operate with the government and – especially – not to start local feuds or behave unjustly towards ordinary people, there would be no need for extra money. He even reduced the annual provincial budget of 72,000 tumans to 24,000 (i.e. to one-third of the central government allocation) and returned the rest to the state coffers. He himself drew no salary, perks or privileges other than the expenses of official entertainments.[16]

The local magnates were far from altruistic in their action. They wanted Musaddiq because they knew he would save them a lot of money in bribes, *pishkish* payments, etc., even if he accepted their collective offer of 68,000 tumans per annum, and that he would protect their persons and property against outside powers, including the state. During and after his premiership, allegations were made that 'the British' had been behind Musaddiq's appointment to Fars. He himself accepted the theory (for there was no evidence for it) on the ground that the British would always prefer to work with honest and efficient people whenever possible.[17] It is more likely that the British consulate in Shiraz, and the autonomous British gendarmerie in the province – the South Persian Rifles (SPR) – simply had no objection to his appointment.

As Governor Musaddiq handled his official duties with care, caution and subtlety. As a matter of official policy (as well as personal sentiment) he could not and did not recognize the SPR.[18] But he established a good working relationship with them, and was especially respected by Colonel Fraser. With Major Meade, the Irish patriot and British consul, however, he struck up a deep bond of friendship. It is not difficult to see why. His honesty and efficiency as well as his blend of high Iranian and European learning were unusual among Iranian politicians at the time, and these qualities must have impressed the British officers in the province on both moral and practical grounds.

For instance, towards the end of his governorship a local landowner complained to him that the SPR intended to use his farm as a temporary racecourse, and refused Musaddiq's solution (which was accepted by the SPR) that full compensation should be paid for any damage. As it happened, he was himself awaiting the acceptance of his resignation in Tehran, and wondered what more a caretaker governor could do in the circumstances. But he found the solution when Fraser invited him to watch the race, and he wrote back saying he could not accept the invitation when the race was being held without the proprietor's consent. The colonel immediately offered his apologies, saying that he had been 'taught a lesson', and the matter was settled to everyone's satisfaction.[19]

The 1921 coup and after

This event happened in March 1921, a few weeks after the *coup d'état* of February, led by Sayyed Zia and Reza Khan. The riddle of who organized the 1921 coup has not yet been completely solved. There can be no doubt about the involvement of British army officers – Smyth and Ironside in particular – in arranging its execution. It is also tempting to regard the coup as the price for Curzon's failure over the 1919 Agreement, especially now that Kolchak and Denikin had lost the Russian Civil War to Lenin and Trotsky. But there is no evidence of this in the existing British records. On the other hand, there is sufficient Iranian evidence that Smart and Havard at the British legation in Tehran were involved in organizing the coup, although Norman, the British minister and head of the legation, has not been named in this connection. This is confirmed by a letter from General Dickson of the British Mission to a member of the American legation in Tehran (dated 6 June 1921). He writes that Colonel Smyth had 'admitted' to him that he had been the organizer of the coup on the military side: 'He also told me that he had done it with the knowledge of the British legation in Tehran. He did not say that Mr Norman had had a hand in it but admitted that Smart had. I am rather inclined to think that Smart, Haig and Co. ran the business without letting Norman in on the secret.'[20] One wonders if Curzon himself had been kept completely in the dark on the matter, both in view of the collapse of his earlier 'Persian policy', and given the fact that he no longer had any confidence in Norman. The coup was led by Brigadier Reza Khan at the head of his *qazzaq* ('Cossack') troops in a march from Qazvin to Tehran. The day before the march on Tehran, Sayyed Zia had paid 2,000 tumans to Reza Khan, and distributed 20,000 among his 2,000 men. No Iranian could have raised such a substantial amount of cash over a short period of time.[21]

Son of Sayyed Ali Aqa Yazdi – an anti-constitutionalist preacher turned constitutionalist at the right moment – Sayyed Zia was a thirty-year-old journalist who had previously received some of the £130,000 paid by the British to Vusuq al-Dawleh and his close associates, Nusrat al-Dawleh and Sarim al-Dawleh to 'facilitate' the passage of the 1919 Agreement, and who had zealously defended it in his newspaper, *Ra'd*. He was personally in contact with both Smart and Havard, and had been openly talking to others about the coup, weeks before it happened. They included poet-laureate Bahar, Sardar Mu'azzam-i Khurasani (later known as Abdulhusain Taimur-Tash), as well as important members of the establishment ranging from General Abdullah Khan Amir-Tahmasibi (commander of the royal guards) to Sepahdar-i Rashti, the prime minister who resigned the day before the coup to make way for the goodwill mission from Qazvin.[22]

Sayyed Zia's young comrades-in-arms were Major Mas'ud Khan (Kayhan) and Captain Kazim Khan (Sayyah), the young gendarmeric officers who travelled up to Qazvin to join the march on Tehran. Apart from Colonel Smyth, General Ironside had also been directly involved in organizing Reza Khan's cossacks for the move on Tehran. On 12 February, he had personally told Reza Khan that the British expeditionary force 'would not oppose any effort by him to seize power provided that the Shah was not deposed'.[23] The cossacks and the gendarmerie were the two main (and rival) military forces at the time. The gendarmerie was dominant in Tehran itself, and had it agreed to become involved in the coup, there would have been no need for 2,000 cossacks to be brought from Qazvin to Tehran. Indeed, the gendarmes were not even issued with bullets to put up a resistance against Reza Khan's men, although they themselves as well as the government knew that an attack was imminent.

There are conflicting reports about the reaction of the shah and the establishment to the events, just before the coup took place. The shah is said to have authorized the march of 500 men from Qazvin, whereas it is certain that he sent three envoys later on to Karaj to talk the *putschists* out of their plan. He might at first have been advised to go along with the idea, then got cold feet at the news of the size of the force coming to Tehran, and finally submitted, after the failure of the mission to Karaj. In any event, the official lack of resistance would have been unlikely, had it not been believed that the British were behind the coup.

The public statements put out by Sayyed Zia and Reza Khan were unprecedented – in the history of Iranian government – in the nationalism of their tone and content. This, together with the internment of the establishment figures, was sufficient for nationalist intellectuals to forgive and forget Sayyed Zia's campaign in favour of the 1919 Agreement, especially as he himself declared its abrogation within a short period. The fact that there was no British protest against this unilateral action is not without significance. Indeed, Norman who – in his official despatches – had welcomed the coup, went on praising the new regime, and regretted the Sayyed's fall. This happened almost exactly three months after the coup, when the triumvirate of Sayyed Zia, Mas'ud Khan (who had already lost the war ministry to Reza Khan) and Kazim Khan left Iran for Europe, not to return for 20 years or more.

According to a famous Iranian legend, this, too, had been the work of the British ('*Ingilisha*'). In fact, Sayyed Zia fell because he had not left himself a single friend in influential circles, confident that the support of the British legation in Tehran was all that he needed by way of protection. He was hated both by the shah and the establishment and by constitutionalist and popular politicians. And Reza Khan – now entitled Sardar-Sepah, and in full command of the army – had no reason to defend an opinionated rival who was falling from grace.

Immediately after the coup, many important conservative as well as constitutionalist politicians – including Farmanfarma, his son Nusrat al-Dawleh and Mudarris, a leading religious leader and democratic politician – were put behind bars. Musaddiq first heard of the coup when the shah himself telegraphed the news to him, and asked him to submit to the new government and put out the news officially in the province. He refused. The new prime minister also sent him a cable, carrying overtones of the arrogance which was to become his undoing within three months. Sayyed Zia mentioned that he thought well of Musaddiq and that the new regime needed the help and support of men like him, but he also emphasized in no uncertain terms the fate of 'those who would stand in the way' of the new order. Musaddiq did not reply to his cable and, instead, telegraphed his resignation to the shah which it took the latter three weeks to accept. Orders having been put out for his arrest, he took refuge with a few friends among the Bakhtiyari chieftains until the danger passed.

The coup was popular with nationalists, modernists and radicals, to the point that months after the fall of Sayyed Zia, Abulqasim Arif – the romantic nationalist poet, song-writer and musician – was still yearning for the return of his 'Black Cabinet'.[24] Most of the hated old-school politicians were imprisoned. Qavam, then governor of

Khurasan, who, like Musaddiq, had refused to co-operate with the new regime, was not so lucky as him. He was arrested by the young nationaist gendarmerie chief of the Khurasan province, Colonel Mohammad Taqi Khan Pesyan, and this action lay behind the latter's tragic end when Qavam succeeded to the premiership after the sudden removal of Sayyid Zia.

Qavam then named Musaddiq as his minister of finance, but the latter agreed to serve only when Armitage-Smith (the British financial adviser to the Treasury under the 1919 Agreement, which had now been 'abrogated' by Sayyed Zia) withdrew from his post. Reza Khan, the powerful war minister, personally prevailed on him to accept the position. Musaddiq asked the Majlis to delegate special powers to him for a period of three months for rapid administrative and financial reforms which he would then submit to them for approval or rejection. This the Majlis agreed to with great reluctance.[25] But no sooner had he begun his reforms – and especially his abolition or reduction of old stipends and grants to members of the establishment – than the royal court together with the majority of the Majlis, were up in arms against him. The Prince Regent was particularly angry that Musaddiq had substantially cut both his public stipend and that of the shah (who was absent from the country). Many important persons among his friends and acquaintances would no longer talk to him because of their financial losses resulting from his reforms.[26] Qavam's government eventually gave way on account of Musaddiq's unpopularity as minister of finance. The new prime minister (Mushir al-Dawleh, his friend and a popular politician) then offered him the foreign ministry, but he turned it down on the ground that if he was not good enough for finance he would not be good enough for foreign affairs either.

Having thus been frustrated by another setback, he reacted by deciding to leave the scene completely, for (as we have already seen, and will see again below) it was characteristic of him to want to beat a retreat the minute he felt he was alone or deserted. Indeed, his thoughts returned to his plan of a year before to emigrate to Switzerland. But fate would have it otherwise.

Turmoil in Azerbaijan necessitated the appointment of a good governor and, with the reputation of his governorship of Fars behind him, both Mushir and Reza Khan insisted on posting him there. He agreed, but only after obtaining Reza's word that, as in Fars, the provincial army would be under his own direct command in security matters. The account of his efforts to bring peace and security to the province would take us further afield than we can go here.[27] Two incidents are, however, worth a brief mention. One was his enforcement of Iranian law in the case of a Soviet citizen in Tabriz despite the Soviet consul's protestations, for although the Irano-Soviet Agreement of 1921 had formally abolished the capitulation agreements, they were still in force in practice. The other was the recurrence of his nervous disease – which he himself put down to the bad climate as well as his frailty and frustration – this time manifesting itself by bleeding in the mouth. He had to move to a house in the country, and talk as little as possible for a whole month.[28]

The belief that Reza Khan was going back on his word about the control of the provincial army led to Musaddiq sending in his resignation. Back in the capital, he stood as a candidate for Tehran in the elections for the Fifth Majlis. Meanwhile, Mustawfi's government had fallen through Mudarris's manoeuvres. Mudarris brought down Mustawfi's cabinet at the close of the Fourth Majlis (in 1924) solely because he felt that it was not capable of putting Reza Khan firmly in his place. That is why he compared Qavam (whom he unsuccessfully tried to bring back to office), as a 'sabre' which was indispensable for war, with Mustawfi's 'jewelled sword' which was good only for peacetime.[29] Musaddiq was made foreign Minister in a new cabinet formed by Mushir. He was also elected a Majlis deputy for Tehran, but could not take his seat while he was in the cabinet, on account of the constitutional separation of powers.

As foreign minister, he established good relations with the envoys of 'our northern and southern neighbours', as Russia and Britain were normally described. Indeed, he became a personal friend of the British ambassador, Sir Percy Loraine, and always remembered him with warmth as well as respect in later times. The only major problem with Britain at this time was the legal claim of a British subject to the concession for the shipping monopoly in Lake Urmiyyeh. Musaddiq obtained cabinet approval for financial compensation up to 350,000 tumans, and finally settled for 320,000. He preferred to pay out cash rather than allow the foreign concession to run its course, although there was no financial return to the government from the withdrawal of the concession.

Shumiyatsky, the new Soviet envoy, was unhappy about the fact that Soviet citizens could be tried in Iranian courts, especially against the background of Musaddiq's enforcement of the new Agreement in Tabriz. His argument, according to Musaddiq, made sense: in view of the persistence of the jurisdiction of *shari'a* courts in criminal cases (although a modern system did exist on paper), according to what law would Soviet offenders be punished in Iran? Musaddiq talked to the prime minister who obtained Majlis approval for a bill to introduce a new penal code, and in the hope of forestalling the *ulama*'s opposition to it, he decided to talk to some of them before the event. His first contact was with Haj Aqa Jamal Isfahani – a powerful *Mujtahid* (high-ranking religious leader) in Tehran – who refused to budge even if the new code was applied only in the case of Europeans because, he said, 'it would leak', i.e. Iranians themselves would become subject to it in time. When Musaddiq explained that the absence of such a code could mean the re-establishment of extra-territorial rights for European powers, the divine responded simply by saying 'To hell with it!'[30] The reforming foreign minister then felt that there was no point in contacting other spiritual leaders on the subject.

For quite some time Reza Khan had been being groomed by his military and civilian supporters to take over the government. Meanwhile, a preacher had stated from the pulpit that, with Mushir as premier and Musaddiq as foreign minister, the country lacked any defence against the infidels. Musaddiq got wind that Reza was now impatiently awaiting the inevitable, and made direct inquiries which confirmed his intuition. He therefore advised Mushir to resign before things began to turn sour, and the latter took his friend's advice. On becoming premier, Reza Khan asked Musaddiq to serve in his cabinet, but he refused because – as he himself said – he knew he would have had to quit after a short period.[31] He was soon to find himself in total opposition to the new regime.

3

Opposition and isolation
(1924–41)

The reluctant peace-maker

Musaddiq now took his seat in the Majlis for the first time. This proved to be the position which best suited his temperament as a master debater combining seriousness of purpose with an unusual degree of openness, using a formal and respectful language marked by flashing sparks of a highly individual wit and humour.

These were turbulent times. The Qajars were unpopular. They were blamed for the country's present backwardness, and attacked for the mistakes and follies of former Qajar rulers. The shah was weak and preferred to spend his time in the south of France if only as a means of escaping from his troubles. The Prince Regent was more of a politician, but he was no reformer and became increasingly isolated. The old establishment was corrupt, divided, and lacked initiative and ideas. The army, senior civil servants, writers, poets, and intellectuals, all sought change and modernity with revolutionary fanaticism; they were romantic nationalists of various right- or left-wing colours. The religious establishment feared any modernization which, they thought, would damage Islam and weaken their power base. Between these extremes, there was a group of democratic Constitutionalists who themselves fell into two categories.

The first group were the followers of Sayyed Hasan Mudarris – Bahar, Ashtiyani, Kaziruni, Firuz-Abadi, Hayerizadeh, etc. – in the Majlis. They had a large urban power base, and from 1922 had adopted a policy of confrontation with Reza Khan. An electrifying orator, Mudarris was a learned scholar and professor of Islamic jurisprudence; a fearless, self-assured and, hence, open and often tactless politician who – like most politicians – was not too particular about his choice of means, although he would never compromise his ends. He was effectively isolated from the religious establishment, was not opposed to a certain degree of modernization and social change, and regarded the defence of basic freedoms as well as constitutional government as no less important than the protection of the Islamic faith.

The second group comprised popular, incorruptible, highly principled (and, hence, relatively handicapped), courteous, modern-minded (though not anti-traditional), democratic politicians like Mustawfi, Mushir, Mu'tamin al-Mulk, Dawlat-Abadi, Taqizadeh, Musaddiq, etc. Their attitude towards Reza Khan – over the short but crucial period, 1922–5 – was a mixture of appreciation of his intelligence, energy, ability and apparent patriotism, and concern over his increasingly autocratic methods. They were ready to let him have as much constitutional power as possible, on condition that he did not act in an absolute and arbitrary manner. It was Musaddiq himself – the most respected modern doctor of law at the time – who advised the Majlis as well as the Prince Regent that, as prime minister, Reza was entitled to the practical (as opposed to purely ceremonial) command of the armed forces.[1] Hence, the group was described as Independents (*munfaridin*) in the Majlis lobbies.

Early in his premiership, Reza Khan used the leading figures of this group collectively in an informal advisory capacity, mainly in order to keep them quiet until their potential disquiet had ceased to be dangerous. His campaign in 1924–5 for the establishment of a republican regime would have been successful had it not been for Mudarris's fearless and energetic opposition, plus one or two small miracles. Yet, it was both symbolic and ironic that the movement's formal collapse was preceded by a public rebuke of Reza Khan from Mu'tamin, Speaker of the Majlis and head of the legislature, and a leading Independent. Reza resigned and retreated to one of his estates to the east of Tehran, but – once the army generals had made their feelings public and issued threats about their potential course of action – a large group of politicians and civil dignitaries (including Musaddiq) escorted him back to Tehran, and to office, with pomp and ceremony.[2] There were several reasons for this. Reza Khan still had the army, the higher civil service, the Majlis majority and the nationalist-modernist forces behind him. The popular democrats still hoped that it would be possible to contain him within the constitutional framework. In any case, neither they nor the Qajars and the conservative politicians (who by then had lost credibility) had the will or the means to take over from him. Indeed, Mudarris himself came to a hasty compromise with Reza Khan after his return to power.

Having tactfully reassured the religious establishment of his good Islamic intentions by visiting the *ulama* in Qum, making friendly contacts with those in the Atabat (the holy Shi'a cities in Iraq), and attending *ta'zieh* (ritual penitence) processions in Tehran, Reza Khan now made a successful bid for the throne itself. But this time nothing was left to chance. Two nights before he and his followers were due to surprise the opposition with a Majlis Bill for the removal of the Qajars and their replacement by Reza himself (i.e. on 29 October 1925), undercover agents were sent to assassinate poet-laureate Bahar outside the Majlis, but – in a classic case of mistaken identity – killed an unfortunate Qazvin journalist instead.[3] The following night all the wavering deputies were taken, one by one, to the home of Ali-Akbar Davar, Reza's chief supporter in the Majlis and later to become minister of justice, to ensure their full co-operation via persuasion or intimidation. Dawlat-Abadi, who had wrongly been included in the list, publicized the story afterwards.[4] Mirpanj Ahmad Aqa (later General Amir-Ahmadi) stood at the Majlis gates next day, reminding the deputies of the consequences of non-co-operation. However, when he found Mohammad Vali Khan Asadi (a Khurasan deputy) un-impressed, he told him that the life of his close friend, Amir Shuka al-Mulk (Alam), would be in danger if he did not toe the line. Asadi gave in, little knowing that Reza would one day have him hanged on an unproven political charge.[5] Next morning, Mustawfi (then the reluctant Majlis Speaker) telephoned Musaddiq to tell him of the impending move in the Majlis. Musaddiq agreed that there was not much they could do in the circumstances, but insisted to a dispirited Mustawfi that they were still obliged to fulfil their duty to their constituents. They tried a delaying tactic which in fact boomeranged.

With Sayyed Mohammad Tadayyun – deputy Speaker and Reza Khan's Majlis campaign manager – in the chair, the opposition's argument that Mustawfi's resignation from the Speakership should – by the standing orders – be considered first was brushed aside, and they were left to face a hostile, rather than a sympathetic, chairman of the meeting. Shouting 'Even if you take a hundred thousand votes it would still be unconstitutional', Mudarris stormed out of the meeting before the debate began. As the first deputy to speak against the Bill, Musaddiq gave up his place to Taqizadeh when he left the meeting and tried, unsuccessfully, to persuade Mudarris to return and make a formal speech against the Bill. Taqizadeh's opposition speech was fairly short, firm but polite and even subtle; he ended by quoting the verse, 'What is evident is in no need of description'. Dawlat-Abadi and

Ala also spoke against the motion, though they (and especially Ala) were noticeably less forthcoming than the first two speakers.

Musaddiq's speech was the longest, best reasoned and most emotionally charged. First, he established his authority in a hostile meeting by making the deputies rise and show their respect for the Koran, a copy of which he produced from his pocket, to remind them of their oath of allegiance to the state and the constitution when they were sworn in. Then he began by enumerating Reza Khan's services in bringing security and stability to the country. Reza would still have his support as prime minister, he said, but he would be useless as a constitutional monarch and to turn him into a powerless head of state would be tantamount to 'the severance of the country's hands'. However, if the idea was to turn him into a royal dictator, then (and here he shouted): 'If they cut off my head and mutilate my body, I would never agree to such a decision. After twenty years of bloodletting [for freedom and democracy] do you now believe that someone in the country should be both shah and prime minister and ruler?' If this was the intention, then it would be 'pure reaction, pure *istibdad*', a system which did 'not exist even in Zanzibar'.[6] The opposition speakers left the House one by one as soon as their speeches were over, feeling it safer to leave before the meeting broke up.[7]

The Bill was predictably carried and later ratified by a hastily concocted constituent assembly. Only Sulaiman Mirza Iskandari (the parliamentary socialist leader, who only then saw through his own aspirations for Reza Khan as a progressive leader) dared to vote against the amendment to the Constitution, thereafter vanishing from the Iranian political scene (with one brief but significant exception) until his death in 1945. But the appearance in that assembly of Sayyed Abulqasim (later Ayatullah) Kashani, and his full support for the establishment of the new dynasty, was indicative of the *ulama*'s attitude at the time towards Reza Khan.

Iranian legend has it that Britain had been grooming Reza Khan for royal dictatorship since 1921. However, this theory completely overlooks Reza's own energy and efforts, the support given him by Iranian nationalists and modernists of various descriptions, and the mistakes made by his opponents. It also contradicts the evidence that the British Foreign Office was divided in its attitude, and that only in the end, and with some misgivings, did it decide not to stand in his way. It further ignores the consistent Soviet support given to Reza Khan from 1921 until 1928. It is true that British civil and military officers in Iran had been involved in the 1921 coup, but they had little role in Reza's later political successes.[8]

Meanwhile, Musaddiq had been devoting some time to writing as well as to cultural activities. In 1923, the Majlis set up an independent Commission for Culture and Education (Kumisiyun-i Mu'arif) and elected Musaddiq as a member. The Commission's task was not clearly defined; it was charged with initiating and supervising cultural and educational activities in the direction of modern scholarships and science. One of its most useful achievements was its sponsorship of translations of good European texts in various fields.

At the same time, Musaddiq published six articles on law, the constitution and public finance. The article on the role of European parliaments in budgetary allocations and expenditures was a short review of the rules and conventions governing the subject in England, France, Germany, etc. (where he also made a few mistakes about English history).[9] The upshot of his argument was that both budgetary allocations and expenditures must be under parliamentary control, especially of the Lower Chamber.[10] The short piece, 'Citizenship in Iran',[11] was no more than a systematic exposition of the laws of national citizenship and naturalization in the country at the time. 'The Fundamental Principles of Civil and Commercial Law in Iran' was a longer article, which reviewed such basic legal categories as contract, inheritance, and property rights in Iran, with occasional comparisons with their counterparts in European countries.[12]

The lengthy article on parliamentary elections in Europe and Iran was much more substantial, and included analysis and interpretation as well as recommendations for electoral reform in Iran. It contained a comprehensive review of election rights and procedures, from statutory qualifications for voters and candidates to the importance of party politics, and the 'pros' and 'cons' of constituency and proportional representation. Although the emphasis was not direct, his review of the development of election rules and procedures in different European countries was (at least partly) intended to show that full franchise in Europe was a recent phenomenon, and that therefore democratic government was itself an evolving system: for example, property qualifications for voting as well as candidacy existed in England and France until the twentieth century, and there was disqualification in Italy (at the time) of illiterate voters below the age of thirty.

Apart from purely technical suggestions to ensure the honesty and efficiency of general elections, his main recommendations centred (a) on the need for proportional representation based on voting for party candidates; and (b) on a literacy qualification for voting. Regarding party politics, his point was simply wishful thinking but his hint — for it was not much more than that — of the desirability of a literacy qualification for voting was important, and gave a foretaste of his later views on this subject in the early 1940s. (see chapter 5). Point (11) of his list of recommendations read as follows:

> Entry of every literate voter *on his own* into the ballot box; or – in the case of an illiterate voter – together with a literate person (*assuming that there was no literacy qualification for voting*) but on the proviso that no one literate person would enter the name of the candidates for two illiterate voters.[13]

His concern for the secrecy and honesty of the voting procedure was obvious. So was his bias in favour of a literacy qualification or, instead, a change to an electoral college system 'until such time as the spread of education would have prepared the ground for direct elections'.[14] Whatever the reader may think about these particular qualifications, it is clear that the intention behind them was to enhance, not limit, real democratic control.

The new shah appointed Furughi, a loyal supporter, as a caretaker premier. By June 1926, however, he was well-established as the new monarch and ready to extend the social base of his regime. He therefore invited Mustawfi to form a government, and asked him to sound out Musaddiq for the post of foreign minister. But the latter refused the offer despite his friend's strong personal pressures. He went even further and opposed the popular old politician's Cabinet when it was introduced in the Majlis, because of its inclusion of Vusuq and Furughi, whom he attacked for their role in concluding and defending the hated 1919 Agreement, and Vusuq, in particular, for his dictatorial regime during that episode. His openness in describing them as traitors might sound over-harsh to Western ears, but this was not unusual for Iran at the time, and – at any rate – its redeeming feature was that it was meant with the utmost sincerity: it was neither rhetoric nor humbug.[15]

Musaddiq refused to co-operate because he was convinced that the shah would not tolerate independent advice – a view which Mustawfi confirmed to him shortly after his resignation in June 1927. Musaddiq became an independent member of the opposition in the Sixth Majlis (1926–8), showing an even greater consistency than Mudarris. To begin with, he refused to take the conventional oath of allegiance to the shah and the constitution, and – with characteristic stubbornness – managed to get away with it. His regular defence of basic freedoms was no surprise to anyone, but his criticisms of the seemingly modernizing projects of the new regime were surprising to many at first, and were later misinterpreted by his Iranian and Western critics alike as a sign of social conservatism, if not traditionalism. In fact, his attitude was entirely consistent with the spirit of his 1914 book, *Kapitulasion va Iran*, as well as his political views in practice; for example, his unsuccessful effort to establish a modern penal code when he was foreign minister.

Musaddiq and others like him (such as Mustawfi and Mushir) were neither frightened of modern ideas and techniques – as was the religious establishment – nor were they mesmerized and captivated by them, as were the modernists (in fact, pseudo-modernists) of both Right and Left. Their understanding of both Iranian and European societies was rational and realistic; they believed that lasting progress was possible only through methods which would produce a comprehensive as well as synthetic change. An important aspect of this attitude was their firm belief in freedom, law and democracy, perhaps even more than in technical progress. And this meant that technical and socio-economic progress must involve the people's consent, conviction and co-operation. Hence Musaddiq's emphasis on *Iraniyat va Islamiyat* (the Iranian and Islamic way of life) in several of his Majlis speeches at the time (and later in the Fourteenth Majlis).

Far from showing a reactionary attitude towards technical progress, Musaddiq's opposition to the Trans-Iranian Railway Bill was an example of such realistic analysis and assessment. He was not opposed to railways as such, but was in favour of a rational allocation of the country's resources for the construction of a modern transport system. He did suspect (rightly or wrongly) that the specific project to connect the Caspian Sea to the Persian Gulf was intended to facilitate British access to the Soviet border, but his public arguments against the Bill were purely rational, economic and technical in nature.

First, he pointed out that the construction of a modern road network would be much cheaper in local currency, and immensely so in precious foreign exchange. Secondly – and assuming a railway network had to be built – he showed that the proposed line would be a complete waste of resources, because (a) hardly any international or domestic cargo was carried along that route, (b) the demand for its passenger services was even less, and (c) it was particularly costly to construct because of the rugged terrain of the north and southwest. Instead, he suggested the construction of an international transit line to connect the Turkish railways in the northwest and the Indian railways in the southeast, which was cheaper to build, and for which there was much greater domestic and international demand for trade and passenger services. His arguments were entirely ignored, and it is small wonder that he put this down to Britain's (presumed) secret insistence on the Trans-Iranian.[16]

Musaddiq's opposition to Davar's Bill to modernize the judicial system was based on the same approach, although this time his argument was less readily comprehensible. He was in favour of judicial reform but against the procedures and methods proposed in the Bill. His greatest objection was to the employment of French legal advisers to provide a blue-print for reform within a short period of time. He emphasized the great differences between the two cultures, and pointed out that a mechanical design for such an important social institution drafted by French lawyers who otherwise knew nothing of the country's past and present needs and requirements would be more likely to fail than succeed. He even gave an example of the pitfalls in an uncritical application of French medicine in Iran, when he quoted his own experience in having worsened his illness once in Tehran by keeping strictly to the diet which had previously been prescribed for the same illness in Paris. Apart from that, he objected to the complete closure of the machinery of justice – as Davar had suggested, and later carried out – while the proposed modernization was taking place. The people needed recourse to justice, and 'judges must not be intimidated'.[17]

On another occasion he criticized the ways and means by which towns and cities were being modernized. Urban renewal was absolutely necessary, but historical monuments and buildings should not be destroyed simply because they looked non-European; new roads and streets did not need to be perfectly straight, necessitating the demolition of everything in their way; and family homes and local communities should not be destroyed arbitrarily and without prior study and consultation.[18] Thus he comes through like a European modernizer who is trying to teach non-European pseudo-modernists how to go about modernization and progress.

When official orders were issued for men to change their various kinds of traditional head-gear for the French military cap (locally described as 'the Pahlavi hat'), he stayed at home for eight months – since wearing a hat in public was then a traditional social requirement – until the order was turned into a legal compulsion.[19] He was one of the few men in his social category who were opposed to Reza Shah's order in 1936 that all women should immediately go bareheaded[20] or face verbal and physical violence followed by arrest and punishment. Some civil servants committed suicide when they were told to bring their wives to official celebrations held everywhere to celebrate the great event. Others entered into temporary marriages with prostitutes whom they then took to these parties as their wives. Many urban women over the age of forty stayed indoors until 1941, when, upon Reza Shah's abdication, the order was lifted. However, by 1936 Musaddiq had been a village recluse for many years. He had to wait until 1945 for an opportunity to express his critical views on the matter.

The shah had not yet given up hope of bringing Musaddiq into the new mould. He tried – unsuccessfully – to persuade him to replace Mustawfi. As a matter of interest, when the latter resigned and was replaced by Haj Mukhbir al-Saltaneh (Hedayat), he told Musaddiq that he had told his successor: 'I sank into the mud up to my chin; make sure you don't drown in it right up to the top of your head'. The last offer came from Davar when he asked Musaddiq to become President of the Supreme Court (and head of the judiciary) for a higher-than-normal salary, but he declined this offer as well.[21]

As the Sixth Majlis drew to a close in 1928, Musaddiq was convinced that he would not be allowed to be elected for the next session. The Sixth Majlis elections had been rigged by the state everywhere except in Tehran where there was much greater political awareness and participation. This time, however, the state was powerful enough to do the same in the capital as well. Musaddiq therefore seized his last opportunity in the Majlis to produce documentary evidence for official election rigging in the previous elections, and to predict a worse performance in those which were impending.[22] He was destined to remain out in the cold for the next fifteen years.

Nevertheless, the Tehran elections were a cause for official concern, and Taimurtash (the powerful Minister of Court) entered into negotiations with Musaddiq on how to manage the results. He suggested that, of the twelve deputies for Tehran, six should be nominated by '*dawlat*' (the state), and six by '*mellat*' (the people). He mentioned Mudarris, Mushir, Mustawfi, Mu'tamin, Taqizadeh and Musaddiq himself as the six *melli* deputies.[23] Musaddiq's response can easily be guessed. But the regime did not want to lose face completely. They 'elected' Mushir and Mu'tamin, although the latter did not stand for the elections, and in any case refused to serve, but Mudarris and Musaddiq who *did* stand as candidates were not elected. Indeed, Mudarris told Brigadier Dargahi, the police chief: 'I assume all the 14,000 people who had voted for me in the previous elections changed their minds; but what happened to the vote which I cast for myself?'[24]

Mustawfi died soon afterwards. Mushir, Mu'tamin, Dawlat-Abadi, Bahar, Firuz-Abadi, Kaziruni, etc., withdrew from the political scene, though Bahar was persecuted, jailed or exiled until 1936. Taqizadeh crossed over and became finance minister. In 1933 he was forced – as he himself said later – by the shah to sign the new oil agreement. Eventually, he ended up in self-exile in England until 1941 when he became head of Iran's diplomatic legation in London. But Mudarris would not give up the fight, and could not hold his tongue. He was arrested a year later (in 1929), beaten up to the point of losing consciousness, bundled into a car, and sent to the medieval prison citadel in Birjand, at the far edge of the Khurasan desert. His jail was later changed to Khaf (or Khvaf) nearby; and in 1938 he was taken to a private house in Kashmar (also nearby) to be put to death on the shah's orders.[25]

However, the politicians, generals and intellectuals who had helped, supported, or acquiesced in, the rise of Reza Khan and Reza Shah did not fare much better. Taimurtash was dismissed in disgrace, tried, imprisoned, and murdered in jail before he had served his full sentence. Nusrat al-Dawleh (Firuz), (Farmanfarma's powerful eldest son) was strangled in a police station many years after he had been taken straight from his ministerial seat to a court where he was tried and convicted for embezzling 3,000 tumans. Shaikh Khaz'al was strangled at his own dinner table; Davar was driven to suicide. General Amir-Tahmasibi was assassinated in Kurdistan. Brigadier Dargahi was dismissed, beaten up by the shah himself, and jailed with an unknown fate. General Ayrum managed to flee the country just before his turn came. Sardar As'ad (formerly Sardar Bahadur) Bakhtiyari (one-time commanding general of an army in which the shah had served as a sergeant) and Sawlat al-Dawleh Qashqa'i were murdered in jail. Farrukhi-Yazdi, first a supporter, then an opponent, then a reluctant fellow-traveller, was jailed, and eventually murdered in prison. Asadi was hanged in Mashad on the unproven charge of having instigated the revolt in that city against the compulsory order for men to wear – this time – the European (instead of the 'Pahlavi') hat. General Jahanbani was put in prison, and the whole of the Jahanbani 'clan' were forced to change their surnames (literally meaning 'founder of the world') into Shahbandeh ('the shah's slave'). Bahrami (Dabir-i 'Azam), Hedayat and Furughi fell from grace, one after the other. And this is just the list of the best known and most important official victims of the new order. Thus, the shah became an absolute and arbitrary ruler much in the almost unbroken line of Iranian *istibdad*; and he was left with virtually no one other than dictaphones, sycophants and human automata. He himself was to become the last victim of his own system when he could no longer tell fact from fiction.

Musaddiq was forty-five when his political career and social existence came to an indefinite halt. Realizing that there was nothing *he* could do in this situation he beat a quick and complete retreat into his own private shell. He was not the stuff martyrs are made of as long as he could help it. He would neither throw himself into a desperate gamble nor compromise over his principles. On 19 August 1953, while his house was under siege by rebel troops and hirelings, he hoisted a white flag and said he did not wish to continue the fight; but when the commander of the troops demanded his resignation first, he refused to give it, and continued the fight to the finish; he was prepared to surrender, but he would rather be killed than resign (see chapter 13).

The same psychology lay behind his conduct between 1928 and 1941. He completely withdrew from the social and political scene, but took no steps ¬ not even when the shah had become the absolute arbiter of all life and property in the land – even to pretend that he was anything other than an internal *émigré* (to use Isaac Deutscher's eloquent term), a rebel in silence. And that was the reason for his imprisonment and exile in 1940. He took great care to ensure that his name was not even mentioned in public; and, within a couple of years, he effectively became a permanent self-exile in Ahmad-Abad, his estate to the west of Tehran. Although he was incensed at the news of the conclusion of the 1933 Oil Agreement, he apparently discussed it with no one except Mushir al-Dawleh who initiated the exchange of views on the subject. He himself said that he lived in constant anxiety during those years, almost daily expecting a knock at his door at dawn.

There can be no better justification than the above brief account of the fate of Reza Shah's friends and loyal servants – let alone his foes and opponents – for Musaddiq's unceasing fears of a similar end, although, as we shall shortly see, death itself was not so much the cause of his fears as were the prospects of an undignified end. Furthermore, he was, by nature as well as nurture, prone to nervous frailties which normally result in physical disorders as well. And the objective and subjective factors – the environmental terror and the nervous frailty – must have reinforced each other to produce an intolerable vicious circle of anxiety. By this time, he had lost a mother to whom he was unusually attached, and he had been reduced from a highly successful and greatly respected rebel of the old establishment to the position of a rural recluse, living in permanent fear of death with indignity.

It was no less than the loss of the only world in which he had lived since infancy, and in emotional terms it went far beyond mere loss of power, prestige and even social fulfilment. Almost all his friends, relatives, acquaintances – even enemies – had been destroyed, imprisoned, exiled, or turned into social unpersons. No more Mustawfi, Mushir, Mu'tamin, or Mudarris; no more Samsam, Qavam, or Vusuq either; nor Taqizadeh, Furughi, or Hedayat; not even Davar, Nusrat, Taimurtash and Sulaiman Mirza. It all looked like a vanished civilization.

He began to bleed through his mouth again. It was treated in Tehran and stopped for a time, but it soon recurred with greater force, and he went to Germany in 1936 for treatment. He was seen by a throat specialist first, then a consultant physician. They both said it was nothing, and did not even issue any prescriptions or other instructions. Afterwards, the bleeding stopped occurring through the mouth, and changed its direction. 'In this very prison I have passed so much blood in my urine that I am alarmed by its threat to my life', he wrote in 1955.[26] He was to die, in the end, of bleeding of the stomach, the physical 'nothing' which had important neurological origins.

Musaddiq was arrested in 1940. His home was ransacked in search of 'evidence' (any scrap of paper or old letter complaining about prices would have been sufficient) but without success. He told Sarpas Mukhtari, the police chief, that he could hold him without charge for twenty-four hours, as expounded in the law books. But when he learned that he was to be imprisoned in Birjand for an indefinite period and without any charges brought against him, he lost control, cursed the shah while pointing at his huge picture on the wall, declared himself a rebel against a lawless state, and had to be dragged into the car which was taking him to his new abode. He took an overdose of tranquillizers on the way, but could not hold them because of the roughness of the long unpaved road from Tehran to Mashad. He was still in a coma when they pulled up at a local clinic in Shahrud and saved his life.[27]

He continued to try to harm himself in the medieval desert citadel, and the prison governor had to be personally present when he shaved in the mornings. The Mashad police chief wrote in an official letter to the police headquarters in Tehran that the prisoner had been 'suffering from chronic hysteria (*bimari-yi ghash*)' ever since his arrival in Birjand.[28] Once, when the governor was on sick leave, Musaddiq went on indefinite hunger strike which he terminated after ten days only when the hapless governor turned up to beg him to think of what would happen to his (i.e. the governor's) children if he died. Predictably, his wife and children were gravely concerned about the threat to his life, both from himself and from the authorities. Then, sheer luck brought Ernest Perron – a Swiss national and close personal friend of the Crown Prince (later Mohammad Reza Shah) – to the Najmiyeh Hospital for treatment. The hospital had been endowed by Musaddiq's mother, and was being run by his son (Dr Gholam-Hossein) at the time. Perron's treatment was successful, and the younger Dr Musaddiq waived all the fees. When Perron asked him what favour he could do for him through his influence at court, he asked him to persuade the young Prince Mohammad Reza to intervene on his father's behalf. As a result Musaddiq was transferred to his home in Ahmad-Abad under house arrest. The confinement was lifted in September 1941 by a general amnesty declared shortly after the shah's abdication. Yet it took the old hand almost two years to emerge from a long and unhappy period of total political inaction.

The episode of his rough treatment by the regime did not pass without taking its toll on the family. Khadijeh, the youngest daughter, fell into a deep mental depression from which she was never to recover. She might have had a native tendency towards the illness, especially in view of Musaddiq's own nervous problems. Even so, it was the fear of her father's murder in jail that brought it out in full force, to the extent that she once attempted to throw herself under the shah's car on a public occasion. She has been living in various Swiss psychiatric hospitals since 1942.

The fall of Reza Shah

The origins of Reza Shah's failure must be sought in his success in establishing himself as an absolute and arbitrary ruler. For that is how he managed to turn all social classes and groups – landlords, merchants, the *ulama* and the religious community, the traditionalists as well as the modern educated people, etc., – into his personal enemies, and how he deprived himself of independent information and advice. There is a close analogy with the case of his son, Mohammad Reza, whose similar failure had no external origins, notwithstanding legends to the contrary.

Reza Khan had owed his initial 'break' to the British-designed 1921 coup. Yet, from the very beginning, he 'hated HMG', as Armitage-Smith bluntly put it in his report to the Foreign Office as early as 1922.[29] Indeed, in 1924, Reza himself had boasted to Musaddiq, Dawlat-Abadi and other Independents that the British had brought him to power.[30] Not only did his nationalist sentiments cause him to be unhappy about Britain's extraordinary influence in the country; this was also consistent with his psychology as a ruler who wanted an absolutely free hand in his own domain. Besides, there was the question of royalties from Iranian oil, of which he needed as much as he could possibly get both for his own pocket and in order to fulfil his ambitions for the country.

Many Iranians (Musaddiq included) believed, and still believe, that the 1933 Oil Agreement was the product of a carefully designed British plot which was executed by Reza Shah with unrivalled cynicism. According to this theory, the Anglo-Persian (later, Anglo-Iranian) Oil Company would first drastically reduce Iran's royalties (as it in fact did) – relative to previous years – on some technical and commercial pretext. There would then be a concocted press campaign (as there was, mainly through the newspaper *Ittila'at*) apparently demanding a full rectification of Iran's rights from APOC and the D'Arcy concession. The haggling would drag on, and APOC's response would be largely dismissive if not contemptuous. The shah would then appear to have lost his patience, and would order the sudden abrogation of the concession. Britain would respond – precisely in the same way as in 1951, over the oil nationalization – both by sabre-rattling and by taking the matter to the League of Nations. With the tacit co-operation of the Iranian delegation (led by Davar) at the League, the latter would resolve to recommend the settlement of the dispute through bilateral negotiations. The negotiations would then end up with the 1933 Agreement which extended the concessionary period for thirty years, and was otherwise no better (if no worse) for Iran than the D'Arcy concession.[31]

This is a fascinating theory, and it makes much sense in view of the general circumstances of the country and, especially, the way the oil dispute emerged and was settled. But stronger reason and evidence point to its invalidity. Efforts for the revision of the concession originally granted in 1901 began as early as 1927. Until 1929, Taimurtash was in complete charge of negotiations, but Davar and Firuz were later brought into the process. At one stage, there was a good chance that Iran's position would be substantially improved – perhaps even to the extent of 25 per cent of the oil company's shares being freely transferred to the Iranian government – in exchange for the extension of the concessionary period. But the opportunity was not seized, and negotiations became protracted and quite often acrimonious. The shah's growing loss of patience with Taimurtash (which had many other causes, including fear and jealousy) did not help Iran's position, because the Company was aware of his waning authority.

In April 1931, Taimurtash's 14-point proposal was turned down by the company's chairman, Sir John Cadman. Between November 1931 and January 1932, a settlement was about to be reached but was confounded by Cadman's rejection of Taimurtash's bill for Iran's outstanding claims. Yet in February 1932 both the shah and Taimurtash sued for an amicable settlement, and a draft contract reached Tehran the following June. Suddenly, however, it was announced in London that Iran's royalties for that year had fallen to a quarter of the previous one. There has never been, and there is unlikely to be, a convincing explanation for this, short of the view that it had been intended as a deliberate act of provocation by the oil company.[32]

The angry shah ordered the annulment of the D'Arcy concession followed by public celebrations. Britain began sabre rattling while, at the same time, taking the matter to the League of Nations. The Iranian delegation, led by Davar, did not present a strong case, perhaps because, by this time, the reality of British power had been clearly seen through the facade of the legal wrangle. The result was the 1933 Oil Agreement to which the shah consented at a meeting with Cadman in Tehran, before cabinet approval, Majlis debate or any public knowledge of its terms. It extended the concessionary period by 32 years, in return for relatively marginal improvements for Iran in royalty and other rights.[33]

The shah may have played straight into the company's hands, but he was not their man. Even Taqizadeh, the hapless finance minister who later declared that he had signed the Agreement against his will, was careful to emphasize that the shah himself had been close to tears in submitting to it. But no effective lesson was learned about the dangers of arbitrary rule, not even by the ruler himself. On the contrary, the process of arbitrary decision-making began to become more rapid and comprehensive from then onwards.

The new agreement was signed in the same year as the Nazis took over in Germany. A strong pro-German sentiment among Iranian nationalists of various descriptions dated back to the First World War. Apart from that, many modern and modernized Iranians (whether they supported or opposed Reza Khan and Reza Shah) had been deeply impressed with twentieth-century theories of European nationalism, especially in view of their emphasis on the superiority of the Aryan race. The two factors – pro-German feelings and Aryan nationalism – later became embodied in an almost completely emotional commitment to Nazi Germany, the rising power which was both anti-Russian and anti-British.

The shah was looking for a countervailing power to that of Britain, and this could not possibly have been Russia – Soviet or otherwise. Given the twin featured pro-German sentiments of himself, the army and the modern elite, the rise of Nazi Germany under a fanatical dictator could only have been regarded as an extra bonus. The import of goods and technology from Germany had already been growing since earlier times. From 1926 when the shah began to send students to Europe on a regular basis, they were all sent to Germany, France and Belgium, and Germany's share rose rapidly in the 1930s. Again, German technology played by far the most important role in the construction of the Trans-Iranian Railway: the ceiling of Tehran railway station's great hall was even decorated – though with some subtlety – with large swastikas. By 1937 Germany was Iran's dominant economic partner. One year later, the country's international name was officially changed from Perse, Persia, etc., to Iran, on the advice of the ambassador to Berlin.[34] The Second World War broke out a year after that, and Iran declared itself neutral.

However, the country was soon infested with German undercover agents. Rashid Ali Gilani's brief and unsuccessful revolt against Britain in Iraq could hardly have been reassuring for the Western Allies. Rommel's drive through North Africa posed a definite threat to Egypt, and had the potential aim of cutting through to Palestine and on towards the Persian Gulf. Almost at the same time, Field-Marshal von Bock's Army Group South captured Kiev, and was looking southwards towards the Caucasus on the Iranian border. In the event, Hitler vetoed both courses of action, at least partly because of his parochial European ambitions.[35] But this was not known (nor did it look likely) at the time, and – given the official as well as popular pro-German feelings in Iran – both London and Moscow must have been alarmed at the prospect.

When the Western Allies began to issue warnings to Iran about its tolerance of German war activities in the country, there was no one who could either gauge the situation correctly or who had the courage to explain it to the shah. He responded to the warnings with simple denials and dismissals, and by the time the Allies were poised to cross the Iranian border, it was too late to stop them. Even then, things could have been different if the shah had had a genuine domestic power base, a point which did not escape Musaddiq's notice when he commented on the event. Whatever one may think of the present Islamic Republic, the real reason for its survival in the face of uniform hostility from great and small powers alike lies in its reliance on a strong power base within the country, even though it still faces substantial domestic opposition. In other words, even if Iran's occupation during the Second World War had been inevitable, the shah would not have had to abdicate in disgrace had he had real internal backing.[36] The shah himself became the last victim of his own absolute and arbitrary rule; for where there are no rights there are no obligations either.

4

Occupation and interregnum

Foreign occupation

Reza Shah left the country almost within a month after the Allies entered Iran. Abbasquli Gulsha'iyan's valuable diary, which has only recently come to light, gives a day-by-day account of cabinet meetings in the shah's presence, and other important events. At first, the shah and the cabinet tried to reassure the Allies in the hope of forestalling the invasion. Then they began to look for a solution short of the shah's abdication. Later, as Soviet troops were reported to be about to reach Karaj (some forty-two kilometres west of Tehran), the shah thought of moving south to Isfahan, but was talked out of the idea by Furughi and other advisers. The Majlis had been told to assume its full constitutional powers, but as soon as it began to do so, the shah publicly reprimanded the Speaker. The people were first stunned, then angry and rebellious. Then came the news that the Russians were advancing on Tehran. The shah asked Furughi (who had become prime minister in the meantime) for advice, and he told him to abdicate in favour of the crown prince. This he did – according to Furughi – with courage and dignity.[1]

The Allies' main purpose in occupying Iran was to prevent the country (and the region) from falling into the hands of pro-German forces from within or without. But it also guaranteed the continued flow of oil to Britain from the Persian Gulf, and made possible the shipment of vital supplies to the Soviet Union, mainly via the Trans-Iranian railway.

Having quickly pacified the Iranian army, neutralized the country, and forced Reza Shah to abdicate, the Allies had to decide on a kind of internal political settlement which was both tolerable for the Iranians and acceptable to Britain and the Soviet Union alike, although Britain was bound to have a larger say in the matter both because of the existence of the Anglo-Iranian Oil Company in the south, and because many Iranians were more concerned about communism than about British influence in the country. Eden even toyed with the idea of restoring the Qajar dynasty, but finding a suitable candidate for the throne was difficult for he had to be both young and untainted by past history, and well-adjusted and attuned to the social and political circumstances of the country. Eden went so far as to contact Mohammad Hasan Mirza (the former prince Regent) to discuss the possibility of putting his son, Hamid Mirza, on the throne. Both father and son were permanently settled in England at the time. But the proposal collapsed when Harold Nicolson (Eden's go-between in the matter) discovered that the young Iranian could not speak one word of Persian.[2] Stalin, on the other hand, was more in favour of Crown Prince Mohammad Reza's succession because of the Qajars' closer relationship with Britain at the time. This was also the Iranian establishment's preference and it soon became a foregone conclusion for all parties concerned.

Had Reza Shah fallen without direct foreign intervention and occupation, the public reaction would have been much stronger and the consequences more far-reaching. This has been the pattern in Iranian history, and a direct product of the system of absolute *and* arbitrary rule (*istibdad*) itself. The swift and total collapse of the Achaeminid, Ashkanid and Sassanian Empires in ancient times, and of the Khwarazm-shahid and Safavid Empires in the Islamic era, are too well-known to merit elaboration. But a more detailed study of foreign and domestic upheavals and revolutions in Iranian history will also reveal much the same pattern.

The system of absolute *and* arbitrary rule was based on the state monopoly of property *rights*, and the concentration of economic, bureaucratic and military power to which it gave rise. There could be no *rights* of private property, only *privileges* which were granted to individuals by the state, and which, therefore, could be withdrawn at a clap of the hands. There always existed social classes in terms of differences of wealth, position and occupation – landlords, merchants, artisans, peasants, etc. However, (unlike European societies) the composition of these classes was changing rapidly through time, because the state could arbitrarily withdraw a privilege from a person, family, clan or community, and grant it to others. Consequently, there could be no established peerage or aristocracy, and there was an unusually high degree of mobility both up and down the social ladder.

An absence of law and politics was the institutional counterpart to this sociological base. Where there are no rights there is no law. In other words, where the law consists of little more than the arbitrary decisions, whims or desires of the law-giver, the concept of law itself becomes redundant. It is only independent rights, not dependent privileges, which can form the basis for real economic and social power on the part of individuals and social classes. Hence, the absence of rights results in the absence of law, and the absence of law must mean the absence of politics. Note that it is not *just* laws and *rational* politics (usually associated with the rise of modern European society in the last few centuries) which are absent, but law and politics themselves – 'just' or unjust, traditional or 'rational'. Therefore, the society is *pre*-legal (or *pre*-constitutional) as well as *pre*-political. And that is how the state (*dawlat*) stands above as well as opposite to the people or society (*mellat*).

These sociological and institutional structures and phenomena – which contain an unusually strong element of insecurity and unpredictability – have been the main reasons behind the absence of feudalism (as this is known from European history) in Iranian society. Furthermore, they provided the strongest barriers against the accumulation of financial and (later) physical capital in industry and agriculture alike, for history and experience had shown that money and possessions could easily be lost, not infrequently together with the lives of those who possessed them.

The resulting social psychology and pattern of public behaviour are, thus, easy to discern. *Dawlat* is, in principle, regarded as the actual or potential enemy both by individuals and social classes, including its own servants. Both the systemic arbitrariness (*istibdad*) and the resulting individual examples of injustice (*zulm*) create an acute sense of fear and insecurity, mistrust, disbelief, frustration, resentment and alienation. There may be loyalty and attachment to one's own family and community, the popular (i.e. non-state) culture, or even the whole of the country. But, once a given regime has managed to identify the arbitrary system with itself it persists not by consent nor by sectional or class loyalty, nor even by otherwise overriding considerations concerning the defence of the realm, but merely by the dialectics of force and fear. Therefore, the moment that this seemingly inexorable force begins to weaken, the state loses its grip, and its force quickly gives way to fear, while, at the same time, the communal fear turns into explosive energy, giving rise to a new force.

This is not a matter for 'purely' psychological analysis. Since the state monopolizes all rights, it must also monopolize all obligations. Contrariwise, the society, having no rights, feels no obligation towards the state. It follows that, at times of acute domestic or external crisis, the people either side with the enemies of the state or refuse to 'pull its chestnuts out of the fire'. In fact, when it is (rightly or wrongly) thought that the state is about to fall, the public reaction is such that it either helps bring it about where it might otherwise have been averted, or shortens the pace of its death agony.[3]

The social psychology of Iranian upheavals and revolutions – the suddenly emerging sense of a strong public bond among individuals and classes, the oneness of purpose, the idealism, heroism and self-sacrifice, etc. – is not much different from those elsewhere. The real difference lies in (a) the unity of *all* the communities and social classes, as such, to bring down the regime which then represents the arbitrary state; (b) the implicit belief that once the regime collapses the entire arbitrary state will have been destroyed; (c) the role of an individual leader as saviour, the 'good' counterpart to the 'evil' person they confront; and (d) the consequent lack of a programme *for dismantling the arbitrary state itself*.[4] Consequently the arbitrary state tends to survive in the new regime, or in what will soon replace it.

This brief account is not intended to encapsulate Iran's long history. Nor does it intend to imply (and how could it?) that there has never been any change in Iranian society. Rather, it should be read as an abstract and simple theory to help make sense of the general tendencies during that history. Compared with Europe, Iran has gone through too many rather than too few changes – a fact which is at least partly due to the basic social features described above. The change that is yet to occur, however, is the final and complete destruction of the arbitrary state.

The origins of the Popular Movement are, in fact, in the resistance to arbitrary rule in the late nineteenth century, which later erupted into a full-scale revolution for constitutional government. The Tobacco Movement of 1890–1 demanded the withdrawal of yet another concession granted to foreigners, but its greater historical significance lay in the fact that – for the first time in Iranian history – *mellat* was challenging an arbitrary decision by *dawlat*. And, given the continuing domination of Iran by foreign powers, the interrelated issues of independence and democracy became the overriding political objectives of the Popular Movement in the twentieth century.

The Constitutional Revolution began with a demand for law itself, and its initial successes quickly led to further demands for constitutional monarchy as a form of democratic government. Anti-Russian feelings among the revolutionaries were certainly intense both for historical reasons and because Russian troops were present in the country, and were defending the arbitrary state. But there was no widespread nationalist feeling (except in a relatively small circle of modern intellectuals) harking back to the country's Aryan origins, and the pre-Islamic Persian empires. However, the disillusionment with the results of the revolution and the intensification of foreign domination during the First World War helped spread romantic nationalist sentiments rapidly among modern educated people. The rise of Reza Shah owed a great deal to this new ideology, and the Pahlavi state was its official offspring.

The struggle of the old constitutionalists such as Mudarris, Musaddiq, Mustawfi, etc., against Reza Khan's dictatorship was much in the spirit of the mainstream of the Constitutional Revolution. They were not opposed to modernization and change, but they regarded the rule of law, and government by consent, as the most cherished achievements of the revolution which had to be defended at all costs. And, as Reza Shah's dictatorship degenerated into arbitrary rule, and his weakness *vis-à-vis* foreign powers was exposed (especially through the 1933 Oil Agreement), the twin issues of independence and democracy once again became the clearest and most important aims of the Popular Movement. It was understood that democracy would not be possible without full independence, and the latter would not be possible as long as the Iranian government and politics were manipulated by foreign concessionaries and their governments (see further chapter 18).

When Reza Shah left Iran, independence and democracy were the most popular political demands in the country. For a short period it looked as if the Tudeh party would be the organizer and standard-bearer of the Popular Movement. But (for reasons that will be explained below) it fell to Musaddiq and the National Front to continue the struggle for independence without, and democracy within, the country.

The absence of law and politics under Reza Shah would have led to an equally lawless and pre-political behaviour by the public had his regime fallen to purely internal forces. But the Allies were there to ensure the establishment of law and order, at least in their own interest. This led both to a restoration of basic rights and freedoms to the people at large, and the emergence of the higher social classes as powerful socio-political entities. Landed property began to become secure once again, as had been the case between the Constitutional Revolution and the early 1930s. The landlords became powerful in the provinces where they had rural estates, and they could send deputies to the Majlis to share in the global power. The merchants could now replace the state in its monopolies of domestic as well as international trade, and use their wealth to acquire political power. Likewise, the religious leadership and the faithful could now freely operate in society in their own various traditional ways.

However, until 1945, the fact that Britain and the Soviet Union were now allies had one redeeming feature, namely, the fact that lack of *acute* rivalry between them in domestic Iranian politics kept in abeyance an important source of political conflict and corruption which had been there for almost a century. From the mid-nineteenth century onwards Britain and Russia had competed with each other for political and economic concessions in Iran, except just before and during the First World War when they were allied against the Kaiser's Germany. They still played the same old political games, but – until the mid-1940s – the stakes were not so high as to provoke a confrontation of domestic forces on behalf of one or other foreign power. Yet the winds of the Cold War began to blow from that part of the world even before the fires of the Second World War had been completely extinguished. The interregnum brought about by the occupation of the Allies in 1941 was to last – albeit not uniformly – for twelve years. The 1953 coup led to a dictatorship which, from 1963 onwards, turned into an authentic regime of absolute and arbitrary power. That regime fell as a result of the 1977–9 revolution in the same authentically Iranian way.[5]

The political establishment

There was, and there could be, no political establishment in the usual sense of this term under Reza Shah. But its elements were there, if only because Reza Shah's *istibdad* was short-lived, and had been preceded by many years of Constitutionalism. Apart from the young shah and his court, they included some of the old conservative Constitutionalists such as Ahmad Qavam and Husain Ala, some of the more able politicians and generals who had been associated with Reza Shah, e.g. Furughi, Dashti and Amir-Ahmadi, and some leading religious figures in Qum and Tehran, for example, Sayyed Mohammad Bihbahani. They were ready to assume power, especially as the shadow of foreign occupation had prevented a total upheaval and provided the broader framework for law and order. That is the only reason why the Twelfth Majlis – packed as it was with the former regime's appointees – was able to survive, and even become the strongest single political entity in the land. By the same logic, the Majlis deputies quickly changed colour, vying with each other in denouncing the injustices (*mazalim*) and lawlessness (*istibdad*) of the fallen shah. It would be enough to read the text of Ali Dashti's speeches against Reza Shah – and not least about the latter's alleged theft of some of the Crown Jewels – to be able to gauge the new mood. Here is an excerpt from his Majlis speech on 23 September 1941, less than a month after the shah's abdication:

> From what I heard yesterday, His Majesty the former Shah is due to leave [the country] . . . The very day Mr Furughi [the prime minister] communicated his decision to abdicate to the Majlis, I pointed out to him that he [the shah] should not be allowed to leave before settling the accounts of his twenty-year rule as well as that of the Crown Jewels . . . If in ten days' time it was discovered that some of the Jewels are missing would the government and Mr Furughi accept responsibility for it? Would Mr Furughi, the other ministers and the minister of finance, pledge themselves to be fully responsible for the Crown Jewels?

And on a more fundamental note:

> A question to which the government would have to address itself is the problem of the weakness of property rights in Iran which is a very important issue, and in which the people have much interest. The right of property ownership is one of the most noble and most ancient rights of civilized human societies . . . But in these past twenty years it has been so badly violated in ways which know no limits.[6]

The new power quickly and inevitably led to the emergence of factionalism – an age-old feature of Iranian politics in the absence of the arbitrary state. In the course of less than two years a number of governments came and went, including those of Furughi, Suhaili and Qavam. The latter had returned from seventeen years of enforced foreign exile to face his old enemy, Sayyed Zia, who had likewise returned after twenty years and more. The Sayyed was now a completely 'reformed' man. Gone was the aggressive nationalist and modernist tone of his short premiership, as if his own fate and, especially, that of his old partner (Reza Shah) had taught him a hard lesson on how to succeed as well as survive in Iranian politics. He wore the traditional Persian hat which was then acquiring a kind of religious symbolism; he established good contacts with the religious leadership;

and (having buried the old anti-Pahlavi hatchet) he decided to throw in his lot with the new shah. The only old political habit which he (openly and unashamedly) retained was to co-operate with Britain, which he believed to be the strongest as well as the best foreign power involved in Iranian affairs.

Qavam was a man of a very different type, although there was no major difference between his and the Sayyed's basically conservative as well as pragmatic approach to Iranian society and politics. But he was vain if not arrogant, anti-Pahlavi for both personal and socio-political reasons, more able than the Sayyed in political manoeuvring, and more shifty in his attitude towards the foreign powers. These are some of the reasons why he managed to become prime minister four times in the course of those twelve years, despite the shah's equally negative sentiments towards him. The Sayyed, on the other hand, did not manage to make it at all, in spite of the shah's support, and his own great efforts. But he had another important disadvantage in having been a co-leader of the 1921 coup, and the politician who was most believed to be a direct agent of the British interest in Iran.

Not much was left of the old guard of the Fifth and Sixth Majlis opposition. The Mudarris group – i.e. the opposition led by Mudarris in the Fifth Majlis – had all but disappeared as a recognizably organized force. Poet laureate Bahar remained on the fringes of literary politics, and became minister of education for a short period under Qavam with whom he had always had close personal ties. Mushir al-Dawleh was dead, and his venerable brother, Mu'tamin al-Mulk, rejected all pressure from his friends and political advisers (including Musaddiq) to stand for the Fourteenth Majlis elections. He too was to die within a few years.

After seven years of self-enforced, but highly prudent, exile in England (and teaching at the University of London's School of Oriental Studies) Taqizadeh had been made head of the Iranian legation in London. He had evidently lost his old fire, hoping for a gradual change of Iranian society. There is no doubt that, by this time, he had become much impressed by the basically conservative British outlook towards politics and social change. But the charge against him (to which Musaddiq also subscribed) of being a 'British agent' was unfair. It was the price of his co-operation with Reza Shah and, especially, his signing of the 1933 Oil Agreement against his will, as he was to declare later in 1948 and again in 1952.[7] A long confidential appraisal of Iran's relationship with its Arab (and Turkish) neighbours revealed much about his contemporary attitude to politics and administration. He began by saying that, far from posing a danger to Iran, the contemporary ideal of the formation of a United Arab State might be helpful to other 'Eastern and Islamic' countries in 'liberating them from the claws of Western and Christian countries which milk and exploit them'. He went on to hope that Iran would not one day catch the disease of 'nationalist madness' or it would have to say farewell to most of its inhabitants. The right policy was to treat 'our own Khuzistani brothers' with fairness as well as kindness, let them promote their own language and culture, give them a better share of the country's wealth, and choose the provincial officials from those who knew Arabic and liked Arabs (and were not 'Zoroastrianists'). Furthermore, civilization did not mean 'lifts, *café-dansants*, drinking whisky, wearing European outfits, owning motor-cars, or even the wearing or not wearing of *hijab* by ladies'; it meant culture, higher education, modern technology, etc.[8]

Of the remnants of the Constitutional era, Vusuq had decided he had had enough of politics, and kept himself to himself. Hakim al-Mulk (Ibrahim Hakimi), Husain Ala, Husain Sami'i (Adib al-Saltaneh), etc., had all become moderate conservatives, hoping to keep the new shah on his throne within a broadly constitutional framework. They were not active politicians (even though Hakimi formed two caretaker governments in the 1940s), and usually served the shah at court, as personal advisers, and on foreign missions.

The younger and more able men who had directly served Reza Shah – Ali Suhaili being the best example – had been tainted and (after the first one or two years) could be effective only behind the scenes. But there was a still younger, able, and untainted breed of judges and administrators – many of them trained and raised by Ali-Akbar Davar – who held important posts in the twelve-year period. These included Abbasquli Gulsha'iyan (of whom more in chapter 6 below), Allahyar Saleh – the leading figure in the Iran Party who was later to join Musaddiq – Mohammad Sururi (minister of justice and of finance in the 1940s, and Senator and President of the Supreme Court under Musaddiq), and Abulqasim Najm al-Mulk, several times minister as well as Senator. There were also others of similar age, background and (sometimes) ability who were more adept at political intrigue and sycophancy. The chief example of this group is Abdulhusain Hazhir (Princess Ashraf's favourite politician) who was courtier, prime minister and minister of the royal court, before his assassination in October 1949 at the hands of a member of the Islamic extremists, the Fada'iyan-i Islam.

The young Mohammad Reza Shah was, in many ways, in an unenviable position, although the support of experienced politicians such as Furughi and Suhaili made his accession much easier. During his father's reign, he had spent a few years in an exclusive boarding school in Switzerland, before returning to Iran to attend the military academy in Tehran. At the age of twenty he had married Princess Fawzyya of Egypt by arrangement. And he was not yet twenty-two when his father's abdication exposed him to the pressures of foreign occupation and domestic strife. According to the evidence of Dr Qasim Ghani – physician, man of letters, ambassador, and loyal but not uncritical towards the shah – the new shah was surrounded by, and largely under the influence of, a group of self-seeking sycophants as well as his twin sister, Princess Ashraf. This is largely confirmed by the views of many of Ghani's important correspondents at the time, including Ala, Sami'i, Husain Shukuh (Shukuh al-Mulk), Mahmud Jam, and others. Indeed, both the shah's public behaviour and the personal impressions of his loyal well-wishers at the time provide a telling picture of his psychology.[9] It was that of a young, timid as well as intimidated man, suffering from a basic sense of insecurity which was further exacerbated by his own superficiality as well as lack of knowledge and experience. He disliked older men of knowledge and wisdom because he felt dwarfed by them. He enjoyed the company of women and of sycophants but did not trust them. He was acutely worried about a foreign (mainly British) plot to dislodge him, and he therefore took extreme care not to displease them. He had an idealistic view of the United States, not just as a potential patron and benefactor, but also as the best and most advanced society on earth. He wished to increase his personal hold over the country, but lacked courage and decisiveness, and hoped that others would do it for him. It is not difficult to see that, as his fortunes began to rise in the last decades of his rule, this background was to have an apparently different but even more destructive impact on his judgement and behaviour.

The Tudeh party

The Tudeh party was formed shortly after Reza Shah's abdication, with the tacit approval of the occupying powers. But the claim, made by some including the shah himself, that it was a joint product of an Anglo-Russian conspiracy, is untrue. Clearly, no major political party could survive in the first years of the occupation against the express wishes of either of the two occupying powers. But the political forces which made up the Tudeh party at the time had been there already, and the Anglo-Soviet alliance ensured that they did not overstep the mark one way or the other. More than that, Soviet officials told the leading Marxist elements in the party that a Communist, even Marxist, organization would not have their blessing. This was part of Stalin's extremely cautious attitude towards the new alliance with the US and Britain which even led to the dismantling of the Comintern, and Soviet directives to such established Communist parties as those of France, Italy, and Yugoslavia to co-operate loyally with all democratic and/or anti-Nazi forces wherever they operated.

Thus, at the time of its formation, the Tudeh party was a popular or democratic front. Its symbolic founder and titular head, Sulaiman Mirza Iskandari – an old democrat turned socialist – could hardly be described as a Communist of the new breed. Its leadership, until 1947, was mixed, although the Marxist elements still had more than their fair share because of the heroism with which the individuals concerned were – as members of the Group of Fifty-Three[10] – associated. Its original membership consisted of a large number of educated and intellectual men (and a few women) almost all of whom were below the age of forty, and very few of whom remained in the party by 1949. Its political programme supplied a broad democratic framework, confirming the party's loyalty to the constitution and constitutional monarchy, emphasizing that it was a representative coalition of various social classes, and calling for administrative and political as well as social reform.[11]

The party began to attract the young and progressive, the educated, and the intellectuals because of its modern, democratic and popular ideals, the large number of reputable Marxist and non-Marxist individuals in its leadership and among its cadres, and the growing popularity of the Soviet Union towards which it was clearly (but not yet slavishly) inclined. But – perhaps most important of all – it provided channels for airing and publishing modern European ideas, and a home for those who talked, wrote and read about them. It was no coincidence that such intellectuals as Alavi, Al-i Ahmad, Nushin, Maleki, Tabari, Khameh'i, Malek, Chubak, Hedayat, etc., were all there – sooner or later – either as members or sympathisers. In the first party congress (August 1944) the leadership fell entirely into the hands of the Marxist elements, but (to a considerable extent) even this was due to their active presence and participation in various party organs.

The party's response to the Soviet demand for the North Iranian oil concession (of which more below) led to the first serious conflict and crisis of conscience, both within and outside the party itself in regard to its attitude towards the Soviet Union. But this episode passed without either a rift in its ranks or a blot on its name at the time. On the other hand the Azerbaijan crisis of 1945–6 led to both. By then the winds of change had begun to blow between the West and the Soviet Union. Victory against the Axis powers having been assured, the Allies were now thinking ahead about the future geo-political map of the world. The lines were being drawn, and ranks closed everywhere. Soon, there would be only two possible worlds of Good and Evil: the progressive masses facing capitalist imperialism and its lackeys; or the free world confronted by the Iron Curtain, its masters, and its agents and fellow travellers. And the wretched of the earth would be caught in the cross-fire. It was this international climate which (more than any other factor) helped convert the Tudeh party to the local evangelical force of the Stalinist faith by 1949.

The above brief account gives an outline of the more or less organized political forces which exerted considerable influence through the Majlis, the government, the press and the religious establishment. But there were other important, though not yet organized, social and political forces, such as the bazaar, the shop-keepers, and the bulk of the middle-ranking civil servants and other professionals, later to be joined by many actual or potential Tudeh supporters and sympathisers to make up the activists and the social base of the National Front. During the Fourteenth Majlis Musaddiq was the mouthpiece of much of the unorganized political public who opposed corruption and dictatorship, and wished to be free from the domination of any foreign power. And this was implicit in his famous policy of passive balance.

5

The first deputy

The one-man parliamentary faction (1944–6)

Musaddiq's return to active politics was slow and sluggish. It was characteristic of him to become active only after he had received a certain amount of encouragement, but to be fully committed the moment he had decided to assume the political role expected of him. The Thirteenth Majlis elections had been largely completed before Reza Shah's abdication. Both the occupying forces and the political establishment thought it wiser to let it run its normal course than to dismiss it straightaway and hold new elections. Hence, the Fourteenth Majlis elections were held in 1943, and it began its work only at the beginning of 1944. During this period, Musaddiq maintained a low political profile, though when he saw energetic support for him to stand as a candidate for Tehran he stepped forward and was duly elected, winning more votes than any of the remaining eleven Tehran deputies and thus becoming known as the first deputy for Tehran.

His first action in the new Majlis was to oppose Sayyed Zia's confirmation as a deputy by the whole House. This was a clever move which killed several birds with one stone: it launched him right from the start as the leading spokesman for the country's 'freedom and independence'; it exposed the origins of the 1921 coup and its undemocratic consequences; and it was also a major blow to the Sayyed's aspirations for premiership at the head of a coalition of conservative forces backed by the shah. The speech was well received across a wider spectrum of political opinion, including the Tudeh party, and other important contenders for power, notably Qavam.[1] Its central theme was, however, familiar, and was to remain Musaddiq's principal political objective for the rest of his life — namely independence without, and democracy within, the country:

The Iranian people want independence and will not give it up at any price. They wish the foreign powers would absolutely refrain from interfering in our affairs, and respect our independence in words as well as deeds ... Gentlemen! Please do not allow a repetition of misery and misfortune. Please have pity on society. Please do not allow the torture of the young and progressive intellectuals of this country. Please do not deliver the standard-bearers of freedom to the agents of reaction.[2]

A characteristic of Musaddiq which has been seldom recognized is that he was an 'outsider', or a 'radical' in the old sense of the term. An 'outsider' is an individual who does not quite fit in with prevailing social and intellectual frameworks; 'radicals' are individuals who speak their minds and present their views regardless of the sensitivities of the existing power centres. In politics, this goes far beyond simply being in opposition to the existing government or even the established regime. For oppositions, too, have their own framework, their own rules of 'proper' conduct, their own internal censorship. But radicals and outsiders do not recognize such boundaries, even if they are formally affiliated to them, and sooner or later they leave or are expelled.

Therefore, in both science and society, radicals or outsiders are original, in the traditional meaning of the word in the history of art, science and political thought. They tend to be critical of almost all established norms and prejudices, and have no power centre of their own to which they can attract converts, clients and fellow travellers, or from which they can make an impact on their environment. Most do not succeed in their own lifetime, and usually receive recognition only from future generations. Not all outsiders are prophets, saints, founders of great religions or ideological schools, or immortal men of letters or of science. But almost all of the latter have been outsiders in their own lifetime. Musaddiq and Khalil Maleki (of whom more below) are the most prominent outsiders of modern Iranian politics. Indeed, Maleki was even more of an outsider than Musaddiq (see chapters 8 and 18).[3]

Musaddiq had always been an outsider and was to remain so until a rare combination of factors made it possible for him to create his own framework. Having once made a few complimentary remarks about him to Ahmad Matin-Daftary (Musaddiq's grand-nephew and son-in-law), Mudarris had added: 'But this uncle of yours [sic] is quite an indigestible meal'. In his youth he had joined one or two Constitutionalist groups, but not for long. His affiliation to the radical wing of the Democratic party (during the First World War) had also been transitory. Before entering the Majlis he had always been a 'loner' in politics and government. After becoming a deputy in 1924, he remained an Independent until 1926, and became his own one-man opposition until 1928, when he was chased out of politics altogether. And now in the Fourteenth Majlis he was once again a one-man opposition among various political factions of right, left and centre, including the Tudeh party's eight-man parliamentary group.

Like most individuals and organizations in Iran at the time he had no comprehensive political programme. Furthermore, he acted and reacted to men and events on their own merits alone. And that was why he was one day praised, another day denounced, and yet again praised both by the Tudeh party and by the conservative forces. But although he was thus regarded as an outsider by the existing political frameworks and establishments of right and left alike, he had a vast constituency among the unorganized political public who were to supply the popular base for his campaigns. He appealed to them directly and over the heads of the existing power centres, but he lacked the art as well as the machinery to organize them into a power centre of his own. And he even lacked the art of creating that machinery.

Predictably, a recurring theme of his parliamentary speeches was the twin evils of *istibdad* and foreign dependence, on the one hand, and the virtues of independence and democratic government on the other. For example in a speech on 7 March 1944:

If patriotism (*vatan-parasti*) is undesirable, then why is it that the great powers seek the best for their own countries? If democracy (*dimukrasi*) is not desirable why do they fully subscribe to it in their own countries? If press freedom is damaging, why do they not interfere in the press in those [Western democratic] countries?

No nation ever got anywhere under *istibdad* [i.e., absolute *and* arbitrary rule]. It would be a mistake to compare the present times (when we have only just heard the name of freedom) unfavourably with the [Reza Shah] period. For one would still need many more years to get rid of the [destructive but inevitable] reactions to the events of that period . . .

A dictator is just like a father who prevents his child's normal development, and, when he dies, leaves an inexperienced and underdeveloped child behind. Therefore, it would take some time before his child fully develops and gains experience . . .

We should either claim that individuals are worth nothing, and ought to be ruled over by one person alone. There is no difference between this and traditional *istibdad* – why, then, did we create a

Majlis and a constitution? Or we should say that there is a democratic system (*hukumat-i melli*), in which case there is no need for a Leader or Saviour . . .

If there is only one captain the boat would be in danger every time he is ill, and sink the minute he dies. But if captains were numerous the illness and death of one individual would not alter the course of the boat.[4]

And on 15 October 1944:

If I am a Majlis deputy it is not for the sake of the shah but for that of the country. . . . According to the constitution the shah is not answerable and [therefore] he has no right whatsoever to interfere in the country's affairs. And why? I submit, in the shah's own interest. If the shah were answerable [for political decisions and their consequences] then he would eventually have to go. But when the shah is not answerable, he will remain, and the shah should remain . . .

Therefore, the shah's position is ceremonial, that is the shah should assent to acts of parliament in a symbolic and ceremonial sense, for if you eliminate its ceremonial nature we would no longer have a constitutional government. If the shah were to appoint and dismiss the ministers then there would be no Majlis, the constitutional regime, and all that Your Excellency [the acting minister of war] says about democratic government?[5]

The issue of democratic government came up frequently with regard to government policy and the conduct of the executive. But its most memorable example in the Fourteenth Majlis occurred when Muhsin Sadr, Sadr al-Ashraf, became prime minister primarily in the hope that he could deal with the deepening crisis in Azerbaijan (of which more below). Sadr's record was plainly undemocratic and reactionary. He had been both the chief state prosecutor against Constitutionalist leaders during Mohammad Ali Shah's coup against the Constitutional Revolution, and a leading functionary during the most undemocratic period of Reza Shah's rule.

Furthermore, it was well-known that Sayyed Zia had played an important role in bringing Sadr (as well as his unpopular army chief of staff, General Hasan Arfa') to power. There were genuine fears of an extreme right-wing coup among many politicians and parties, including a considerable number of moderate conservatives. The Tudeh party was so alarmed that it issued a public statement through its official newspaper describing Sadr as an 'executioner', warning that the Constitutional system itself was in serious danger, and proposing the formation of a 'united democratic (*melli*) front' for a 'ruthless struggle' against Sadr's government.[6]

Sadr's cabinet had been approved by the Majlis meeting of 26 May 1945, which had lacked the necessary quorum, and various opposition groupings within the House demanded another formal meeting for the sole purpose of approving the government. Sadr refused and there followed a fascinating episode in Iran's parliamentary history. The opposition – including the Tudeh faction – united tactically under Musaddiq's leadership in order to bring the government to book. Musaddiq suggested that they should all retaliate against Sadr by refusing to co-operate with the government and causing 'obstruction' to parliamentary business. Each time the government was about to introduce a matter, the united opposition would walk out of the Chamber, thus removing the quorum. After much public and private bargaining, Sadr promised to resign if and when forty deputies voted against him. But when this happened (on 29 September 1945), he went back on his word though his government fell for other reasons three weeks later.[7]

Another important issue which Musaddiq pursued in this Majlis – much as he had done before in his political career – was the struggle against financial corruption by politicians and civil servants. Official corruption – embezzlement, bribery, misappropriation of public funds, etc. – was a social evil which (not infrequently) tended to reach epidemic proportions. Musaddiq believed that the best if not the only effective way of attacking this problem was to eliminate it at the higher political and bureaucratic levels. But this was obviously a tall order. Once, in 1921, when he was minister of finance, he had managed to bring down the whole government as a result of his direct assault on the financial privileges of the most important people in the country (including the shah and the Prince Regent) (see chapter 2).

In 1944, a judicial investigation into allegations of financial corruption and election rigging against a recent prime minister, Ali Suhaili, and a former minister of supply, Sayyed Mohammad Tadayyun, ended up by dismissing the case against them. Musaddiq suspected – as did many others – that there might have been illicit intervention by the royal court on their behalf. He therefore asked the Majlis for a mandate – which the Chamber had the power to give him – to examine the case against the accused with full access to their dossiers. The Majlis majority refused to grant his request. Musaddiq lost his temper, described the Assembly as a 'den of thieves',[8] and walked out in disgust. A crowd then gathered outside his house and carried him back shoulder-high to the Majlis (once again), although the event did not pass without official violence and bloodshed.[9]

North-Iranian oil and passive balance

The peak of Musaddiq's performance in the Fourteenth Majlis was – both at the time and in historical perspective – undoubtedly his unique role in the rejection of the Soviet demand for a concession for oil exploration and exploitation in northern Iran. The Soviet occupying forces were still much in evidence when, in late September 1944, Kaftaradze (a Soviet deputy foreign minister) visited Iran in public pursuit of the concession. The concessionary area was to include the entire northern provinces which the old and apparently defunct Anglo-Russian Agreement of 1907 had recognized as Tsarist Russia's zone of influence. Mohammad Sa'id's government and the Majlis majority were obviously against the idea but, being both unpopular and regarded as 'British agents', they could hardly excite public emotions against it. The Tudeh party at first adopted a cautious attitude towards the proposal (partly because of their own internal divisions), but went on to support it both inside and outside the Majlis. Thus it fell to one individual alone to turn the tide.

This episode was, incidentally, also the instrument for Musaddiq's formulation, or rather articulation, of his foreign policy of 'passive balance' (*Siyasat-i Muvazeneh-yi Manfi*).[10] The idea had first been put forward by Mudarris in the Fifth Majlis when he criticized Mustawfi's friendly relations with Soviet Russia. He had used the terms *tavazun-i adami* (for passive balance) and *tavazun-i vujudi* (for active balance).[11] Musaddiq's policy was inspired by Iran's past as well as ongoing experience in its relations with Britain and Russia, and must be understood (as it seldom has been) within that context. The argument can be summarized as follows. Foreign trade concessions dating back to the nineteenth century had led to (direct and indirect) British and Russian interference in domestic Iranian politics to safeguard as well as extend their economic interests in the country. This inhibited the attainment of full independence, the establishment of the rule of law, the promotion of democracy and progress, and the realization of popular rights and freedoms, in spite of all the popular efforts and sacrifices for them, notably in the Constitutional Revolution. The future would be much the same unless no more foreign concessions were granted, and efforts made to minimize the effects of (and possibly remove) the existing ones. Such an argument contained the seeds of the future oil nationalization policy as well as Musaddiq's refusal to allow the AIOC to return to Iran in any form and at any price, a determination which led to his downfall in 1953.

Notwithstanding their own factional differences, the conservative Majlis majority welcomed Musaddiq's impassioned but reasoned opposition to the Soviet demand, an opposition which also contained many friendly gestures and overtures to the Soviet Union. To the consternation of the conservatives, however, he seized the opportunity (which they had hitherto denied him) to launch an attack on the 1933 Oil Agreement, and expose the damage it had done to the country. All this, together with the arguments for the policy of passive balance, they swallowed in order to give him a free rein to lead a campaign which, for different reasons, they all desperately desired. Furthermore, and in one sitting (on 2 December 1944), they passed the single-article Bill, forbidding all future governments from granting foreign concessions without prior debate and ultimate approval by the Majlis, which Musaddiq suddenly drew out of his political hat as a general guarantee for his policy. The Tudeh deputies after some hesitation voted against the Bill. Meanwhile, Musaddiq had been offered the premiership by the Majlis majority, but had turned it down because the deputies refused to underwrite their offer by giving him special leave to return to his Majlis seat if his government was brought down before the end of the parliamentary session in March 1945. Because of the principle of separation of powers, Majlis deputies had to resign their seats before joining the government, and Musaddiq was certain that his premiership would not last long.[12]

The Tudeh party's attitude and conduct in this affair have been strongly criticized by many commentators. But the matter must be put in perspective. When Kaftaradze arrived in Tehran, the Tudeh organized a public demonstration in support of his demand under the protection of Soviet troops, which, both then and later, was publicly viewed as a shameful tactic.[13] They opposed Musaddiq's Bill both inside and outside the Majlis, even though Dr Reza Radmanesh, their parliamentary group leader, had said (on behalf of his own party) that they were opposed to the granting of any oil concessions to foreigners prior to the Soviet demand. And, in the process, they accused Musaddiq of double-dealing (if not outright pro-British motivation) even though until then they had been describing him as a democratic and anti-imperialist politician. Meanwhile, and in the process of justifying the Soviet demand, they went so far as to describe (from the pen of Ihsan Tabari) the southern and northern parts of Iran – respectively – as the legitimate 'zones of [British and Soviet] security'.[14] It is now clear that the idea came straight from Kaftaradze's own mouth, when, in a private conversation with Sa'id, the prime minister, he told him: 'We want a security zone. By northern Iran we don't just mean [North] Iran's oil, but that this area should be under our influence, and be our security zone'.[15]

On the other hand, the time was 1944, the Allied forces were in Iran, there was no prospect at all of reclaiming Iran's southern oil from Britain, and the Soviet Union was enjoying worldwide popularity among socialist and democratic parties and politicians. Britain had been the dominant foreign power in Iran since the Bolshevik revolution, and many Iranians were looking for a countervailing power to reduce the scale of British influence in Iranian politics. It was therefore not surprising that Tudeh party feelings began to run particularly high against Musaddiq and his possible motives, when he turned down a radical, non-Tudeh, deputy's suggestion to him to put his signature also to another single-article Bill which would abrogate the 1933 Oil Agreement forthwith. Why the apparent inconsistency? they cried. The deputy in question was Ghulamhusain Rahimiyan. After the Majlis meeting, Musaddiq explained to him confidentially that such a Bill was bound to be rejected by a large Majlis majority, and that this would appear to provide a legal and legitimate base for the Agreement which, up to then, had been based only on the personal decision of Reza Shah rather than the approval of a proper constitutional body.[16] However, the later criticisms of the Tudeh party's conduct in this matter are heavily coloured by hindsight, especially given their role in the ensuing Azerbaijan crisis, and later during Musaddiq's premiership.

Azerbaijan and the Majlis elections

The Azerbaijan crisis came at the close of the Fourteenth Majlis. When the regime's various manoeuvres proved futile, the shah consented to Qavam's premiership under Soviet pressure. Sadr al-Ashraf's and Hakimi's short-lived governments fell one after the other, because the former was too unpopular and the latter too ineffective to be able to cope with the situation. Musaddiq did not agree with the Azerbaijan Democrats' specific demand for home rule, but was in favour of sympathetic negotiations with them, and advocated the implementation of the Constitution's neglected provisions for the geographical decentralization of government and administration throughout the country.[17] However, it was decided not to hold general elections for the next Majlis, on the ground that it was not possible to hold proper elections in Azerbaijan. Musaddiq launched his last campaign of the session by opposing this decision:[18]

> I am afraid of [a long] recess. I have had unpleasant experiences of parliamentary recesses. Whatever calamity has befallen the country has been due to recess. Agreements [cf. the 1919 Agreement] were concluded as a result of parliamentary recess. Coups [cf. the 1921 coup] were made during a recess . . . Do not close the Majlis gates; leave the Majlis open before you leave.

He suggested various alternative schemes to meet the apparent election problems caused by the Azerbaijan crisis, including the extension of the life of the existing parliament. But the minds of the powers that be were already made up: neither the shah nor Qavam nor the Tudeh party wanted an immediate general election.

A full description and analysis of the Azerbaijan crisis is beyond the scope of this study. The people of Azerbaijan had many grievances against the central government's attitude and policy towards them under Reza Shah. As a Turkic-speaking people they were not happy about official Aryanism, including the fact that they were not allowed to learn to read and write their own mother tongue. They were also unhappy about the state's discriminatory policies towards them – e.g. the government's compulsory purchase of their corn products at arbitrary prices – and the fact that the state offices in their province were run by non-Azerbaijanis. Reza Shah's abdication made it possible for the province to begin to air its grievances. But the movement quickly fell into the hands of the Democratic party of Azerbaijan, which in turn was controlled by the Azerbaijani communists who themselves were being manipulated by the Soviet authorities, especially by Mir Baqir Baqirov, the Communist party chief in Soviet Azerbaijan. The Soviets also put pressure on the Tudeh party to give unconditional backing to the Democrats' demand for home rule, though in fact this would have meant the province's secession from Iran, and its possible integration into Soviet Azerbaijan.

Qavam entered a temporary coalition with the Tudeh party, and made some friendly gestures towards the Azerbaijani leaders. At the same time, he negotiated with the Soviet authorities, both in Moscow and in Tehran, and finally entered an agreement with them which effectively exchanged the withdrawal of Soviet troops from Iran for the promise of Northern Iran's oil concession, *subject* (as Musaddiq's Bill had ensured) to Majlis approval. After the Soviet troops had left Iran, it was a simple matter for the Iranian army to move into Azerbaijan and rout its demoralized provincial army and government.[19] The Azerbaijan Democrats ultimately lost because their organization and strategy were dependent on the Soviet Union. The Tudeh party lost because it gave in to Soviet demands to go the whole way with the Democrats in blind faith, contrary to strong pressures (led by Khalil Maleki) from within the party.

However, Qavam's 'magic' in 'duping' Stalin into exchanging his Azerbaijan policy for the promise of the northern oil concession has been much exaggerated: he did his best both for himself and for the resolution of the crisis, although the almost universally accepted hypothesis (normally proclaimed as self-evident truth) that he had *intended* to cheat the Russians later over the oil concession is theoretically weak and empirically unproven. The Soviet Union ordered its troops to withdraw, and the Democrats not to resist, because of President Truman's secret ultimatum to Stalin. Within this constraint, the Soviet authorities felt that Qavam (rather than the Tudeh party) would be their most realistic bet in Iran, with the possible prize of the oil concession. They were no fools. Qavam did not intend or manage to deceive them, and he might well have played the role of the Soviet Union's good neighbour had he not alienated all and sundry, including the shah, in domestic politics. In fact, the mutual hatred between Qavam and the shah was already legendary.

Qavam's organized rigging of the Fifteenth Majlis elections, which were held in 1947, had seen no equal since 1941. They remind the historian of the British 'coupon elections' after the First World War, although here real coupons were an instrument for buying large pro-Qavam votes by speculators, to whom illicit privileges over staple food supplies were doled out in reward.[20] Musaddiq stood as a candidate for Tehran at the time when a thoroughly demoralized and conflict-ridden Tudeh party had decided to keep a low profile and boycott the elections. He organized and led a public campaign against official election rigging, addressed political meetings, took *bast* (i.e. 'sat-in') in the royal palace with a group of leading dissidents, but in the end gave up in despair, left Tehran for Ahmad-Abad, and (unconvincingly, as his later campaigns were to show) announced his 'retirement' from politics.

In January 1948 the Tudeh party split, and in February 1949 it was banned by the Majlis on the charge of complicity in the attempted assassination of the shah at Tehran University. The charge was correct to the extent that the assassination attempt had been organized by a

Tudeh terrorist group (led by Khusraw Ruzbeh and Nur al-Din Kiyanuri), but without the prior knowledge of the party central committee, while General Ali Razmara, the army chief of staff, was strongly suspected of having been involved in the plot (see further chapter 6).[21] Most of its traditional leaders were rounded up, while others managed to cross the Soviet border in time. But the imprisoned Tudeh leaders, too, quickly broke jail and escaped to the Soviet Union by means of a plan jointly drawn up by the party (civil and military) apparatus, in which, once again, General Razmara (now prime minister) was widely believed to have been involved. Thenceforth the Tudeh party became, in all but name, a fully-fledged member of the international Communist camp. Its *formal* espousal of (pro-Soviet) international Communism in the 1950s was merely to amend the text of the 1941 party constitution which had long been superseded by the party's full conversion.

The Tudeh party thus having failed to provide a broad democratic front for independence and democracy, the resulting vacuum was quickly filled by the National Front led by Musaddiq.

6

The Supplemental Agreement and the National Front

Qavam's government fell in December 1947, and the Majlis' 'straw vote' in search of a new prime minister resulted in 54 votes for Ibrahim Hakimi (Hakim al-Mulk) and 53 for Musaddiq, although Musaddiq was still at Ahmad-Abad and was not canvassing for nomination. Hakimi was not exactly a popular figure, but he had few real enemies among the public, and the votes in his favour (as well as those for Musaddiq) showed that the Majlis was in the mood for a general reconciliation after Qavam and the Azerbaijan episode. Yet the circumstances were such that the moderate but ineffectual Hakimi could not last in office for long; the shah did not particularly want him to be prime minister, and his sister – the 27-year-old Princess Ashraf – was keen to put Abdulhusain Hazhir in that office.

Dr Qasim Ghani's contemporary appraisal of the country's political situation, and – in particular – the sorry state to which the shah, the royal court and the political establishment had fallen, makes fascinating reading. It occurs in the private entries in his diary for the period November 1948 to January 1949. The shah, he wrote, was surrounded by individuals not all of whom were evil, but most of whom did not care about him or the country. The shah's association with them, and his promotion of their interests, tended to reduce his own popularity among the people. 'Among members of the royal family, Ashraf Pahlavi is completely in charge. She has an unusual degree of influence over her royal brother', and was the driving force behind Hazhir's appointment to the premiership.

Ghani goes on to say that Hazhir had done his best to bring down Hakimi's cabinet (of which he himself was a member) in June 1948 and take over the government. He had submitted to the demands of every corrupt Majlis deputy, and had made false promises to them which he could not deliver. Yet he failed to hold the 'corrupt Majlis majority' behind his government in spite of great efforts made (by Princess Ashraf?) on his behalf.

> Iranians in general are a nice people, but their ruling class, and especially those who are professional lackeys of the state,[1] are typically corrupt, thievish and roguish people – be they ministers, deputy ministers, departmental heads, Majlis deputies, journalists, or those who are around them. And it is this small group of people who ruin the Iranian people's reputation and good name.[2]

The cabinet of Abdulhusain Hazhir had been intended to remain in office for some time, but he had many important enemies and the fact that Princess Ashraf had put him there did not help. In fact, her use of every tactic to keep her man in power worked, on the whole, against rather than for him.

In November 1948 Hazhir's government suddenly resigned, in spite of the large vote of confidence which it had just been given by the Majlis after a censure-motion debate. Almost certainly the reason was the need for a new accord with the Anglo-Iranian Oil Company. The domestic and foreign powers that be preferred Mohammad Sa'id to handle this delicate problem on account of his greater dexterity as well as his much wider political appeal within the political and religious establishment. An elder statesman and former prime minister, and a moderate conservative with considerable diplomatic abilities, he was suspected of favouring Britain, although less so than Hazhir. Abbasquli Gulsh'iyan (one of Ali-Akbar Davar's bright boys) was made finance minister, and charged with the task of renegotiating the terms of the 1933 Oil Agreement. The result was the famous Gass-Gulsha'iyan Supplemental Agreement which was never to pass through the Majlis (see further below).

The Anglo-Iranian Oil Company

The Anglo-Iranian (formerly Anglo-Persian) Oil Company had come into existence as a result of the D'Arcy concession of 1901 and the successful discovery of oil in 1908; in 1913, the British government had acquired 51 per cent of the company's shares. Relations between the company and successive Iranian governments had seldom been good. The attempts at obtaining a better deal for Iran had resulted in the 1933 Agreement which (as we saw in chapter 3) had been far from satisfactory from the Iranian viewpoint. The unhappy relationship was to continue until the nationalization of Iranian oil in 1951.

Iranian grievances against the AIOC were numerous and covered many aspects of the relationship. Their most fundamental grievance was that the company had not only turned an important part of the country into almost an autonomous colony, but that it indirectly ran the country as well. But the less spectacular and more tangible complaints were more widely understood at the time. There was frustration at the imposition of the 1933 Agreement itself which had extended the concessionary period by thirty years without improving Iran's economic returns from its own oil resources. The company was still paying Iran 4 shillings per ton of crude, whereas the 1933 Agreement had tied Iran's royalties to the price of gold, and the gold value of the pound sterling had fallen considerably since the signing of the agreement. It also refused to show its accounts to the Iranian government; as late as 1951 it refused to show them even to the British Lord Privy Seal and chief negotiator in the Anglo-Iranian oil dispute.[3] It would also not say how much oil it sold to the Royal Navy and at what discount.

It treated its Iranian employees unfairly and with contempt. The pay and conditions for Iranian and British employees were considerably different. There was discrimination in the use of all services – houses, clubs, cinemas, shops, even buses. The situation was so bad that Mustafa Fateh, the most senior Iranian employee, who had spent his whole career with the company and was no radical, has accused it of racism.[4] The company violated the terms of the 1933 Agreement in various ways. One of these, which affected its relationship with its Iranian labour force, was its refusal to implement Article 16 of the Agreement by increasing its Iranian employees 'progressively and in the shortest possible time'. Its argument was that, according to the same Article, operations had to be run in 'the most effective and economical way', and this required continuing to use British labour, rather than replacing it by qualified Iranians. The Iranian government had battled with the company over the issue for three years, but, in the end, signed an agreement against its own interest because it 'coincided with some other negotiations between the government and the Company, which were of a private nature':

The Company attached so much importance to this accord, and was so keen for its own view to prevail, that Sir William Fraser [the Company chairman] personally came to Tehran, and after long negotiations with the then minister of finance (the late Ali-Akbar Davar) imposed the Company's view on the government. *Unfortunately, these negotiations coincided with some other negotiations between the government and the Company, which were of a private nature, and the minister of finance had to sacrifice the rights of many of the Company's [Iranian] employees for the sake of success in the other negotiations.*[5]

Fateh published his memoirs (in 1956) in Iran, and – both here and elsewhere in his book – he could not have been more open and explicit about the behaviour of the company and the Iranian government and officials.

From 1944 right up to 1953 the company discovered a useful whipping boy in the shape of the Tudeh party. Playing on the fear of communism which rapidly gripped the West from 1946 onwards, it dismissed the grievances of its Iranian employees as little more than communist propaganda, and explained its bad labour relations as a product of Tudeh agitation. It became so good at this that it ultimately succeeded even in representing Musaddiq and the Popular Movement as instruments of Soviet communism and expansionism, both to the British public and – through the Foreign Office – to the American government.

Early in 1944 the Aghajary district workers went on strike. The company blamed the Tudeh party. The Iranian government's commission of inquiry discovered that the workers were demanding drinking-water supplies, a few midwives to deliver their babies, and a modest pay differential because of the extraordinarily harsh working environment in Aghajary at the time. The company was forced to oblige, but its attitude did not change, if it did not harden. Thus, the gunpowder was left ready for the explosion of July 1946.

The company ignored Iranian labour laws, including those which obliged employers to pay 'the Friday wage'. The reason behind this legislation was that the daily wage was so low that it could not cover the workers' subsistence on Fridays as well. The refusal to pay the Friday wage was the main factor behind the strike by 6,000 Iranian oil workers on 2 July, although other demands were also made. On 13 July there was a full stoppage across the industry in Khuzistan. Within two hours after the strike was made official – and under pressure from the company – Qavam's government declared martial law in the province, the security forces occupied the headquarters of the oil workers' union, and troop reinforcements were dispatched from Tehran. On the evening of 14 July some Persian workers clashed with some Khuzistan Arabs, because – in the midst of the strike – the latter had been celebrating the foundation of the Arab Association. Troops intervened because the government was anxious to avoid giving a welcome pretext to the company that 'British lives and property were in danger'. This angered the workers who felt they had clear evidence that their own government was acting as the company's loyal servant. The battle raged for several hours, leaving 47 dead and 173 wounded.

The Tudeh party at that time supported Qavam, and was about to enter a coalition government under his premiership. Two of its leaders therefore, together with two government ministers, went to Khuzistan next day and helped break the strike. Yet the company described the motives of the strikers as 'purely political'. Moreover, and as if the Iranian government had not sufficiently fulfilled its obligations, the Royal Navy began to 'show the flag' in the Persian Gulf, and troops in India were put on alert to defend 'British, Indian and Arab lives' in Iran. According to Fateh, 'one of the Company's gravest mistakes was that it did not treat its Iranian workers and employees well. There is no doubt that if it had not made this mistake, it could at least have enjoyed the support of its own employees and, hence, mitigated the effect of events which were about to occur.[6]

On 21 October 1947 the Fifteenth Majlis rejected Qavam's Bill for the granting of North Iran's oil concession to the Soviet Union.[7] This was the Bill which Qavam had promised the Soviet Union in return for the withdrawal of their troops during the Azerbaijan crisis. At the same time, it explicitly charged the government to negotiate with the AIOC for a more reasonable agreement between the two parties. This led to the signing of the famous Supplemental Agreement which was destined to stir up greater frustration, and eventually be rejected by the Majlis.

The Supplemental Agreement

Qavam was still prime minister when the Majlis instructed the government to open negotiations with the AIOC for a better deal. Consequently, in November 1947, Sir Neville Gass came to Iran to negotiate on behalf of the AIOC. After the fall of three successive governments (Qavam's, Hakimi's and Hazhir's) the negotiations with Gass were continued by Gulsha'iyan, Sa'id's minister of finance, and the Gass-Gulsha'iyan (or Supplemental) Agreement was signed in July 1949. But public opinion had already been aroused against it, both inside and outside the Majlis. The Agreement was both too little and too late. Its most important concession was to increase Iran's royalties from 4 to 6 shillings per ton of crude, which itself fell far short of the so-called 50-50 agreement which Aramco, the American concessionaire, had already concluded with Saudi Arabia. According to a highly revealing private letter written by Gulsha'iyan just after signing the new agreement, he had been under pressure from the shah and Sa'id as well as the AIOC to settle for less than he could have obtained:

> Thank God the oil business is over and the [Supplemental] Agreement has now been signed ... But I should tell you one thing in confidence. If it had not been for the interferences of the prime minister and the person of His Majesty, I would have hoped for more [than this Agreement]. Unfortunately, these gentlemen's political considerations, and their regard for political expedience, reduced the freedom of action which I had enjoyed in the earlier months [of the negotiations]. And the fellows [i.e. the British], too, had realized that I was all on my own, and that [the shah and Sa'id] no longer supported my views as much as they should have done. Otherwise they would have gone even higher than this amount.[8]

The Majlis majority would have passed the corresponding Bill sent to them by the government had it not been for the vehement and vocal campaigns which (already for some time) a few deputies had been leading for a considerably better deal from the AIOC. To this day, it is difficult to know Abbas Iskandari's motive in his impassioned airing of Iran's grievances in January 1949, six months before the draft Agreement was put to the Majlis. For he was very close to Qavam, and later collaborated with the British agents in Iran to bring down Musaddiq's government (see chapters 9 and 13). Had Qavam himself put him up to it in the hope of frightening the Anglo-American powers into helping him back to power? He said:

> The British government needs oil and will not easily let us sell this oil to someone else. But we need money ... The [1933] Oil Agreement has no legal basis to it, and I hope that it will be cancelled through the knowledge, experience and patience of our patriotic statesmen [an allusion to Musaddiq and Qavam]. If Britain takes our oil we shall not try to sell it to someone else — but takes it at what price? At least at the price which Saudi Arabia sells its oil to America [i.e. on a 50-50 basis].

And then, all of a sudden:

> *The government must nationalize the oil industry and extract the crude itself. But of course it should then sell the oil to Britain at the just price which prevails in the Gulf of Mexico.*[9]

With hindsight, the idea may sound prophetic, but at the time hardly anyone picked up the reference to nationalization. Moreover, his concrete proposals ranged between a 50-50 agreement and the higher Gulf of Mexico price. The speech (together with its strong overtones) was delivered in support of a censure motion which Iskandari himself had tabled against Sa'id's government. And it was in the course of the same debate that he challenged Taqizadeh – the *ex officio* Iranian signatory of the 1933 Agreement – to step forward and repudiate that agreement.

Taqizadeh obliged. He told a baffled and bemused Assembly that he had had 'nothing to do with this Agreement other than the fact that it bears my signature'. Even if he had refused to sign, someone else would have done so and the result would have been the same. There might have been an 'oversight' or a 'mistake' in signing the agreement under pressure, but:

> I was never happy about extending the [D'Arcy] Concession [by another thirty years]. And if there has been an oversight or a mistake, it is not the fault of the instrument [i.e. himself]; rather, it is the fault of the man in charge [i.e. Reza Shah] who, unfortunately, made a mistake, and could not undo it.[10]

The public took Taqizadeh's revelations as clear proof of the illegality of the 1933 Agreement and, as things turned out, his statement sealed the fate of the Supplemental Agreement.

Yet, despite his strong opening shots, it was not Iskandari who continued the struggle in the Majlis; as mentioned above, he was an unlikely candidate to lead a crusade on the oil question. The issue led to the emergence of an informal opposition group made up of Dr Muzaffar Baqa'i, Husain Makki, Sayyed Abdulhasan Hayerizadeh, Abdulqadir Azad and Ghulamreza Rahimiyan, who took the matter into their own hands and led a noisy and relentless campaign both inside and outside the Majlis. Dr Abdullah Mu'azzami and Ahmad Razavi – both of whom later became senior leaders of the Popular Movement – also joined in the debate and gained their support.

At the session of 30 January 1949 Makki read out a letter from Musaddiq in reply to one of his own. In it Musaddiq mentioned his own 'silence [since] the defeat of the Iranian people in the Fifteenth Majlis elections', but added that the issue in hand was too important to be passed over in silence. His conclusion was moderate even to the point of advising withdrawal of the censure motion which was still on the table. But he spoke of Taqizadeh's revelation of the 'high treason which has been committed against our dear land during the dictatorship [of Reza Shah]', and advised the deputies to continue their pursuit of Iran's oil interests.

A few days later an attempt on the shah's life failed when he was attending the annual ceremony of the anniversary of the independence of the University of Tehran. It is now certain that a Tudeh terrorist group (led by Khusraw Ruzbeh and Nur al-Din Kiyanuri) had been behind the attempt, although the party central committee as such had not known about it.[11] It is also highly probable that General Razmara was involved with the Tudeh plotters. The rumour about Razmara's involvement in the attempt went far and wide immediately after the event, and was believed by many (including conservative) politicians and dignitaries. Apart from the strong oral tradition on this matter, a few published sources make it clear that the shah and the establishment had seen Razmara's hand in the affair. Thus, according to Mohammad Sa'id (then prime minister, and a close confidant of the shah), Razmara had seen Sa'id that evening and told him that he had had Ayatullah Kashani, Qavam and Sayyed Zia arrested as the prime suspects:

> However, since I believed that the source of the matter lay elsewhere, I told Razmara that the internment of Sayyed Zia and Qavam al-Saltaneh is not in our interest . . .
>
> Razmara wanted to take the greatest possible advantage of the [University of Tehran] incident which he had arranged by the hands of foreigners, in the sense that by arresting and imprisoning influential people he was trying to clear the way for his own premiership.[12]

Having described in detail the incident to which he himself was a witness, Ali Akbar Siyasi, then president of the University of Tehran, pointed out that — after the assassin had been disarmed and badly beaten by the guards — the prefect general of the police suddenly drew his gun and 'shot a bullet into the head of the half-alive assailant, perhaps in order to ensure that he would die instantly, and there would be no longer any need for the trouble of interrogations and investigations'. And he went on:

> Another interesting point which may help clarify the roots of this assassination attempt is that the chief of general staff [i.e. Razmara] was not present in the meeting that day, although he had always been present in such meetings, including the occasions [of the anniversary of the university's independence day]. I remember well that, before the shah's arrival, Mahmud Jam, the minister of court, noted this [i.e. Razmara's] absence, and said to me: 'Where is the army chief of staff? His Majesty will be arriving any minute, but he is not here yet.' Later on, one of the accounts regarding the attempt on the shah's life was that Razmara, the army chief of staff, had been involved in the plot, and had been waiting in his office to take charge of the country immediately after hearing the news of its success. At any rate the successful attempt which was later made on his own life has been viewed as a confirmation of the above theory.[13]

Here, Siyasi is alluding to the even stronger possibility that the shah was later involved in Razmara's own assassination in March 1951 when he was prime minister (see chapter 7). The case of the attempt on the shah's life, and Razmara's implications in it, has been discussed in great detail by Anvar Khameh'i, to whose book the interested reader is referred for more information.[14]

However, both the Tudeh party as a whole, and Ayatullah Kashani were blamed. The former was quickly banned, and the latter hurriedly banished to Beirut. With the Tudeh leaders in jail, a new oil agreement in the making, and conflict in the Majlis, a constituent assembly was called (in May) which amended the constitution to give the shah the power to dismiss parliament. It enjoyed the support of the religious establishment in Qum and Tehran, who were alarmed at the attempt on the shah's life and pleased with the demise of the Tudeh party.[15]

The idea had already been floated among the shah's friends and well-wishers, and had come out at a meeting between Abulhasan Ibtihaj, then head of Bank Melli, and Dr Qasim Ghani in October 1948.[16] The motives of the shah and the establishment in this are clear. They both wanted to increase the shah's power, and to use the amendment as a threat to secure a quick passage for the Supplemental Bill which was currently in the making. But Razmara's co-operation had a more complex motive behind it, which will be discussed below.

The Majlis opposition led by Baqa'i reacted angrily against the move, and censured the government for it. Kashani wrote from Beirut condemning both the assembly and the amendment. Musaddiq came out against it (after the event) in his important public statement in September, when he described it as a weapon to frighten the Majlis into submission over the impending new oil agreement. Qavam wrote directly to the shah from Europe, and denounced the amendment as a blow to constitutional government. The shah reacted violently and withdrew the title of *Jinab-i Ashraf* which he had given him for his role in the Azerbaijan episode. Qavam retaliated by circulating a strong reply among members of the political establishment.[17]

The Supplemental Agreement Bill was sent to the Fifteenth Majlis on 19 July, a few days before the end of the parliament's life. The government hoped to railroad it quickly through the House in the face of the uncertainties of the next general elections. The Bill's second reading was launched three days before the recess. The opposition – Baqa'i and Makki especially – stalled and filibustered. They fought hard and with great courage, but they owed their success in preventing the passage of the Bill to public opinion which they themselves had helped arouse. The press had been alerted to the oil issue more than ever before, the bazaar leaders had become active, students were drawn into the campaign, and public meetings were frequently held in support of the Majlis opposition. By the time of the general elections Makki and Baqa'i had sought Musaddiq out of his 'political retirement' to lead the Movement.

The National Front

Two factors were particularly helpful in the emergence of a popular movement on the oil issue and the subsequent formation of the National Front. Firstly, the failure and demoralization of the Tudeh party over the Azerbaijan crisis, its boycott of the Fifteenth Majlis elections, the internal strife which led to the party split of January 1948, and its subsequent banning in February 1949. Secondly, the fall of Qavam, and his withdrawal from the political scene except for a brief period in July 1952.

When the Fifteenth Majlis came to an end, ranks closed and battle lines were drawn on all sides. Outside Tehran, the elections were largely in the hands of the central and local powers – the shah, Razmara, the army chiefs, the landlords and the provincial magnates. But the twelve deputies for Tehran commanded much more authority and respect than the others, because of the weight of the candidates, the public vigilance against election rigging and (hence) the fact that the Tehran election results would more accurately reflect the mood of the country. Furthermore, the opposition candidates in these elections were a formidable group of men, and their presence in the House would provide (as in fact it did) both a power base and a focal point for organizing the amorphous political public which lay outside the reach of both the establishment and the Tudeh party, namely, the unused social base for a 'third force'.

In the summer of 1949 two new daily newspapers came into being: Dr Husain Fatemi's *Bakhtar-i Imruz* and Dr Muzaffar Baqa'i's *Shahed*. The first issue of *Bakhtar-i Imruz* was published on 30 July with a leading article entitled 'Freedom or Death' written by Fatemi himself. The newspaper thus had a clear political stance but it was not a political newspaper in the narrow sense of the term. It was intended as a wide-circulation daily, able to compete (as it eventually did) with *Ittila'at* and *Kayhan*, the establishment's 'twins'. On the other hand, *Shahed* (which was first published on 12 September) looked more like a party newspaper even though the party had still to be founded. Significantly, it was the first serious newspaper of its kind to be published outside the Tudeh umbrella since 1941.

Musaddiq was fast emerging as the leader of an opposition within a broad constitutional framework. It was a position which no one (including himself) had quite occupied since Mudarris. The small Fifteenth Majlis opposition group (Makki, Baqa''i, Hayerizadeh, Azad) had now been joined by other figures, some of whom already enjoyed good reputations and had held important public positions. Allahyar Saleh, the *de facto* leader of the Iran party, had been an important judge as well as a minister of justice. Dr Ali Shaigan held the chair of civil law at the University of Tehran, had been a dean of that faculty and a minister of education. Mahmud Nariman was an exceptionally able and reputable senior civil servant at the ministry of finance. Dr Karim Sanjaby was a leading member of the Iran party and a professor of law at Tehran University. Dr Husain Fatemi, a young and talented journalist, had just returned from Europe where he had recently completed his academic studies. Others such as Ahmad Razavi, Kazim Hasibi, Mehdi Bazargan, Ahmad Zirakzadeh, etc. (most of whom were also foreign-educated university professors) were not yet in the limelight, but were nevertheless active in the Movement.

On 13 October 1949 a large crowd gathered outside Musaddiq's home and followed him to the main gates of the shah's palace nearby, where he handed in a statement claiming wholesale rigging of the elections in the provinces, and demanding their annulment. The public was deeply suspicious of the motives of Sa'id (the prime minister), Dr Manuchehr Iqbal (minister of the interior) and Abdulhusain Hazhir (now minister of the royal court), all of whom belonged to the shah's party. But they were even more worried about General Razmara and his increasing power both within and outside the army. It also looked as if the chief prefect of the police, Brigadier Saffari, was completely in Razmara's hands, although later events give the impression that Saffari might have been the shah's stool pigeon inside Razmara's nest.

The crowd and its leaders were seeking permission to take *bast* in the palace grounds. Both Hazhir and Colonel Shafaqqat (the commander of the Imperial Guards) explained that this was not possible. In the end, they agreed to let Musaddiq, who was greeted with a military salute, and nineteen others into the palace. Of these, seven (i.e. Shaigan, Sanjaby, Fatemi, Nariman, Amir-Ala'i, Zirak-zadeh and Kaviyani) continued to back Musaddiq until the 1953 coup; five (Baqa'i, Makki, Hayerizadeh, Azad and Mushar) later split off, and opposed Musaddiq's government; four (Sayyed Ja'far Gharavi, Arsalan Khal'atbari, Hasan Sadr and Jalali-Na'ini) sat on the fence, or became mild critics of Musaddiq; and the remainder (Amidi-Nuri, Ahmad Maleki and Abbas Khalili) were to fall out with the Movement within a short period of time.

Having spent two eventless days in the palace, the *bastis* decided to intensify their protest by going on hunger strike. But it did not last long because Musaddiq and a couple of the others were feeling unwell. On 17 October they therefore issued a long statement regarding their fears lest election rigging should result in the misappropriation of 'Iran's dearest assets',[18] namely oil, and left the palace apparently empty-handed. They then met at Musaddiq's house to take a decision which was to prove more far-reaching than the electoral campaign itself. Until then, they had been a group of reputable politicians leading a large crowd. True, even as a group they were (politically as well as otherwise) not nameless or rootless; they were generally described by the historical term *melliyun* (i.e. 'of the people' as opposed to the despotic state and its foreign backers) by friend and foe alike. But they now felt that – as well as a name and a political platform – they needed a political framework; *melli* did not mean 'nationalist': it meant both 'popular' or 'democratic', as well as 'national' or 'non-foreign'. And it neatly described the Movement's aim to attain the country's full independence in order to be able to establish and extend democratic government.[19]

There was some disagreement about the nature and type of political organization they were looking for. This found an echo in Husain Fatemi's leading article in *Bakhtar-i Imruz* of 23 October 1949 when he wrote that what was needed was 'either a strong party or a powerful front'. In the end, the consensus came down in favour of the latter. There was also discussion on organizational questions; in particular, whether the Front should be composed of individual members or of existing and future parties and organizations. The issue was quickly resolved in favour of the latter, but it was to reappear forcefully many years later in the context of the Second and Third National Fronts (see chapters 16 and 17). Apart from the individual founding members, the Front's leadership consisted of representatives of its affiliated organizations. At the time, these were the Iran party, Baqa'i's Action Group for the Freedom of Elections, and the bazaar's Committee of the Guilds. They were to be joined by some other (existing or emerging) political parties, notably the Zahmatkishan party (see chapter 7).

The Front's formation was announced on 23 October. On the same day, the Tudeh party's secret newspaper described its leaders as agents both of imperialism and of the royal court.[20] Ten days later, Sayyed Husain Imami, a member of the Fada'iyan-i Islam, shot and killed Abdulhusain Hazhir in the Sepahsalar Mosque where he was distributing gifts among *ta'zieh* leaders in a religious congregation held in the name of the royal court. Hazhir was known to be on very good terms with the religious establishment in Qum and Tehran, and as a favour to them had once used his influence to save Imami from justice after his assassination of Ahmad Kasravi.

The motive behind the assassination was political. The Sepahsalar Mosque was the central polling station in Tehran. There were genuine fears of whole ballot boxes being replaced, and some National Front leaders, notably Makki and Nariman, were keeping a close watch on all movements in the mosque, day and night. Hazhir had been deeply involved in the ballot rigging process, though his presence in the mosque at the time had a different purpose. The Front's leaders had had no knowledge of the Fada'iyan's intention to assassinate Hazhir because of his general unpopularity (and suspicion of being a 'British agent') and because of his involvement in election rigging. But the regime used the occasion to take measures against the Front, and contain their activities. The Fifteenth Majlis opposition – Baqa'i, Makki, Azad and Hayerizadeh – were rounded up, and Musaddiq was banished to Ahmad-Abad.

The shah was behind Sa'id's pro-British government which in turn was behind the election rigging. But he was more afraid of Razmara than of Musaddiq. In addition, he was ready to listen to the Americans, and hoped to draw them into Iranian politics, both as a countervailing power against Britain and the Soviet Union and as a generous aid-giver. The US State Department had been observing the Iranian elections fairly closely, and four American Senators visited Tehran a few days after Hazhir's assassination.[21] Their visit was followed by the annulment of the Tehran elections which had not yet been completed, and the dismissal of Brigadier Saffari, the police chief, who was replaced by General Zahedi, the shah's close ally and Razmara's adversary in the army. Three days later, George McGhee, the young liberal American Under Secretary of State, visited Tehran. This was followed by the release of Baqa'i and the others from jail, and the lifting of the ban on Musaddiq's movements.[22] Baqa'i was arrested again in less than four weeks on the last day of 1949. At his court-martial (no less) on charges of sedition among the armed forces, he defended himself fearlessly, and was given a long prison sentence, but he was released within a few weeks.

In the meantime the shah's attitude towards Musaddiq and the National Front began to show some noticeable change, both because of his fear of Razmara and because of liberal American opinion. In September 1948, Husain Ala, the Iranian ambassador to Washington, had written to his close friend, Qasim Ghani:

> The impression that one gains here from private conversations with American leaders is that they are not very pleased with the conduct of our shah and government ... The use of British influence for the constitutional amendment to increase the shah's powers [i.e. the power to dismiss the Majlis, etc., which was eventually obtained early in 1949] has left a bad impression here ... Thirdly, they view the situation in Azerbaijan – i.e. the ill-treatment of the people there by the army ... with grave misgivings.[23]

Ala was then a well-wisher and loyal adviser of the shah, and is certain to have sent him this information and more, both in his own personal capacity and as ambassador. On his return from a visit to the United States, the shah had a long meeting with Musaddiq, and gave him his word to oppose election rigging in Tehran. The Sixteenth Majlis was opened while the new Tehran elections were still in progress. But the political climate had now tangibly improved for the National Front and its leader. Sa'id backed down on the Tehran elections, Zahedi did not organize ballot rigging, and six of the Front's leaders – Musaddiq, Baqa'i, Makki, Hayerizadeh, Nariman and Shaigan – were returned as deputies. Ayatullah Kashani, who was also on the Front's list of candidates, was elected *in absentia*, although he was never to take his seat in this or the following Majlis. In addition, Allahyar Saleh was returned as deputy for his native Kashan where a similar battle against election rigging had been fought. It was a small team; but it was the strongest parliamentary opposition group yet in the Majlis' history.

By their tactical retreat over the Tehran elections, the shah and the establishment had hoped to kill several birds with one stone: to appease Musaddiq, the Front and their large following; to erect an outside barrier against Razmara who was getting help from the Tudeh party; and to keep Sa'id's government in power in order to push through the Supplemental Agreement. This did not work. The National Front saw Sa'id as an irredeemably pro-British prime minister with whom there could be no real deal over oil or democracy. On the other hand, Razmara was quietly preparing the ground for his own premiership. Hence, Sa'id's new ministry did not last even a month. It fell on 19 March, almost exactly a year before the Oil Nationalization Bill was to be passed by the Majlis.

Ali Mansur (Mansur al-Mulk) replaced Sa'id as an interim prime minister. He was conservative, had been convicted for embezzlement under Reza Shah, and was suspected of pro-British motives. The British Embassy in Tehran brought pressure on him to get the Supplemental Agreement Bill off the floor of the Majlis but he did not have the stomach to face a crusade against himself both inside and outside the Chamber. On the other hand, he did not want to cross swords with the AIOC and the British government.[24] He found the solution in setting up an *ad hoc* Majlis oil committee to investigate and report on the proposed agreement to the full Chamber. Dr Hasan Alavi, a hard-line conservative, proposed the idea from the floor of the House. Musaddiq suspected a trick to take the debate out of the public view, and opposed the suggestion. It is an irony of history that the same committee was to become the instrument for the rejection of the Bill and the nationalization of Iranian oil (see chapter 7).

The eighteen-man committee was elected on 20 June 1950. Five days later, Razmara managed to dislodge Mansur and – as prime minister – to come out into the open as the country's most powerful leader. The whole of the Popular Movement suspected a creeping coup. On the day Razmara introduced his cabinet to the Majlis, Musaddiq and the parliamentary opposition group made such a loud noise in the Chamber as had not been heard since the struggle against Reza Khan's republic.[25] Kashani, who had been allowed back into the country two weeks before, prepared himself for action.[26] Baqa'i's *Shahed* became the most vocal organ of opposition, and when the police and hired men began to interfere with its sale — they could not ban it because of Baqa'i's parliamentary immunity — he, together with Nariman, Makki and (occasionally) Hayerizadeh, began to distribute it themselves in the streets of Tehran.

This was the time when Musaddiq headed the opposition inside the Majlis and Baqa'i led the campaign out into the streets of Tehran. Although he had still to have a political party of his own, he had kept the former Action Group for the Freedom of Elections intact, and was being aided by volunteers from the ranks of the Movement. In December 1950 a group of roughs attacked the offices of *Shahed*, to teach a lesson to Baqa'i himself who was spending his nights on the premises. According to Baqa'i, they were helped and protected by the police who were now commanded by General Mohammad Daftary (a Musaddiq relative, of whom more in chapters 12 and 13 below). Baqa'i barricaded the building, alerted the public, led the defence and the counter-offensive, and became the hero of the hour.[27] From this moment he emerged as the Movement's young and able heir-apparent until his opposition to Musaddiq's government in 1952.

The argument on oil had been going on for some time, but it was Razmara who acted as the catalyst for the rise of the Popular Movement in its full sense. It was, in many ways, their finest hour.

7

The Popular Movement and oil nationalization

Razmara's premiership

Ali Razmara was forty-seven when he became prime minister. He was by far the youngest lieutenant-general, which was then the highest military rank in the country. He had received his military training in the French military academy, and had risen from the rank of third lieutenant to become chief of the general staff, and the most powerful commander in the Iranian army. Apart from his obvious intelligence and ability, he was extremely hard-working, and combined boundless physical energy and stamina with an unusually strong nerve.

His public appearance and behaviour were that of an educated, polite, tactful – almost urbane – individual. In contrast to this outward image, within the army itself he was known as a tough – even harsh – disciplinarian. He was popular among officers below the rank of general for his efficiency and commitment, but was disliked by most other generals because of his power and success. This would also have been quite sufficient for him to be disliked by the shah, even if the latter had been completely unaware of the young general's ambitions.[1]

Razmara was an educated officer from the middle class. But he was a replica of Reza Khan in almost every other respect – intelligent, tough, bold, ruthless, singleminded, and politically astute. Like Reza Khan, Razmara saw himself as a nationalist, destined to save the country from chaos and backwardness. His conception of modernization was superficial and based on a self-conscious attitude towards the Europeans: two of his famous 'reforms' while he was prime minister were the removal of street vendors from around the Tehran bazaar, and the imposition of a fine for appearing outdoors in pyjamas and similarly informal dress (which was then quite normal in the narrow alleys of the traditional districts). He had a natural distaste for democracy and freedom; and he wished to establish his own total power in the country since he was certain that what was good for Razmara was also good for Iran.

His style, approach and techniques also resembled those of Reza Khan. By sheer hard work and good diplomacy he had established a position for himself within the armed forces that made him look almost indispensable to their existence and development. Many officers believed that their own personal positions and prospects (as well as those of the army and the country) were bound up with his. Just as Reza Khan had once got rid of Swedish officers in the gendarmerie, so Razmara re-took full command of that paramilitary force from the US adviser, General Schwarzkopf, thus getting rid of a close friend of the shah and General Zahedi, and increasing his own power and prestige at a single stroke.

He had no roots within the political establishment, and yet he had managed to find himself many important allies within it, because they believed he was a winning horse, and because they were afraid of losing power to the *melliyun* and the Tudeh party. At the same time, his pseudo-modernism appealed to the Tudeh party as well as the Westernist right.

The Tudeh party saw in him (much like the old socialists and communists had seen in Reza Khan) a kind of 'bourgeois-democratic' leader with whom they could ally against the shah and the conservatives. This was in part because of his careful cultivation of friendly relations with the Soviet Union. There was even a new Irano-Soviet commercial treaty, reminiscent of that signed by Reza Khan in 1927. While both the Soviet Union and the Tudeh party believed he was a 'British agent', that was nowhere as intolerable for them as the prospects of the growth of American influence in the country.[2] In fact, Razmara was careful to cultivate all three powers in the interest of his own plans, and the evidence shows that (just like Reza Khan between 1924 and 1926) they all saw him as their best available alternative in Iran. He had had American backing (via their advice to the shah) in becoming prime minister, and the United States was ready to give foreign aid to Iran under his leadership. On the other hand, a brief from the British Foreign Office to Attlee's cabinet on the situation in Iran shows that they too were content with Razmara's premiership, though it does not show that he was their 'agent'.[3]

Both the Soviet Union and the Tudeh party accused the United States of having arranged Razmara's assassination. *Pravda*, the daily organ of the CPSU, wrote that he was 'killed by the circle who are close to the Americans . . . It was Razmara alone who was trying to improve the Irano-Soviet relationship ... the Americans alone were interested in destroying Razmara'.[4] Their theory was that Razmara had tried to settle the oil question in favour of Britain, and to the exclusion of the United States; hence the Americans were behind his assassination. The argument was reproduced by *Bisu-yi Ayandeh* (the Tudeh party's public daily) a month later: 'As soon as it became clear that Razmara's being at the helm is not welcome to the Americans, a few shots were fired in the Tehran Mosque [sic] which ended the life of the Iranian prime minister'.[5] Furthermore, this also proved that Musaddiq and the National Front were 'agents of American imperialism' and had been put in power to deliver Iran's oil to the American oil companies. It was an unintelligent and incorrect theory in both respects.

Razmara had the army behind him, although the shah's allies among the generals – notably Major-General Fazlullah Zahedi – still carried a reasonable amount of influence within it. The shah and the National Front, each for their own reasons, were against him. So was the entire religious leadership and community, whether the conservative religious establishment or the radical religious tendencies (led by Kashani) which, at the time, had the support of the Fada'iyan Islam.

On 27 May 1950, Zahedi resigned from his position as head of the country's police following a quarrel with Razmara. That evening Ahmad Dihqan was assassinated. Dihqan was a powerful newspaper publisher, theatre owner and Majlis deputy to whose power and influence eight other deputies owed their seats. The convicted assassin was Hasan Ja'fari, a secret Tudeh member who belonged to the same Kiyanuri-Ruzbeh faction which had arranged the assassination of the fiery and unscrupulous journalist Mohammad Mass'ud, and the attempt on the shah's life. However, many believed that the assassination had been a product of co-operation between Razmara and the Tudeh party. Indeed, Baqa'i who was one of the defence counsels in Ja'fari's trial – there could then be lay counsels in criminal cases – just stopped short of naming Razmara as the culprit.[6] A month after Dihqan's assassination Razmara became prime minister.

The attempt on the shah's life had led to an official ban on the Tudeh party and the arrest of many of its leaders. On 15 December 1950, and as a result of Razmara's suspected co-operation with the Tudeh military network, they broke jail and eventually crossed into the Soviet Union. Both the shah and the conservatives and the National Front believed that Razmara had helped them escape. Thus, Fatemi attacked and taunted Razmara (though without actually naming him) in a leader in his own newspaper on 17 December. How was it possible

for an officer and several NCOs to pick up the ten prisoners from jail
(and even be seen off to the door by two officers of the prison guard)
without leaving the slightest trace behind them except for an army cap?

> You may regard this jail break as an ordinary event which is
> unrelated to the behind-the-scenes activities of the government.
> But we cannot take the matter as simply as that ... The most
> grotesque claim of them all was that of [the Persian service of] the
> BBC, last night, that officers opposed to Razmara have been
> responsible for this ...

One week later, Baqa'i went much further, and (in a formal Majlis
meeting where Razmara was present), named him as the culprit: 'And
now the exalted general and respected prime minister has helped those
political prisoners escape'.[7]

Razmara's co-operation with the Tudeh party had no ideological
connotations, and was entirely a part of his power game. But his
suspected involvement in the Tudeh leaders' jail break was the last
straw for many of his conservative friends, and alarmed the religious
establishment. The increasingly dominant theory among the conservatives (echoed by no less a person than Jamal Imami in the Majlis oil
committee) was that there had been an explicit Anglo-Soviet accord
over Iran which was about to divide the country into zones of influence
as in 1907.[8] The shah was additionally – and much more realistically –
afraid of losing his throne. There were even rumours circulating among
the establishment of an imminent Razmara coup.[9] On the other hand,
the National Front leaders were certain that, having obtained the tacit
support of the Tudeh party and having pacified the Soviet Union,
Razmara was anxious to settle the oil problem with Britain, receive
substantial aid from the US, and establish a military dictatorship in the
country.

So, as time went by, the shah and the conservatives seemed to be
moving closer to the National Front in the same way as Razmara and
the Tudeh party were increasingly identified in the public eye. There
had been no explicit deal between the conservatives and the National
Front over Razmara. But when, for example, one compares Baqa'i's
deliberately complimentary words about the shah (in his Majlis speech
on 21 December, just five days after the Tudeh jail break) with his
crusade against the constituent assembly a few months earlier, it
becomes clear how fast events had been moving. The popular leaders
had then seen the constitutional amendment as a joint product of both
the shah and the conservatives and Razmara. But they could now see

the genuine contest between the two sides, and they regarded Razmara as the more dangerous rival and adversary. The shah thought the same.

Exactly what the shah and the conservatives were up to in connection with the (physical or otherwise) elimination of this dangerous enemy is not known. They must have been busy plotting against him both in and outside the army, with General Zahedi leading the campaign in the military sphere. Zahedi was an old 'Reza-Shah general', and during the war had been working as a German agent in Isfahan, where he was arrested by the British army with a suitcase full of money, drugs and pornographic pictures. He was appreciably senior in age and formerly in rank to Razamara – 'the young upstart' – and had personal ambitions of his own.[10] He was self-regarding and no 'lackey' of the shah. But neither his natural abilities nor his personal ambitions were comparable to those of Razmara; and he saw his prospects as being consistent (not in conflict) with the shah's interests, though only up to the point that he would keep his own independence.[11] At any rate, it was the rivalry with Razmara which had motivated Zahedi not to rig the Sixteenth Majlis elections against the Popular Movement candidates when, for a brief period, he became the country's police chief. And it was for the same reason that Razmara had replaced him in that post by Brigadier-General Daftary.

Just as Razmara's position in the army and his success in dealing with the three foreign powers had alarmed the shah, Musaddiq's increasing public support began to alarm Razmara. Nevertheless Razmara, like the shah, saw Musaddiq as a less dangerous enemy, and they both began to try and neutralize (or enter an agreement with) him. But he could not be manipulated by either of them. Razmara had several private meetings with Musaddiq, and even put a number of cabinet posts at his disposal, but the latter refused to take advantage of the situation. During the weeks running up to Razmara's assassination, the shah sent Jamal Imami to Musaddiq three times, offering to sack Razmara if he was willing to become prime minister.[12]

The shah's calculation was correct. The conservative deputies would not easily have dismissed Razmara, given his strong army support and good relations with the foreign powers. The shah's trump card at the time was Sayyed Zia who had the active backing of the religious establishment. Zia could have managed to obtain a 'straw vote' in his favour from the conservative Majlis majority. He was also acceptable to Britain. But he was wholly unacceptable to the Popular Movement, and – to a lesser extent – to the Tudeh party and the Soviet Union. In the circumstances, he could not have taken on both Razmara and Musaddiq at the same time. Therefore, the shah had no choice but to try and defeat Razmara through Musaddiq, in the hope of later outsmarting Musaddiq with Sayyed Zia's support. But Musaddiq refused to budge. There were several reasons for this, the most important being that he suspected that the same majority which would vote him into office would then refuse to pass the oil nationalization bill. He would then have to resign, and the whole Movement would collapse. Musaddiq having thus refused to co-operate, the shah and his friends began to think of other means of dealing with the fearsome general.

Razmara was assassinated on 7 March 1951 while attending a funeral service at a mosque in Tehran. The self-confessed assassin was Khalil Tahmasibi, a member of the Fada'iyan-i Islam. But there is a strong probability that the shah was involved in the plot, just as it is generally believed that Razmara had known about the unsuccessful attempt on the shah's life two years earlier (see chapter 6 above). It is clear from the above analysis that the shah so desperately wanted to get rid of Razmara that he had been sending Jamal Imami to Musaddiq with the offer of premiership while Razmara was still prime minister.

Immediately after the assassination, Sayyed Zia had confided in his friends that he believed that the shah was involved in the incident. The Sayyed had related that he was with the shah when Asadullah Alam – who had accompanied Razmara to the mosque where he was shot dead – had hurriedly arrived at the palace, and joyfully told the shah: 'They killed him and we are relieved.'[13] But the belief in the shah's involvement in the affair was much more widespread, and went as far as Musaddiq himself who was neither a friend of Sayyed Zia nor of Razmara. For example, in a Majlis meeting of May 1951, shortly after he had been named prime minister, Musaddiq strongly hinted that the shah had been behind the general's assassination. We thus read in the entry for 14 May 1951, in Nasir Qashqa'i's recently published diaries:

Arbab [Bahram] Shahrukh [a close confidant of the shah] . . . said afterwards: His Majesty is extremely angry because yesterday Dr Musaddiq had said in the Majlis . . . when the shah told him he had issued orders for his [i.e. Musaddiq's] protection, Musaddiq had replied: [the guards] will not be more trustworthy than those of Razmara, meaning that the shah had been involved in the killing of Razmara. This has made the shah very angry.[14]

At the same time, there had been rumours that the bullets fired at Razmara did not match, and that an army NCO had fired the fatal

shots from a Colt (which was available only to military personnel) at
the same time as Tahmasibi had opened fire with his low-calibre hand
gun. However, Colonel Musavvar-Rahmani's detailed discussion of the
event in his recent memoirs has left little room for speculation that
the plot had had different sides to it. Thus he writes:

> An army sergeant, in civilian clothes, was chosen for the deed . . .
> He had been told to shoot and kill Razmara with a Colt, the
> moment Tahmasibi began to shoot . . . Those who had examined
> the wounds in Razmara's body were in no doubt that he had been
> killed by a Colt bullet, not by the bullet of a weak gun.[15]

Furthermore, Musavvar-Rahmani relates his conversations with
Colonel Daihimi shortly after the event, and the letter from Daihimi to
the shah which the latter had read out to him, ending with the
following words (which Rahmani emphasizes he is paraphrasing from
memory): 'As Your Majesty knows very well, no one had a greater role
in getting rid of General Razmara than Mr [Asadullah] Alam and this
servant.'[16] Finally, Anvar Khameh'i has also concluded that 'there are
many reasons in hand that the shah had also been involved in this [i.e.
Razmara's] assassination'.[17]

The Tudeh party

The 1948 split had removed all 'dangerous' argument from within the
Tudeh party, ensured the leadership's grip over organizational and
policy questions, and affirmed and enhanced the party's Soviet
connections. The banning of the party in 1949, and the subsequent
arrest and escape of most of its traditional leaders, completed this
process. There were still factions and fighting within the party, but this
was now almost exclusively confined to differences in the character and
personality of the remaining leaders in Tehran, the personal rivalry
among them, and their views on tactical questions. There was no more
argument about party democracy, politics and ideology, or the
relationship with the Soviet Union. The dominant faction was that of
Kiyanuri, its rival being the faction led by the party's youth leader,
Nadir Sharmini, while the rest of the local leadership – led by
Dr Mohammad Bahrami, the general secretary – was caught in the
middle.[18]

Whatever their other differences, there is no evidence of any
disagreement within the top party leadership over their assessment of

the country's political forces, and the strategy which grew out of it. This would indicate that their Soviet contacts saw the position and prospects in much the same light. Razmara was their best available choice while Musaddiq and the Popular Movement were the most dangerous elements on the scene – more so, even, than the shah, because they were viewed as direct agents of American (*not* British) imperialism. The oil nationalization policy was simply meant to replace the British by the Americans with regard to Iran's southern oil, while at the same time robbing the Soviet Union of its ambitions for northern oil. Furthermore, it would open the gate to the United States' long-term involvement in Iran's political, economic and military affairs, and strengthen its local and global position vis-à-vis the Soviet Union. Therefore, any other trend – Razmara, the shah, Qavam, Sayyed Zia, etc. – was preferable to the 'hotch-potch' led by Musaddiq. Late in November 1950, while Razmara was prime minister and the battle over oil was raging in the Majlis Oil Committee, *Bisu-yi Ayandeh* stated:

> The people know very well what kind of a hotch-potch the 'National Front' is [and] how it has been created by imperialism in order to deceive the people . . .

And a year after the nationalization of oil and Musaddiq's premiership their *Nashriyeh Ta'limati* (no. 12) wrote:

> This so-called nationalization is supposed to expel British imperialism from Iran in order to make room for the dominant American imperialism . . . The National Front would like the people to be so busy *fighting the British* that they would totally forget the exploitative imperialism of America.

It was a basically similar approach and reasoning which, three decades later, led the Tudeh party into giving total support to the Islamic Republic, and paying an even heavier penalty for it than they had for their Azerbaijan policy and their attitude and conduct towards the Popular Movement.

Given the tactical alliance between them and Razmara, the general gave the Tudeh a free hand to continue their secret activities without running any real risks, to set up several front organizations – notably the Democratic Youth, and the Peace Club – to publish and circulate their official newspaper – *Mardum* – through their clandestine press, and to publish a number of daily and weekly newspapers and journals under

other names – *Bisu-yi Ayandeh, Naisyan, Chilingar, Shahbaz, Sharqi*
etc.

The Popular Movement parties

The Iran party

The Iran party had been set up during the occupation by a number of
young modern Iranian technocrats. Most of its leaders had been
educated in Europe, and taught at the University of Tehran, especially
in the faculties of law and engineering. The party had liberal and
social-democratic leanings, was opposed to dictatorship, foreign
domination and bureaucratic corruption, and (along with many
democratic and liberal-minded individuals and groups at the time) had
a relatively sympathetic attitude towards the Tudeh party and the
Soviet Union. In 1946, it joined Qavam's coalition cabinet together
with the Tudeh party, when Allahyar Saleh, its most prominent leader,
became minister of justice.

In other ways, however, it was not much like modern political
parties in terms of membership, organization and publications.
Although its membership grew in consequence of its affiliation to the
National Front, it never became a large political party as did
Zahmatkishan (later, Third Force). It was a 'top-heavy' party with
many of its members occupying (then exclusive) academic and
technocratic posts. Many of its leaders were rather too conscious of
their personal public image. Hence, some of them were described by
their detractors as demagogues (*Avamfarib*) but friendly critics thought
of them as honest and well-meaning individuals who lacked political
acumen and the qualities of leadership. The combination of these
various characteristics gave the Iran party a disproportionate say in the
Movement – especially in the Majlis and government departments, and
as close advisers to Musaddiq – and this did not always serve the
Movement's best interests. Apart from Saleh, the party's most
prominent leaders were Dr Karim Sanjaby, Kazim Hasibi and Ahmad
Zirakzadeh. The latter was the party chairman, and played an
important – and sometimes divisive – role in fixing important political,
bureaucratic and military appointments.[19]

The Society for the Freedom of the Iranian People (JAMA) was a
splinter group of the Iran party. They described themselves as Socialist
Deists (*Khudaparastan-i Susiyalist*), but were much weaker than their
mother organization in terms of both quantity and quality. They were

led by Mohammad Nakhshab who was to die prematurely, in the 1960s, in his American self-exile. In the same period, their radical wing was reorganized under the leadership of Kazim Sami and Habibullah Payman, both of whom were to play fairly prominent roles in the revolution of 1977–9.

Zahmatkishan and Third Force

This was the product of a formal coalition between Dr Baqa'i and his Action Group for Free Elections, on the one hand, and Khalil Maleki and the bulk of the Tudeh party splinter group on the other. Baqa'i, a charismatic and fearless journalist and orator, became its public political figure; Maleki, an acute political theorist and strategist without public political ambitions, became its theorist and internal organizer. It rapidly attracted large numbers of workers and students, and became the only Popular Movement party which could compete, in many ways, with the Tudeh party. It was the most effective modern political instrument for the Movement as a whole both then and later in 1952 when – after the departure of Baqa'i and his personal following – the party became popularly known as *Niru-yi Sevvum*, Third Force. A more detailed description and appraisal of this party's contribution to the Movement will follow in chapter 8.

The bazaar

This was a traditional socio-political entity with its own peculiar ways, rules and networks for social action. For this reason, it would be difficult either to describe its organization in detail or to do justice to its role in the Popular Movement. There has been a tendency therefore to underestimate its real significance in modern historical accounts and political analyses. The bazaar is one of the most ancient urban communities in Iran, and has many distinct economic, cultural and sociological features. At the time, much of the dues paid to the religious establishment as well as the radical religious leaders such as Kashani and the Zanjani brothers came from the bazaar. It had both a direct and indirect role in organizing religious events and festivals and – more regularly – running Shi'ite congregations in mosques as well as private homes. In general, they belonged to the radical and *melli* wing of the religious community, though a relatively small minority of them – usually the most well-to-do – were closer to the religious establishment.

The bulk of the Popular Movement's finance was raised by the bazaar, especially in Tehran, Mashad and Isfahan. Haj Hasan Shamshiri, Haj Mahmud Maniyan and various members of the Lebaschi family were at the time among those who were most active for the Movement in the Tehran bazaar, but the number of activists and participants was almost as large as that of the individual traders.

The bazaar itself was made up of many guilds (*asnaf*) and a Committee of the Bazaar Guilds (*Kumiteh-yi Asnaf-i Bazar*) acted as the central organ for the whole community. This Committee – as we have seen – became one of the member organizations of the National Front as soon as it was formed. A basic mistake of Kashani, Baqa'i and the others who first opposed and then confronted Musaddiq's government was their hope of carrying the bulk of the bazaar with them. In the event, it proved to be a gross miscalculation. The bazaar remained loyal to Musaddiq and the Movement right up to the coup, and even beyond it. Many of its leaders went to jail and were financially discriminated against by the government because they continued to remain active, or refused to co-operate with the new regime. They gave financial and other support to the National Resistance Movement set up after the coup to resist Zahedi's government. And, from time to time, his regime responded to their strikes by openly demolishing the roofs, or (more covertly) setting fire to parts of the vast interconnected arcades which made up the central bazaar in Tehran (see chapter 15).

The nationalist parties

In the wake of Iran's occupation during the Second World War a youth movement was founded by a few young idealists with intensely nationalist views and emotions. It called itself the Pan-Iranist party and was anti-British and anti-Russian, as well as anti-communist. They were a relatively small group of young zealots, but were active in meetings and street warfare. At first they devoted their energies to anti-Tudeh campaigns – even to the point of throwing a petrol bomb at the house of Dr Firaidun Kishavarz, the Tudeh deputy – but when the Popular Movement began to grow they were attracted by it.

There was a problem, however, in their subscription to the Popular Movement. The bulk of the Movement and its leadership were anti-imperialists, constitutionalists, democrats, patriots and socialists of various descriptions. But they were not nationalists in the sense of the Pan-Iranian movement, which had its origins in the late nineteenth and early twentieth centuries and had found its official expression in the ideology of the Pahlavi era. The Popular Movement sought freedom and independence for the country, but they did not unduly emphasize ancient Iranian empires, were not alienated from its living culture, were not anti-Islam, anti-Arab and anti-Turk, and did not plan to recover lost Iranian territories which are now either independent or a part of the Soviet Union. Hence the young pan-Iranists either had to revise some of their aims and slogans or leave the Popular Movement. As the differences between the shah and Musaddiq began to surface, the party wing led by Dariyush Furuhar detached itself from the rest, reorganized itself as the Iranian People's Party, and stayed in the Movement. The remainder, led by Muhsin Pizishkpur, went on supporting the shah until 1978.

The most extreme nationalist group of this period was the National-Socialist Workers Party of Iran, SUMKA. This was a small but highly excitable – even violent – group of Iranian Nazis who wore black uniforms complete with swastikas printed on their sleeves. Their leader was Dr Davud Munshizadeh, a German-educated philosopher whose father had been executed by one of Vusuq al-Dawleh's governments as a leader of Karim Davatgar's nationalist-terrorist Committee for Punishment (*Kumiteh-yi Mujazat*). He had returned to Iran precisely in the hope of seizing his opportunity for a Nazi – anti-Soviet, anti-British and anti-American – campaign in Iran from within the Movement. But both he and his group were soon to be disappointed, and they vehemently opposed the Popular Movement. The group broke up after the coup, their leader left Iran once again, and some of its cadres became functionaries in the shah's regime. Dariyush Homayon – onetime minister of information under the shah – is one of the better known of this group.

The religious leadership and community

After Reza Shah's abdication, the conservative religious leaders rallied behind the young shah because he took a conciliatory turn towards them and had the support of most landlords and conservative politicians. Their fear of the Soviet Union, communism, and the Tudeh party had inclined them towards both Britain and Sayyed Zia who – quite unlike his erstwhile modernist nationalism – was now emphasizing the importance of religion. He was also one of the shah's close advisers, and his favourite for the premiership. Hence, the religious establishment did not lend any support to the National Front, did not endorse the oil nationalization policy, and both tacitly and explicitly opposed Musaddiq's government.

Kashani and a group of radical *mujtahids*, on the other hand, were actively involved in the Movement, and helped rally the public for oil nationalization. In 1952 Kashani first opposed Musaddiq and then broke with the Movement, but most of the others stayed in it even beyond the 1953 coup.

The Fada'iyan-i Islam supported Musaddiq and Kashani until Musaddiq became prime minister, but they fell out with them immediately afterwards. Kashani's later opposition to Musaddiq did not result in a *rapprochement* between him and the Fada'iyan, even though they all supported the coup and Zahedi's government for a while. The role of religious leaders and activists will be more fully discussed in chapter 12 below.

The oil committee and nationalization

At first the National Front lacked a clear alternative policy to the Supplemental Agreement. Implicit in their earlier campaigns was the possibility of the abrogation of the 1933 Oil Agreement, but the experience of Reza Shah's abrogation of the D'Arcy concession and its results was present in their minds, and they knew that abrogation based on proof of the agreement's illegality was no easy task. Then, in November 1949, Dr Husain Fatemi came up with a new formula. As he told Musaddiq: why not nationalize the oil industry and compensate AIOC, in the same way as the Labour government (which was still in office) had nationalized a number of important industries in Britain? Within a week, oil nationalization became the Front's unanimous policy, though not without serious hesitation on the part of some members. The timing was just right, for the Majlis oil committee was now discussing the Supplemental Agreement.[20] Mansur had hoped to take the heat off by referring the Supplemental Agreement Bill (to which his cabinet was not formally committed) to an *ad hoc* committee of the Majlis. Hence the fact that no less than five (out of eight) National Front deputies were elected to the 18-member Committee.[21]

The Committee first met on the same day (25 June 1950) that Mansur's government fell and was replaced by Razmara's. Razmara wanted to use it in the same way as Mansur had intended. But very soon things began to go wrong for the government: the committee became the most important channel of debate over the whole issue of Iranian oil; and its conservative majority (who were at first willing to co-operate with Razmara) began to turn against the government half-way through its proceedings. This turn-about was due partly to the government's poor tactics within the committee itself, and partly to public opinion, but mainly it was because, as we have seen, the conservatives suspected that Razmara was (or had become) the instrument of an Anglo-Soviet accord (reminiscent of the 1907 agreement) over Iran. It was the fear of 'the north' being turned into a Soviet zone of influence which frightened them most.[22]

At the first meeting of the committee Musaddiq was elected its chairman (despite his own express reluctance) by fourteen out of the fifteen members present. The next meeting was held about a month later, but the frequency of meetings then increased rapidly to twice and three times a week. In the first couple of meetings the committee was groping in the dark, trying to clarify its own specific function and terms of reference. At first Dr Husain Pirniya, the deputy finance minister, attended in a 'consultative capacity', but as soon as the committee began to emerge as a powerful political as well as parliamentary entity, the finance minister himself (Ghulamhusain Furuhar) joined its meetings.

The opposition's attitude towards the Supplemental Agreement was absolutely clear from the outset. It was the gradual, but radical, change of attitude on the part of the conservative members of the committee – led by Jamal Imami – which turned the tables on the government. When the new Irano-Soviet trade agreement was concluded, Razmara himself attended the committee meeting of 4 November 1950 at Imami's personal invitation. He openly committed the government to the Supplemental Agreement, but also mentioned that 'further negotiations' were still going on between the government and the oil company, although he was not prepared to specify what they were.[23] In the next few meetings, Imami spoke openly against the Agreement, on the grounds that Razmara had told them that he was still negotiating for a better deal. Much more significantly, however, he made indirect references to the presumed Anglo-Soviet accord over Iran, saying the British 'are bringing the Soviet Union forward in order to frighten us'.[24]

On 10 December, Makki reported to the full House on the committee's findings, and presented the committee's *unanimous* resolution that the Supplemental Agreement 'is not sufficient for a rectification of Iran's rights and interests. Therefore the Committee declares its opposition to it.' Five days later, the Tudeh party leaders broke out of jail with Razmara's help. In the next few days came the attack on the premises of *Shahed* (Baqa'i's newspaper) and Imami then began to give open support, in the Majlis, to Baqa'i and the National Front against press censorship and the imprisonment of the *melli* journalists. Baqa'i, in return, thanked Imami – who, he specified, 'used to back Razmara's government' – several times for his support. For good measure he also praised the shah, and even put in a good word for Reza Shah as well. Clearly then, there was an implicit (almost spontaneous) realignment of forces to get rid of Razmara, though there was no further agreement on any other important matter. In the meantime, following Makki's report to the full House, the government tried to withdraw the Supplemental Agreement Bill in order to prevent its formal defeat. The tactic backfired, however, especially as – in the course of the debate – Furuhar openly and emphatically defended the legality of the 1933 Oil Agreement. This was the last nail in Razmara's coffin. It was then, in January 1951, that the oil company offered him the 50-50 'profit-sharing' formula (plus £2 million) which, to their apparent amazement, he asked them to keep confidential, and did not himself make public.[25] It is difficult to discuss his motives for this in the absence of any evidence, but it seems likely that he wanted to use it as a winning card in a major strategic counter-attack.

The fact that the National Front deputies were primarily concerned with the politics (rather than the economics) of oil shows up in the course of the debate in remarks made by different individuals. Thus, Musaddiq said at one point that 'the moral aspect of oil nationalization is more important than its economic aspect'.[26] For Hayerizadeh, 'whatever is wrong with the country is the oil company's doing, and it would be better for the oil to be destroyed by fire rather than remain in the oil company's hands'.[27] Makki, speaking in a meeting of the full House, preferred to 'seal over the oil wells'[28] rather than let the company remain in Iran. And Baqa'i wished that Iran's oil deposits would be destroyed by 'an atom bomb' if the company was here to stay.[29] This was the main reason why (later on, under Musaddiq's government) they were not prepared to enter into a settlement with Britain which included the company's return in one form or another, and had to resort to the strategy of non-oil economics (see chapter 11).

Oil nationalization and Musaddiq's premiership

The National Front's Bill for the nationalization of Iranian oil, north and south, was passed on 20 March 1951 – the Persian New Year's Eve – unanimously by the Majlis and the Senate amid public jubilation. The new caretaker cabinet let by Husain Ala could not and did not last long. Musaddiq moved quickly and tabled his nine-article Bill for the implementation of nationalization, briefly described as Repossession (*Khal'-i Yad*). The shah and the establishment were well aware that this was a much taller order, and were bent on stemming the tide of the Movement.

The shah privately told Ala to step down in favour of Sayyed Zia, who was ready to form a tough, no-nonsense, government, dismiss the Majlis under the shah's new powers, face the public and their leaders in a head-on clash, and settle the oil issue amicably with Britain. The plan had been drawn up in such a way as to catch everyone on the other side by surprise. An unscheduled meeting of the Majlis was suddenly called on Saturday, 28 April 1951,[30] at which – in Ala's absence – the news of his resignation was circulated. Owing to the absence of real party politics, it had become the convention for the Majlis to take a 'straw vote' (*ra'y-yi tamayul*) in favour of anyone nominated by any deputy for the premiership. The shah would then be told the name of the candidate with the most votes, and he was obliged to suggest his appointment to the Majlis. The prime minister-designate would then present his cabinet and his programme to the House, and be confirmed by a vote of confidence.

Sayyed Zia was, at that very moment, with the shah at the palace, waiting for Jamal Imami to obtain a majority vote in his favour at the extraordinary Majlis meeting. Imami was a shrewd politician. He knew that to propose the Sayyed outright would be tactless and, probably, self-defeating. On the other hand, he had previously sounded out Musaddiq for the premiership, and the latter had declined the offer.[31] He therefore personally asked Musaddiq to step forward and take full responsibility for the country's affairs. The tactic boomeranged, however, and Musaddiq immediately accepted the offer amidst cheers from the crowd of deputies. Before Imami and his close colleagues could regain their composure, Musaddiq called for an immediate session of the Assembly, and instead of a straw vote, insisted on a secret ballot. Thus, he was effectively made prime minister prior to the shah's formal proposal, though with twenty-one abstentions.

Imami's otherwise mathematically correct equation had gone wrong because the plan had leaked. Musaddiq had been baffled to learn of Ala's resignation because, during a long private negotiation between the two of them only a couple of days before, Ala had given him every reason to believe that he intended to remain at the helm. When, after arriving in the Majlis, he expressed complete surprise at the new development, Dr Abdullah Mu'azzami – then an independent moderate democrat – told him the full story, including the fact that Sayyed Zia was waiting at the palace for the news of his nomination.

In turn, he had heard about the plan from Khushraw Qashqa'i who had got the story from the Sayyed himself. Hence, Musaddiq lost no time in accepting it when the offer was made to him.[32]

Musaddiq was afraid that the same majority which had voted for his premiership would vote against his Repossession Bill, and oblige him to resign. He therefore made the formal assumption of office conditional on the *prior* passage of the Bill by the Majlis. And the conservative Majlis and Senate majority duly obliged. Having lost the initiative, they could not resist the tide of public opinion.

8

Khalil Maleki and the Theory of the Popular Movement of Iran

The fact that the Popular Movement did not begin with an established theoretical framework was no accident. For the Movement was an Iranian phenomenon which had to be explained by suitably new theories, rather than by a direct and uncritical application of theoretical and ideological frameworks imported from Europe. Therefore, once the Movement had emerged, it was necessary for it to be analysed, explained and enriched through rational political discourse. It fell to Khalil Maleki to fulfil this task, and he did so with an acuteness and originality which have seldom been matched by modern Iranian political thinkers.

Maleki and the Tudeh party

Khalil Maleki was born in Tabriz in 1901 in a family of well-to-do merchants who were very active in the Constitutional Revolution. Changes in family circumstances found the young Khalil in Sultan-Abad (later, Arak) where he went to the traditional schools, *Maktab* and *Madreseh*. In the 1920s he attended the German Technical College in Tehran, and succeeded in the difficult competition for a state scholarship in Europe. He had already been attracted to politics and socialism in Tehran, and his interest was to be extended both because of the rising political conflict in Europe (which at the time was best represented in Berlin where he studied chemistry), and because of contacts with other radical Iranian students, notably Dr Taqi Arani. But his education in Germany was to be interrupted. The much valued state scholarship was withdrawn, after a student had been driven to suicide by the Iranian embassy staff in Berlin, and Maleki refused to

95

co-operate with them over a cover-up. They reported that he was a Communist (which he was not) and he was shortly back in Tehran.

In 1937 he was put in jail among the young radicals known as the Fifty-three. He was not yet a Marxist when arrested, but he became one in prison. By all accounts, he behaved with exceptional courage and dignity while in jail. But he was disappointed and disillusioned with many of his comrades, hence his refusal to become a founding member of the Tudeh party in 1941. On the other hand, he could never be a bystander in political affairs, and – over a period of time – the cream of the party's young intellectuals persuaded him to join the party with the express purpose of helping them to reform its leadership and programme. The party opposition thus became known as the Reformist Wing (*Hinah-i Islah-talab*) of the party. Their grievances could be summarized as (a) the leadership's bureaucratic attitude within, and conservative policy outside, the party and (b) its subservient relationship with the Soviet Embassy in Tehran. Maleki was to discover the phenomenon of Stalinism quite independently later on in 1948, but at the time he put the behaviour of the party leaders down to their own personal characteristics, as well as pressures from the Soviet embassy staff.

The party somehow managed to survive its ongoing internal conflicts, notably those over the first party congress (1944), and the Soviet demand for an oil concession. But the Azerbaijan crisis brought matters to a head. As the head of the provincial Tudeh party in Azerbaijan, Maleki had been highly critical of the attitude and behaviour of both the Russian occupying army and Pishehvari's Democrats. For this reason he was 'exiled' from his own land back to Tehran. There he opposed both the Tudeh party's formal affiliation to the Democrats in Azerbaijan, and its coalition with Qavam in Tehran. The catastrophic failure of these policies demoralized the party leadership and their local Soviet contacts for a short period. The central committee resigned *en masse*. Maleki was elected to the provisional executive committee which had been given full powers pending the decision of the second party congress. He was one of the three secretaries of the new committee but refused to act as the First Secretary because he would then have had to be the party's official contact with the Soviet embassy in Tehran.

The 1947 Tehran provincial party conference revealed the extent of the Reformist Wing's power and influence. Tehran was the centre of operations, and – by the party constitution – its provincial party supplied two-thirds of the delegates to the full party congress. The Reformists demanded a full congress, and the leadership (now including some former members of the Reformist Wing such as Kiyanuri, Tabari, Qasimi, and Jawdat) was in fear of losing its grip. The young intellectuals – Jalal Al-i Ahmad, Husain Malek, etc. – were under the influence of both the young and fiery theorist, Eprime Ishaq, and the 'elder' statesman of the party opposition, Khalil Maleki. It was they who persuaded Maleki to lead the famous split of January 1948.

The split was immediately denounced by the Soviet Union, and its leaders were branded as British spies and agents. They therefore decided to lie low for a time. A combination of observation and reflection quickly led Maleki into discovering the roots of the problem in Soviet Stalinism, on the one hand, and Marxist-Leninist ideology on the other. He denounced the former, and grew out of the latter without formally denouncing it. But some of his comrades in the Tudeh splinter group (e.g. Anvar Khameh'i) denounced him as a revisionist and opportunist, though many years later they themselves came round to the same views. Maleki was then ready for the Popular Movement to emerge.[1]

Maleki and the Popular Movement

Shortly after Baqa'i launched *Shahed* in 1949, Jalal Al-i Ahmad (who always regarded Maleki as his political mentor) joined its staff and persuaded Maleki to write for the newspaper.[2] A series of articles explaining why he had first joined and then left the Tudeh party were subsequently published in a separate volume, the famous *Conflict of Ideas and Opinions*, the Persian title of which (*Barkhurd-i Aqayed va Ara*) became one of the many social and political terms and phrases invented by Maleki and currently used in the Persian language. In it he described the attractiveness of communism *as a faith*, and the Soviet Union *as a power centre*, for modern intellectuals, especially in a country like Iran where there was no other alternative: 'we did not choose communism but were chosen by it'. He also described the moral and intellectual reserves within himself, which finally helped him to break free from his ideological fetters at great social and psychological cost. He predicted that the Tudeh party would make a bigger mistake over the Popular Movement than it had in the case of the Azerbaijan crisis, and – more significantly – described the factors in the party's character which would lead it into this mistake.[3]

The co-operation within *Shahed* continued and – in May 1951 – led to the formation of the *Zahmatkishan-i Mellat-i Iran* (Toilers of Iran) party. At first, the new party was dominated by the relics of Baqa'i's Action Group, but Maleki and the bulk of the Tudeh splinters who had entered this coalition began to attract growing numbers of the young, university students, workers and intellectuals to the party. Baqa'i led the party in the Majlis and at open-air meetings. Maleki, on the other hand, was the party theorist and organizer in addition to being in charge of its publications. *Shahed* became the party's daily organ. *Niru-yi Sevvum* (Third Force) was published every Friday as the organ of the party's youth organization. *Ilm va Zindigi* (Science and Living)[4] was the party's intellectual monthly periodical, though not as an official organ; it explicitly invited and published contributions by non-party writers. Maleki was its chief editor; Jalal Al-i Ahmad, Nadir Nadirpur (the famous poet) and Amir Pichdad (later a professor of medicine at Paris University) were successively its executive editors. The editorial board and regular contributors included Simin Danish-var, Mohammad Ali Khunji, Firaidun Tavalluli and Ali-Asghar Haj-Sayyed-Javadi.

Maleki was keen to keep Baqa'i in the Zahmatkishan party and the Popular Movement. He sympathized with Baqa'i over some of his personal grievances against Musaddiq, and himself was quite critical of some of Musaddiq's domestic and foreign policies (of which more below). But he regarded an open confrontation with Musaddiq's government as no less than catastrophic, and he would never allow Baqa'i to turn their party into an anti-government instrument. Baqa'i was not too surprised to find Maleki unco-operative over his new anti-Musaddiq strategy, but he was alarmed when he learned that the large majority of the party activists − workers, students and intellectuals, almost to a man − were solidly behind Maleki. Any doubts to the contrary were removed by the meeting of the party activists of 9 October 1952, which he himself had hastily summoned to get majority support for his proposed new strategy. He resigned from the party there and then. A few days later, however, he arranged for his toughs, together with those of Kashani, to attack the party headquarters and throw its activists out, and he then withdrew his resignation (see chapter 12).[5]

After the British lost the game with Qavam as their trump card, they turned to General Zahedi whom George Middleton, the British chargé d'affaires, had been secretly grooming[6] (see chapters 10 and 13). Zahedi began to mobilize his forces everywhere, including inside the Popular Movement where Baqa'i and Hayerizadeh were especially keen to listen. They had both had good relations with Zahedi in the past; and Hayerizadeh was to be actively involved in the 1953 coup, and be rewarded by Zahedi afterwards. Baqa'i had not told Maleki about his contacts with Zahedi, but the matter had been leaked, and it tied in well with Baqa'i's growing (though still private) anti-Musaddiq stance. Maleki was later to give a strong hint at this in his long open letter to Kashani in the first issue of the daily *Niru-yi Sevvum* (the newspaper of the new Zahmatkishan, Third Force, party) which was published on the day after the attack on the party headquarters:

> At any rate, it is certain that neither the Zahmatkishan party nor I
> . . . could turn a blind eye to plots which we believe to have
> dangerous consequences for the country. *I do not regard [the
> leadership of] a General Negib as acceptable for Iran, even
> assuming that it would be good for Egypt. Dr Musaddiq's
> personality has relieved us from the need for the General Negib
> types who might even be truly 'noble and dignified'.*[7] *And no
> 'noble and dignified' Iranian general would take any steps against
> Dr Musaddiq.*[8]

Baqa'i, of course, continued to dismiss Maleki's revelations about his anti-Musaddiq strategy, and claimed that the reason for the internal party rift was that Maleki was 'a non-Moscow communist'.[9] But he began to reveal his opposition to Musaddiq from then on, and soon became the most outspoken member of the opposition in the Majlis. In time, his party shrank to a small band of personal devotees, many of whom were from his native Kirman. But Third Force grew fast, launched a new (and daring) Progressive Women's Organization (*Sazman-i Zanan-i Pishraw*), increased its publications and other activities, and gave the government its unwavering support along with policy advice and solid (but loyal) criticism (see further below). Their moment of glory came on 28 February 1953, when they helped win the day for Musaddiq (see chapter 13).

After the 1953 coup, Maleki was jailed (deliberately, he believed) along with a group of Tudeh leaders, workers and intellectuals in the Falakul-aflak, a medieval citadel in Khurramabad.[10] In 1960 he led the formation of the Socialist League of the Popular Movement of Iran (see chapter 16). Five years later he was again arrested, tried in a military court on the customary charge of planning to overthrow the constitutional regime, and sentenced to three years' imprisonment. But he was released after he had served half his sentence because of continuing pressure on the shah by human rights groups and European socialist parties and governments (including the Austrian president). Two years later he died in isolation, depression and destitution.

The theory of the Third Force

When Maleki formulated his Third Force theory, the winds of the Cold War had been blowing for some time. A couple of years before, the USSR had almost come to blows with its wartime allies in Berlin. In 1949, Mao Tse-Tung had driven Chiang Kai-Shek out of China, and turned the United States into his regime's most bitter enemy. The war in Korea was raging, and that in Vietnam creeping. In 1948, the Communist takeover in Czechoslovakia had added that country to Stalin's war prizes without much fuss. Churchill had already made his famous speech about an iron curtain falling across Europe, though when it came to Western imperialism it was all explained (or explained away) in the name of freedom. India's independence had brought hope to the colonial and semi-colonial countries of Asia and Africa, but Nehru and his team were viewed with suspicion by both the United States and the Soviet Union. Tito's Yugoslavia had already broken free from the international communist movement. The West was naturally pleased about this as far as it went, but otherwise they had no more enthusiasm for Tito than they had for communism in their own territories. On the other hand, Moscow and its international brotherhood (including the Tudeh party) denounced Tito, Djilas and the rest of the Yugoslav leadership in terms which are now almost unprintable.[11]

Ever since 1943, there had been two main political camps in Iran: the pro-Soviet camp, represented by the Tudeh party, and the pro-Western camp, represented by the political establishment. The Western country which had by far the greatest power and influence in Iran was Britain, and the British could rely on the services, support, self-interest, or good will of various politicians ranging from Sayyed Zia and Qavam to Sa'id and Taqizadeh. There were now, however, hopes among some conservatives, including the shah and Zahedi, for a direct alliance with the United States.

Maleki's Third Force theory must be studied against this domestic and international background. He first developed the theory in a series of articles (written in 1951 and early 1952) which he later published under the titles 'The Third Force Will Triumph' (*Niru-yi Sevvum Piruz Mishavad*) and 'What is the Third Force?' (*Niru-yi Sevvum Chist?*), although he had developed and used its main concepts and ideas in many of his other writings. He introduced two broad categories, 'The Third Force in General' and 'The Third Force in Particular'. The 'general' concept referred to attempts to break free from the two (socialist and capitalist) stereotypes everywhere outside the USSR and the United States. The 'particular' category described the specifically socialist roads to progress, which were independent from the Eastern bloc and discovered by each country on the basis of its own culture and historical experience.

The Third Force in the world context

At the time the world political map was divided into two blocks: the 'socialist' and the 'imperialist' camps, 'the iron curtain countries' and 'the free world'. Maleki divided it into three: the West, the East, and the countries which many years later became known as 'the third world'. These were countries which 'neither feel free in Mr Truman's free world nor do they see any sign of socialism in the Soviet Union's Socialist camp. These masses of people in Asia, Europe, Africa and elsewhere wish – indeed most of them are determined – to co-operate with each other, and (despite the two world powers, and by taking advantage of the conflict between them) *protect their own national and social character and identity.*'[12] It was clear at the outset, then, that the Third Force theory went far beyond a mere articulation of the foreign policy of non-alignment, though this itself was quite an original idea at the time and formed a small part of Maleki's theory. According to this theory, the apparently solid and homogeneous front put forward by the West was misleading. Western Europe, in particular, was an advanced cultural and historical entity of its own which would soon recover its separate identity from the United States, but without crossing over to Soviet communism:

> The Western [European] civilization with its deep historical, economic, industrial and scientific roots will eventually recover from its [present] weaknesses, and will not surrender to either of these two simple and superficial civilizations which themselves have sprung up from Europe, but which have developed in the less advanced circumstances of Russia and America.[13]

This he described as the West European 'Third Force *in general*'. It was still based on capitalism, but one which was significantly different from American capitalism, and drew heavily on the rich European culture, and was likely to lead to the formation of a West European social and economic union. On the other hand, the West European Third Force *in particular* referred to the socialist methods of solving the social problems which result from the contradictions of capitalist society:

In Europe, 'the Third Force in particular' finds expression in a socialist approach which is consistent with the progressive tenets of European democracy . . .[14] Vis-à-vis American capitalism and its numerous European fellow-travellers, and Soviet state capitalism (which claims to be socialist, but which has destroyed economic, political and personal freedoms in Russia), a European road to socialism in the particular sense of the Third Force is now emerging and developing.[15]

Similar tendencies also existed within Eastern bloc countries, but Soviet suppression prevented their public expression and development:

Whenever the Third Force has dared raise its head in Eastern bloc countries it has been condemned and destroyed as deviationism, and as an agent and spy of imperialism. The only exception to this rule among the Balkan countries is Yúgoslavia, because this country has not been conquered – or, as the Cominform would put it, liberated – by the Red Army.[16]

Maleki's special regard for Yugoslavia was both because of its courageous stand against Stalin and (as a part of it) its own independent approach to socialism. But he did not necessarily agree with the Yugoslav system even for that country, let alone for Iran. In particular, he was critical of limitations on freedom in Yugoslavia and became even more critical when the regime began to persecute Djilas for the sake of peace with Khruschchev's Russia. The reference to 'the Balkan countries' in the above passage was not accidental. It would have looked very odd, almost unbelievable – at the time, and for many years to come – to claim that China too was likely to go down the road of Yugoslavia some time in the future, given the apparent Stalinist orthodoxy of its regime. But this was precisely what Maleki predicted would happen in the end because China's new regime was the product of a genuine and popular revolution rather than of Soviet conquest. He made the point elsewhere in a more exclusive article written at about the same time:

The Movement which Dr Sun-yat-sen began on the basis of his three basic principles, and which Mao Tse-tung now continues, will not in the end remain a satellite of the Soviet Union. Indeed, it can be confidently predicted that similar developments to those in Yugoslavia will also take place in China. The forms which these developments will take will doubtless be different from what happened in Yugoslavia. But their substance would be the same resistance against [Soviet] pressures and expansionist behaviour.[17]

In short, Western Europe's 'Third Force in general' was an attempt to protect its great traditions, identity and independence from both Russification and Americanization. Its 'Third Force in particular' was expressed through the development of democratic socialism based on Europe's own advanced experiences in both fields. Within the Soviet orbit, the Third Force in general and in particular were one and the same thing, namely, efforts to break free from Soviet domination and build an independent road to socialism on the basis of each country's peculiar culture and traditions. Yugoslavia was the actual, and China the potential, example of this movement, although even the former left much to be desired with regard to personal freedoms and democratic control.

There remained 'the colonial and semi-colonial countries'. Here, the Third Force in general had emerged in the form of popular and anti-imperialist movements which wished to throw off the shackles of colonialism, but had no intention of replacing them with Soviet domination. The Western powers were prepared to bring about certain reforms and changes in these countries through their ruling establishments, in the hope of permanently maintaining their own general hold over them. Their notion of 'freedom' for these countries meant little but the maintenance of the *status quo* – including their own political and economic domination – even though this might be combined with a certain amount of window-dressing. On the other hand, Soviet communism and its fraternity within these third world countries put forward the Stalinist theory that all efforts should be put in the service of the Soviet Union as 'the headquarters of the world proletariat'. According to this theory, the destiny of the world proletariat was directly bound up with the fortunes of the Soviet Union. The progressive and democratic forces in every country – big and small, rich and poor – must therefore give complete priority to the promotion of Soviet power in its global contest with the United States.

Thus, in both Western and Soviet eyes, any movement in colonial countries which did not toe their own particular line was bound to be an agent of the other side. They were both wrong, however; in spite of the local ruling establishments and the communist parties, which together made up a small (though powerful) numerical minority, there existed the independent force of the people of these countries – including their culture and history – harnessed by indigenous leaders and intellectuals who were not committed to any of those global powers, nor did they subscribe to their specific ideologies. This was 'the Third Force in general' – the non-communist movement for freedom and independence – within colonial and semi-colonial countries.[18]

But there was also a 'Third Force in particular', composed of the left wing of these popular movements, who wished to spread them further in time and space, and bring about political progress and economic development via their own peculiar roads to socialism. It would be best to discuss this tendency in the context of the Third Force in Iran.

The Third Force in Iran

It follows from the above brief account that the Popular Movement was Iran's example of 'the Third Force in general', and the democratic socialist forces within that Movement (which had developed Iranian models of socialism for application after the Movement's success in its broader democratic aims) made up the particular Third Force in Iran. Regarding the Iranian Third Force in general:

> All those who have no hope in the decadent ruling establishment, and no expectations from the leaders of the Tudeh party . . . , belong to the Third Force. All those who support the nationalization of Iranian oil everywhere in the country [i.e. not only in the south, as the Tudeh party wanted it], that is the nationalization of all the resources and industries which either Britain or Russia hopes to possess at one and the same time, are part of the Third Force. All those who find it possible to maintain Iran's political and economic independence without its attachment to the Eastern or Western Bloc, who believe in the power of their own people, and the ability of their own leaders, and who think it possible for the people of Iran to hold their destiny without blindly following this or that foreign power, belong to the Third Force. . .

But there were those who did not belong:

> The gentlemen of the Tudeh party as well as those in the service of the ruling establishment ought to be taught to overcome their sense of weakness and inferiority, and recognize their own existence, and the power of their own people; that is, the Third Force. Those who have not managed to recognize their own

existence and independence have failed to understand the reality of the Popular Movement of Iran.[19]

As the symbol of the Third Force in general, Dr Musaddiq is the most obvious, the most intelligent, and the most worthy personality which modern Iranian history has put forward before expansionists of all colours and creeds.[20]

The Third Force in Iran was not only the force which resisted both Western and Soviet domination of the country, but also, and at the same time,

> *an alternative social model, a mode of national and social living distinct from both the American and the Russian models which they try to impose on us.* The Third Force is the modern manifestation of the will of freedom-loving people in Iran, itself reflecting a great deal of historical experience through the centuries of Iranian civilization.[21]

Despite the Tudeh party theorists, the National Front was neither an instrument of imperialism nor even a 'bourgeois or petty-bourgeois' movement. It was a coalition of forces, all of which wished to promote freedom, independence and democracy, and the left wing of which had developed a specifically Iranian model for social and economic renovation, progress and justice. This model did indeed draw on Europe's experience of industrialization, democracy and socialism, but it was not an imported blueprint and was firmly based on Iran's own past history and present resources. The Zahmatkishan party was a *melli* force, i.e. one which was both 'national' (as opposed to foreign-inspired) and 'popular' (as opposed to *dawlati* or *mustabid*). But it was *not* nationalist in the racialist, chauvinist or expansionist sense of this term.

> It is therefore evident that the Zahmatkishan party is in one sense absolutely *melli*. That is, it seeks its social base among the great masses of the people, and the labouring and productive classes of this country; it rejects any development or movement which does not originate within the mass of the people; it is conscious of the fact that real social progress must find its source and origin in the capacity and potential of the people themselves, and use that potential to produce a programme which is consistent with the country's resources and with the stage of social development.[22]

Apart from this vision of an Iranian democracy and socialism, Maleki's main contributions in this period centred around two themes: one, the Popular Movement's policies and programmes; two, philosophy of history, socialist theory, and the phenomenon of the Soviet Union. It is impossible to do justice to either of these two topics in this limited account; in what follows, only a bare outline is given (the interested reader is referred to Maleki's original works).

Government policy and programme

The recurring themes in Maleki's strategic advice to Musaddiq and his government were briefly as follows: (a) to settle the oil dispute on the best *possible* terms within a reasonable period of time; (b) to launch a series of major social reforms – especially land reform, reform of the state bureaucracy, and the application of other redistributive measures; (c) to stand up to the destructive activities of foreign agents, the Tudeh party as well as the conservative (military and non-military) elements who were trying to bring down the goverment by illegal means; and (d) to establish good relations with both the West and the Soviet Union, but to refuse to enter any military alliance with either of them.

On the settlement of the oil dispute, Maleki's logic was in line with Musaddiq's own view of the Movement. Oil nationalization was, in the first instance, a strategy towards attaining the country's independence and establishing a democratic regime. Iran was too weak to go every inch of the way over the oil dispute, given the United States' ultimate backing for Britain, and the Soviet Union's unhelpful attitude. Besides, there was the enemy within in the shape of the ruling establishment and the Tudeh party. He backed World Bank mediation (see chapter 12), and was later the only major voice within the Movement who dared to emphasize the necessity of a settlement for the survival of the whole Movement. An honourable settlement (even though it would be short of the ideal) would remove international pressure, normalize the country's economic situation, increase the government's financial power, and enable it to spend on projects for social and economic development. This would start a virtuous circle in favour of the Popular Movement, and against its enemies in the country.

Land reform was, and remained, one of Maleki's two favourite themes for social reform, the other being the emancipation of women. He advocated a comprehensive reform of Iran's system of land tenure, both for reasons of justice and morality and in the interest of social and economic development. He welcomed Musaddiq's attempt at a partial redistribution of income from landlords to peasants (see chapter 10) but viewed it as no more than a temporary measure. We shall briefly discuss his own particular formula for a comprehensive land reform later in chapter 16. On the question of women, he did not miss an occasion to advocate (a) the full franchise and integration into civil society of 'the one-half of society which brings up the other half in its lap', and (b) the need to mobilize the country's full capacity and potential by bringing its women into the sphere of public economic and social activity.

The conservatives would lose much of their foreign support and encouragement the minute the oil dispute was settled. The Tudeh party would also be neutralized as soon as the government entered into a fair and cordial relationship with the Soviet Union on an equal footing. But, in the meantime, the government should apply the law (as it did not) to put a stop to undemocratic and conspiratorial activities – sabotage, disruption of public life, defamatory propaganda, etc. – by its domestic enemies. Furthermore, it would be a grave mistake to succumb to Tudeh temptations (propagated through one of their open organizations which described itself as 'The Popular Society for Anti-colonial Struggle') for a 'United Anti-imperialist Front'. The Tudeh party had no independent will of its own, and the best way of stopping its disruptive activities – even gaining its co-operation, perhaps – was to establish good relations with the Soviet Union.

On the whole, the Iran party leaders (and some of Musaddiq's other close advisers) were not very enthusiastic about these ideas. Some of them were opposed to any settlement of the oil dispute short of total victory, because they were afraid of losing popularity. They did not advocate socio-economic reform and development, and said nothing about land reform and women's emancipation. They were not too keen on the efficient enforcement of the law, because they were extremely averse to making personal enemies, conservative, Tudeh, or any other. And, for similar reasons, they were prepared to be more responsive to Tudeh overtures, although Maleki and his party managed to prevent the development of any serious relationship between the Movement and that party's front organizations. For they saw their aim as none other than the penetration and eventual domination of the whole Movement now that it had a large and independent social base, in spite of their vehement campaigns against it.

The programme outlined above could best be applied as a package, as had in fact been intended. In particular, a comprehensive land reform would not have been possible without the prior settlement of the oil dispute. But the law could have been enforced before a settlement with Britain; indeed, it was probably more imperative while the government faced financial hardship within, and a hostile attitude towards itself outside, the country. This should not have involved ham-fisted or illiberal behaviour on the part of the government. It would not have been necessary to ban right-wing political parties and clubs, or the front organizations and publications of the Tudeh party. Nor would it have been necessary to resort to wholesale arrests and containment. It would have been enough to bring suspected law-breakers to justice, keep order in the streets, and enforce the libel laws. That aside, when, from April 1953, everyone was convinced that a coup against the government was imminent, Zahmatkishan-Third Force suggested the formation of Popular Movement district com-mittees, and a Popular Movement Guard to defend the government, and managed to set up two such committees themselves.[23] But the government did not agree to their proposal, or support them in their voluntary action. The government's inertia in enforcing the law and preparing to defend itself was one of the principal reasons behind the defeat of Musaddiq and the Popular Movement when they were seemingly in power.

History, socialism and the Soviet Union

At the time, Soviet Marxism was the only interpretation of Marxism with wide currency in the realm of political theory and practice throughout the world. An important aspect of this interpretation (even in its Trotskyist version) was the belief in an iron historical necessity, a determinism which was almost indistinguishable from fatalism. Maleki, by contrast, emphasized the importance of both individual and social consciousness in shaping events. What would have happened if Razmara had not been assassinated?, he once asked.[24] What would have happened if Reza Khan *had been*? he could equally well have asked.

The concept of 'historical necessity' was not invented by Marx. In modern political thought it goes back at least to Vico, Herder and Montesquieu. Other thinkers – Maleki mentioned Hegel, Monod, Guizot, Mignet and Spencer – later developed the same idea in the eighteenth and nineteenth centuries into hard determinism. But 'realistic socialists' (he meant Marx) 'corrected' their excesses.

For a progressive and socially-conscious individual, history is a description and analysis of the present, based on past experiences, in the hope of creating a better and more advanced future.

There might be natural laws and historical constraints, but these did not in themselves condemn any individual or society to a certain destiny:

> Those who understand the laws of nature can impose their own will on them. Those who know past history and are familiar with its laws . . . are able to govern future history.[25]

Britain's control of Iran's oil industry might have been a historical necessity; that is, a product of its industry and empire. But so was the Popular Movement of Iran and its reaction against it:

> So long as individuals and peoples are not conscious of social laws and social relations they will be enslaved by the system which rules over them. But when the masses of the people understood those social laws . . . and realized that they were not due to celestial forces, it would be possible to undo the laws themselves. Hence, they move from the realm of necessity into the realm of freedom.[26]

There were two distinct concepts of necessity: scientific and metaphysical. The metaphysical concept was not merely found among the followers of traditional religions, but was shared by some modern ideologies as well. The elementary principles of democracy required that social change be based on the needs of the great masses of the people; and 'socialism is unthinkable without democracy'. Therefore, socialist necessity arose from democratic choice, not the dicta of impersonal history.[27]

Maleki's theoretical attack on the notion of 'historical inevitability', like all his other theoretical discussions, had a firm basis in political practice and experience. Four years earlier, and exactly at the time of the split in the Tudeh party, he had written a long pamphlet on behalf of the critics who were about to leave the party, in which he had firmly rejected the Tudeh leadership's use of fatalistic arguments in the hope of justifying their own mistakes as well as reassuring their membership that victory would inevitably be theirs:

> In the Executive Committee's statement, and as a part of a long argument intended to prove the inevitability of past mistakes, it

has been said: 'The party leadership is part of this same [Iranian] society . . . and its shortcomings cannot be isolated from the larger society and its limitations. . .' Those who – for the sake of justifying a few of the party's leaders – wish to base future decisions on the same mistaken methods of the past do the party no service at all . . . In their view, historical inevitability would, willy nilly, take us to socialism. Therefore, they neither believe in an able and intelligent leadership, nor in a conscious and active struggle. As they themselves put it, they have 'faith' in the International Democratic Front, which is apparently supposed to succeed mechanically, and without any effort on the part of the national movements.

On the other hand, freedom of choice should not be confused with the naive as well as dangerous concept of voluntarism which was the other side of the coin. The programme of every popular movement for social change 'must be consistent both with the existing social constraints, and with the actual forces which wish to bring it about'.[28] Voluntarism and political romanticism were doomed to failure, in part because they would use any means to achieve their ends, whereas – both for moral and scientific reasons – ends and means could not possibly be separated from each other:

In principle, the only standard by which the aims of a political party ought to be judged is the means which it employs. And if these do not correspond to its declared aims, we must conclude that the party in question does not pursue its alleged objectives. On the contrary, its real objectives are those which are placed at the end of the path which it treads.[29]

The Soviet Union was a complex phenomenon. Stalinism had almost managed to destroy every fundamental tenet of socialism, and every democratic vestige of the Russian Revolution. In its foreign relations, the Soviet behaviour towards its 'allies' and 'fraternal parties' was no less exploitative than that of Western imperialism towards non-European countries. Stalin's interpretation of Lenin's internationalism was that the world proletariat and their parties should sacrifice their own interests for the sake of 'the citadel of socialism', 'the headquarters of the world proletariat', the Soviet Union. Hence, they now had an ideological justification for exploitation whereby the faithful volunteers should let themselves be sacrificed in the hope of realizing the millennium at an indeterminate time in the future.

Furthermore, Stalinism was not just a foreign policy or a pro-Russian theory of internationalism. 'The hypothesis that the Soviet Union is a socialist country cannot justify or absolve the anti-socialist realities of the Soviet state.' For, apart from the colonial relationship between the Soviet Union and its satellite parties and countries, the Soviet workers and peasants were exploited, there were extreme inequalities in the standard of living, and the Soviet state ruled the country with an iron fist.

In his *State and Revolution*, Lenin had promised that the moment the socialist state was created it 'begins to wither away'. But the reality was the absolute opposite. It was not socialism; it was state capitalism:

In socialism, the tendency is towards democracy and decentralization; in state capitalism, it is towards 'the strengthening of the state at any cost'. In the former, the proletariat gradually replaces the party. In the latter, the party and – eventually – a few of its leaders usurp the seat of the working class, and an oligarchy, or even absolute rule by one individual, becomes established.[30]

Furthermore, the Soviet system was state capitalism because, while the state owned the productive capital, the workers were exploited in the same Marxian sense of creating surplus value for their employers. It might have been possible to justify this on the basis of Marx's theory of capital accumulation and economic development had there been a tendency towards industrial democracy and redistribution of income in Russia. But here as well the trend was the other way round. The state bureaucracy was expanding to the point of there being 'overmanning' (or 'disguised unemployment') within it, and a growing gap between its standard of living and that of the ordinary people.

Regarding the Popular Movement of Iran, the Soviet Union applied the same old 'General Line' as it did everywhere else. Both Russia and the Tudeh party described Musaddiq as an agent of American imperialism simply because the Movement which he led was independent of themselves. Even the Movement's objective struggle against British imperialism was not good enough for them, partly because the nationalization of oil everywhere in the country had robbed them of the hope of getting North Iran's oil concession, and partly because they preferred to deal with Britain in the Middle East, rather than face the possibility of its replacement by the United States. In fact, the Soviet Union's global strategy, its international network, its seductive ideology, and its local organization in the shape of the Tudeh party, posed 'the greatest danger for the Popular Movement':

The Soviet Union . . . has a global strategy for the implementation of which the parties which call themselves communist, and their fellow-travellers, are its executive branches. As we know, every popular movement, and every attempt at establishing social justice and struggling against imperialism which is not within the general framework of the Cominform is described – in Stalin's dictionary of Leninism – as an instrument of imperialism. Since our Popular Movement is not part of this whole, the headquarters of the Cominform regards the fight against this Movement as one of its most fundamental duties, which it conducts by means of its Iranian branch, i.e. the Tudeh party. . .

By misusing and deforming socialism which is the most advanced system and school [of politics], the Cominform has turned it into an instrument of the Soviet Union's expansionist policy. Thus, for the first time in history, an expansionist and aggressive power is using a weapon which has no rival of its kind. Tens and hundreds of thousands – even millions – of simple-minded people believe that they are struggling for the greatest and most sacred human ideal. Whereas, in reality, they have fallen into the trap of a state which does not hold the slightest value for their freedom and independence.[31]

The above is a brief and partial account of Maleki's ideas and efforts at the time, from which he never departed. But he was to continue his thoughts and actions beyond the 1953 coup, and we shall see him again in later chapters of this book.

9

Musaddiq's first government (May 1951–July 1952)

The cabinet

Musaddiq's first cabinet went beyond the National Front coalition, and included outsiders, notably General Zahedi, as minister of the interior. There were two reasons behind this. Tactically, he wanted to reassure the shah and the conservatives as much as possible, in a calculated move to minimize trouble and keep his reluctant Majlis majority in one piece. The longer-term reason was that (with one or two major exceptions) Musaddiq always appointed his ministers from among administrative, technocratic and largely apolitical individuals, while, for purely political decisions, he relied mainly on the advice of his National Front colleagues in the Majlis, who were more needed there, and themselves preferred to be in the legislative chamber rather than have an executive position. Indeed, Dr Sanjaby, who was minister of education in Musaddiq's first government, became a Majlis deputy in the next parliamentary session; and Mahmud Nariman who left the Majlis to become minister of finance (in a cabinet reshuffle) went back to it in the following session. Fatemi, on the other hand, was first elected to the Seventeenth Majlis, and then joined the government as minister without portfolio and, after 21 July, foreign minister. The only other political (as opposed to administrative and technocratic) members of Musaddiq's cabinets were Allahyar Saleh, Shams al-Din Amir-Ala'i, Dr Ghulamhusain Sadiqi and – to a lesser extent – Baqir Kazemi (Muhazzib al-Dawleh). Saleh replaced Zahedi as minister of the interior, but ended up as Iran's ambassador to the United States. Amir-Ala'i was minister of justice for a short period, then governor in Khuzistan during the operations for the repossession of the oil industry (*Khal'-i Yad*) in Abadan, but ended up as Iran's ambassador to

113

Belgium. Sadiqi was made minister of posts and telegraphs before becoming minister of the interior as well as deputy prime minister. Kazemi was foreign and finance minister, and deputy prime minister, at various stages, but finished up as ambassaor in Paris.

But despite the broad base of Musaddiq's first cabinet the shah was still unhappy. Many appointments, such as those of provincial governorships, had been made without his consent.[1] Foreign policy had slipped out of his hands, and ambassadors no longer reported direct to the royal court as before, although that practice had not been strictly constitutional. He was worried by the extensive and increasing Tudeh party activity in various guises, as well as their open press and publications under other names. This was a legacy of Razmara who – as we have already seen – had been in a tactical alliance with the Tudeh leaders since 1948. It continued and intensified under Musaddiq for two reasons: there was no easy way to curtail such activities *legally* because they were not conducted in the name of the Tudeh party (which had already been banned); and the banning of any political party would not have been consistent with Musaddiq's political ideals. On the other hand, the fact that his government did not use the full force of the law to prevent campaigns of defamation, disruption and destruction against itself, was equally true of both Right *and* Left, though the shah would not have wished to see firmness shown equally to the undemocratic Right as well as to the Left.

14 July 1951 (23 Tir 1330)

In fact, the shah had even more serious worries. He had seen how the British government had brought his father to his knees in 1933 and sent him into exile in 1941, and had also thought of replacing the Pahlavis by the Qajars and only reluctantly tolerated his own succession. He was under pressure from the British and their local agents and associates to stand up to Musaddiq, and this ran against his native lack of self-confidence. Moreover, regarding his personal psychology, he was (and was to become even more) intensely jealous of the old man's knowledge, experience, self-assuredness and, in particular, his great public appeal. So desperately anxious was he that, only three weeks after Musaddiq's premiership began, he sent Husain Ala (now minister of the royal court) to tell him his fears lest there should be a constitutional change in favour of a republic. Musaddiq took the point, reassured Ala, and (on 25 May) wrote to the shah asking him to nominate the chief prefect of the police himself. The shah suggested Major-General (later Senator) Baqa'i, and the latter was given the post.[2]

This provided the means for Musaddiq's opponents to make their first major move against him. On 14 July, Averell Harriman – President Truman's intermediary in the Anglo-Iranian oil negotiations – arrived in Tehran. The US government, in principle opposed to old-style imperialism and wishing to extend its power and influence in Iran, as well as stem the tide of universal communism, and having nothing to lose (if not something to gain), was hoping to steer a middle course, and find a solution acceptable to its British allies as well as the Iranians. Dr Henry Grady, the US ambassador to Iran, and George McGhee, the young Assistant Secretary of State, played an important role in formulating this policy, before they lost their posts largely through pressure from the Conservative government soon to be returned to power in Britain.

The Tudeh party and the Soviet Union saw the matter in a different light. The Tudeh party, which had vehemently opposed the National Front's oil nationalization programme under Razmara, at first described it as a British plot which their domestic agents (Musaddiq and his colleagues) had been commissioned to pursue. In the early months of Musaddiq's premiership, the analysis changed, and the Popular Movement was described as an American conspiracy – led by Musaddiq and other US agents – to expel the British from Iran and its oil industry, and replace them both. To the Tudeh party, this was a far greater sin than complicity with Britain. The United States was the Soviet Union's and, therefore, the world proletariat's chief enemy and rival. It would be much more desirable for the British to stay in Iran and the Middle East, than be replaced by Americans.[3] Hence the party's persistent press campaigns and street demonstrations – full as they were of verbal and physical violence – against Musaddiq and his government and supporters, and their tacit or explicit co-operation with the Right to bring his government down. The documents discovered in June 1951 in the AIOC's Central Information Bureau in Tehran, and at the house of the company's chief representative in Tehran, N. R. Seddon, revealed that the company was aiding the Tudeh press explicitly to render their opposition more effective. They were also using the Peace Club, a Tudeh front organization which was largely led by members of the conservative establishment.[4] Hence, also, Musaddiq's coining of the original and eloquent term 'Oil Communist' (*Tudeh-Nafti*).

The moment Harriman's visit was announced, the Tudeh party

described it as proof of a complete sell-out to the United States, and planned street demonstrations for the day of his arrival. These were banned by the government, but the party decided to break the law and go ahead with them. Musaddiq had personally instructed the police chief, General Baqa'i, to stop the demonstrations but not to use firearms without obtaining prior permission from himself. Harriman arrived on 14 July, the demonstrations were held in full force, and Baqa'i ordered the police to open fire (without Musaddiq's knowledge or approval) leaving a number of casualties. Baqa'i as well as General Zahedi (the minister of the interior) were dismissed, and Baqa'i was committed for military trial which predictably cleared him of any misconduct. Musaddiq did not resign (as had been hoped by the architects of the event), but it was a serious blow to his position and prestige, especially outside Iran. Whether or not there had been direct co-ordination between the Right and the Tudeh leaders is uncertain, although one or two of them – such as Nur al-Din Kiyanuri – may have liaised with the Right even without the other leaders' knowledge. We have already seen that Kiyanuri, at any rate, was quite experienced in using his own initiative in such decisions.

Repossession

On 19 June the Iranian flag was hoisted in Abadan from the top of the largest refinery in the world. The five-man Provisional Board of the National Iranian Oil Company (headed by Mehdi Bazargan, and including Husain Makki) had already arrived there to take over the AIOC's assets. But the AIOC officials were in no mood for co-operating with them. They refused to show them the files or give them any administrative or technical information about running the industry. They had already turned off the taps, and refused to give government officials a simple receipt against current liftings and loadings. The government feared that they were looking for an incident which would justify the intervention of British troops in the name of defending British lives and property. Indeed, Musaddiq, Makki and Amir-Ala'i had had to issue personal appeals to the Iranian employees not to allow themselves to be provoked.

The oil company had no intention of coming to a settlement little short of a complete reversal of fortunes, and the attitude of the British Foreign Office was generally in line with this. Sir Francis Shepherd, the British ambassador, had been anti-National Front from the start, and despised Musaddiq personally, to the extent that, as early as 6 May

1951, he described him as looking like a 'cab horse', and unjustly accused him of being a drug addict.[5]

The government, however, was still hoping for a quick and amicable settlement, though – with the benefit of hindsight – this seems to have been somewhat naive. Harriman and Grady prepared the ground for the British negotiating team, led by Richard Stokes, Lord Privy Seal in the Labour government. Musaddiq went out of his way to receive them as the country's honoured guests, put them at their ease, and talked to them in a friendly fashion – which must have been partly the reason for Stokes's kind gesture in sending him a Christmas card in jail two-and-a-half years later.[6] Before the arrival of Stokes's mission, and with Harriman's active help, Musaddiq had obtained a formal acceptance of the principle of the oil nationalization from the British government '*qua* itself, and on behalf of the Anglo-Iranian Oil Company'.

Attlee's government was tired and in disarray, and the successful handling of this blow to British interest and prestige was beyond its capacity. The Conservative opposition and the British press, both quality and popular, were howling for blood, and – in Eden's later words – wanted to 'restore the stolen property'.[7] Beyond the sheer legal and technical argument, the British were seriously worried about the spread of the disease of 'Musaddiqism' in the Arab Middle East which they still controlled, and a similar threat to their position in the Suez Canal, especially in view of Musaddiq's immense popularity in those countries.[8] The nationalization of Iranian oil appeared to be a serious blow to the British Empire's position and prestige the world over, and it undoubtedly hurt national pride.

The failure of Stokes's mission must be seen against these British and Iranian perspectives, although – in all fairness – Stokes, and perhaps Attlee himself, did not entirely share the AIOC's view of the dispute. The negotiations were broken off (though not yet formally ended) on 22 August, Stokes left Iran, and attitudes hardened on both sides (see chapter 11). However, no sooner had Stokes left than – in the wake of Iran's occupation of the oil zone – his conscience began to worry him. He wrote a letter to Attlee early in September, in which he effectively condemned the past as well as present behaviour and attitude of the AIOC, and pointed out that the 50–50 offer to the Iranians was no longer fair. As he was about to dispatch the letter, he received a letter from the Agha Khan, expressing much the same views, which he enclosed with his own for the prime minister's information.[9]

The Iranian government was left with no choice but to continue its repossession operations in Khuzistan. In an address to the British technicians and skilled staff, Musaddiq invited them to stay at their posts with the same pay and conditions, but they refused the offer. Eventually, they were issued with notice to leave the country, and late in September the oil zone was occupied by Iranian troops. By this time the battle lines had been clearly drawn. Attlee's cabinet was divided on how to react to the new developments. Herbert Morrison, the number two man in the Labour cabinet, was angered by this treatment of 'poor whites' and, together with Emmanuel (later, Lord) Shinwell, advocated the use of military force.[10] Attlee tactfully sat on the fence and let others (especially Hugh Gaitskell who, as the party leader, was to confront Eden over Suez in 1956) outmanoeuvre the Labour hawks.

Britain had already applied for, and obtained, an injunction from the International Court at the Hague (on 6 July 1951) to forestall repossession, pending the result of its litigation against Iran. The Iranian government rejected the Court's injunction, however, on the legal argument that – since the 1933 Agreement had been concluded, not between the two governments, but between the Iranian government and an independent company – the International Court lacked jurisdiction in the case.[11] On 28 September, Britain complained to the UN Security Council about Iran's disregard of the injunction. Meanwhile, the AIOC was refusing to pay its outstanding debts and royalties to Iran, and Iranian assets at the Bank of England were frozen.

The British general elections in October brought the Conservatives to power, with Eden as the new foreign secretary. A letter from President Truman to Musaddiq gave him the impression (falsely, as we now know) that he wanted to talk to him personally in Washington.[12] This was why the old and ailing prime minister himself led the Iranian delegation to the Security Council, paying his own expenses (75,000 rials in all) from his private purse.[13] They put their legal case on the International Court's decision, and, perhaps more effectively, supplied documentary evidence about Reza Shah's dictatorship and the arbitrary way in which the 1933 Agreement had been concluded. Furthermore, they presented the documents obtained from the AIOC's Information Bureau and Seddon's house about their involvement in internal Iranian affairs. The Council decided in their favour and postponed any decision, pending the result of the Court's ruling over its jurisdiction in the case. While in the United States, Musaddiq met President Truman, Dean Acheson (the Secretary of State) and, several times, George McGhee. McGhee came up with a brilliant formula to resolve the dispute, which Musaddiq accepted. Acheson then took the proposal to Paris to obtain Eden's approval, while Musaddiq waited for the result. But Eden turned it down and told Acheson to 'send him home'.[14] Musaddiq returned home via Egypt, where his tumultuous welcome by the Egyptian people was noted by the British Foreign Office as further evidence of the soundness of their strategy towards him.

The general elections

Back in Iran, he was faced with two major issues: the state of the economy in the absence of oil revenues and foreign aid, and the impending general elections for the Seventeenth Majlis. A free vote would have returned a comfortable majority for the government. But the realities were different: the provincial magnates – most of whom were anti-government – would interfere in the elections with the aid and support of the provincial army and gendarmerie chiefs who still took their orders from the shah; and the Tudeh party would resort to any means, mainly in Tehran (but also in Isfahan, Rasht, Pahlavi, and one or two other urban centres where they had sufficient following), to get its candidates elected. The government's only major concern was to try and prevent election rigging as well as violence and disruption in its process. But this, in itself, was a monumental task.

Musaddiq took the diplomatic step of first discussing the whole election issue with the shah, although this was not constitutionally necessary. He told the shah that the elections ought to be free. The shah agreed, but then asked 'What about the Tudeh party?' Musaddiq explained that it, too, had a right to its own vote, but he assured the shah that it had very little chance of success; even assuming it managed to send a few deputies to the Majlis, what danger could they possibly pose to the government and the country?[15] Apparently, he did not add that such an event ought even to be welcomed, because the Tudeh's presence in the Majlis would inevitably restrict its members' undemocratic conduct when they were complete outsiders, and force them to act more in the manner and style of a democratic opposition.

The shah was seemingly unconvinced. But the real issue behind it all was that both men wanted to send their own candidates to the chamber; Musaddiq, by the people's free vote, the shah, mainly by direct and indirect interference. Therefore, the ranks were tacitly closed, and the battle stations prepared for action. However, one redeeming feature was that all the interested parties were actively watching each other's moves and methods, ready to expose any irregularity committed by their rivals.

Because of the vastness of the country and the poor means of communication in many places, elections in Iran were always a long and arduous process. They were conducted relatively quickly in the major cities, but it took weeks and months for the results of small towns and rural constituencies to be returned. The results were therefore announced as they came in. The Popular Movement candidates won in almost all the large cities and towns, although not all of them (even in the case of Tehran) were fully committed to the Movement – a fact which was later to cause problems for the government, specially from January to August 1953. The (twelve) National Front candidates for Tehran were elected to a man: Makki, Kashani, Baga'i, Shaigan, Zirak-zadeh, Hasibi, Hayerizadeh, Zuhari, Mushar, Rashid and Parsa. The Tudeh party's vote was well down: its first candidate for Tehran scored considerably less than the National Front's twelfth deputy-elect. But the conservatives came last, their first candidate, in turn, scoring less than the Tudeh party's twelfth.

The picture in small towns and rural areas was considerably different, however: the Tudeh party had little or no strength in these areas, and it was much more difficult for the government to stop the efforts of the shah and his conservative allies to rig the elections. For example, having failed to become an official National Front candidate for Tehran, Dr Sayyed Hasan Imami – the *Imam-Jum'eh* of Tehran, and a nephew of Musaddiq's wife – was (on the shah's recommendation) returned for Mahabad by the territorial army. Mahabad was the small Kurdish capital which had been under military control since the fall of an autonomous Kurdish government in the city in 1946. The *Imam Jum'eh* had had no base whatsoever there or anywhere in the region; and, moreover, as a semi-official Shi'ite dignitary, he was at a great additional disadvantage in a purely Sunni town. In Abadan, the three-cornered fight – but especially that between the Popular Movement and the Tudeh party – claimed death and injury every day, and the government was forced to stop the election process altogether even though its own candidate would have won the vote easily.

In the circumstances, the names of 80 deputies-elect (out of 136 for the whole of the country) had been announced by June 1952, when Musaddiq was due to lead the Iranian delegation to The Hague for the International Court's hearing of the British lawsuit. He decided to stop the rest of the elections until his return, but the worsening strife in the remaining constituencies was to prevent the completion of the process. The non-completion of the elections was not illegal; but if the incomplete Majlis which made up about two-thirds of the full House had told him to continue the elections, he would have had to oblige.

Nevertheless, it was his first major defeat by the country's powerful undemocratic traditions and social institutions.

Musaddiq personally opened the case for the defence at the International Court and then rushed back home for the formal opening of the new Majlis,[16] leaving the rest of the case in the hands of Henri Rollin, a distinguished Belgian lawyer who was acting as Iran's chief counsel. By the time the majority of judges voted in Iran's favour, Musaddiq had begun his second term of office, then resigned, and subsequently been swept back to power by a public uprising.

The 21 July uprising

When the Seventeenth Majlis began its business, Musaddiq resigned by convention to allow the new parliament to choose its own government. Both in the Majlis and in the Senate the straw vote went in his favour unopposed, but the shah made sure that the Senators (half of whom were directly appointed by himself) did not give Musaddiq a firm vote of confidence. He remained the only candidate proposed from the floor of the Senate, but a large number of those present abstained in their straw vote. The shah had been under pressure from Britain and its Iranian agents and assistants to put Qavam (whom he did not like) into office.

As we shall see below, Musaddiq himself was looking for an excuse to quit. But his advisers (who were unaware of his real reason) swept aside his protests about the insufficiency of the Senate vote, on the ground both that the Senate was a weak and relatively unrepresentative chamber, and that it would be a grave political mistake to quit on such a flimsy issue.[17] Nevertheless, the shah provided Musaddiq with a better excuse to resign and, by yet another irony of history, he came back to power with a greater prestige and popularity than ever before.

When Robin Zaehner, the Oxford Persian scholar and undercover Foreign Office agent, came to Tehran in the summer of 1951, he concluded that Qavam was the best man to replace Musaddiq and settle the oil issue with Britain. In the minutes of his conversations with Abbas Iskandari – a staunch Qavam supporter who himself had fired the opening shots against the 1933 Agreement in the Fifteenth Majlis (see chapter 6) – Zaehner wrote:

After concluding our discussion on the ways and means of overthrowing Musaddiq, Iskandari went on to reassure me (in Persian) that it was Qavam's desire to work closely with the

British and to preserve their legitimate interests in Persia without jeopardizing Persia's political and economic independence.

Furthermore:

> Qavam-us-Saltaneh greatly preferred that British influence should be exercised in Persia, rather than that of the Americans (who were foolish and without experience), or of the Russians who were Persia's enemies . . . If we [i.e. the British] were prepared to accept Qavam-us-Saltaneh's assurance that he would come to an agreement satisfactory to both sides, we must give him a free hand in the use of methods. . .[18]

Qavam himself had made some personal contacts with right-wing British politicians such as Julian Amery.[19]

The shah had therefore agreed to replace Musaddiq by Qavam. But how? The Popular Movement coalition was still intact, and Musaddiq's public support was unswerving. The shah's attempt at election rigging in the provinces had been only partially successful. Musaddiq did not have a permanent majority in the Majlis but he had a large, united and organized minority of the deputies behind him with which no other ministerial candidate could compete. And, in the circumstances, a military coup would have been doomed to failure from the start. Suddenly, Heaven seemed to come to the shah's aid when, on 16 July, Musaddiq went to the palace to discuss the composition of his new cabinet before presenting it to the Majlis.

Musaddiq had already been contacted by the Patriotic Officers (of whom more in chapter 10) about corruption, disloyalty and acts of sabotage in the army. He was also well aware of the role played by the provincial army (as well as the gendarmerie which was a parliamentary force) during the elections. By convention, the shah used to appoint the minister of war, though this was unconstitutional. Musaddiq therefore decided to claim his constitutional right as the prime minister to choose the minister of war himself. The shah's choice was always an army general, but, for a number of reasons – and, in particular, in order not to alarm the shah that he wanted to take full command of the army – Musaddiq politely suggested that he should 'supervise' the war ministry himself. The shah reacted angrily by saying that he should 'let [him] pack his suitcase and leave the country first'.[20] He knew that this was his moment to try and engineer Qavam's succession. What he did not suspect, and was never to learn even afterwards, was that Musaddiq, too, was looking for an excuse to quit the stage. For this has only recently come to light through the pages of Musaddiq's memoirs, and even then in the shape of a fleeting remark within a totally different context.

When leaving for The Hague a couple of weeks earlier, he says, he had been convinced that Britain would win its case at the World Court. He had therefore decided to resign the minute the unfavourable decision was announced by the Court, and never to return to Iran.[21] The reader may recall that, once before in his political career, he had decided to emigrate when the 1919 Agreement had been concluded, and his withdrawal to Ahmad-Abad after the failure of his campaign for free elections in 1947 had been part of the same psychological pattern. It was precisely the same psychology which a year later led him into another – this time fatal – mistake by holding a referendum to dissolve the Majlis (see chapter 13).

Before The Hague decision had been made, however, he had had to return to Tehran for the formalities of the new parliamentary session, though he still believed that the Court's vote would go against Iran. Therefore, the moment the shah opposed his suggestion of running the war ministry himself, he made for the door. The shah was frightened into thinking that he would rally his forces inside and outside the Majlis against him. There followed the comical scene of the prime minister wishing to leave the room, and the shah blocking his way by leaning against the door. Having failed to persuade the shah to get out of the way, the old man fainted, either because of the pressure on his frail nerves or because it was the most diplomatic way out of the impasse. When he came round, the two agreed that unless Musaddiq heard from the shah before 8 pm that day, he should send in his formal resignation. And that is exactly what happened. He resigned on 16 July without telling any of his friends, colleagues, advisers or ministers about the decision. He had had his own reason for wanting to go, as we have seen, and did not want to put up a fight as he would certainly have been advised to do by his colleagues and advisers.[22] He did not even make a radio broadcast before leaving Tehran for Ahmad-Abad. He must have heaved a sigh of relief.

Next day the news of Musaddiq's resignation and Qavam's appointment was announced. Everyone was stunned. The element of surprise had made it possible for the shah to concoct a majority straw vote for Qavam. The thirty Popular Movement deputies were thrown off-guard, not knowing what to do, partly because it took some time for them to learn the apparent reason for Musaddiq's resignation. Things would have developed differently had the shah nominated one of their own leading figures – for example, the mild and respected

Dr Abdullah Mu'azzami or Allahyar Saleh. But their names had not been put forward by Britain. The Popular Movement deputies' first reaction therefore was to think of an alternative government of their own, and Mu'azzami's name was being mentioned when, according to Baqa'i's own testimony, he shook them all off by shouting 'Our prime minister is none other than Dr Musaddiq'.[23]

Things went wrong for the shah and Qavam for many reasons, but Qavam's fateful radio broadcast (written by Muvarrikh al-Dawleh, whom Qavam himself had had banished to Kashan during his previous government) was the most fatal of them all. In it he threatened to 'court-martial' the opposition and deliver them into the 'heartless and pitiless hands of the law'. Furthermore, he spoke of his hatred for 'hypocrisy and duplicity in religious matters', and promised to 'keep religion apart from politics, and . . . prevent the spread of superstition, and retrogressive ideas'.[24] The message was received and understood by the whole of the Movement, and not least by Ayatullah Kashani for whose ears the above words had been especially intended.[25] He published a reply, putting Qavam down in commensurate terms, and calling on the people to prepare for resistance. Qavam offered to let him fill half the cabinet posts in return for his co-operation. But his envoys – Dr Ali Amini and Hasan Arsanjani – returned empty-handed. The shah sent Ala (the court minister) on a similar mission which also failed. Worse still, the Ayatullah wrote to the shah via Ala stating that he should either restore Musaddiq to office or face the prospect of Kashani leading the rebellion personally.[26]

Meanwhile, the bazaar and the Popular Movement parties and deputies were recovering their composure, and preparing for a counter-attack. Fatemi's leading articles in his daily *Bakhtar-i Imruz* were increasing in boldness,[27] and Baqa'i's *Shahed* (now the Zahmat-kishan party's daily organ) had become the most effective medium for the struggle. Its leading article of 20 July, written and signed by Baqa'i himself, was headed by the following audacious verse: 'Although the arrow goes through the bow, any intelligent person would see the archer's finger behind it'. It was the most daring dart thrown at the shah by a Popular Movement leader up to that date.

A general strike began to spread on 20 July, and became complete as well as formal by the next day. The ground had been prepared both by the press campaigns mentioned above, and by the *bast* of all of the Popular Movement deputies in the Majlis. But the strike and public demonstrations were almost spontaneous, although Zahmatkishan played an important role in organizing and leading the crowd once they were out in the streets. The police having failed to deal with the situation the previous day, the troops were called out on 21 July. Some of the officers fired on the crowds without mercy, some of the others hesitated, while a few went over to the demonstrators. In Tehran alone, there were 17 deaths and many more casualties. The shah got cold feet and, at about 4 pm, asked Qavam to resign and reappointed Musaddiq. Another reason for his quick turnabout has only recently come to light: he had received word that the Patriotic Officers in the army and (especially) the air force were about to mutiny.[28]

The Tudeh party's reaction to these events was predictable. The American agent Musaddiq had been replaced with the British agent Qavam. The latter was preferable, especially as he had had a tradition of good relations with the Russians, and a deal with Britain might even carry some good news about North Iran's oil for the Soviet Union. The Tudeh press therefore responded to Qavam's premiership by attacking Musaddiq,[29] but there was no formal statement from the party, which did not participate in the uprising.

Having been restored to office in triumph, Musaddiq was then at the pinnacle of his popularity and power, especially as, the next day, the news came of the International Court's decision in Iran's favour. He treated the shah with magnanimity and – being the only man in the whole country who could do so – wasted no time in repairing his badly-damaged public image. Without doubt, he could then have got rid of the shah forever, but this was no part of his design even in spite of the shah's hostile attitude towards him. Now that he had taken over the ministry of war (and renamed it the ministry of national defence) he even asked the shah to introduce three generals whom he personally trusted as his (Musaddiq's) special advisers. But the shah, Britain and (now) the United States were not to abandon their plan to overthrow Musaddiq simply because the Qavam option had been spent. On the contrary, their minds became increasingly occupied with the idea of a *coup d'état*, and their eyes rapidly turned towards General Zahedi as its leader. It took them almost a year to succeed, and then they managed it only by the skin of their teeth (see chapter 13).

10

Musaddiq's second government
(August 1952–August 1953)

Delegated powers

An important reason why Musaddiq would rather have left the political scene than face the consequences of defeat at the International Court was the domestic difficulties with which he had to cope. It was now certain that the United States and US banks would not lend to Iran – 'at any rate of interest' – before the settlement of the oil dispute. Neither were the Russians in a mood to help his government even to the extent of repaying their considerable war debts to Iran. By means of strict import controls, currency depreciation and public expenditure cuts, the government had managed to contain the external and internal disequilibrium resulting from the loss of oil revenues. There was need for legislation on monetary, fiscal and other important economic matters. But there were other pressing problems as well. The government had promised electoral reform as well as 'the strengthening of the foundations of Constitutional government'. The latter had been interpreted to mean wide-ranging judicial and administrative reforms, in addition to social legislation to extend public welfare in town and country. The Zahmatkishan party had already been demanding various measures for land and income redistribution,[1] and Third Force was soon to press for the franchise as well as other rights for women. The Patriotic Officers were also asking for extensive reforms in the army.

On the other hand, the government faced barriers to social and political reform which went far beyond shortage of funds. The shah and the conservative forces (both military and civilian) were constantly encouraged by Britain and (later) the United States to do their best to destabilize it. In addition, for constitutional as well as historical reasons, the Majlis was an unusually powerful legislative body. For example, not only the issuance of new money (or even the release of some of the existing funds from the reserves) but many, much more trivial, decisions had to have its prior approval. Serious though it was, this problem might have been possible to live with had the government had a coherent majority in the Majlis. But the problem went even beyond that. Most of the deputies did not belong to disciplined political parties with whom formal coalitions or legislative agreements could be made: in the case of almost every bill, a majority had to be negotiated from amongst a number of loose groupings as well as independent deputies. Not even the Popular Movement parliamentary group itself – which, though strictly in a minority, was the most coherent faction in the Majlis – behaved like parliamentary factions in modern democracies. For example, all the twelve deputies for Tehran had been elected on the Popular Movement platform, but five of them – Makki, Baqa'i, Hayerizadeh, Zuhari and Mushar – opposed the government with growing hostility from October 1952 onwards. And there were other defections from the ranks of Popular Movement deputies for the provinces.

Since independence, India has occasionally suspended its constitution in considerably less difficult circumstances. Instead, Musaddiq asked the Majlis to delegate some of its legislative powers to the government for a period of six months, after which the resulting bills could be debated for approval or rejection. The idea had already been floated before, but had not yet been put to the test, and it could well have proved difficult to sell to the Senate, half of whose members were directly appointed by the shah and the other half elected through an electoral college. The government knew that without some such powers it would be impossible to hold the hostile forces – both domestic and external – at bay, and the arguments for delegated powers were forcefully set out by Fatemi in his leading articles in *Bakhtar-i Imruz*, before the 21 July uprising. 'In order to be able to balance the budget', he wrote in the issue of 13 July, 'Dr Musaddiq's government has prepared some useful financial bills':

When the country's budget was balanced, and the government was not dependent upon oil revenues for its current and development expenditures, and the country could stand on its own feet, the oil problem would then be resolved according to the wishes of the Iranian people. But as long as the budget is unbalanced, and London expects the bankruptcy of the Iranian treasury at any moment, and the government's hands are tied for lack of money, Britain's financial pressures and economic blockade will continue.

And on 15 July:

> For ten years now, the general budget has been approved [on a
> monthly basis] as one-twelfth [of the previous year's expenditure],
> and each year there has been a considerable amount of deficit.
> Governments have borrowed millions from Bank Melli [Iran]
> without being able to repay a penny of it. Besides, they have spent
> the oil revenues, and squandered the foreign reserves. Today, the
> government is facing a financial crisis, and if past methods are to
> continue, the result will be bankruptcy. Should the poor and the
> needy go on paying taxes and the rich and wealthy be exempt
> from them? Should bureaucratic behaviour and attitude continue
> in public administration, and the rusty wheels of the government
> departments (which are in need of repairs and reform) stay as
> corrupt as they are? If so, then Dr Musaddiq has no need for
> delegated powers.

The July uprising coupled with the unexpected success at The Hague
tipped the parliamentary balance. On 30 July, Musaddiq's government
was given a unananimous vote of confidence by the Majlis. Within a
month, the Delegated Powers Bill was passed by the Majlis and Senate,
and received the royal assent. The powers were delegated 'to the
person of His Excellency Dr Mohammad Musaddiq, the prime
minister'. They empowered the government to revise the electoral laws
governing the Majlis and municipal elections, and to reform the fiscal
and monetary system, public administration and the armed forces, the
judiciary, public health and education, etc. The Act came up for
renewal in January 1953, and was extended for a further year after a
heated debate both inside and outside the Majlis (see chapter 12).

Social legislation and reform

The pressure for land reform came mainly from the Zahmatkishan
(and, later, Third Force) party. Khalil Maleki had been demanding the
redistribution of land in the party's press and publications, and Baqa'i
had delivered a formal speech in the Majlis (written by Maleki) in
favour of a comprehensive reform (see chapter 8). For obvious reasons,
such a policy would not have been possible as long as the oil dispute
remained unsettled. Instead, a Bill under the delegated powers was
approved in October 1952 which obliged landlords to return 10 per
cent of their own share of the crop to the peasants, and pay a further

10 per cent into a fund for rural development, which elected village councils were to use for extending transport, education and social services in the rural sector. This law was abolished after the 1953 coup.

Another pressing problem was the high cost of housing for the urban lower classes. In August 1952 the ministry of finance was authorized to sell off urban land belonging to the state to individual buyers in small plots on which they could build houses for themselves. At the time, almost all new private houses were built individually by their owners after purchasing a plot of land from urban proprietors, the cost of which made up a large proportion of the total costs. Early in 1953, and partly as a result of a campaign by the *Niru-yi Sevvum* newspaper, rents on middle to poor accommodation were reduced by 10 per cent; the newspaper continued its efforts on behalf of urban tenants beyond this legislation. The newly-established Construction Bank had been created by the government to increase the supply of low-cost housing; it managed to complete two fairly extensive projects in Tehran, one in Narmak, for lower income groups, the other in Naziabad, for the poor.

Musaddiq's legislation of October 1952 for the protection of workers and employees is so comprehensive that it defies any attempt at a brief summary. Composed of 96 articles, it provided for the foundation of the Workers' Social Security Organization. This covered sickness as well as accident insurance for all workers and their families, important cash obligations – e.g. those arising from marriage, birth of children, and funerals – supplementary welfare benefits for workers with large families, and unemployment benefits where none had ever existed before. In addition, detailed rules and regulations were laid down for sickness benefits and retirement and family pensions. The scheme was financed, in part, by transferring funds from various government departments and the state insurance company, and in part by contributions from industry itself, one-third paid by employees and two-thirds by employers.

The promised electoral reform was publicly discussed and a Bill drafted, but it got no further, largely because of the opposition of powerful conservative religious leaders – notably, Burujirdi in Qum and Bihbahani in Tehran – to women's suffrage. The Third Force, and especially its women's section (which, in practice, was the Popular Movement's women's organization) were publicly pressing for such a reform, and Musaddiq received a delegation from them when the draft Bill was being debated. He told them that if the people supported the idea he would be all for it, thus hinting at how the religious leaders could appeal to the people's traditionalist instincts and rally them against the government over the issue.[2] In the event, no new electoral law was passed under Musaddiq except that affecting municipal government which returned to the public much of the powers hitherto exercised by the state. But this, too, did not last beyond the 1953 coup.

There were a number of other measures, including tax reform, which there is not scope to discuss in this book. However, the reforms of the army and the judiciary are too important to be overlooked.[3]

Reform of the armed forces

The intrusion of the Second World War into Iran had bruised the Iranian army in both body and spirit. The army's response to the Allied invasion was not glorious, though this was more of a political than a military failure.[4] The occupation and interregnum had led to a considerable fall in military expenditure. As the army chief of staff, Razmara had tried to improve its organization, and as prime minister he had hoped to increase its budget, but he was killed before he could get far with these aims. The younger officers' pay and prospects had diminished badly. Corruption was rife, and by the end of the decade the price for a colonel to be promoted to brigadier was 50,000 rials, plus a pair of silk rugs.[5]

For these and other reasons the younger army officers had become considerably politicized. The sense of patriotic outrage led some of them – by familiar stages – to ideological conversion, and they organized the Tudeh party's military network. Some of the others – with greater representation from the air force – set up the network of Patriotic Officers early in 1952. Ideology apart, there were some important differences between the two groups. In particular, the Patriotic Officers were not members of a political party (except for a couple who owed some allegiance to the Iran party). Furthermore, no political party had had any part in organizing them, and they were thus a completely autonomous body. They included many more senior officers, and at least six brigadier-generals within their camp. On the other hand, they lacked the force of a millenarian ideology with a powerful international brotherhood behind them, and the organization and discipline that movements based on such ideologies possess.

Their *de facto* leader was Brigadier Mahmud Afshartus, who enjoyed an excellent reputation within the army itself for his honesty and ability. He was destined to be murdered by the government's opponents in April 1953 when he was prefect-general of the police (see chapter 13). At this time, it was rumoured that he had behaved unjustly towards the peasants of Reza Shah's estates in Mazandaran in the 1930s, in order to promote his own career. However, no evidence to this effect was put forward then or afterwards. The group's executive committee was made up of Afshartus himself and four colonels, including (air force) Colonel Musavvar-Rahmani. Another important and highly-respected member of the group was Brigadier Mahmud Amini (Dr Ali Amini's brother), and Brigadier Husain Azmudeh – who was later to defect to the extent of acting as the prosecutor in Musaddiq's military trials – was also a founding member (see chapter 14).

According to Musavvar-Rahmani, the Patriotic Officers set them-selves four principal aims: to help promote democratic government; to support Musaddiq 'because his government was democratic'; to help detach the armed forces from the shah's personal rule, and safeguard their constitutional status; and to try and purge the army of corrupt officers and other personnel.[6] They voluntarily contacted Musaddiq and made a series of suggestions to him for helping them promote these objectives, the first being that he should run the war ministry himself. Musaddiq agreed in principle, and promised to act on their other proposals once he had taken personal charge of the war ministry in his forthcoming cabinet. In the event, the shah opposed the idea, and the matter was settled only after the 21 July uprising (see chapter 9). One of the reasons why the shah backed down was the news of an imminent mutiny in the air force plus the refusal of some tank commanders to shoot at the crowd, and the defection of a couple of them to their side.

After Musaddiq assumed direct responsibility for the ministry of national defence the Patriotic Officers suggested that he should dismiss most of the army generals (because they were claimed to be either corrupt or actively disloyal to the government), set up machinery from within the army to purge all corrupt, disloyal or inefficient elements, and appoint brigadier Amini as chief of staff, and Brigadier Afshartus as police chief among other top military appointments. Afshartus was made police chief, but only late in February 1953. General Baharmast (who was trusted by the shah) was kept as army chief of staff until his active disloyalty towards Musaddiq was proved in the 28 February incident; he was then replaced, not by Amini but by another Patriotic Officer, Brigadier Taqi Riyahi, an Iran party member, and a close friend of its chairman Ahmad Zirakzadeh.

According to Musavvar-Rahmani, Musaddiq had at first 'expressed horror' at the suggestion that most army generals should be dismissed;

in the end, many of them were retired on full pension. As for the rest of the military personnel, he asked each military unit to elect representatives to a board of inquiry, which ultimately recommended the prosecution, dismissal, and retirement of 1,360 military personnel. With the full participation and approval of his three defence advisers nominated by the shah, Musaddiq agreed only to a final list of 136 retirements on full pension.[7] This made matters worse for the government, for many of those still under suspicion remained in the army, while the retired officers were organized by Zahedi and other retired generals (in the Retired Officers' Club) to go into action. For some time, their daily public demonstrations outside the prime minister's home and office made a mockery of the normal conduct of government business. Many of them became actively involved in plots and coups against the government, including the 28 February assault on Musaddiq's house, the murder of General Afshartus and the successive coups of August 1953 (see chapter 13).

Reform of the judiciary

This was a pressing problem. There was much corruption and inefficiency in the justice department which had always been regarded as the cornerstone of Constitutionalism, and was especially close to the hearts of Musaddiq and his lieutenants, many of whom were among the country's leading lawyers and jurists. Musaddiq appointed Abdul'ali Lutfi minister of justice and Mohammad Sururi President of the Supreme Court and head of the judiciary. Neither of them was a member of the National Front. Lutfi was a highly respected senior judge who had never occupied a political post. Sururi had been an equally reputable judge who had become minister of justice and of finance in the 1940s, but had refused the shah's offer of the premiership in 1949, and was to do the same in 1963 and 1978. Early in 1952, he strongly urged Musaddiq to accept the World Bank's proposal for mediation over the oil dispute with Britain (see chapter 11).

Using the powers delegated to him by the Majlis, Musaddiq reformed the machinery of justice as well as the legal process in various ways. The new Supreme Court headed by Sururi included some of the most respected and independent judges of the land. Some of them – e.g. Baqir Rassa, presiding judge in Division 3 of the Court – were even brought out of retirement for the purpose.[8] A judicial commission was set up to investigate allegations of corruption against the judges, and the minister of justice was empowered to act on its report. Hitherto, judges were appointed by the minister, and could be transferred at his will. The new law laid down that all new appointments must be approved by a committee composed of the President and two elected members of the Supreme Court, and no judge could be removed or transferred by the minister. All extraordinary, special and administrative courts – notably the Department of Military Prosecutions – were abolished, and their business handed back to the ordinary law courts.[9] This included the justice department's own administrative court for hearing complaints against the judges. Instead, the High Court of Judicial Discipline was created. The government may seem to have been somewhat idealistic in carrying its judicial reforms thus far. But it goes some way to show their strong commitment to democratic government. Besides, most of these decisions were taken by the government and the judiciary without there being any public pressure for them, as only a small percentage of the electorate could appreciate their social and political meaning.

On the contrary, there was much pressure from the conservatives to prevent these reforms. Immediately after the August 1953 coup, Sururi and all the new Supreme Court judges were dismissd without ceremony, although there was then no parliament which, by law, was the only authority with the right to appoint and dismiss Supreme Court judges. Lutfi, the justice minister, paid much more dearly for his reforms. He could not be jailed for long because he was clearly apolitical. Once released, however, he was attacked at his home by a mob, led by a notorious mobster and an equally notorious former judge who had been dismissed as a result of his judicial reforms. They blinded him and broke his ribs without any regard for his advanced age, and he died later in hospital of his wounds. His attackers went unpunished, though the regime was fully aware of their identity. One of their two leaders later became a minister of the interior, and both amassed fabulous fortunes in later years and went on to live in Europe.

The nationalization of Caspian shipping

In January 1953 the Soviet concession for the monopoly of fishing in the Iranian port on the Caspian Sea came up for review. The concession had first been granted to a Russian citizen (Lianozov) up to 1925. During the First World War, Samsam al-Saltaneh's government cancelled the Lianozov concession on the ground that the concessionaires had not honoured their rent obligations to the government.

Later, in 1921, the matter was referred to arbitration, and the concessionaires were given back their monopoly rights for a longer term. In 1927, Reza Shah approved the transfer of the concession to the Soviet Union for a further 25 years – a measure opposed by Musaddiq in the Majlis at the time[10] However, before its lapse at the end of January 1953, the Soviet government asked for the Agreement's renewal for a further term. Musaddiq turned down the request, telling the Soviet ambassador that Iran should not be expected to renew a Russian concession which had fallen due, while it had nationalized a British concession decades before it was due to lapse.[11]

On the day on which the Caspian Fishing Company passed into Iranian hands, *Niru-yi Sevvum*'s leader ran the following:

> The Iranian government's refusal to renew the Soviet fishing concession must not be put down to an unfriendly attitude [towards the Soviet Union]. The Iranian people wish to have a friendly relationship with the Soviet people, and maintain their political, economic and cultural links with them . . . The Soviet government can be absolutely sure that the Iranian people have no wish to break up their friendship with the Soviet Union. But this friendship must not be based on the old lines. If the Soviet government does not respect the freedom and independence of the Iranian people, it should not expect a friendly attitude from them.

Next day 2 February 1953, *Bisu-yi Ayandeh*, the Tudeh party's leading daily newspaper, attacked the decision, and wrote that 'to defend the Soviet Union is to defend peace, freedom and national independence'. The day after it went much further. Having declared that 'the Third Force [party] spies' intended to disrupt Irano-Soviet relations and 'prepare the ground for an even greater expansion of the destructive influence of American imperialism in our country', it had the following to say about Musaddiq and his government:

> The truth of the matter is that the Iranian government represents the feudals [*sic*], large landowners and big capitalists who are dependent on imperialism; and it does not reflect the interest of the Iranian people. That is why it cannot be in agreement with Soviet policy, which is the policy of securing peace, freedom and happiness for the masses of all nations [of the world].

Both *Bisu-yi Ayandeh* and *Shahbaz* (another Tudeh newspaper) at first denied that the Russians had asked for a renewal of the concession, but they had to retract their denials after Tass confirmed that the demand had indeed been made. Then *Mardum* (the official organ of the Tudeh party's central committee which was published clandestinely, but circulated with little difficulty) put the party's official view on the matter on 11 February:

On 31 January 1953, because of the lapse of the activities of the Iranian Fishing Company [*sic*], the Soviet government made a proposal [to the Iranian government] for the renewal of the Company's activities [*sic*] for a further period [which was] fully and entirely in the interest of our people, and beneficial to our country. Yet, and despite these obvious truths, Musaddiq's government – against the interest of our people and country, and in keeping with the orders of its own foreign masters – formally responded to the Soviet government's proposals by declaring that his government had decided not to renew the activities of the bi-national Irano-Soviet Fishing Company because the period of its activities [i.e. the concessionary period] had lapsed. The Iranian people regard as an ugly decision this anti-people (*zidd-i melli*) action of Musaddiq, and believe that it has been motivated by enmity towards the people's interests, and the pursuit of the wishes of the imperialist masters of those who run Iran's present politics.

Apart from the matter in hand, the above account provides some evidence of the Tudeh party's attitude towards Musaddiq's government almost a fortnight before the events of 28 February 1953, whereas it is sometimes claimed (both by the party and by Musaddiq's conservative opponents) that the party supported Musaddiq after the uprising of July 1952.

Not a great deal of social and economic development (especially in their technical sense) took place during the turbulent two years and four months of Musaddiq's government, although significantly more was done than his critics and detractors have been prepared to admit. This was partly due to the great shortage of domestic funds and foreign exchange (because of the international boycott of Iran's oil) which will be discussed in the following chapter. But it was also because of the strong domestic and international campaigns of destabilization and destruction (by Britain and the United States, the shah and the Iranian conservatives, and the Tudeh party) which made it virtually impossible to open up large new domestic issues and, for example, provoke *fatvas* from the religious leadership that land redistribution and women's suffrage were contrary to the *shari'a*. What was impressive, however, was Musaddiq's legislation for the decentralization of political power and decision-making, public participation in social and political processes, democratization of the law, bureaucracy and the army, and measures for the protection of ordinary people. As subsequent history was to prove, these achievements were much more fundamental to social progress and economic development in Iran than any amount of expenditure on hydro-electric dams and assembly-line industries in their absence.

11

The oil dispute and non-oil economics

The political nature of the oil dispute

The oil dispute might well have been resolved had the Labour Party returned to power in the British general election of October 1951. At no time did Attlee's government show any sign that they would accept a settlement without the grant of another concession. But their acceptance of the principle of the oil nationalization was itself a conciliatory gesture which the Conservatives would not have initiated; and there are indications (including the letter from Stokes to Attlee, cited in chapter 9) that Labour might eventually have agreed to some form of compensation short of the grant of another full concession.

The Conservatives, on the other hand, were in no mood to make any settlement with Musaddiq unless he was made to eat his own words, and let the British return. A review both of the British press at the time and of Eden's subsequent memoirs shows that the Conservatives were extremely angry with Musaddiq. And declassified documents make it plain that they were plotting to bring his government down by any means. They were therefore not prepared to return to the negotiating table, and instead successfully brought the Americans into line against Musaddiq and the Popular Movement.

Musaddiq and his colleagues were explicit that the most important reason for the oil nationalization was political rather than economic. Indeed, during Razmara's premiership, Baqa'i had gone so far – in a Majlis debate – as to wish that Iran's oil resources should be destroyed by an atom bomb rather than remain in the AIOC's hands.[1] The policy had been formulated on the basis of the following historico-political analysis.

It had been proved time and again that, as long as foreign concessionaires were operating on Iranian soil, any effort to establish democracy, freedom and the rule of law, eradicate political and financial corruption, and achieve social and economic progress would be thwarted. Not even the Constitutional Revolution nor the dissolution of Reza Shah's *istibdad* were sufficient to make any such effort fruitful. The increasing interference of Britain and Russia in Iran's domestic affairs in the nineteenth century was, in the main, bound up with the attainment of, and further demands for, trade concessions. In turn, the concessionaires and their governments increased their meddling into every aspect of the country's affairs, both to keep what they had and to ask for more. Furthermore, as long as one power had, or obtained, a concession, the other power would come in for another, so that an active balance between their interests was maintained or restored.[2]

This meant that the country did not enjoy real independence. Worse still, with the constant corruption and intimidation of Iranian politicians and officials – resulting in election rigging, purchasing of favours, making of governments, breaking of oppositions, etc., etc. – any talk of democracy and its further development was no more than indulgence in romantic self-deception. Therefore – and this was the crucial point – foreign concessionaires had to be removed at all costs, and no more concessions should be granted to non-Iranians to become an autonomous economic and political enclave in the country. Only then would it be possible to uproot *istibdad* and backwardness, and struggle against their defenders in domestic politics with a fair chance of success. This was why Musaddiq and his colleagues were prepared to settle the Anglo-Iranian oil dispute at almost any economic price, but were equally determined not to grant another concession at any cost.

The British view was more straightforward, and was better understood both at the time and afterwards. In 1933, the AIOC had agreed to exchange the original D'Arcy concession with the Iranian government by means of a perfectly valid international agreement. In 1951, the Iranian government had illegally nationalized the oil industry and (subsequently) seized the oil installations in Khuzistan. Therefore, the company and the British government had every right to try and regain their previous position, albeit with some modifications. The British attitude, too, had important political dimensions which have already been mentioned.[3]

This attitude was consolidated as soon as the Conservatives came back to power in 1951, and there was no real chance of the British government's settlement with Musaddiq thereafter. When Eden shouted at Anthony Nutting four years later about Nasser, 'I want him removed', this may well have been an echo from the past.[4] How, then, could the Iranians' grievances against the AIOC be considered, let alone understood? The Iranians pointed out that Britain had obtained the 1933 Agreement from an arbitrary ruler by the threat of force, or – as most of them believed – by issuing an order to him as its local agent; that it had been worse than the previous concession and had in fact led to a net financial loss to Iran ever since; that the company had ignored constant Iranian demands to see its general accounts,[5] and to be told of the terms and quantity of its sales to the Royal Navy on special terms. They charged the company, on some objective evidence, with literally stealing crude oil via secret underwater pipelines connected to Iraq. They mentioned the company's effectively autonomous rule in a part of the country, its treatment of the inhabitants as second-class citizens in their own land, its discrimination between expatriate and domestic workers and staff, and its particularly bad labour relations and low wage rates. They showed that they were being paid in royalties up to 10 or 12 per cent of the company's net proceeds, while the amount the company paid to the British government in taxes alone could be as high as 30 per cent.[6]

All this aside, they were asking why a sovereign state could not nationalize one of its industries and compensate its owners. Had the Labour government and many other European countries 'stolen' their own citizens' property by doing the same thing? The answer to this (as argued in *The Daily Express*, itself echoing *The Manchester Guardian*) was that this was altogether a different case, because it involved British property which had been acquired by an international agreement.[7] But the argument proves the opposite. The British citizen's property is, in principle, sacred and inviolable, and his freedom and independence is firmly guaranteed by British law and tradition. What possible legal agreement between two citizens, the citizen and the state, let alone Britain and another country, could be more binding than this? And yet, for perfectly valid legal as well as social reasons, British governments could nationalize, had nationalized, and went on nationalizing their own citizens' properties, even including their personal dwellings. Apart from all that, the Iranians never tired of pointing out that the 1933 Agreement had been concluded between the Iranian government and the Anglo-Persian (later, Iranian) Oil Company, not the British government.

The search for a solution

The failure of the Stokes mission was due to insistence by the British government on the formation of another company along the lines of the consortium which was later created. This went against the political premises on which the nationalization policy was based. Musaddiq had emphasized that the National Iranian Oil Company would sell any amount of oil to Britain and to other traditional buyers of Iranian oil; that the AIOC would be compensated on the basis of the pre-nationalization value of the company's shares (as had been done in Britain and elsewhere in the case of nationalized industries); that the NIOC would be ready to re-employ British technicians in the oil industry; that it would be prepared to employ European, but non-British, managers if this proved technically necessary. Stokes, however, did not agree to any of these proposals, and kept insisting on the formation of a new company.[8]

During Musaddiq's visit to the United States to defend Iran's case in the Security Council, George McGhee came up with a brilliant formula to resolve the dispute: Iran should agree to the supply of oil to Britain at $1.10 per barrel, i.e. 65 cents less than the Persian Gulf price of $1.75, as compensation for the nationalization of the industry. After some discussion in a meeting which included Acheson, Musaddiq agreed to the formula. Acheson left Washington for negotiations with Eden in Paris, and Musaddiq was asked to await his return with the British response to the US formula. They must have been optimistic about selling the proposal to Eden, or they would not have told Musaddiq to wait for a quick answer.[9]

They were to be badly disappointed. Eden rejected the solution and urged the Americans to let Musaddiq hang himself with his own rope (though these were not his words). More specifically, he said that American fears of communism as the only possible alternative to Musaddiq's government were unfounded;[10] that negotiations with Musaddiq were useless; that there were other and better alternatives both to Musaddiq and to communism in Iran, and that these would come forward, given time and support, and (especially) if Musaddiq was seen to be boycotted by the West. He also stressed that the Americans should leave the handling of the matter to Britain. For good measure, he dropped a hint at America's possible participation in Iranian oil in a future settlement, which Acheson graciously declined. As for the old man waiting for 'the good news' in America, Eden simply advised Acheson to 'send him home'.[11] It is important to note that although, in his memoirs, Eden describes the Paris discussions at some length, his only reference to the proposed American formula, and Musaddiq's acceptance of it, is that they 'were anxious to complete an agreement with him if this were possible'.[12]

Musaddiq's ultimate decision to turn down the World Bank's

intervention of February–March 1952 has been widely criticised by writers and commentators, including the present author.[13] For that reason, it requires a closer examination.

The Bank made it plain that it was not offering a formula for the permanent settlement of the dispute. It offered (a) to restart the production and sale of refined as well as crude oil in Abadan for an initial period of two years, subject to its extension on the approval of both parties to the dispute; (b) to sell the crude at $1.75 per barrel, holding 80 cents for the cost of production (i.e. as compensation for Britain pending a settlement), and paying 58 cents to Britain, and 37 cents to Iran;[14] and (c) to use non-Iranian managers and technicians where necessary.

Musaddiq was highly receptive at first. There were some queries about the (lower) Persian Gulf price of $1.75, and the 58 cent 'reduction for the major buyer' (i.e. Britain). But this was not the real bone of contention, and it would have been settled without much fuss. However, the government's more important objections were: (a) to the employment of British managers and technicians by the Bank (although other non-Iranian nationals were readily acceptable). This, too, was not a serious stumbling block and it would have been resolved satisfactorily; and (b) to the Bank's proposal to act solely as a neutral trustee for both sides of the dispute, and not as the agent of the Iranian government. The deal fell on this issue alone.

The objection appears to have been a purely verbal wrangle, but the government argued that the Bank's legally neutral status would by-pass the Iranian repossession of the industry. This was hardly surprising, because the Bank was not in a position to recognize (or denounce) repossession, which was still being disputed in the International Court, and – more importantly, and for similar legal considerations – the British would not have accepted the Bank's (or any other party's) intermediation *as the agent of the Iranian government*. If they had done so, they would have had no case left to pursue. Musaddiq was also put under immense pressure from some of his colleagues, and especially Kazim Hasibi, that if the Bank was not to act 'on behalf of the Iranian government' in the deal, the opposition – and the Tudeh party in particular – would describe the whole agreement as a complete sell-out. Musaddiq gave in to this pressure.[15]

It has been widely believed that Hasibi and (Dr Ali) Shaigan were most instrumental in dissuading Musaddiq from accepting the Bank's proposal. But, in his recent replies to my enquiries, Hasibi has insisted that it was he alone who stood in the way of an agreement.[16] Furthermore, in a conversation with Mohammad Husain Khan

Qashqa'i, he said, without any prompting, that he had been a witness to Shaigan's efforts in favour of accepting the World Bank proposals, and Hasibi's vehement campaign against it. Qashqa'i was then a Popular Movement deputy along with his brothers Khusraw and Nasir.

The Tudeh party led a hysterical press campaign against the acceptance of the Bank's intermediation and, for some time, went on claiming that Musaddiq had accepted it even after it was rejected: 'The masses will accept our views when they are seen to be confirmed by daily events as well. When . . . the wheeling and dealing with the International Bank . . . proved our views about Musaddiq and his demagogic gang, then the mask of the enemies of the people was torn apart, and his [sic] treacherous face was seen by all.'[17]

The tragedy for the government was that, in rejecting the Bank's offer, it did the British government's job for it. The latter did not want a deal with Musaddiq nor to see the normalization of the industry and the end of the financial crisis in Iran, and – Bank or no Bank – it would not have retracted its demand for a new concession, or (what was effectively the same) compensation for the AIOC's loss of profit until 1990. If the Bank's intervention had succeeded, Britain would still have pursued its maximum demands openly, and its aim to unseat Musaddiq by the usual techniques. But the fate of every battle is settled by the tactics of *both* sides. The temporary peace brought by the agreement, and the government's ability to spend as well as proceed with domestic social and political reforms, would have considerably strengthened its hand both inside and outside Iran, and Britain would have been left with little choice but to agree to a reasonable settlement in the process. The decision to turn down the World Bank's mediation was thus Musaddiq's greatest mistake during his premiership, if not in the whole of his political career. Nevertheless, the costs to Musaddiq of the acceptance of the deal should not be underestimated. Those who are familiar with the time-honoured attributes of Iranian politics will know that the acceptance of the proposed price of $1.75 and, especially, its mode of division, plus the legal and political constraints over repossession, could well have turned him – in the eyes of many Iranians – into an agent of Britain, the US or somewhere else overnight.

Musaddiq's unprecedented triumphs in July 1952, due to the July uprising and the International Court's decision in favour of Iran, made him more eager to settle the oil dispute than ever before. On the other hand, the British government's failure both to bring about a radical change of government in Iran and to win the battle in the International Court made it necessary for it to try to look more reasonable – in the first instance, in US eyes – than it had hitherto seemed to be. Therefore, when (on 7 August) the Iranian government demanded repayment of the AIOC's debt of 'several tens of millions of pounds', and the release of Iran's sterling balances at the Bank of England, the British government responded by formulating a new proposal. In fact, it involved no real change in Britain's previous position, but it was a major diplomatic coup, because Britain managed to obtain the United States' public commitment to it. Hence, it became known as the Truman-Churchill proposal.

The proposal's principal point was that Iran should voluntarily agree to the referral of the question of compensation to the International Court, now that the latter had denied its own jurisdiction in the case without Iran's consent. The remaining items – the AIOC's sale of the already produced and stored-up oil, Britain's release of Iran's sterling balances, and an American grant to Iran of $10 million – were all marginal, and clearly intended to sweeten the pill.[18]

The Iranian counter-proposals (of 24 September) were briefly as follows: (a) that Iran would consent to The Hague's arbitration *so long as the amount of compensation to the AIOC was determined on the basis of the market value of its property at the time of nationalization*, the principal point; (b) that the claims of both parties should be considered by the International Court, including the damages so far caused by the British boycott of Iranian oil, etc.; (c) that the AIOC should pay in advance its total debt of £75 million to Iran. Once again, it was point (a) which was the real bone of contention. Britain rejected the Iranian counter-proposals (on 14 October) simply by insisting on compensation for losses resulting from 'the unilateral ending of the 1933 Agreement', i.e. it demanded compensation for the AIOC's profit losses until 1990.

The US ambassador's proposed formula also collapsed simply because Britain would not compromise on its demand for compensation until 1990. Loy Henderson suggested (a) Iran's agreement to the sale of 200,000 tons of crude to Britain over the next ten years at $1.75 a barrel plus 33 per cent reduction, i.e. at $1.17;[19] (b) its consent to refer the compensation problem to the arbitration of the International Court. Musaddiq agreed, *on the proviso that Britain would declare its maximum compensation demand from the outset.* This was a significant retreat from his previous position that the AIOC should be compensated purely on the basis of the market value of its property. Instead, he argued that, in any legal dispute, every creditor is expected to state the full amount which it demands from the debtor in his lawsuit. And Britain should do the same in this case. Predictably, Britain turned down this proviso, because it would have compromised (even though no longer entirely negated) its maximum compensation claim for profit losses until 1990.[20]

Musaddiq did not give up hope of finding a solution in time, although lack of any future settlement with him was by now a foregone conclusion in Britain: Iran and Iranian oil vanished from the front pages of the British press, and from parliamentary debates, until August 1953. Indeed, he was seriously misled by the well-intentioned attempts of two individual oil-men, Ross and Loy, who offered alternative proposals for a settlement almost at the same time in July 1953. He interpreted the two separate contacts as diplomatic feelers, and followed both of them up seriously and immediately, only to discover that it was all a hoax.

The oil dispute: a summing up

Musaddiq was ready to compensate the AIOC, and said so many times. The terms were open to negotiation, but they excluded the possibility of the AIOC's return to Iran in one form or another. Britain, on the other hand, demanded either a new oil concession or compensation to the AIOC that would include the loss of future profits in consequence of its closure by the nationalization act. In other words, the Iranians would have had either to give up the spirit of the nationalization or to compensate the AIOC not just for its investment but for all the oil which it would have produced in the next 40 years.

The question of the legality or illegality of the 1933 Agreement also came into it. Any sovereign state can legitimately nationalize and compensate an industry operating on its soil even though – as is usually the case – its existence and operations are legally impeccable. In other words, whether or not the 1933 Agreement had a legal or moral basis, the Iranian government was well within its rights to nationalize the AIOC and compensate it for its losses. The 'illegality' issue was often invoked in response to the British argument that the AIOC should be compensated for the cancellation of the concession, i.e. for all the oil in the ground which would have been produced for a further 40 years. This would have been analogous to the owners of British coal-mines being compensated not for the market value of their property but for the value of the coal remaining under the ground. That is why Musaddiq's offer to compensate the AIOC on the terms paid to any nationalized company in Europe, including Britain, was also ignored.

If Musaddiq seemed to be inflexible, it was because he insisted on basic principles which would have been observed if the dispute had been between two equal nations. The fact of the matter was, however, that Iran was not powerful enough to maintain its position. The two sides thus dug in for a war of attrition from which Iran finally emerged the loser.

Britain's principal weapon was the boycott of Iranian oil. It was then that the Iranian government realized that the main problem it faced was not the technical difficulty of refining oil, but the politico-economic question of exporting crude oil. The AIOC's argument was that Iranian oil was its property, and its sale (unless authorized by the AIOC) was illegal. Other (mainly US) major oil companies joined the boycott by refusing to handle Iranian oil – in part to help a sister company, but principally to prevent other oil-exporting countries (in whose territories they operated) from learning a 'bad' lesson from Iran's example.

At the same time, oil production elsewhere (notably in Kuwait) was stepped up to compensate for the loss of Iranian oil in the international market. The British naval presence in the region was an effective deterrent against other buyers of Iranian oil, and the efforts of Italian and Japanese companies to import oil from Iran – although bold and daring – did not get far. Thus oil revenues ceased to flow to the Iranian economy in any significant amount until the fall of Musaddiq's government.

The strategy of non-oil economics

Not only Musaddiq and his government, but also his opponents – for a short time taking on a semblance of unanimity in the Majlis – had hoped and believed that the British government would come to an early settlement, and that in the meantime the United States would provide economic aid to Iran. But even before the arrival of the World Bank mission, it was clear that, prior to a settlement of the oil dispute, US aid would not be forthcoming. As early as 24 November 1951, Musaddiq himself indicated (in a report to the Majlis on his recent visit to the United States) the difficulty of obtaining US aid. Jamal Imami, the *de facto* leader of the Majlis opposition, retorted that the whole campaign had been in the hope of receiving higher revenues from oil as well as American aid. Musaddiq replied that he would not compromise Iranian sovereignty and independence merely to obtain American support.[21]

There was great fear of economic hardship in the country, not least among the upper classes who – from the beginning – had been unhappy about the turn of events. Much upper-class complaint rested on the fact that luxury imports had become very expensive or unobtainable. Yet, to some extent it reflected the fact and fiction of the situation as they were perceived by the political public. There is much direct and indirect evidence that the government was itself very conscious of the country's economic difficulties. But there is also evidence that it was determined to overcome these difficulties and free the economy – as the evidence shows it eventually succeeded in doing – from its dependence upon oil revenues. Although Musaddiq was not charged with any economic offence, the matter came up now and again in the course of his military trial. For example, towards the end of his trial he said that one of the reasons why his government had been brought down was because his opponents realized that 'gradually, the Iranian economic situation would improve so that it could sustain itself without oil revenues'.[22]

Prior to the oil nationalization, a Seven Year Plan had been drafted for economic development, consisting of a number of macroeconomic expenditure projects with emphasis on rural development and the socio-economic infrastructure.[23] Oil revenues were to contribute 37.1 per cent of the plan's financial requirements, and another 31.9 per cent was expected to be financed through loans from the World Bank. The virtual standstill in oil operations and exports, the British blockade, the AIOC's refusal to pay the royalties it owed Iran up to the nationalization act, and the freezing of Iran's considerable sterling facilities by the Bank of England were therefore a sudden and substantial shock to the economy. Besides being a source of substantial exports and foreign-exchange earnings, oil revenues could be used to supplement domestic consumption and investment. The loss of the revenues, therefore, presented the government with a balance-of-payments, a fiscal, and a monetary crisis.

Traditionally, the domestic currency had been 'covered' by gold and foreign-exchange reserves. An act of 1942 had set up a 'Currency Supervisory Board' (or Issue Department) with sole authority for the fiduciary issue. The same act had specified that 60 per cent of the currency in circulation should be 'backed' by gold, and the remaining 40 per cent by convertible foreign-exchange reserves. This law was repealed early in 1947, but it was not replaced by another and continued to be enforced in practice. In August 1951, while the Stokes mission was still in Tehran, the Majlis authorized the government to issue new notes against £14 million from the foreign-exchange reserves. This naturally reduced the foreign reserve 'backing' of the currency in circulation.[24]

The loss of substantial oil revenues in foreign exchange was bound to have important external and internal repercussions for the economy. A series of decisions had to be taken in order to meet the difficulties caused both for the balance of payments and for the financing of domestic (current and development) expenditures.

International trade: policy and performance

The balance of payments was the more immediate cause for concern, and the government took steps to contain the foreign payments deficit.

Under Reza Shah, foreign trade – both exports and imports – had been brought under government control by the Trade Monopoly Acts of 1931 and 1932. At the same time, the government was authorized to issue import licences to the private sector for items which it did not wish to import directly. A system of import quotas was introduced which imposed a ceiling on the total value of imports, as well as sub-ceilings for individual items. In addition, there was a complete prohibition on the import of certain items: exportables, foreign products for which there were adequate supplies of domestic substitutes, and luxury goods. The abdication of Reza Shah in 1941 had important economic repercussions, one of which was a much greater participation by the private sector in foreign trade. By 1947, the only major import commodity of which the government still held the monopoly was tea. The import quota system remained intact but, as the country's foreign-exchange reserves improved, there was a tendency for the government both to relax the ceiling figure and to allow substantially higher imports to enter the country.[25]

The year 1952–3 (and the following months up to the coup of 19 August 1953) was the real period of economic crisis. The government was by then seriously concerned about the problems facing the economy, both because no settlement of the oil dispute was in sight, and because of the depletion of the foreign-exchange reserves which could be used for foreign trade payments. As we have seen, Iranian money had to be 'backed' by gold and foreign currency, and so the country's reserves were never wholly available for foreign transactions. This was an unnecessary restriction, both on the use of foreign reserves and on the issues of new money, which had survived from the old-school economics of 20 years before. If it had not been largely adhered to over the period, the problem of external and internal adjustment would have been considerably easier. However, given the situation, the government launched its strategy of 'non-oil economics' (*iqtisad-i bidun-i naft*).

To deal with the foreign-exchange shortage, imports were divided into necessary and luxury goods, and exports into more and less marketable goods. Necessary goods could be imported against more marketable exports, while luxury goods were allowed in against exports of products which were less competitive in the international market. In addition, a large number of items, ranging from meat and poultry to military weapons and rubber and its products, were put on the prohibited imports list. Efforts were stepped up to promote the country's non-oil exports. A number of barter deals were concluded with Germany, France, Italy, Hungary, Poland and Czechoslovakia.[26] At the same time, measures were taken to encourage and facilitate greater exports through the open market. By a stroke of good fortune this was a boom period in the international market for commodities, and hence there was no shortage of demand for Iranian non-oil exports which the depreciation of the rial had made more competitive.

Currency depreciation played a greater role in containing imports and promoting exports than the other steps taken by the government. Although there was an official exchange rate of 32.5 rials to the dollar, the exchange rate was managed according to a complex procedure, and the effective market rate was appreciably less than the official rate of exchange. A system of exchange certificates (*gavahinameh-yi arz*) which could be bought and sold on the market was in operation. Therefore, a decline in the supply of foreign exchange would result in a rise in the market price of the certificates, which would mean a depreciation of the local currency. Key products, for example necessary foods and medicines, were imported at the lower official exchange rates, while other products were imported at the higher market rates of exchange certificates depending on their relative priority. Market exchange rates varied a good deal over the 1950–3 period. The government held a considerable quantity of exchange certificates, and when necessary it bought and sold certificates in order to reduce or raise the market exchange rate. On a number of occasions the government helped increase the exchange value of the rial in this way. But, in general, there was a steady trend for the depreciation of the rial throughout the period: from 40 rials to the dollar in mid-1950 to 100 rials to the dollar in the summer of 1953, a decline of 250 per cent. This depreciation caused domestic import prices to rise, and external export prices to fall, and thus helped improve the balance of payments.

Table 11.1 shows the balance of payments for the period 1949–55. The government's main success was in managing to contain and then reduce the current account deficit over the period 1951–3 when the net contribution of the oil sector to export earnings had all but disappeared. The key to this success was the steady increase in non-oil exports, and the dramatic decline in imports as a consequence of the imposition of import quotas, the increase in customs duties, and – especially – the depreciation of the rial. The question as to whether there was a trade surplus or deficit during this period has attracted a good deal of attention.[27] Export and import values could be converted into rials at various – official and unofficial – rates. Hence, there would be trade surpluses or deficits depending on the rate of exchange used. The table uses the IMF figures which in fact show considerable deficits rather than surpluses.

Table 11.1 *Balance of payments of Iran, 1949–55 in millions of rials*

		1949–50	1950–1	1951–2	1952–3	1953–4	1954–5
Oil sector							
1	Exports	15389	22184	6829	–	90	2798
2	Imports	−2979	−914	−256	–	−226	−270
3	Profits and other payments abroad	−8886	−17590	−5708	–	–	1414
4	Balance (1+2+3)	3524	3680	965	–	136	1114
Non-oil sector							
5	Exports	1244	2110	2710	2807	2958	3912
6	Imports	−6287	−6049	−5434	−3776	−5390	−7425
7	Services (net)	−463	−325	−366	−153	99	−235
8	Balance	−5506	−4264	−3090	−1122	−2506	−3748
A	Current account balance (4+8)	−1982	−584	−2125	−1122	−2442	−2634
B	Capital account balance*	992	874	145	592	3442	2723
C	Overall balance (A & B)	−990	290	−1980	−530	1000	89

* Includes errors and omissions as well as private and official grants.
Source: based on IMF, *International Financial Statistics*, October and December 1955.

Fiscal and monetary policy

Apart from its impact on foreign-exchange reserves and payments – and hence on the foreign trade sector of the economy – the virtual shut-down of oil production and refining was a sudden shock to the domestic sector.

However, by contrast to the foreign trade sector where the impact of the boycott was confined to the loss of the direct oil revenues received in foreign exchange, there was, in the domestic sector, a *revenue* as well as a *cost effect*. The *revenue effect* was the sum of the *direct* revenues foregone and all the *indirect* revenues – for example taxes on the income of the AIOC's foreign employees, and customs revenues from its non-exempt imports – arising from the company's operations, which could be as high as 30 per cent of the direct revenues. The *cost effect*, on the other hand, comprised the cost of the wages and salaries of the AIOC's former Iranian employees, in addition to all the other overhead costs of the National Iranian Oil Company. The *total* revenue effect was about 1.5 billion rials, and the cost effect amounted to 2.0 billion rials. Therefore, other things remaining equal, the government was faced with an annual deficit of about 3.5 billion rials on the oil account, about 38 per cent of the budgeted expenditures for the year 1951–2.

Fiscal measures to increase public revenues took several forms. Steps were taken to increase income tax receipts, but they were unlikely to have much success because of the inadequate administrative machinery for their collection. However, the government managed to increase its revenues from indirect taxes, and especially customs duties. Between 1949–50 and 1953–4, receipts from customs revenues increased from 43 to 71 per cent of dutiable imports, in spite of the fact that imports were declining and the import quotas discriminated against luxury imports which carried higher tariff rates. Another source of increased revenue was the rise in the price of goods, especially tobacco, tea, sugar and opium, produced by state monopolies. This was in the nature of an implicit excise tax, and it enabled the monopolies to gain considerably higher profits.

The sale of foreign exchange for raising public revenue was – generally – not a policy option because of the note coverage convention. In this respect, the government had to make do with the transfer of £14 million from the reserves authorized in August 1951. As early as September 1951, the Majlis authorized the issue of public bonds up to the value of 2 billion rials, (or $50 million at the official exchange rate) described as 'popular [or national] debt', carrying a 6 per cent 'prize' (i.e. interest), and redeemable after two years. They were to be issued at 500 rials each, and sold in four lots of 500 million rials. In practice, only the first lot was issued. The country was poor and becoming poorer because of the loss of oil revenues: the rich were not particularly concerned to help the government; and the nominal rate of interest which the bonds carried was considerably less than the formal and informal market rates.

Theoretically, foreign borrowing would have been a useful option. However, apart from its routine aid and technical assistance through Point IV, the United States was not prepared to provide financial support to Musaddiq's government. Nor did the Soviet Union provide any help; it even refused to repay its war debt to Musaddiq's government. In the early days of oil nationalization there were hopes of a loan of $25 million, at a 3.5 per cent rate of interest, from the Export-Import Bank of America. For this, as for many other routine executive decisions in that period, parliamentary approval was necessary. Accordingly, in July 1951, a Bill was submitted to both houses to authorize the borrowing. Shortly afterwards, the Anglo-Iranian negotiations failed to produce a solution to the oil dispute, and in September the oil installations were taken over. From then on the Americans made the granting of aid conditional on the resolution of the oil dispute on terms acceptable to both parties, and contrary to common belief the $25 million loan from the Export-Import Bank did not materialize.[28]

The government was left with little choice but to balance its budget deficits by means of various domestic fiscal and monetary policies, including an increase in the fiduciary note issue. In September 1952, Musaddiq invited Dr Schacht, the German financial expert, to Iran for consultation. It is not known whether Schacht ultimately presented a formal report on monetary policy in Iran, but the indirect remarks which he made to the Iranian press gave the impression that he did not attach much importance to the traditional note coverage policy.[29] Schacht had been a practitioner of 'Keynesian' policies before Keynes's *General Theory*, and it would come as no surprise for him to recommend an active monetary policy when effective demand had been considerably reduced due to the loss of oil revenues.

Table 11.2   *Summary of the budget 1951–4 (1330–2) in billions of rials*

		1 1951–2 (1330)	2 1952–3 (1331)	3 1953–4 (1332)
1	Revenues	7.8	7.8	9.5
2	Expenditures	9.7	10.3	10.0
3	Deficit	−1.9	−2.5	−0.5

Sources: Bank Melli Iran, *Bulletin*, various issues and dates; Bank Markazi Iran, *Bulletin* and *Annual Report and Balance Sheet*, various issues and dates up to 1969; Plan Organization, *Review of the Second Seven-Year Plan Programme of Iran* (Tehran, 1960). *Ruznameh-i Rasmi-yi Kishvar*, several issues, 1951–5.

Table 11.2 shows the budget summaries for the years 1951–2 to 1953–4 (1330–2). In both 1951–2 (1330) and 1952–3 (1331), government revenues were 7.8 billion rials. However, the figure for 1951–2 includes about 0.8 billion rials from direct and indirect oil revenues in that year, so that the domestic, non-oil revenues were in fact about 7.0 billion rials. The following year (1331), when there were virtually no oil revenues, the efforts to increase non-oil revenues made up for the loss. In the formal budget Bill of 1953–4 (1332), the revenue *estimate* was significantly increased to an optimistic 9.5 billion rials, indicating the government's confidence in the economic and financial prospects.

On the other hand, there were no substantial variations in the annual expenditures for the three years, though they now included substantial payments towards the upkeep of the oil industry which were no part of the ordinary budget. Hence, there had in fact been a substantial *cut* in ordinary public expenditure.

The most interesting aspect of the table is the annual deficits. As Dr Ali Amini – Zahedi's finance minister – pointed out in the Eighteenth Majlis, the Musaddiq government had to finance a total budget deficit of 4.4 billion rials in its 27 months of office.[30] The problem of financing this deficit caused it much economic and political difficulty. Having reduced the potential deficit of 1951–2 (1330) to 1.9 billion rials, it managed to meet the deficit from the authorized sale of £14 million (1.3 billion rials) from the reserves, plus the $8.75 million (0.6 billion rials) loan from the World Bank (see Table 11.3). In the following year, however, the deficit rose to 2.5 billion rials for which there was no deficit finance available. The hopes of raising 2 billion rials from the sale of public bonds having been largely dashed, the government then issued a provisional Bill under the Delegated Powers Act, and increased the fiduciary note issue by 3.1 billion rials. But this did not necessarily reduce the foreign-exchange 'backing' of the local currency, because the depreciation of the rial had substantially increased the value of the foreign-exchange reserves in local currency items. This therefore left a balance of 1.1 billion rials in the Treasury, which would have been more than adequate to finance the projected deficit of 0.5 billion rials for 1953–4 (see Table 11.2). A moment's reflection on the figures in Table 11.3 therefore shows that Dr Amini's claim that, at the time of the overthrow of Musaddiq's government, 'there was not a farthing in the government's hands' was a gross exaggeration.

This brings us to a consideration of the government's monetary policy. It has been observed that, between 1951 and 1953, government debt to Bank Melli increased by 1.8 billion rials, or, in other words, the government borrowed this sum of money from the bank over the period. This observation is technically correct, but it needs to be qualified in some important ways. First, the borrowing was done by the National Iranian Oil Company for the payment of 1.2 billion rials of its annual 2.0 billion rials deficit. It therefore had no part in financing the government's budget deficits. On the contrary, it was the government that made up the remaining 0.8 billion rials from the ordinary budget. Secondly, it was borrowed, *on a monthly basis*, from April 1952 to May 1953. Thirdly, 0.3 billion rials of the loan were repaid on a regular monthly basis, so that the *net* NIOC borrowing from Bank Melli over the 15-month period (April 1952 to July 1953), was 1.5 million rials – a monthly average sum of 0.1 billion rials.[31] Also, the money supply increased from 14.1 billion rials in 1950–1 (1329) to 22.3 billion rials in 1953–4 (1332). But the money supply figure of 22.3 billion rials for 1953–4 refers to April 1954 when Zahedi's government had been in power for seven months. Therefore, Dr Amini's subsequent reference to Musaddiq's 'inflationary policy' was in fact much more true of his own: during the whole of Musaddiq's period in office, the money supply increased by 3.9 billion rials, whereas in the first seven months of Zahedi's government it rose by 4.3 billion rials.

Table 11.3 *Budget deficit and deficit finance, 1951–3 (April 1330–August 1332) in billions of rials*

	Budget deficit	Deficit finance	Balance
1 (April 1951–August 1952)	−1.9	1.9	0.0
(i) Sale of £14 million	−	(1.3)	−
(ii) World Bank loan	−	(0.6)	−
2 (April 1952–August 1953)	−2.5	3.6	1.1
(i) Note issue	−	(3.1)	−
(ii) Public bonds	−	(0.5)	−
3 Total: 1 + 2	−4.4	5.5	1.1

Source: Table 2 and the sources therein: Musaddiq, *Memoirs*, Book II; Buzurgmehr, *Dr Mohammad Musaddiq dar Dadgah-i Tajdid-i Nazar-i Nizami*.

The expansion of the money supply and the depreciation of the rial (which inevitably led to higher import costs) had the greatest influence in raising general price levels. But the evidence suggests that later (vague and non-quantitative) criticisms of the government's 'inflationary policy' have been exaggerated. Table 11.4 shows changes in various price indices from 1951 to 1955. The average annual change in the wholesale price index for the two years 1952–3 was 8.6 per cent, and the average annual increase for home-produced goods was 7.0 per cent. However, the cost of living index increased at an average annual rate of 6.5 per cent. By comparison, prices had been falling sharply in 1950–1 to a large extent as a consequence of the fall in import costs brought about by the 1949 devaluation of sterling. However, in 1953–4, when the post-*coup d'etat* government was no longer in financial difficulty, the first two indices rose much more sharply than in any of the two previous years, while the rise in the cost of living index was still higher than in 1951–2. In a word, the evidence shows that, especially in the circumstances, the rates of inflation were moderate and manageable.[32]

Table 11.4 *Changes in various price indices 1951–5 (percentages)*

	Wholesale	Home-produced goods	Cost of living*	
1951–52	12.7	6.0	4.5	(6.3)
1952–53	4.5	7.9	8.6	(7.1)
1953–54	20.4	13.7	5.9	(9.2)
Average				
1951–53	8.6	7.0	6.5	(6.2)
1954–5	18.7	23.1	16.8	(14.4)

* Figures in brackets are based on Bank Markazi Iran, *The Revised Cost of Living Index* (Tehran, 1962).
Source: based on International Monetary Fund, *International Financial Statistics*, various issues.

The absence of reliable GNP figures makes it difficult to comment on the overall production and growth performance of the economy with any reasonable confidence. According to one estimate, from 1950–1 to 1953–4, the average annual money growth rate of GNP was 11.0 per cent.[33] Compared with the average annual increase in the cost of living index, this would mean an annual *real* growth rate of 3.7 per cent which, in the circumstances, would be a significant – and in fact unlikely – achievement. What can be said with confidence is that the economy had not been declining in consequence of the loss of oil revenues and the resulting economic problems.

The strategy of non-oil economics was controversial among different political groupings. Not only did the conservative press sharply disagree with it but even the Tudeh party's satirical publication, *Chilingar*, told Musaddiq to 'take a bucket and sell the oil'.[34] Doubts about the possible success of this strategy also existed within government circles, and among their supporters, although they were not expressed publicly. In a sense, the strategy could be said to have been 'forced' on the government by circumstances. But it was not inevitable, and a settlement of the oil dispute outside the basic Iranian terms would have been the obvious alternative. Musaddiq, therefore, consciously opted for running the economy without the oil revenues, and in so doing he had the support of most of his ministers and National Front colleagues.

From the above discussion of specific policies designed to make the economic strategy work, it might appear that they were based on a coherent and comprehensive policy framework. There is no evidence that such a framework existed, and, in fact, it is likely that policies were a good deal less systematic than would appear from this brief analysis. Yet, all the various measures were taken with a view to meeting the (external and internal) effects of the loss of oil revenues. In this sense credit must be given to the government for the fact that the different policies tended to complement and reinforce each other. Finally, the government's tough austerity measures inevitably led to a fall in public welfare. It was the government's great popularity which enabled it to take such unpopular measures without provoking a backlash of public opinion against itself.[35]

12

Religion and rift in the Movement

Ayatullah Kashani was the leading religious figure in the Popular Movement. He was also one of the most important leaders of the Movement who subsequently broke away from it, and eventually went over to the other side. The Fada'iyan-i Islam also supported the Movement at first, but fell out with it as soon as it came to power. Hence the link between the two aspects of this chapter's topic.

Religion and the Popular Movement

When in February 1949 an attempt was made on the shah's life, Kashani was suspected of complicity and exiled from the country, although in fact he had had no hand in the affair. At the same time, Ayatullah Burujirdi sent a telegram to the shah regretting the incident and praying for his continued reign. During the campaign for the nationalization of oil, Kashani issued numerous public statements of support both for the idea, and for Musaddiq and the National Front. He also helped raise funds for the Movement and organized the radical religious community behind it. But Burujirdi in Qum and Ayatullah Bihbahani in Tehran remained silent.

When Musaddiq resigned in July 1952 and Qavam became prime minister, Kashani was the only religious figure of his rank and stature to confront Qavam and the royal court, although a few other important *mujtahids* – notably the brothers Haj Sayyed Abulfazl and Haj Aqa Reza Zanjani, and Shaikh Baha al-Din Mahallati – were behind him. Burujirdi remained silent, and Bihbahani's opposition to Musaddiq had been known for some time.

In January 1953, the argument ostensibly over the extension of the

156

delegated powers which the Majlis had granted to Musaddiq ended with Kashani's open attack on the prime minister. But Burujirdi and Bihbahani maintained public silence, presumably because they regarded the matter more as a civil war within the Popular Movement itself.

On 28 February 1953, when the shah announced his decision to go abroad, both Kashani and Bihbahani issued statements of support for him and were involved in organizing the anti-Musaddiq demonstrations and riots of that day. There was no official statement from Qum, however, partly because the whole episode took no more than a few hours, and partly because of their indirect representation through Bihbahani in Tehran.

In July and August 1953, Musaddiq's referendum for the dissolution of the Seventeenth Majlis led to both Kashani's and Bihbahani's strongest attacks yet on him and his government, but there was no word directly from Qum. This came only after the shah's return from Europe, in the wake of the 19 August coup, when Burujirdi himself greeted him with a welcoming telegram. In the meantime, Bihbahani had helped organize the mob attack on Musaddiq's house on 19 August, and – as recent evidence seems to indicate – Kashani may have been involved in getting American funds to help bring down the government (see further below, and chapter 13). At any rate, the three religious leaders were, at the time, united in their opposition to Musaddiq and support for efforts to bring him down. In this they had the active support of the small but highly excitable group of the Fada'iyan-i Islam.

Three fairly distinct tendencies among religious leaders and activists can thus be distinguished. The *conservatives*, led by Bihbahani with Qum's implicit blessing, supported neither oil nationalization nor Musaddiq, and were politically in line with the shah and the establishment. The *radicals*, led by Kashani, were part of the Popular Movement at first, but split up into a pro-Musaddiq and an anti-Musaddiq camp afterwards. The *militants* – that is, the Fada'iyan-i Islam – actively supported the Movement until Musaddiq became prime minister, and fought against it from that moment onwards.

A note on Kashani's life

Sayyed Abulqasim Kashani was born in 1882, though it is not quite certain whether in Iran or Mesapotamia. He was taught by his father (who was himself a *mujtahid*) and reportedly attended some of the lectures of Haj Mirza Husain (*najl-i* Mirza Kalil) Tehrani and Akhund

Mulla Kazim Khurasani. But he obtained his degree (or *ijazeh* for *ijtihad*) from a relatively unknown *mujtahid* in Najaf by the name of Aqa Zia al-Din Iraqi. Later, when he had made a name for himself as a result of his opposition to the British occupation of Mesapotamia, he obtained letters of introduction from the great teacher Shaikh al-Shari'a (Shari'at-i) Isfahani, and Aqa Sayyed Abulhasan Isfahani, later to become a *marja' al-taqlid* (Supreme Religious Guide). They both described him as a *mujtahid*, but these references do not constitute degrees of *ijtihad* obtained from their authors.[1] During the First World War, Kashani became increasingly active against the British occupation of Islamic lands, and a price was put on information leading to his arrest. In 1920, he managed to escape and made his way to Tehran.

The early 1920s found the *ulama* in disarray if not retreat. They were unhappy about the domination of the Middle East by Britain and France, and alarmed by the rise of pan-Turanian and pan-Iranian sentiments and politics in Turkey and Iran. They still regarded the Qajar court and the old establishment as their natural allies. But they were disunited in their perception of current trends and useful ways of responding to them. And the fact that Najaf was no longer a solid base for religious leadership, and that Qum was yet to become an important centre, did not help. In the end, they tacitly supported the foundation of the new Pahlavi dynasty.

Kashani managed to contact Tehran's major *ulama*, including the Bihbahanis, the Tabataba'is, and the Ashtiyanis, as well as *Imam-Jum'eh* Khu'i and Haj Aqa Jamal Isfahani. But his most important politico-religious contact was Sayyed Hasan Mudarris who (as we saw in chapter 3) was about to become the leader of the parliamentary opposition to Reza Khan.

In 1924, both Mudarris and the religious establishment opposed the Reza Khan-inspired campaign for a republic: the former, mainly because he wanted to stop Reza Khan's rise to total power; the latter, mainly because they were afraid of the rise of modernism and the decline of religious influence. They were even concerned about Soviet support for Reza Khan. Kashani took an active part in the campaign against the republican movement and was involved in organizing the demonstrations outside the Majlis which ended up with Reza Khan's tactical resignation and retreat.[2]

However, after the movement's failure, Reza Khan made conciliatory contacts with the *ulama* in Qum as well as the *Atabat*, displayed religious fervour in public and received gifts and messages of support from them with pomp and ceremony. Thus the leading *ulama* tacitly approved of the change of dynasty from Qajar to Pahlavi. This made it easier for many religious figures in the Majlis to support the move, and more difficult for the old establishment to resist it. Mudarris, Musaddiq and others who did put up a fight were (as we have seen) left to their own devices. This was one important reason why both Kashani and Sayyed Abulhasan Hayerizadeh (who was later to become a pro-Kashani deputy during the Popular Movement) entered the constituent assembly which followed the Majlis resolution, and voted to ratify the proposed change of dynasty. The elections for that assembly were not free, and there were many other religious figures elected, but the role of Kashani and Hayerizadeh was especially significant because both of them had been pro-Mudarris and anti-Reza Khan. Indeed, Hayerizadeh had belonged to Mudarris's parliamentary group until the day of the Majlis vote.

Kashani cannot have been happy about the turn of events under Reza Shah, and this was true of almost every religious leader who did not defect or surrender to the new system. But the fact that even his most enthusiastic followers have not claimed anti-Reza Shah activity on his part must be sufficient proof that he refrained from political activity. During the Allied occupation of Iran in the 1940s he was arrested and held for some time on suspicion of pro-German activities. When released, he became increasingly vocal in politics until his arrest and exile in February 1949.

Conservatism or 'quietism'?

Far from protesting against Kashani's exile, the religious establishment called a conference in Qum (at exactly the same time) to forbid political activity by religious leaders. It is probably true that Burujirdi had a natural dislike for involvement in politics. Shaikh Abdulkarim Hayeri (his mentor and predecessor) had had the same attitude. But the Qum decision together with its subsequent attitude – which is sometimes described as 'quietism' – must be put in their proper context. The February 1949 decision against involvement in politics was largely intended as a rebuff to Kashani, and an expression of support for the shah and the political establishment. Burujirdi's later refusal to support the oil nationalization (even in the face of challenges and taunts from the Fada'iyan-i Islam) was in any case in line with the views of the conservative political establishment. Apart from that, Ayatullah Bihbahani, who did not hesitate to express his political views when necessary, was generally regarded as the link between the political establishment in Tehran and the religious establishment in Qum. It was the contents of a letter from Burujirdi to Bihbahani which in 1960 (a year before Burujirdi's death) was published as a *fatva* against land reform.[3] Burujirdi was certainly not a political leader or campaigner. But there is a tendency for Kashani's *radicalism* to be described as political 'activism', and Burujirdi's and Bihbahani's *conservatism* as political 'quietism'. Yet, these are two different political views rather than two different views of politics.

Kashani retorted to Qum's apparent decision against political involvement by issuing a statement from his exile in Beirut attacking the constituent assembly (which gave the shah the power to dismiss parliament) and warning against an unacceptable new agreement with the Anglo-Iranian Oil Company (see chapter 6). He was later (and *in absentia*) elected deputy for Tehran, although he never took his seat in the Majlis. After he was allowed to return to Tehran in June 1950, he issued numerous public statements in favour of oil nationalization and the National Front, and Musaddiq personally read out in the Majlis two of his letters addressed to the deputies. He was the only important religious leader at the time who committed himself to the Movement and the oil nationalization policy. Burujirdi, Bihbahani and all the other important religious leaders – Ayatullahs Hujjat, Sadr and Fayz, in particular – were, and remained, silent on the issue.[4]

After Razmara's assassination, however, others stepped forward. Ayatullah Mohammad Taqi Khansari, Shaikh Baha al-Din Mahallati, Sayyed Mahmud Ruhani, Shaikh Abbasali Shahrudi and Sayyed Mohammad Reza Kalbasi issued statements of support for the oil nationalization policy.[5] Khansari was a major religious leader; all the others were to become known as Ayatullahs, and Ruhani became well-known, but the most politically active of this group was Mahallati who maintained his support for the Popular Movement until the end. On the other hand, the Zanjani brothers, both of whom were important *mujtahids* in Tehran, had been actively behind the Movement from the beginning. So had Sayyed Mahmud (later Ayatullah) Taliqani, Sayyed Ja'far Gharavi, Sayyed Zia al-Din Haj-Sayyed-Javadi, Jalali-Musavi, etc., many of whom became deputies in the Seventeenth Majlis.

Fada'iyan-i Islam

This emotional group of Islamic activists struggled for the creation of an Islamic state and had strong sympathies with the Egyptian Muslim Brotherhood, and wider ambitions for the unification of all Islamic states. They were led by Sayyed Mujtaba Mirlawhi, better known as Navvab-i Safavi, and included the Vahidi brothers, Ibrahim Karim-Abadi and Abdullah Karbaschiyan, among their leading figures. Their principal weapon was assassination. There was no formal contact between Qum and the Fada'iyan, though there had been informal contacts with some relatively junior members of the Qum hierarchy, including Ruhullah Musavi (later, Ayatullah) Khomaini. The latter had been generally pleased with the Fada'iyan's assassination of Ahmad Kasravi in 1946, but displeased with that of Abdulhusain Hazhir. Later, the Fada'iyan shot and permanently wounded Dr Husain Fatemi; still later (in 1955) — and despite their active participation in the coup — they made an unsuccessful attempt on the life of Husain Ala, then prime minister. This led to their arrest and execution as well as Kashani's internment for a short period. The religious establishment did nothing for them, and little for Kashani.

The Fada'iyan supported the Popular Movement and the oil nationalization policy until the moment Musaddiq took over the government, when they quickly broke with him as well as with Kashani.[6] Their differences with both leaders were doctrinal. They had been hoping for an Islamic revolution which neither of the two leaders had promised or even aspired to. Indeed, Kashani's response to some partial demands towards Islamic rule was so succinct that it is worth a direct quotation:

> [The British colonialists] are now using other tactics in order to weaken our struggle. Currently, I am receiving signed letters asking why we do not ban the sale of alcohol, expel women employees from government departments, or order the ladies to wear the *chadur*. The authors of these letters are either direct agents of Britain, or have their own axe to grind, or are stupid.[7]

The Fada'iyan were equally uncomplimentary, but much more open, about Kashani and Musaddiq. Thus their leader declared that they were 'opposed to the policies of Kashani, Dr Musaddiq and members of the National Front':

> In my meeting with Kashani I made it clear to him that . . . their duty was to try and impose the Islamic rules, but Kashani raised some excuses, and my views made no impression on him . . . We told Kashani: your attitude is not a religious one; nor is your mode of living a religious one; you must change your attitude, and your children must observe the religious rules, but these

views did not impress him . . . I have no doubt that, right now, all
my dear brothers who are in jail [i.e. the seven Fada'iyan
members, who had been arrested after Razmara's assassination]
are there on the orders of Dr Musaddiq, Kashani and the
National Front. . .[8]

The Fada'iyan's personal attacks on Musaddiq, Kashani, Baqa'i,
Fatemi and other important Popular Movement leaders continued
throughout Musaddiq's premiership. They called Kashani a British
agent and also accused him of financial corruption. Significantly,
Kashani's later rift with Musaddiq – even his outright opposition in
January 1953, and his alienation from the Movement after the
28 February incident – did not bring him any closer to the Fada'iyan.
As late as May 1953 they dismissed rumours of their collaboration
with Kashani with contempt, describing their own leader as 'the
venerable Navvab-i Safavi', and the Ayatullah simply as 'Kashani'.[9]
Thus, at the beginning of Musaddiq's premiership we find Qum
apparently quiet; Kashani and the radical *mujtahids* and preachers
actively supporting the government; and the Fada'iyan describing
Musaddiq as a liar,[10] and publicly threatening to assassinate him.
When a suspected attempt was aborted outside the Marble Palace,
Musaddiq took *bast* in the Majlis and was visited there by Kashani.[11]
Later, Kashani said in a statement that he was not interfering in
government affairs and did not want any share in official appointments.[12]

Baqa'i, Makki and Hayerizadeh

Of the old Fifteenth Majlis opposition group, Abdulqadir Azad had
quarrelled with the Movement within a couple of months after
Musaddiq's premiership. The others – Makki, Baqa'i and Hayerizadeh
– were to hold out much longer. The fact that it was *they* who
(together with Kashani) broke with Musaddiq was no accident, for
they saw themselves not as Musaddiq's disciples but as the most
important leaders of the Movement after him. Baqa'i had been elected
the second deputy for Tehran (Musaddiq was first) in the Sixteenth
Majlis, and was universally regarded as the Movement's heir apparent.
Makki was to become Tehran's first deputy in the Seventeenth Majlis.
Hayerizadeh was not so young or so popular; but he was an old hand
from earlier times, a one-time religious figure who had known Kashani
for decades. These men together with Kashani turned against Musaddiq

at the same time and for the same reasons, and their break with Musaddiq had little if anything to do with religion.

Disagreements between Baqa'i and Makki, on the one hand, and Musaddiq, on the other, began as early as July 1951. At that time Musaddiq dismissed General Zahedi from his cabinet for disloyalty or negligence with regard to the demonstration on the day of Averell Harriman's arrival in Tehran which left many dead and wounded. But he was astonished to learn from Makki and Baqa'i that they had hitherto regarded Zahedi as an alternative prime minister should anything suddenly happen to him.[13] The conflict over Matin-Daftary was, however, the first serious test of their relationship. Senator Ahmad Matin-Daftary was Musaddiq's son-in-law and grand-nephew. He was a distinguished professor of law, and had been both minister of justice and prime minister under Reza Shah at a time when the latter tolerated no independent thought or action. Later, the Allies had put him under arrest for suspected pro-German activities, along with Kashani, Zahedi and a few other public figures. There was documentary evidence that – as a favour to the Anglo-Iranian Oil Company – he had used his influence with Musaddiq to direct the movements of the provincial governor of Khuzistan during the repossession of the oil industry in Abadan. Indeed, Musaddiq had to apologise to Amir-Ala'i, the governor in question, for having insisted on his instructions to him at the time, which had been based on information confidentially supplied by Matin-Daftary. During this incident, Makki had been at the centre of operations in Abadan, and Baqa'i had printed the relevant documents in *Shahed*.[14] Briefly, the documents in question show that the AIOC representatives in Tehran had asked for and obtained the co-operation of Matin-Daftary in trying to direct Amir-Ala'i's movements. Something like this had in fact happened on Musaddiq's express orders (and despite Amir-Ala'i's own advice against it), before the documents were discovered in Richard Seddon's house in Tehran. But Baqa'i's other specific charges against Matin cannot be taken seriously.[15]

A couple of months later, having discovered that Matin-Daftary was on the list of delegates in Musaddiq's delegation to the UN Security Council, Baqa'i threatened to make a scene by refusing to go, but was persuaded by Khalil Maleki to raise the matter with Musaddiq himself. Musaddiq told him plainly that he was under pressure from his wife to take their son-in-law with them. Baqa'i backed down, but neither he nor Makki (who was extremely hurt by his own exclusion from the delegation) was entirely convinced, and they seldom stopped referring to the matter after the rift in the Movement became apparent.

Arguments over other appointments increasingly poisoned the atmosphere between the two sides. Makki and Baqa'i were unhappy about the appointment of Murtiza-Quli Bayat (Saham al-Sultan) to the chairmanship of the National Iranian Oil Company, and of Dr Reza Fallah to run the refinery in Abadan. A Musaddiq relative and one-time prime minister, Bayat enjoyed a good public reputation, notwithstanding Makki's and Baqa'i's contrary views. But he did not belong to the Movement, remained at his post after the coup, and participated in the negotiations which led to the Consortium Oil Agreement. Fallah, on the other hand, was suspected of having strong sympathies with the AIOC. Dr Shahpour Bakhtiyar's appointment as deputy minister of labour was also controversial, and he did make one or two serious mistakes in that post. But Baqa'i's and Makki's insistence, then and ever since, that he had been a British agent can be dismissed as ridiculous. There is no evidence that Kashani had any objections to the above appointments. Nevertheless, as will be seen below, he had his own quarrels with Musaddiq over official appointments.

Baqa'i, Makki and Hayerizadeh – as the old Fifteenth Majlis opposition – expected special treatment: it was *they* who had initiated the argument in the Majlis, and *they* who had persuaded Musaddiq to lead the Movement; they were his colleagues not his protégés. Instead, they saw the newcomers – the Iran party leaders, etc. – winning all the prizes. This was at least in part the result of a vicious circle which they themselves did little to break, for as they went on quarrelling with Musaddiq, he tended to listen to those who were more accommodating to him. Musaddiq was not the most flexible of men; but they, too, were quarrelsome.

Baqa'i was by far the most outstanding of the three. The son of Aqa Mirza Shahab Kirmani, an important Constitutionalist leader in Kirman, he was, and always remained, the natural deputy for that old city. Although a career academic, he was not noted for his intellectual depth any more than his adversaries in the Iran party. But he was a charismatic leader, with boundless physical energy, exceptional courage, and an unbreakable spirit; a highly effective orator and rhetorician with an excellent command over Persian language and culture; and an almost ascetic individual who shunned material possessions, and did not seek power purely for its own sake. On the other hand, he was extremely self-regarding, opinionated, even arrogant, and (deliberately or otherwise) regarded the use of almost any means (including the destruction of other people's reputation) as legitimate, so long as he judged the ends to be in the public interest. He could be both charming to friends and highly vindictive towards opponents. His real grievance against Musaddiq was what he saw as his imperious attitude towards his colleagues and advisers. But he himself was quite intolerant of contrary opinion, which was why he broke with his own party, and ended up with a diminishing band of personal devotees.

After the July uprising

Disagreements and conflicts within the leadership had been going on for a long time, although none of them came into the open before the 21 July uprising. According to Fatemi's testimony, Makki and Sanjaby had once almost come to blows over informal squabblings within the National Front.[17] On 12 July (only nine days before the uprising) Baqa'i sent a secret circular to the Zahmatkishan's senior leaders. In it he talked about 'a treacherous as well as strong band' which – 'as a result of His Excellency Dr Musaddiq's oversights and regard for expediency' – had penetrated the Movement. Therefore, 'the party leadership intends to raise the problems faced by the party with His Excellency Dr Musaddiq, and present him with an ultimatum, but in a language which would not help him try and dodge the issue'.[18] The 'treacherous band' to which Baqa'i characteristically referred must have included a couple of Iran party leaders, and possibly Shaigan as well. But it is certain to have been headed by Husain Fatemi whom Baqa'i claimed to be nothing less than a British agent.[19]

As we have seen, both Kashani and Baqa'i (especially in his role as the Zahmatkishan party leader) played an extremely important role in determining the outcome of Musaddiq's resignation in July 1952. Kashani called the general strike, and refused to reach a settlement with the shah and Qavam; Baqa'i insisted that the Popular Movement deputies should demand no less than Musaddiq's reinstatement, and his party organized the crowd in the street demonstrations.[20] But the position has been at times overstated. It is arguable that without Kashani's uncompromising stand Musaddiq would not have returned to power. But it is also arguable that without the *bast* by the Popular Movement deputies, and without the organization of the crowd by the Movement's political parties (and especially Zahmatkishan), Kashani's efforts would have been of little consequence. At any rate, all these efforts were successful because of the great public backing which Musaddiq enjoyed. For, within a few months, Kashani's word no longer carried much weight with the public because of his opposition to Musaddiq.

The mournings and celebrations had barely come to an end when Kashani shot his first arrow at the prime minister. Why did you appoint General Vusuq, Nusratullah Amini and Dr Akhavi to important posts? he asked. Vusuq had commanded the gendarmerie under Qavam for three days, Akhavi was not suited to his post (though he did not say why), and Amini Araki was inefficient, he argued. But it was his threat to leave Tehran and even the country, which showed the seriousness of the position. Musaddiq was somewhat more restrained in his reply, but hardly more compromising. Vusuq and Akhavi had volunteered to work without pay, he said, and Amini Araki had been one of the best members of the cabinet office (before being made mayor of Tehran). He had to be free of interference to be able to carry out his reforms. Otherwise, he would be ready to relinquish power instead of the Ayatullah leaving town.[21]

Musaddiq's subtle use of the phrase *umur-i madani*, which literally means 'civil affairs', has led some of Kashani's later admirers and apologists, notably Hasan Ayat, to advance the theory of a grand conspiracy by Musaddiq, Qavam, the British government and Freemasonry to prevent the religious community and its leaders from participation in politics. It is a curious hypothesis, given Musaddiq's and Kashani's co-operation at the centre of Iran's politics for some time. But, in any case, it does not make sense. It is clear from the context that Musaddiq wished to make his official appointments without constant comments on their suitability. There is no evidence from that period, or before or after, that he believed in the desirability or possibility of preventing anyone – let alone the Muslim community – from political participation on account of religion or ideology. Kashani, in any case, was elected Majlis Speaker and head of the legislature with Musaddiq's blessing within a few days of this exchange of letters, although two other Movement leaders (Mu'azzami and Shaigan) also contended for the position, and Mu'azzami eventually replaced Kashani in the post.

Kashani had not in fact issued his dire threats simply because of these three uneventful appointments. Nor could Baqa'i have been particularly unhappy about them. But he was likely to have egged on the Ayatullah to show his teeth to Musaddiq, and even supplied the pretext for it.[22] There was at least one example of personal differences between the two leaders going back to a few months earlier. Two of Kashani's sons, Sayyed Mohammad and Sayyed Abulmu'ali, were candidates for the Seventeenth Majlis. But neither of them succeeded, and one of them did not even meet the age qualification, just like Musaddiq himself in the First Majlis.

On the question of official appointments, Kashani's greatest grievance was the appointment of General Mohammad Daftary as commander of the Customs Division, and the removal of Dr Reza Shervin from the leadership of the Religious Endowments Office. Daftary was a relative of Musaddiq and – as prefect-general of the police – he had been despised by Kashani as well as Baqa'i.[23] He was later to abandon Musaddiq as his police chief on 19 August, 1953 (see chapter 13). The removal of Shervin was another blow to Kashani. He was a Kashani partisan, and owed his post to him. His dismissal was engineered by Ahmad Zirakzadeh, the Iran party chairman, who was quite active in distributing posts to personal or party friends.[24]

The Zahmatkishan split

Still, Baqa'i was somewhat ahead of Kashani in bringing the conflict out into the open. His own later testimony suggests that, by August 1952, he had become restless. In September, he entered hospital for a few weeks to cure a mysterious illness (though, many years later, he said it was a coincidence of diabetes and paratyphoid).[25] Whatever the real reason, this afforded him time and privacy to meet with his own personal confidants in the Zahmatkishan leadership, and some of the leading opponents of Musaddiq, including General Zahedi. The rest of the Zahmatkishan coalition, led by Khalil Maleki, became alarmed. They were by no means averse to criticizing Musaddiq's government, and they said so in public at the time of Baqa'i's break with them, but they regarded a confrontation with that government as detrimental to the whole Movement.[26]

After all discreet discussions and negotiations between Baqa'i and Maleki, and within the Executive and the Central Committee, had failed, a meeting of the party activists was held on 9 October 1952, to settle the outstanding questions. Having quickly realized that he was in a minority, Baqa'i broke up the meeting and announced his own resignation from the party. Four days later, his toughs, together with others from Mujahidin-i Islam (i.e. Kashani's activists), attacked the party headquarters with knives and clubs, and expelled its numerical majority, who were immediately to form the Third Force party. Baqa'i then withdrew his 'resignation' and remained the leader of what was left of the Zahmatkishan party.[27] Two days earlier, General Hejazi and all three Rashidiyan brothers had been put under arrest for aiding 'a foreign embassy' to overthrow the government. General Zahedi was also implicated, though he could not be arrested because of his parliamentary immunity as a Senator. It is now known that the charges were correct, although none of the accused was formally charged. But Iran broke off diplomatic relations with Britain. Neither Kashani nor the old Fifteenth Majlis opposition was directly in league with any foreign power. But the evidence indicates that all of them (with the probable exception of Makki) allowed themselves to be used by those who collaborated with Britain and the United States to bring down the government.

At first, Baqa'i hid the real reasons for the internal party dispute, pretending that Maleki and the rest of the party activists had been too left-wing for him to tolerate.[28] But he had already ceased to see Musaddiq since August,[29] and he soon began to attack the government in public with increasing ferocity. The length of time that he and the other two were allowed to remain in the Movement's parliamentary group despite open campaigns against the government is surprising. Baqa'i had already attacked the composition of the new cabinet (and especially the appointments of Generals Vusuq and Daftary) in the Majlis. He now began to seize on the issue of Qavam's prosecution (which he never dropped, and of which more below) as well as other subjects such as the Social Security Bill. The Bill was introduced following the arrest of Hejazi and the Rashidiyans in order to strengthen public order and security. Both Baqa'i and Kashani attacked it in terms which cannot be taken seriously.

It is no kindness to Musaddiq to describe his government as so lax that it was to prove its own undoing. The press enjoyed a degree of freedom which they do not enjoy in Britain; the Rashidiyan brothers, and others like them, proceeded with their activities with impunity; the American embassy was organizing revolt against the government under its very nose; the Tudeh party was engaged in a campaign of disruption and defamation; the prime minister was almost killed by a mob twice in one day and no one was charged; the prefect-general of the police was kidnapped and murdered while the chief defendant in the case – General Zahedi – was allowed to take *bast* in the Majlis, and escape prosecution. Yet the government had taken on (in Musaddiq's own words) 'the greatest empire on earth', and no one more than Baqa'i and his party had insisted on the efficient enforcement of the law, before he broke with the Movement.

It can be demonstrated that such attacks by Kashani, Baqa'i and the others were motivated by their frustration with Musaddiq rather than a conflict over principles. To explain the rift in the Movement in the usual 'ideological terms' – e.g. Musaddiq's 'left' versus Kashani's 'right' – would lead to a serious historical misunderstanding. No Popular Movement deputy other than Baqa'i ever advocated comprehensive land reform or redistribution of income.[30] Likewise, Kashani did not oppose social reforms (including land reform) as the conservative religious leaders did. The Iran party leaders' softer attitude towards the Tudeh party was partly because they knew and understood the party less well than Baqa'i and Maleki, and partly because they put a high premium on their own personal popularity. How, then, could Baqa'i's 'right wing' continue to cause so much embarrassment to the government by its relentless attacks on it for not 'avenging the blood of the 21 July martyrs' on Qavam and his men?

Baqa'i was an unforgiving man, it is true. But even here, he was motivated more by an urge to embarrass Musaddiq than to pursue Qavam. He cannot seriously have believed (as he said on many occasions) that Musaddiq's treatment of Qavam was determined by the fact that they were distantly related. Musaddiq had not seen Qavam and his elder brother Vusuq for decades; he had campaigned vigorously against Qavam's election rigging in 1947, and had decided to leave politics as a result of Qavam's victory on that occasion; he had once described Vusuq as a 'traitor' at a Majlis meeting where Vusuq was present. The problem was that, although Qavam had raised strong public feelings against himself because of the bloodshed on 21 July, he had broken no law, and this was the real reason why Musaddiq ultimately took no measures against him.[31]

Therefore – and from the point of view of the principles involved – it is extremely difficult to reconcile Baqa'i's persistent attacks on the government for not punishing Qavam with his making such heavy weather of the Social Security Bill which was supposed to reduce the level of real public disorder and insecurity. The apparent conflict is resolved once it is understood that Baqa'i's real motive in taking up both issues was to embarrass the government. In fact, as a result of Baqa'i's vigorous campaign, the passage of the Law of Penalty for the Disruption of Public Order and Security was delayed until March 1953, and was replaced by another – the Formation and Powers of the Commission for Social Security – the following July.

The Law ultimately laid down that anyone suspected of disruption and sabotage should be brought before a security commission. If convicted, he would have the right to appeal to an ordinary court of appeal. If the verdict was upheld, there was a mandatory sentence of either six to twelve months' imprisonment, or banishment to another part of the country – but not both. It is anybody's guess how many people were actually convicted under this procedure; and Baqa'i's later pronouncements that this law formed the basis of SAVAK is correct only to the extent that the Persian word for 'security' occurs in both of them. Baqa'i lost no opportunity, then or later, to insist that the law had made 'intention' (*niyat*) itself a crime. It was not *niyat* or *qasd* but *conspiracy* (of a number of people together) to commit a crime which was at issue. (This itself is a crime in all advanced penal codes.) Kashani's attack on the Bill was meant to support Baqa'i. Their arguments were absolutely out of proportion with the subject and its context; they attacked the Bill because they were unhappy with Musaddiq for other reasons.[32]

The rift becomes complete

The rupture in the Movement began to turn into a total schism in January 1953 over the extension of the delegated powers. These were not emergency powers in the sense of suspension of a part of the Constitution. The Majlis had delegated the right to the government to legislate and enforce certain laws for six months before submitting them to parliament for ratification or rejection. And now, in January 1953, Musaddiq was asking for the extension of these powers for another year. Meanwhile, the Majlis was meeting regularly and was far from a docile or inactive body. Baqa'i, Hayerizadeh and Makki vehemently opposed the extension despite their own support for the delegated powers six months before (see chapter 10). Kashani had then been elected Speaker of the Majlis (and head of the legislature) perhaps partly in the hope of softening his attitude towards the government. But he still refused to attend the Majlis meetings. Instead, he wrote a letter to the Management Committee of the Majlis forbidding them to make time for the Bill because, he said, it was unconstitutional. The Committee (many of whom were opposed to the government) wrote back in extremely polite, almost reverential, terms saying why they were bound to let the Bill be debated.[33] It was eventually passed. Baqa'i, Makki and Hayerizadeh campaigned vigorously against it, but they abstained in the division because it was tied to a vote of confidence for the government. Having failed to impress either the Majlis or the bazaar, Kashani tended to back down for a time. There even was a meeting between the two leaders to settle their differences, but it did not work.

Neither the religious leaders in Qum nor Bihbahani contributed to this controversy, but their opposition to the delegated powers was well known. Recently, they had won the day against Musaddiq's attempt to replace the official trustee of the shrine in Qum, even though Kashani had backed Musaddiq on this issue.[34] They had also opposed women's franchise which was being discussed within the context of an electoral reform bill. Both Musaddiq and Kashani pleaded with the left wing of the Movement not to press the matter, because they were afraid that it would provide a powerful weapon for both the religious and the political establishment to use against the Movement. Zahmatkishan, Third Force, were leading a vigorous campaign for women's suffrage. Khalil Maleki wrote three articles entitled 'The Right of Women, One-half of the Human Race' in *Niru-yi Sevvum* (14, 15 and 16 December 1952). This was followed by a leading article in the same newspaper on 22 December, and an article by Hajar Tarbiyat on 25 December. A delegation of the Third Force party's women's section (*Nihzat-i Zanan-i Pishraw*) was then sympathetically received by Musaddiq who told them that the reform was not expedient at that time.[35]

By the end of January 1953, Kashani seemed to have become isolated among the religious leadership and community who supported the Popular Movement. He may have had Ruhani's and Shahrudi's sympathies, but they were not saying much in public. On the other hand, Mahallati, the Zanjani brothers, and Taliqani (who was not so well known at the time) remained behind the Movement. From a practical point of view, Kashani's failure to carry with him the religious figures in the Majlis was more significant. The Majlis *ulama* did not include any prominent *mujtahids*. This had been the general pattern since the Second Majlis. But they could have helped Kashani's cause tremendously had they solidly backed him against Musaddiq. Jalali, Angaji, Haj-Sayyed-Javadi, Shabistari and Milani remained with the Movement. Qanat-Abadi was Kashani's mouthpiece from the start, though he was to abandon him later under Zahedi. Safa'i, on the other hand, tended to represent the religious establishment. Thus, Kashani was increasingly dependent upon, and identified with, the conservative religious and political camp to which he did not really belong. And this was even more true of Baqa'i, Hayerizadeh and Makki, his close political allies.

The 28 February riots

The news of the shah's impending foreign trip on 28 February was an important turning point. A careful examination of the evidence shows

that the decision had been the shah's own, although the impression
was given that Musaddiq was forcing him to leave the country (see
further, chapter 13). Kashani may not have been privy to the game, but
Bihbahani is likely to have been involved in it. The anti-Musaddiq
demonstrations outside the palace and the mob's attack on the prime
minister's house cannot have been spontaneous, but the contribution of
Kashani's and Baqa'i's toughs might have been because they
genuinely believed that Musaddiq was pushing the shah out of the
country. Kashani wrote two letters of support to the shah that day, and
issued two public statements on the matter. The following is an excerpt
from the less well-known of the two statements:

> People, be warned! Treacherous decisions have resulted in the
> decision of our beloved and democratic (*dimukrat*) shah to leave
> the country . . . You should realize that if the shah goes, whatever
> we have will go with him. Rise up and stop him, and make him
> change his mind. Because, today, our existence and independence
> depend on the very person of His Majesty Mohammed Reza Shah
> Pahlavi, and no one else.[36]

Bihbahani's involvement in the plan is likely but not certain. Indeed,
if one were to rely on documentary evidence alone, it might look as if
he and his circle had been 'quiet' for quite some time. In fact, they had
been active both in unpublicized campaigns against the government,
and in devious methods of organizing public opposition to it. For
example, Mohammad Taqi Falsafi – the famous preacher who was
known to reflect Bihbahani's views – had for a long time been leading
an anti-government campaign through his perorations from the pulpit.
On one of these occasions he had to be rescued from the crowd (in a
congregation in the Shah Mosque) who were incensed with his attacks
on Musaddiq. And this had happened well before the rift in the
Movement; even before the 21 July uprising. On 28 February, in any
event, Bihbahani set his apparent 'quietism' on one side. Accompanied
by Shaikh (later Ayatullah) Baha al-Din Nuri, he personally visited the
shah, and – even more significantly – addressed the anti-Musaddiq
demonstrators outside the palace. Thenceforth, Bihbahani's active
campaign against the government became more obvious, and Qum's
involvement in it more entrenched.

Late in April 1953, General Mahmud Afshartus – the prefect-
general of police – was kidnapped and murdered in a cave outside
Tehran. Four retired generals were arrested in connection with the
charge. Baqa'i was deeply implicated but could not be arrested on

account of his parliamentary immunity (see chapter 13). Zahedi was about to be interned when he took *bast* inside the Majlis building. Kashani was still Majlis Speaker and head of the legislature, although he had not set foot in the building for a long time. He personally visited Zahedi in the Majlis, kissed his cheek, told him that he was welcome to stay in the Majlis 'for as long as he wished', and ordered the Majlis staff to 'take care of our dear guest'. It is sometimes believed that the point of no return between Kashani and Musaddiq was reached over the referendum for the dissolution of the Majlis. In fact, it had definitely been reached by this time.

The ulama and the coup

It was clear by now that both the religious establishment and Kashani were actively and irrevocably opposed to the government. In the following months, rumours of an imminent coup were rife.[37] In July and August Musaddiq decided to hold a referendum to dissolve the Majlis and hold new general elections, against the advice of his top advisers and well-wishers. Both Kashani and Bihbahani declared the decision to be unconstitutional as well as *haram* (forbidden by the Shari'a). Although it was a bad decision, it was not unconstitutional (see chapter 13). However, Kashani had now firmly placed himself within the conservative camp.

Both Kashani and the religious establishment passed over the attempted coup of 15–16 August in silence. Bihbahani was involved in organizing the mob during the 19 August coup. Evidence has recently come to light that Kashani may have received American money through Ahmad Aramish for the express purpose of bringing Musaddiq's government down. The evidence can be described as strong though not conclusive.[38]

In 1979, an exchange of letters between Kashani and Musaddiq was published by a member of Kashani's family who claimed that he himself had acted as the courier. Both were dated 18 August, the eve of the second and final coup. After complaining bitterly about Musaddiq's behaviour towards himself, Kashani bade him join hands with him to fend off 'the coup', although it was unclear which coup he had in mind. Musaddiq's reply was sardonic: 'Your Worship's letter was received through Mr Hasan Aqa Salemi. I put my trust in the support of the Iranian people. That is all.' There has been much controversy about the authenticity of the letters. Critics have wondered in particular why Kashani's letter (which was written in his own hand) was still in the possession of his family. The letters would seem to be authentic because Kashani's handwriting and style are almost unmistakable, and this is even more true of Musaddiq's style, although his letter was typed.[39]

On the other hand, the argument that the letters clear Kashani of any suspicion of support for the coup, and prove Musaddiq's foolishness in not taking heed, is not acceptable. On 18 August, the coup of two days before had already been aborted; and if Kashani's reference was to the 19 August coup, then he was unlikely to have written a letter about an imminent coup in which he would have had to be involved to know about it. Any reasonable person could have seen the purpose behind the letter as an attempt by Kashani to save what was left – and there was not much – in the wake of what must have been seen by him as a complete victory for Musaddiq.[40]

The religious establishment left no room for speculation about their attitude to the coup when Burujirdi went against his apparent 'quietism' and welcomed the shah back to the country in glowing terms. The day after the coup, the Fada'iyan-i Islam's newspaper described it as an Islamic revolution.

> Yesterday Tehran was shaking under the manly feet of the soldiers of the Muslim and anti-foreign army. Musaddiq, the old blood-sucking ghoul, resigned . . . under the annihilating blows of the Muslims . . . All governmental centres were captured by the Muslims and the Islamic army. . .[41]

Two weeks later, Kashani said in an interview that Musaddiq was guilty of high treason and had to be punished by death.[42] The religious establishment, Kashani and Fada'iyan-i Islam were thus all united in their support for the coup and Zahedi's government, although that unity was not to last long. On the other hand, the rest of the religious leadership and community, led by the Zanjani brothers aided by Taliqani, joined hands with the Popular Movement parties to organize the National Resistance Movement against the coup. That, however, is another story (see chapter 15).

A concluding note

The religious establishment gained from the coup for a few years before the conflict over land reform and the shah's bid for total power. Having helped set up a conservative regime, they could then retreat into their apparent 'quietism' and let the political establishment deal with Musaddiq, the Popular Movement, Communism, Baha'ism, and other perceived enemies of Islam at the time. They thus maintained their base among the landlords but without losing it in the bazaar, although – just after the coup – some sections of the bazaar had issued threats to withhold their religious payments to Qum. Kashani, on the other hand, was a complete loser. He had left his political base in the Popular Movement, but did not belong in the conservative establishment. He had also alienated many of his supporters in the bazaar without having any base at all among the landlords. Neither Musaddiq nor he could organize effective opposition against the new regime: Musaddiq, because he was in jail; Kashani, because he had lost his public appeal. As for Fada'iyan-i Islam, they had no social or power base to lose. So they lost their lives at the hands of the regime which they themselves had helped bring to power.

Makki and Hayerizadeh would not have led a campaign against Musaddiq without Kashani and Baqa'i. And, although it might seem difficult to believe, neither would Kashani, without Baqa'i's support (if not encouragement). Here, personality traits were of great importance. Hayerizadeh was less popular or principled than the rest of them; and he was later to abandon them, too, for favours from Zahedi. Makki's opposition to Musaddiq was not so vehement, and within weeks he was to be quite embarrassed by the coup and its aftermath. Kashani did have the self-regard to be outraged by what he considered to be Musaddiq's contemptuous attitude towards himself. He also had the fearless spirit to lead himself down the path of isolation. But Baqa'i's role in cultivating this attitude in him was important. Moreover, Kashani would not have broken with Musaddiq without the support of a political spokesman of Baqa'i's rank, stature and unusual qualities from within the Movement itself.

Baqa'i's role was thus absolutely central both to the rift in the Movement, and to its escalation over time. He alone had *all* the qualities and qualifications necessary and sufficient to bring about the confrontation with Musaddiq. He had an unbreakable spirit, but one which was not always used in a constructive way, because his unusual strength of character would demand that he should be the decision-maker *par excellence*. Once (in 1953), in a parliamentary debate, he described himself as a dog who savages friend and foe alike.[43] And, purely in the metaphorical terms which he himself had intended it, he was not far from the truth.

In the end, they hurt themselves a great deal more than they did Musaddiq. But much of the damage they caused the Movement could have been avoided had Musaddiq been more accommodating towards them. In one candid moment Baqa'i later wished that Musaddiq was more appreciative of men like himself.[44] But he could equally have put it the other way round.

13

The ways and means of overthrowing Musaddiq

The title of this chapter has been extracted from the minutes written by Robin Zaehner for the Foreign Office of his conversation with Abbas Iskandari, in the summer of 1951, which make it clear that at the same time as the British government was taking its case to the Security Council, it was planning Musaddiq's downfall by secret intervention in Iranian politics. Shortly afterwards Eden turned down the American solution for a settlement (which Musaddiq had accepted), told the US Secretary of State that there were better Iranian alternatives both to Musaddiq and to the Tudeh party, and advised him to 'send [Musaddiq] home'.[1]

Eden was determined not to come to any settlement with Musaddiq (see chapter 11). The intelligence staff at the British embassy in Tehran were reinforced, and their domestic contacts mobilized for action against the government. An important Foreign Office strategy was to frighten the US government into the belief that Musaddiq would deliver Iran into the hands of the Soviet Union. The CIA co-operated in thus misleading their own government into taking hostile action against Musaddiq.[2]

There was a snowball effect. The rigid British and hardening American attitudes towards Musaddiq helped extend and intensify the opposition of the shah and the Iranian conservatives against him, if only because they believed that he was doomed to failure. This trend was encouraged by direct British and (later) American pressures on them to act against Musaddiq. The government's lack of firmness in dealing with them and with the Tudeh party did not help. It virtually gave them a free hand to organize the anti-government campaign; it played straight into Britain's hands as regards labelling the Movement; it also frightened the landlords, the religious establishment and other conservative groups. The opposition from within the Movement completed the circuit. It did not manage to divide, let alone break up, the Movement. But, as the seemingly most legitimate opposition to the government, the constant bickerings of its leaders – and Baqa'i, in particular – caused the government much concern and acute embarrassment, and made it considerably more difficult for it to govern. Given this vast array of forces against Musaddiq's government, it seems quite extraordinary that it did not fall sooner than August 1953.

Zaehner's mission has already been mentioned several times above. Middleton, the British chargé d'affaires in Tehran, had begun to prompt Major-General Zahedi into action early in 1952. C. M. Woodhouse (of Britain's MI6) was running the operation to overthrow the government (code-named Operation Ajax). The American embassy in Tehran took direct command of these activities in October 1952, when the Iranian government closed down the British embassy precisely in the hope of curtailing British plotting. Britain's efforts have now been so well-documented in books, memoirs, documentary programmes, etc., that it is unnecessary to reproduce the details in the present volume.[3]

28 February 1953

On 28 February 1953, a rumour was suddenly spread around that the shah was about to leave the country for a visit abroad, the impression being given that Musaddiq was forcing him to leave the country. For the first time, Kashani and Baqa'i joined forces with the right-wing civil and military opposition in taking violent action against Musaddiq. The evidence suggests that there had been an elaborate plan to deliver a major blow against the government. Whether or not this had included the killing of Musaddiq himself cannot be known for certain, but the fact that he managed to survive was almost a miracle.

The habitual interference of the royal court in politics and the administration was well known. The most active and effective among them were the shah's mother and his twin sister Princess Ashraf, both of whom held separate courts. Ashraf in particular had an extensive network of influential people popularly known as 'Ashraf's band'. Ever since Musaddiq had assumed office, both women had been actively campaigning against him. Musaddiq and other Popular Movement leaders had several times made representations to the shah – normally through Husain Ala, the royal court minister – to try and curtail their political activities, but to no avail. In the end, Musaddiq had threatened to discuss the situation in public if no effective action was taken by the shah on the matter.

The shah decided to launch a counter-attack. Several reasons lay behind this. He himself was opposed to Musaddiq and was in contact with the foreign and domestic forces which were engaged in dislodging him; the activities of his sister and mother were thus in line with his own wishes and perceived interest. There was not a great deal he could do to stop them even if he had so wished, because he did not yet wield that kind of power within the royal family; any serious step to contain their efforts could have been seen by the political establishment as well as the British government as an act of disloyalty. Meanwhile, his own bitterness over Musaddiq's insistence on the constitutional principle that 'the shah must reign, not rule' was daily increasing.

Husain Ala had once surprised Musaddiq by saying that the shah had been thinking of going to Europe for some time because 'he was bored with having nothing to do'. Musaddiq had responded with reassuring words, and had advised against the idea.[4] Musaddiq did not in fact seek trouble with the shah because he wished to maintain the system of constitutional monarchy and also hoped to soften the shah's opposition to himself. Many Popular Movement leaders and activists were conscious of the potential damage of a continuing rift between the shah and the government.

Dr Abdullah Mu'azzami was a senior Popular Movement leader and deputy, a well-to-do landlord and professor of law who combined an independent mind with unusually moderate political behaviour. Increasingly, Musaddiq and the court relied on him as the link between them. He saw the shah as well as Ala several times in his efforts to try and reduce their differences. These contacts led to a decision at one of the regular meetings of the Popular Movement parliamentary group to send a formal delegation to the court in pursuit of a *rapprochement* between the shah and the prime minister. Besides Mu'azzami himself, the delegation included Dr Ali Shaigan (independent), Dr Karim Sanjaby and Ali-Asghar Parsa (both from the Iran party), and three of the religious figures among the Popular Movement parliamentary group, Haj-Sayyed-Javadi, Milani and Jalali-Musavi.[5]

Meanwhile, Ala had given Musaddiq another hint (it was no more than that) about the shah and Queen Soraya's thoughts of paying a visit to Europe. The court minister told Musaddiq that the shah and the queen were unhappy about their apparent inability to have children, and wished to seek possible treatment abroad. Musaddiq had suggested that perhaps the queen could go on her own, and the shah could join her later, if there was any real need for it.[6]

On 24 February the seven-man parliamentary team, led by Mu'azzami, was invited to lunch at the court. This time the shah himself joined the party, and the deputies were pleasantly surprised to see him in a friendly mood towards Musaddiq and the Movement. After leaving the palace, they agreed to go straight to Musaddiq's house (which was close by) to give him the good news. There are three versions – Musaddiq's, Mu'azzami's and Sanjaby's – of what immediately followed; they disagree on some details, but concur on the main points.

According to Musaddiq, while the seven deputies were at his house, Mu'azzami was called by the court to the telephone. When he returned to the room, he muttered a few words to Sanjaby, swore everyone to secrecy, and then told them that he had just been told that the shah had decided to go on a foreign visit, although he did not wish to make his decision public. He added that Ala and another court official were on their way to the prime minister's house to discuss the matter. When they arrived, the deputies moved to another room. Musaddiq advised the court representatives against the idea, but was told that the shah's mind was made up. He promised to co-operate in helping organize and finance the trip as well as keeping the decision secret. The shah had insisted on secrecy, 'lest there should be public anxiety and unrest', and he proposed to make a detour by car up to the Iraqi border to avoid prior public detection of his departure.[7] According to Sanjaby, they had already been told of the shah's decision when they were having lunch at the palace, and he did not recall any telephone call from the court to Mu'azzami at Musaddiq's house.[8]

Mu'azzami's recollections of the event have been presented in greater detail, and (for a variety of reasons) are likely to be the most accurate. The matter had indeed been mentioned openly at the royal luncheon but only as a vague possibility. Then he had been called to the telephone at Musaddiq's house and informed that the shah had decided to go on a trip soon. Back in the meeting, he had first told a couple of his colleagues in French about the matter, then (having sworn everyone to secrecy) had broken the news. Ala and Hishmat al-Dawleh had then visited Musaddiq's house, as all three versions agree.[9]

The reason for this detail is the shah's claim in *Mission for My Country* that both the suggestion of the trip and the insistence on keeping it secret had come from Musaddiq himself. But he did not explain why he had agreed to go along with it. At 6 pm on 28 February, after the attack on his house had failed, Musaddiq gave a full report to a 'private' session of the Majlis (i.e. without observers in the public gallery) which contained the points briefly summarized above. Furthermore, on 6 April, he made a long and frank radio broadcast to the nation about the whole issue, in which he once again maintained that the shah himself had decided to go abroad and had insisted on secrecy. The royal court then responded by issuing a statement claiming that the idea had been suggested by 'three [sic] Popular Movement deputies' whom it did not name.[10] This was obviously at variance with the shah's later account in his book. To understand the logic of the events of 28 February, it is essential to know who had decided on the trip, and how the whole thing had been organized. The direct as well as circumstantial evidence discussed above makes it plain that, even if one assumes that it had been intended seriously, the decision had been taken by the shah himself.

On 25 February Ala surprised Musaddiq by calling on him to say that the date of departure had been set for as early as three days afterwards. The course was thus set for Saturday, 28 February, when Musaddiq was to have lunch at the palace at 1.30 pm. Ala also said that the cabinet would attend an official farewell ceremony later in the afternoon. Meanwhile, General Zahedi was taken into custody, on 25 February, on suspicion of secretly conspiring in a security operation totally unrelated to the shah's intended journey. Typically, however, he was released without being charged.[11] On the morning of 28 February, Ayatullah Bihbahani telephoned and asked Musaddiq if rumours of the shah's imminent departure were correct, and why he had agreed to it. Greatly surprised that the matter had apparently been leaked, Musaddiq replied that he could not interfere with a decision which it was the shah's own privilege to make. However, he was even more surprised by a personal telephone call from the shah, after Ala had spoken first, simply to tell him to come to the palace at 12 noon rather than 1.30 pm. After the event, it was natural for him to suspect that the shah had not really intended to leave the country, and that the change of appointment (from which lunch was later omitted without further mention) had been part of a plot to make him leave the palace on his own at a time when the mob had gathered outside to kill him.[12]

At the palace, he found the shah's conduct strange and seemingly disorganized. There was no luncheon nor the full official ceremony with the cabinet, all of whom were duly present. The shah told him of the arrival of a Majlis delegation to talk him out of his journey, and Musaddiq urged him to take their advice. After a brief meeting with them, however, he told the prime minister he had turned down their request. Meanwhile, Musaddiq noted the arrival of Ayatullah Bih-bahani and Shaikh Baha al-din Nuri on a similar mission. Kashani and

Baqa'i had also been very active that day, as we saw in chapter 12. Completely unaware of these developments, Musaddiq received a message (from his office at home, where he always discharged his official duties) that Loy Henderson, the American ambassador, was coming to see him on an urgent matter, though Musaddiq said afterwards that Henderson's business turned out to be trivial. After informing the shah, he set out to leave the palace alone for his home nearby at 109 Kakh (Palace) Street.

As he approached the main palace gates, however, he was astonished to hear loud denunciations of himself outside the gates. By quick thinking and a stroke of luck he managed to leave through another gate which was unlocked on his own initiative by a palace official. The crowd then gave chase to his car, but were prevented by a police cordon from moving towards his home. At this point, Prince Hamid Reza, the shah's youngest brother, intervened and ordered the police to give way. The mob then attacked Musaddiq's house, and that of his son Ahmad next door. The house had an iron gate, and the well-known mobster, Sha'ban the Brainless, (with a retired army colonel sitting next to him) drove an army vehicle against it. At this point, Third Force party youths and activists, led by Jalal Al-i Ahmad, arrived in large numbers, and the crowd was encircled by the guards within, and the Third Force members outside, the house.

On his son's advice, Musaddiq and Fatemi (the foreign minister) climbed over the wall and left through the grounds of the adjacent Point IV office (which happened to be Musaddiq's own property) for army HQ. From there they went straight to an already agitated Majlis meeting, from which the public was excluded, where Musaddiq gave a full account of the incident. A later extended account of his relations with the shah was given in a broadcast to the public on 6 April, in which he recounted that he had heard that, when the news was received of his lucky escape while leaving the palace, the shah had said: 'The bird broke out of the cage.'[13]

As usual, inquiries into the lack of security, in spite of Musaddiq's personal instructions, did not get far. And, as usual, the law was not used to bring the mobsters and rioters to book. Apart from Sha'ban and his gang, there were Baqa'i's and Kashani's toughs and the mob led by Tayyeb Haj-Reza and Husain Ramazan-Yakhi, who usually acted for Bihbahani. Some senior army officers were also actively involved, and others participated in the meetings outside the palace. Thenceforth, Musaddiq became acutely conscious both of the loyalty of the security forces and of his own personal safety. Some time later, Ala resigned as court minister, and was replaced by Abulqasim Amini (younger brother of Dr Ali Amini) in an 'acting' capacity. Musaddiq never again agreed to hold a private meeting with the shah; in other words, he broke off personal relations with him, although the necessary official contacts were maintained. He even turned down the shah's several requests to meet him at the home of his younger son, Dr Gholam-Hossein.[14]

However, on 6 March, the Majlis set up an eight-man team — Mu'azzami and Sanjaby (Popular Movement), Makki, Baqa'i, Hayerizadeh and Rafi' (opposition), and Ganjeh'i and Majdzadeh (independent) — to investigate the differences between the shah and the prime minister. In their unanimous report to the House a week later, they expressed the view that the only bone of contention between the two sides was the question of 'the rights of the monarchy, and the constitutional powers of the cabinet, especially as they affect the armed forces'. This was followed by their own unanimous view on the subject, namely that since according to the constitution the shah was not answerable, the cabinet had the power and responsibility in all executive matters, civil as well as military. However, when it came to the approval of the report by the whole House, Baqa'i and Hayerizadeh led the other opposition deputies against it on the ground that, though the interpretation was valid, its passage by the Majlis would be against the country's interest. It was never passed, because each time it was put to vote, the opposition deputies walked out, and the required quorum did not obtain.[15]

The murder of the police chief

In April a new plan was set in motion to force Musaddiq's resignation. With the shah's knowledge and CIA involvement, it was decided to kidnap key officials and political personalities (including General Riyahi, Dr Fatemi, Dr Mu'azzami and Dr Shaigan) rapidly in succession, thus throwing the country into chaos and insecurity. To date the full list has not come to light. Afshartus the police chief, headed the list, for he was in a truly key position, and was a tough, efficient and loyal officer. It was also easier to lure him into a trap, because of his personal contacts with Baqa'i, in pursuit of his scheme to try to heal the breach between Musaddiq and Kashani.[16] Those directly involved in the plot were Baqa'i, his close personal friend Husain Khatibi (at whose house Afshartus was kidnapped on 19 April), and retired Brigadiers Muzayyeni, Munazzah, Bayandur and Murtiza Zahedi (a relative of the better-known general), assisted by other officers and NCOs, and hired men. Contrary to their expectations, however, the plot was quickly uncovered, and all of them (except Baqa'i who enjoyed parliamentary immunity) were arrested. As soon as Khatibi fell under suspicion, however, they had Afshartus murdered in the cave outside Tehran where he was being kept, in order to destroy the star witness against themselves. Brigadier Muzayyeni was in charge of the murder mission, and Major Baluch-Qara'i executed the order. The former was arrested and shot some time after the coup, whereas the latter was arrested and released after denouncing his Baha'i faith. There was no public account at the time of any interrogations or trials in either case, but in 1953 the results of the investigations were published in the press as they emerged.

In their signed confessions, the four senior officers accused of the plot admitted (in largely consistent detail) the kidnap, and all but Muzayyeni (who had been personally involved in the murder) confirmed the decision to kill Afshartus. The other three described a lunch at Baqa'i's house, where Khatibi (who was then on the run) and Baqa'i made them agree to the killing of Afshartus.[17] Some of the other accused vaguely referred to the marginal involvement of a 'prince' in the kidnap operation, rumours suggesting that it was Prince Ali-Reza, but it could equally well have been Hamid-Reza. Major-General Zahedi was also implicated, but, as noted in chapter 12, he was given protection by Kashani in the Majlis.

From the moment of Khatibi's arrest, Baqa'i went on the attack even more vehemently than usual. He claimed to have personally seen Khatibi being whipped in jail. Later, he also claimed that his servant had been arrested and 'beaten up so badly that he could hardly talk'.[18] But his servant was not charged, and the charge against himself came out of the evidence given by the retired officers involved in the case. Three of them – Munazzah, Bayandur and (Murtiza) Zahedi – wrote and signed their own confessions, implicating Baqa'i in both the kidnap and the murder, and making no complaints at all of any ill-treatment in jail. Muzayyeni, on the other hand, denied the murder charge, but admitted the kidnapping, and Baqa'i's involvement in it. He, too, wrote and signed his statement as well as his replies to the examining magistrate's questions, but he added complaints about his treatment in jail not being consistent with his rank and status.[19]

Baqa'i was arrested on 17 August (i.e. two days before the final coup), but there are no records of any interrogations. The legal process was observed so well that the dossier was not yet complete when the government fell. After the coup, the case against him was dropped (since he had not yet been indicted), but the others were put on a mock trial, and cleared of all the charges against them. No further efforts were made, however, to find the 'real' culprits. Baqa'i consistently dismissed the charge of both kidnap and murder as 'an unchivalrous accusation'.[20] But from 1953 until 1987, when he died a prisoner of the Islamic regime in a Tehran hospital, he did not use a single opportunity to issue a longer statement about the nature of his contacts with Khatibi or the generals who had provided precise details of his involvement in the affair.

From this time rumours of an imminent coup were rife and were encouraged daily by the famous Tudeh slogan, 'We shall turn the coup into a counter-coup'. Since the defection of Kashani and the others, but especially after the 28 February episode (when it had characteristically stayed silent and inactive), the Tudeh party and press somewhat moderated their tone towards the government, though at no stage did they behave like a reasonable democratic opposition. But their demonstrations and public meetings became larger and more ominous. Whether or not the Tudeh leaders themselves knew it, there is now conclusive evidence that CIA money was being regularly used to swell Tudeh meetings with large numbers of hired mobsters,[21] the idea being to prove to the Iranians themselves, as well as to the US government, that Iran was about to fall into the Soviet Union's lap.

The government was largely – and mistakenly – undisturbed by all this, partly because it had won the difficult economic battle and, hence, felt that it could dig in for a long diplomatic war of attrition with Britain. It also laid too much emphasis on its popular support, not realizing that, with the rift within the Movement itself, the growing open and explicit agitation of its domestic and foreign enemies, the increasing agitation within the army and security forces, etc., the times were considerably different from July 1952. Indeed, the legacy of the 21 July uprising was to blur the government's vision of the new realities right up to its fall.

The referendum

Makki, Baqa'i and their small group in the Majlis became increasingly active and vocal, but Musaddiq still had a comfortable, though somewhat reduced, majority in the House. At this point, a fairly insignificant Majlis decision led to a reaction on Musaddiq's part which played straight into the hands of the plotters, and resulted in the 19 August coup. A standing supervisory board, including a few representatives from the Majlis, acted as the watch-dog committee for the issuing of new notes at Bank Melli (then the central bank) of Iran. In June 1953 a vacancy occurred with the departure of one of the Majlis deputies on the board, and the Majlis chose Makki for the post.

According to his own repeated explanations, Musaddiq was alarmed that, once on the board, Makki would learn about the 3.1 billion rials of new notes which had been issued over a period of nine months, and would publicize it with great clamour. We have already seen that the note issue (which was quite moderate in the circumstances) was an economically sound and legally valid decision, which also happened to satisfy the existing prejudices about the close linkage between the volume of the domestic currency and the foreign reserves. Musaddiq has also explained that he was anxious lest the inevitable public row which Makki and the others would create over the matter would result in the shopkeepers putting up their prices. If such were his real fears, they were (technically) largely unfounded. It is likely, however, that he was at least equally worried about the political capital the opposition would have made of this, sounding the death-knell of the economy to an economically innocent public, including even the educated among them.

Then came Ali Zuhari's motion of censure – prompted by Baqa'i – over the alleged torture of the accused in the Afshartus case. Musaddiq was hardly concerned about the subject of Zuhari's censure, but he was frightened into a fatal miscalculation. He believed that the same slender majority which had chosen Makki for the bank post was lined up to vote the government out of office, following the censure motion debate. If this happened, he argued then as later, it would not only mean the end of the Popular Movement, the formation of a dictatorial government, and surrender to Britain over the oil dispute, but much worse, it would all happen, not by illegal means, but by a seemingly constitutional process. The Movement would then be totally demoralized and defeated, having been brought down apparently by its own weapon, i.e. the legal and democratic political process.[22] There was also a psychological side to this reasoning, for while he would (and did) look upon the violent overthrow of his government as almost a personal triumph, he would regard a concocted constitutional defeat of that kind as abject failure, comparable to losing Iran's case in the World Court, the fear of which (exactly a year previously) had made him prepared to emigrate. At any rate, it was the fear of a vote of no confidence alone which lay behind his decision to hold a referendum to dissolve the Majlis and hold new elections forthwith. Many deputies, he pointed out, had been elected on the government platform, but had defected afterwards. Their constituents should therefore be given a chance to review their case.

It was a gross miscalculation, for there was no comparison between sending Makki to the Bank, and bringing the government down over Zuhari's motion. Musaddiq still commanded an absolute majority in the House, not least witnessed by the fact that, when the referendum decision was publicly announced, two-thirds of the deputies voluntarily resigned their seats in support of the government's decision, although some of them, and many committed Popular Movement deputies themselves, had had doubts about the wisdom of the decision. Most of Musaddiq's closest colleagues and supporters – Dr Ghulamhusain Sadiqi, Khalil Maleki, Dr Ali Shaigan and Dr Karim Sanjaby among them – reasoned with him, time and again, that the decision was wrong. They were all afraid that the occasion would be used for the coup attempt which was literally expected any day. When Sadiqi told Musaddiq – in so many words – that the shah would try to dismiss him in the absence of the Majlis, the latter confidently replied that 'he would not dare'.[23] In a famous episode, Khalil Maleki – having failed to convince the old man – came up with these prophetic words: 'The path you are treading will lead straight to hell, but we shall nonetheless accompany you on it.'[24] Musaddiq even told Sanjaby that he must have been smoking 'pot', in view of his argument against the proposed referendum.[25] Dr Abdullah Mu'azzami who had replaced Kashani as the Majlis Speaker (and head of the legislature) resigned his important office in protest against the decision, and immediately left the capital for his home town, Gulpaigan.

The opposition, Kashani, Baqa'i, Makki, Hayerizadeh *et al.*, not to mention the shah and the establishment, immediately had a field day. They issued public statements declaring the decision illegal, dictatorial and – as Bihbahani and Kashani put it – forbidden by the Shari'a. There was no provision in the Constitution for the government's early dissolution of the Majlis (followed by new elections) by referendum. Also, the shah had been given the power to dismiss the parliament four years earlier. But nor was there anything which forbade such a decision, especially given the fact that two-thirds of the deputies had been behind it to the point of voluntarily resigning their seats. Indeed, once they had done so, there was no longer any need for a referendum, as the government had no choice but to hold new elections. Musaddiq's surprising disregard of this obvious fact, which he never even mentioned, must have been for the sake of the formal demonstration of his support. This was another mistake.

The referendum was held – to put it mildly – in bad taste. The rural areas were excluded in order to avoid the long process of collecting and counting their votes twice – once for the referendum, a second time for the new elections. The polling stations for 'yes' and 'no' votes were separated, perhaps with the best of intentions, but it was not and did not reflect well on a democratic government.[26] The government did its best to ensure peaceful and honest voting and counting, but there were occasional intimidations of voters outside the polling stations which (although the matter was largely out of the government's hands) showed the process in a bad light. The result was a huge 'yes' vote, and the government issued the dissolution order. But before it had received the royal assent, 'the royalist coup' (in Eden's words) of 15–16 August was set in motion, 13 days after the polling.

The coup

The plotters had been active without pause. They controlled four-fifths of the press and put out false propaganda as well as anti-government articles, some of which were written by CIA experts.[27] The US government itself was now explicitly committed to the policy of destroying the Popular Movement by force. The American embassy in Tehran, led by Ambassador Henderson and CIA agent Kermit Roosevelt, became the centre of operations. Lessons had been learned from past failures. There was more money, better and more extensive organization, deep penetration inside the army, the police and the martial law administration, and wide contacts among the political and religious establishment. Kashani may have received American money through Ahmad Aramish to organize anti-government activities (see chapter 12). Baqa'i had been co-operating with Zahedi for months, and Hayerizadeh was active in the final coup itself. American pressures on the shah to overcome his native fears had been bearing fruit, and the secret visit of Princess Ashraf to Tehran on 25 July, though discovered, helped ensure his full co-operation. She had come on a mission from Alan Dulles, the CIA chief, like General Schwarzkopf after her, to boost both the shah's and Zahedi's morale. The Majlis recess pending the formal dissolution provided an excellent opportunity for action. Therein had lain the fears of those Popular Movement leaders who had unsuccessfully tried to talk Musaddiq out of the referendum.

The shah and Queen Soraya left for their hunting lodge at Kilardasht on the Caspian Sea, where he signed two blank notices to be filled in at the right time: one for Musaddiq's dismissal, the other for

Zahedi's appointment to his post. The day was set for 13 August when in fact rumours about an impending coup rose to their highest pitch yet, but one or two technicalities led to its postponement to 15 August. The rumours of 13 August were echoed in a leading article in the weekly *Niru-yi Sevvum* next day:

> Nevertheless, the suspicious activities in Tehran of foreign agents during the past two weeks together with their internal counter-parts show that a secret organization is hopelessly working against Dr Musaddiq's government, and the American and British imperialists have not yet lost faith in the use of their last card.

The plan was first to kidnap Fatemi, the foreign minister, and Riyahi, the chief of staff, on the evening of 15 August, in the hope of forestalling civil and military resistance after the event. In the process, two other Popular Movement personalities, who happened to share a house with Riyahi, were also kidnapped, but the chief of staff escaped the ordeal because he had suddenly been summoned by Musaddiq an hour earlier. The four big tanks from the shah's summer palace in Sa'd-Abad were then moved into town, and surrounded Kakh Street, where Musaddiq lived. Finally, Colonel Nasiri (later the SAVAK chief), then the commander of the royal guards, took the royal notice with him to present to Musaddiq at 1.00 am on 16 August, and arrest him there and then. What they intended to do with him afterwards is not known, although the kidnapped Fatemi and others had been told that they would be executed at dawn.

In the event, the royalist coup boomeranged because of 'an indiscretion' (as Eden put it, once again). Since all the operations were to be carried out by the royal guards themselves, the force had been put on alert. Two young officers suspected a move against the government and alerted a member of Musaddiq's staff some time on 15 August.[28] At 7 pm a civilian independently telephoned Musaddiq's house, talked to him in person, and told him in some detail what was afoot, including the transfer of the tanks from Sa'd-Abad. It has only recently come to light that the caller was Mohammad Husain Ashtiyani (Izam al-Dawleh), a higher ranking but retired civil servant at the ministry of finance. Ashtiyani must have got the information – perhaps by chance – from those of his relatives who were close to Princess Ashraf and the royal court.[29]

Musaddiq hastily summoned the chief of staff who was thus saved the indignity of being kidnapped by the royal guards. When Nasiri arrived, defensive tanks were already in position outside Musaddiq's house. After Musaddiq had received and given a receipt for the royal notice, he had the colonel arrested. The coup failed, and the shah and Queen Soraya escaped to Baghdad in a light plane which was standing by, and thence to Rome.

The public received the news of the unsuccessful coup with both anger and jubilation. A large public meeting was immediately organized in Baharistan and addressed by an incensed Fatemi, as well as Shaigan and others. Leaflets (put out by either the Tudeh party or their aides among the foreign agents) were stuck on the walls, demanding the immediate declaration of a 'democratic republic', but were quickly removed on Musaddiq's orders.[30] The government itself did not know quite what to do next, and the idea of setting up a regency council during the shah's absence (led by Ali-Akbar Dehkhuda, the famous etymologist and encyclopaedist) was discussed but not pursued further.

On 17 August, public demonstrations and open meetings continued unabated, and next day there was a near riot. The Tudeh came out in full force (their ranks swollen more than ever by mobs hired with American money), disrupting normal activity in the city, and attacking Reza Shah's numerous statues in public places. Musaddiq was told about this, and sent word to the Popular Movement parties to remove the statues themselves (see chapter 14); the legendary wrestling champion, Ghulamreza Takhti, led the Third Force party members in the operations to remove Reza's statue in Tupkhaneh, the military square. By the evening, however, the government became acutely aware that, both for domestic and external reasons, it had to restore order in the streets of the capital. Musaddiq telephoned the democratic party leaders individually, asking them to keep their troops off the streets the next day.[31] He declared a ban on demonstrations, and ordered the police and the martial law administration to deal firmly with law-breakers. Thus the legend, perpetrated in many English accounts of these events, that Musaddiq himself had allowed the army out, only to be overthrown by it, is entirely without foundation. On the contrary, the fact that he had ordered his own Popular Movement troops to remain off the streets became a surprise bonus for the *putchists*.

Roosevelt had in the meantime sent emissaries to the commanders of the provincial armies in Isfahan and Kirmanshah, encouraging them to move on Tehran. This, incidentally, shows that the plotters were ready to go to any lengths, including a full-scale civil war. The general in Isfahan wavered, but the commander of the Kirmanshah Brigade, Colonel Taimur Bakhtiyar (later to become the first SAVAK chief) was ready for action. At the same time, the money put at Ayatullah Bihbahani's disposal was distributed among toughs and prostitutes to start the riots of the following day. Both the prefect of police (Brigadier Mudabbir) and the martial law administrator (Colonel Ashrafi) were won over, and refused to act on 19 August.[32] The commanding officers who were directly involved in the first coup had been put under arrest, but the others, including General Mohammad Daftary, Brigadier Fuladvand, Captain (later General) Khusrawpanah, etc., were still free to act. Zahedi was in contact with both military and civilian leaders of the coup from his hideout in an American 'safe house' in Tehran.

When the news of the street riots was first heard on 19 August, Musaddiq dismissed his police chief who was not prepared to act, and sent word to Sadiqi (minister of the interior) to appoint General Shahandeh in his place. Meanwhile, the martial law administrator also defected, and Musaddiq personally telephoned Sadiqi to tell him that he had made General Daftary martial law administrator, and that Sadiqi should make him police chief as well. Sadiqi was, in his own words, 'both puzzled and frightened'.[33] Daftary had been Razmara's police chief, and was known to be against the government, though the fact that he was deeply involved in the coup and had already been made police chief by Zahedi was not known at the time. But the fact that he was Zahedi's candidate for the post had already come out in the interrogations of those accused of Afshartus's murder a couple of months before.[34] Musaddiq may not have known or remembered this, and/or he might have felt the need for a tough man like Daftary to meet the occasion. The family tie between them might also have been a factor in his thinking that, unlike the others, Daftary would remain loyal to him. He told Sadiqi 'with tears in his eyes' (next day, when they were still in hiding), that Daftary had personally begged him to give him the job in order to deal with the riots.[35] In any event, he committed all the security forces to the rebels, but he made an even more important – almost indispensable – contribution to the success of the coup, of which more below.

If the first coup had failed through an 'indiscretion', the element of surprise was the winning card of the second. Given the events of the previous couple of days, a certain amount of street agitation and unrest would not have seemed abnormal. At any rate, the police did not interfere with the demonstrations and they quickly spread to many parts of the city. In the first few (and crucial) hours – between 9 am and 1 pm – the whole thing looked like a typical show of force by Bihbahani's, Kashani's and Baqa'i's usual troops, rather than a major coup attempt. Even as late as 2.45 pm, when Sadiqi drove from the interior ministry (which was then situated next to the main bazaar) to the prime minister's house, he did not observe any large demonstrations *en route* to Kakh Street.[36] Others – Shaigan, Nariman, Fatemi, etc. – also arrived at Musaddiq's house that morning. And when Fatemi left at 4 pm because of the news of his young wife's hysterical fit, the house was not yet cut off from the outside world.[37]

An important strategy of the rebels was to seize the radio station. Sadiqi had expressed worries about this a couple of times that day, but nothing was done to defend it. When the station was first attacked, the technical staff simply put on some music, closed down the rest of the facilities, and left. Shortly afterwards, it fell to the rebels and was made operable by the army personnel. Then the voices of leading government opponents – Sayyed Mehdi Mir-Ashrafi and Sayyed Mehdi Pirasteh, for example – came on the air with false claims that the government had already fallen.

Between 4 and 5 pm Musaddiq's house was completely encircled. General Riyahi, the chief of staff, had already been arrested in his office. A few hours earlier he had ordered his own deputy, General Kiyani, to lead an army group consisting of an infantry and a tank battalion into the city from Ishrat-Abad Barracks which was then on the outskirts of Tehran. The effective deployment of this force could have sealed the fate of the coup. Kiyani 'was a good man, but he was not up to the task', as witnessed by Colonel Mumtaz many years afterwards.[38] Here General Daftary played his crucial role. Flanked by a number of rebel officers, he met Kiyani's force on the outskirts of the city with open arms, begging them not to intervene; there followed a 'kissing party', and the entire force was won over.[39] At 4.45 pm, Brigadier Fuladvand, commander of the troops attacking Musaddiq's house, was allowed in, and asked for a cease-fire declaration. Four of the Popular Movement's leaders present issued a statement (with Musaddiq's approval) to the effect that Musaddiq regarded himself as the lawful prime minister, but now that the army had mutinied and his house was declared undefended, the attack on the house must cease. It did not, even after Ahmad Razavi had had a white flag hoisted on the roof. Shortly afterwards it became plain that it had all been a trick for the rebels to announce, as they did, that Musaddiq had resigned.[40]

Between 6 and 7 pm, Musaddiq's colleagues persuaded him to leave the house with them by climbing over the wall. Colonel Izzatullah Mumtaz, the able and loyal commander of his guards, continued to defend the house to the last bullet. It fell at 8 pm, and was looted and ransacked. Musaddiq and his colleagues spent the night at a neighbouring house, whose owners were then away at their summer residence. Next morning, they left, some going their own way, while Musaddiq, Sadiqi, Shaigan and Sayfullah Mu'azzami (Abdullah's brother, and minister of posts and telegraphs) went to Mu'azzami's house nearby. From there they sent word to Zahedi about their whereabouts, but were discovered by security men on a routine check before Zahedi could act on the news.[41] They were taken straight to his temporary headquarters at the Army Officers' Club where they were received and treated with great respect, and put under arrest separately.

Unlike the day before, the Tudeh party was completely inactive on 19 August. Kiyanuri's claim that he had telephoned Musaddiq directly twice during the coup, and that the second time Musaddiq had told him that he was 'alone, alone', and that they were free to do what they thought fit, was undoubtedly false.[42] Many of Musaddiq's colleagues and staff were there, and some of them took him out of the house in the end. They later gave full and largely consistent accounts of the events as witnesses in the military trial, and we now have Sadiqi's most detailed account of them all. Several telephone calls to the house were mentioned, but none from Kiyanuri. And Musaddiq was unlikely to have accepted a personal call from Kiyanuri, whom he did not personally know at all. However, it is not clear what light this story is meant to throw on the Tudeh party's complete inaction on that day, and thereafter for a couple of years when its civilian and military networks were systematically torn apart. The pattern was familiar from the 21 July uprising, and the 28 February mob attack on Musaddiq's house.

14

Musaddiq's trials

Musaddiq was arrested on 20 August 1953. His interrogation began almost a month after, on 17 September, and ended on 29 September. Two days later, the military prosecutor published an indictment against him on charges of treason, but it took another six weeks for the special military court to begin its work. On 21 December they found him guilty as charged, and sentenced him to three years' solitary confinement.[1] Both Musaddiq and the military prosecutor appealed, but the hearings were delayed for almost four months. The retrial in the military court of appeal began on 8 April 1954 and ended just after a month with the court upholding both the verdict and the sentence.[2] A series of tactics were then employed to circumvent the judicial and political embarrassments caused by Musaddiq's appeal to the Supreme Court. In particular, the appeal procedure, the reviewing process, and other matters arising from them were constantly postponed so that Musaddiq received the judgement of the High Court of Judicial Discipline (of which more below) only two weeks before he completed his sentence on 3 August 1956. He was then sent straight to Ahmad-Abad and put under guard for the rest of his life.

Musaddiq's trials must be seen, not as a proper (or improper) judicial process, but as a continuation of the political struggle between the shah and the conservatives, on the one hand, and the Popular Movement, on the other. For this reason his treatment could well have been different, had he made any gesture of accommodation and reconciliation towards his jailers. From the moment he was put under arrest, it was clear that he could have purchased a quiet and respectable life by accepting the coup as a *fait accompli*; that is why his interrogations began four weeks after he was arrested. But the bargaining process went beyond that, and continued throughout the three years which he spent in jail. The four months' gap between the

194

end of the military court of the first instance and the beginning of the military appeal process was in part in the hope of reaching some kind of settlement 'out of court'. The delaying tactics – which were at times little short of grotesque – over the review procedure and process by the Supreme Court were also partly aimed at striking an informal bargain: at one stage, a royal pardon was suggested in exchange for Musaddiq's withdrawal of his appeal to the Supreme Court. The political reasons behind the regime's preference for a quiet settlement need not be mentioned. But there was also a psychological factor: the shah was (and always remained) extremely jealous of Musaddiq's popularity, and unhappy about his assertion of complete independence. But the old man would not, and did not, budge an inch. This was the chief reason for his trial, conviction, imprisonment, and lifelong banishment. It was also the greatest single cause of the shah's psychological problems, apart from the spectre of his powerful, self-confident and self-made father.

The interrogations

The interrogations were spread over five sessions. In all, they took 19 hours and 35 minutes to complete. The minutes of the first session give a distinct impression that the authorities were still testing the ground to see if it was necessary to proceed with indictment and trial.

The official interrogator was an army colonel, who was an engineer and lacked legal training. But the military prosecutor – Brigadier Husain Azmudeh – was present from the first session, and effectively took over the interrogations from the second session onwards. In the first session, the tone and behaviour of both the interrogator and the military prosecutor were polite and respectful. Musaddiq, too, behaved with characteristic politeness, and with legal propriety. But he was firm and unrepentant. When the session ended, a warrant was issued for keeping him in temporary custody, charging him with conspiracy to violate the constitution and sedition against the monarchy. Acknowledging its receipt, Musaddiq wrote underneath it (in line with the judicial procedure at the time): 'I strongly deny the above charges which are absolutely unjust and untrue, and protest against my unlawful imprisonment which is based on these charges.'[3]

Thus, from the second session onwards the atmosphere of the interrogations markedly changed, and Azmudeh took matters in hand personally. Having briefly tested Musaddiq's defiant mood once again, he confronted him with his justice minister, Abul'ali Lutfi, who said that he had not been told of the royal notice of dismissal which Nasiri had delivered to Musaddiq during the attempted coup of 15–16 August. In reply to Azmudeh's question to him as to why a member of the cabinet had not been informed of the royal notice, Musaddiq insisted on a guarantee that his reply would be kept on the record. The prosecutor repeatedly refused to give any such guarantee, however, and Musaddiq continued to refuse to answer the question without it. The tug of war ended with Musaddiq threatening to go on hunger strike; and thus began the long and relentless process of confrontation between the accuser and the accused which was to continue for as long as Musaddiq was in jail.[4]

The whole of the third session was spent in taking Musaddiq's statements about his actions and intentions after receiving the shah's notice on 16 August. In the fourth session the questioning got tougher. At one stage, the prosecutor asked what Musaddiq knew about the pulling down of the shah's and Reza Shah's statues on 17 August, and whether he had issued orders to stop this action and prosecute the offenders. Musaddiq's reply was classic, and reveals much about his own personality, his political convictions, and his style of defence then and later during the trials. He said that he had heard nothing about the removal of the shah's statues (of which there were only a couple in Tehran at the time). As for the statues of Reza Shah, he had indeed been told that Tudeh militants were attacking them, and had sent word to the Popular Movement parties to remove the statues themselves. He had taken this action because Reza Shah had been a dictator and a usurper of the people's property. If the government had prevented the removal of his statues by force it would have offended the public; if they had been removed by the Tudeh, then officially replaced, the government would have been cast in a bad light; and, if they had not been replaced, the government would have been identified with the Tudeh; the government had quite simply asked the democratic parties to do the job themselves.[5] This line of argument must have been the reason why the prosecutor did not pursue the matter further during the trials.

This in fact was the last question asked and answered during the interrogations. On hearing Musaddiq's reply, the prosecutor issued a 'warning' and launched a personal diatribe against him. Musaddiq responded by saying that his statements had gone beyond questioning, and that he should put his views to the court. There followed another 'warning' by Azmudeh that if Musaddiq did not answer his points he would 'carry out [his] legal duties'. The interrogations ended with Musaddiq saying: 'carry out your legal duties'.

Azmudeh issued his indictment against Musaddiq and General Riyahi (his chief of staff) on 1 October 1953. The charge itself was deliberately short: it claimed that they had incited the people to armed rebellion, and that under article 317 of the Military Penal and Procedure Code this carried a mandatory sentence of death. On the other hand, the indictment was quite long, and once again gave a foretaste of the political campaign conducted against Musaddiq both inside and outside the court. It accused Musaddiq of 'treason', referred to his 'apparatus of terror', and claimed that he had tried 'to shake up the people's faith and belief in the country's official religion; that is Islam and the righteous twelver Shi'ite sect'.[6] The evidence for the charges included the claim that Musaddiq had asked his visitors about the activities of 'individuals and authorities', and that he had appointed 'gutless, spineless, conservative [people] who lacked self-esteem' to important and sensitive posts.

Trial in the military court

The miliutary court of the first instance began its work six weeks later. It was made up of a panel of brigadiers (including Taimur Bakhtiyar) led by a major-general. None of the judges had had any legal training. Musaddiq suggested General Naqdi as his counsel, but Naqdi refused. Having learned about the matter, Colonel Jalil Buzurgmehr contacted Naqdi and offered his own services.[7] Buzurgmehr was a trained lawyer, and enjoyed an excellent reputation in the army for efficiency and incorruptibility. At thirty-nine, he was one of the youngest staff colonels in the country at the time, and would soon have been promoted to general had he not acted as Musaddiq's counsel with evident professional integrity. He was formally appointed to his task by the Department of Military Prosecutions. In the beginning, Musaddiq was naturally cautious in his dealings with him, thinking that he might place his loyalty to the army above his duty to his client. During the trial, however, he came to trust him completely, and personally made him his own counsel (against the payment of private fees) in the military court of appeal. Although Musaddiq effectively conducted his own defence in the courts, Buzurgmehr gave him invaluable assistance, not least by providing him with a vital link with his legal advisers and political well-wishers outside the prison.

Musaddiq's defence was both legal and (especially) political. He first objected to a military trial on the grounds that, by law, members of the government could be tried only in the Supreme Court. He personally presented the argument to the court, but the text of his speech had been prepared by Ali Shahidzadeh (the eminent lawyer who became one of his counsels when the case went to the Supreme Court) and smuggled into the prison by Buzurgmehr. However, the court having predictably overruled his objection to their jurisdiction in the case, he proceeded to the substance of the charge.

The prosecutor's legal case (as opposed to his political diatribe, of which more below) rested on the argument that Musaddiq had rebelled against the constitution by ignoring the shah's dismissal notice, and inciting the people to armed insurrection. Musaddiq's defence was (a) that the shah's notice had been delivered in the process of a coup (of which he had had prior warning) at 1.00 am, while the district had been put under siege, and three political dignitaries (including the foreign minister) had been kidnapped from their homes; (b) that the writing in the royal notice revealed that a blank order had been completed in the shah's absence; (c) that he had led no insurrection (armed or otherwise), but had waited to contact or be contacted by the shah about the latter's intentions; (d) that the shah's dismissal notice had been unconstitutional and would, *in any case*, have been rejected by him, firstly because the shah had no such powers in any circumstances, and, secondly, because the Majlis had not yet been formally dissolved, and the deputies who had voluntarily resigned their seats could still withdraw their resignations, since the period of grace for doing so − allowed by the Majlis standing orders − had not yet ended.

The full proceedings of the first trial were published for the first time in 1985 in two volumes. They cover 800 pages, and show that the real purpose of the trial was to conduct a public political campaign, firstly against Musaddiq in person and, secondly, against the Popular Movement. The military prosecutor was effectively in command of the court. He even made veiled threats against the court president on the few occasions when the latter tried to present a semblance of impartiality. He did not miss an opportunity to indulge in vicious personal attacks on the former prime minister, describing him in words such as 'the slave-boy of Qajar courts'.[8] He read out letters to the court from named but unknown correspondents which were full of insults and abuse to the chief defendant. He threatened many times to demand that the court be heard in closed session when he found the old man's revelations and/or verbal audacity − especially about the Pahlavis − too much to tolerate. He planted agitators in the courtroom to hurl abuse and invectives against the prisoner. And, on a lighter note, he kept referring to him − quite seriously − as the 'doctorate' of law who knew nothing about the subject. Musaddiq, in his turn, refused to call him by name, rank or position, merely pointing at him as 'that man'. This was intended as a mark of contempt, although he still had a legal argument for it: as part of his judicial reforms and democratization, the jurisdiction of military tribunals had been reduced to strictly military cases such as court-martial trials, and the Department of Military Prosecutions had been abolished. Hence, no such office as the military prosecutor existed without legislation to reverse his judicial reforms.

A line of both personal and political attack which the military prosecutor frequently used against Musaddiq in the court was that he lacked religious faith, and that he had even blasphemed against Islam in his doctoral thesis (on the last will and testament in Islamic law) forty years before. This referred to a mistranslation into Persian of a single line in the thesis which Musaddiq's enemies had concocted in 1917, when – as deputy finance minister – he was leading a crusade against corruption by influential people in the ministry of finance (see chapter 2). The prosecutor constantly sought informal advice from conservative politicians such as Senator Ibrahim Khajeh-Nuri and Senator Ali Dashti, and in this way obtained the information about Musaddiq's alleged academic blasphemy.[9]

The charge of irreligiosity was intended to keep Qum, Ayatullah Bihbahani and the Fada'iyan-i Islam warm and friendly towards the new regime. And it was more capable of angering Musaddiq than any other insult which the prosecutor hurled at him. For, apart from the fact that he was a religious man, he was fearful (as he explained to his defence counsel) that these allegations were intended to prepare the ground for a religious fanatic assassinating him in the court. His fears were not entirely groundless, for between his two trials the assassination of his foreign minister (Husain Fatemi) by hired thugs was arranged while he was in custody, although he miraculously survived the attack, only to be tried later *in camera* and executed by a firing squad. Fatemi had previously been injured by the bullet of Abd-i Khuda'i, then a youthful member of the Fada'iyan-i Islam (and later a member of the Islamic Majlis in Tehran). The Fada'iyan had vowed to kill Musaddiq almost from the moment he assumed office in 1951, and immediately after the coup their leader was released from jail where he had been for a couple of months on charges of sedition.

Given the political nature of the proceedings, the brunt of Musaddiq's defence inevitably fell on his persistent attempts – against interruptions by the court presidents, the prosecutor, and some observers – to show that he was on trial for political, not legal reasons.

And he finally succeeded — by threatening to ignore the court, by going on hunger strike, by begging, pleading with, and shouting at the court president — in largely making the point. He insisted that he was on trial in consequence of a *coup d'état* which had been financed and organized by the American government; and he even supplied some documentary evidence for his claim, which his friends had managed to put together and send to him through his defence counsel.[10] The following is a short excerpt from his last defence stand in the thirty-fourth and penultimate session of the court on 19 December 1953:

> My only crime, and my great — even greater — crime, is that I nationalized the Iranian oil industry, and removed the network of colonialism, and the political and economic influence of the greatest empire on earth from this land . . . My life, reputation, person and property — and those of others like me — do not have the slightest value compared with the lives, the independence, the greatness and the pride of millions of Iranians, and the future generations of this people. . .
>
> Since from the style of the prosecution as well as the trial process, it is already clear that I shall die in prison, and that they will put down this voice and energy which I have always put in the service of the people . . . I say farewell to the brave and dear people of Iran, men and women, and emphasize that they should not fear any unfortunate incident on the honourable path which they have been treading, and should be confident that God will be their help and support.[11]

At the last moment, the court was sent a message from the shah, which was openly read out, to the effect that he was ready to forgive Musaddiq on his own personal account. This was instantly rejected by Musaddiq with indignation. The court found him guilty as charged, but gave him a three-year (solitary) sentence, explaining their decision against a death sentence, in part, because the law forbade the execution of those aged over sixty, and, in part, because of the shah's apparent decision to forgo his own share of the punishment. A few days later (as noted in chapter 9), Musaddiq received a Christmas card (in prison) from Richard Stokes, the Labour government's Lord Privy Seal who had led the British negotiating team to Tehran in the summer of 1951. It carried formal greetings of the season, but Stokes had added in his own hand: 'may your country see peace and prosperity in 1954'. There followed many more letters of support from Asia, the Arab countries, Germany, the United States and Argentina.[12]

Retrial in the military court of appeal

Immediately after the conclusion of the trial, the battle-lines were drawn for the next round. According to the usual procedures at the time, the defendant had to acknowledge receipt of the court's judgement by signing in the space provided beneath the copy which was handed to him at the end of the closing session of the court. Musaddiq wrote that he did not accept 'this unlawful judgement, made by an unlawful court which lacked jurisdiction in the case', and added that he would appeal against it to the Supreme Court.[13] He did not name the Supreme Court as such, but used the term *farjam* which in legal jargon referred only to appeals to the highest court in the land.

A few days later it became clear that the use of this term had not been a slip of the pen as many had thought at the time. For his three civilian lawyers – Ali Shahidzadeh, Bahram Majdzadeh and Hasan Sadr – sent an affirmation in appeal to the Supreme Court on his behalf, citing the article of the law of military prosecutions according to which there could be only one appeal from the decisions of military courts, to the Supreme Court alone.[14] For reasons that will become clear later in this chapter, the regime had no intention of allowing a proper investigation of the case in the Supreme Court. After a few stalling tactics, the Court's chief administrator wrote to the military prosecutor asking him to send the dossier of the case – 'if you have no more need for it' – to make available to Musaddiq's lawyers, as they had demanded in order to enable them to prepare their case for appeal. The military prosecutor simply wrote back saying that he was unable to comply with the Supreme Court's request. Two months later, Musaddiq wrote to the president of the military court of appeal (where his appeal was later to be heard) asking him to send the dossier to the Supreme Court for it to be made available to his civilian lawyers. But the latter replied that 'at the present time there is no legal basis for your excellency's request to this court to send the dossier to the Supreme Court'.[15]

The regime was still unsettled; it was anxious about Musaddiq's popularity and his greatly enhanced public support (largely in consequence of his conduct at his trial), and was prepared to let him have a quiet life in Ahmad-Abad on condition that he would give up his defiant attitude. Even before his trial, at least one feeler had been put out to him when his weekly health visitor – an army physician and brigadier – had told him that he would be released if he wrote a couple of lines to the American embassy in Tehran asking for their help.[16] Now, the offer became explicit. Yusif Mushar (a minor Popular Front deputy in the Seventeenth Majlis who had later defected to the other side) sent a message from the shah to Musaddiq, via Colonel Buzurgmehr, to the effect that if Musaddiq himself was agreeable the legal procedures would be terminated, and he would be banished to Ahmad-Abad. The offer was turned down.[17]

The case was therefore referred to the military court of appeal, but the stalling tactics continued until April 1954. Two days before the court was due to start the trial in appeal, both Musaddiq and his civilian lawyers wrote to the court president, General Javadi, asking him to allow them to act as his counsels in the court. Javadi replied only to Musaddiq's letter, saying that this would not be allowed. In this case, Musaddiq had asked that they be permitted at least to attend the court and give him private counsel during the short breaks during the proceedings. Javadi wrote (a) that they could try and obtain observers' permits according to the usual procedures, and (b) that permission for private contact during breaks had to be obtained from the military prosecutor.[18]

The second trial was much like the first, with the military prosecutor playing his familiar role, and the court president trying to minimize his own embarrassment. It was held in twenty-six sessions, and took just over a month to complete. Once again, Musaddiq opened his argument on the point that the court had no jurisdiction in the case; and once again, the court decided to the contrary. When they entered the substance of the charges against him, Musaddiq was now better prepared to supply evidence, both from inside and outside the country, to the effect that his lawful government had been overthrown by a *coup d'etat*. At one stage he even quoted the *Tribune des Nations* of 4 September 1953 about the role of Senator Khajeh-Nuri and others in preparing the case against him which was later to be heard in the military courts: and the same newspaper of 14 March 1954, that the recent attempt on his foreign minister's life while in custody had been led by 'the same General Bimukh [i.e. Sha'ban the Brainless]' who had led the mob on the day of the coup. He ended his final defence speech by saying that he wished to inform 'the court as well as my dear compatriots' of the sole objective in the whole of his political career from which he had never departed or deviated:

> Throughout my whole life I have only had one aim, namely, that the people of Iran enjoy independence and dignity, and are not subjected to anybody's rule except the will of the majority. The remarkable struggle of the people against the former [Anglo-Iranian] Oil Company – of which I have been one of the leaders,

and for which, by the grace of God, I can still speak from jail –
has broken, and will break, the chain of colonialism in the Middle
East. Apart from the economic aspects, [i.e.] that the Company
was appropriating our riches, the Popular Movement of Iran was
launched in order that this country would enjoy freedom and
independence in the true sense of this term. Is there anyone who
does not know that the governments before mine were captives in
the hands of the political agents of the former [Anglo-Iranian Oil]
Company?. . .

I thank God that – by virtue of the dark fate which He has
willed for me – this trial became a channel through which . . . the
public's attention could be drawn to the important question as to
whether, in a constitutional and democratic regime, the appointment and dismissal of the prime minister . . . is up to the will of a
single individual or that of the majority of the people.[19]

Predictably, the military court of appeal upheld the verdict and
sentence of the lower court, but stated that the shah's offer to forgo
his share of the punishment could not have been intended, and should
not have been interpreted, as if he was a party to the case. Hence, the
reduction of the sentence to three years' solitary confinement was
purely on account of the defendant's advanced age.

The final appeal

The final appeal to the Supreme Court was, however, quite another
matter. True, the whole of Musaddiq's judicial reforms – through his
old, experienced justice minister, Abdul'ali Lutfi, and the then
Supreme Court president, Mohammad Sururi – had been jettisoned
overnight, and, in particular, many Supreme Court judges had been
replaced by those whose reputations were not quite so impeccable.
This was especially true of the new Supreme Court president, Ali
Hay'at, whom the government itself eventually removed by no less
than a full act of parliament. Yet, these were civilian courts which still
commanded considerable independence, and this was especially true of
the judges of the Supreme Court, the highest court in the land.[20]
Precisely for these reasons, pressures were being applied (though very
unevenly) by both parties concerned: the shah and the government
demanded a quick dismissal of the appeal, while those working for
Musaddiq did not have to ask for more than the enforcement of the

law. The unequal battle lines were drawn, and the campaign got under way.

No one was remotely as active on Musaddiq's behalf as the old man himself. The case was first referred to Division 3 of the Supreme Court, but its judges quickly let it be known (albeit through private contacts with Hay'at, the Supreme Court president) that they were not ready to oblige the government.[21] It was then moved to Division 9 without any explanation. There followed eleven months of complete inaction – on the pretence that there were too many cases in line – until 10 July 1955, when Musaddiq broke silence and wrote to Hay'at asking why he had not yet been summoned to the court to present his case:

> Since 5 September of last year when I presented my affirmations in appeals [i.e. appeal for cassation], I have been waiting to be summoned [to that court] by virtue of article 452 of the Principles of Penal Procedure Code,[22] and defend my case according to article 451 of the same law.[23]
>
> Everyone witnessed what kind of abuse members of the Taj [Sports] Club[24] showered on me whenever I tried to present my defence in the Saltanat-Abad [military] courts, and the newspapers reported the number of times I was threatened [by the military prosecutor] that the hearings would be held in camera [if I said everything that was necessaary for my defence]. Hence, according to the wisdom 'If they cannot take it all, say that part of it which they can',[25] and to avoid private hearings which would have left the public completely in the dark about the proceedings, I decided not to spell out some of the facts.

The Supreme Court in Iran, as in many other countries, was limited to the judgement of the case on points of law. But there were various articles of the law – fully and repeatedly cited in this as well as the rest of his protracted and increasingly acrimonious correspondence with the judicial authorities – which gave Musaddiq the right to attend the court and present his arguments for appeal (on points of law) in person. Thus, he concluded his first letter with the following words:

> My arguments [for appeal] are not such as can all be communicated by letter, and must be presented by word of mouth. It is now virtually two years that I have endured solitary confinement despite old age and ill health in the hope that one day I would be able to attend that Court, and plead the case for my innocence.[26]

This was to be the last, most simple, open, and effective public demonstration of his legal and political case against the regime. Therefore, it had to be prevented at all costs. The president of the Supreme Court wrote back, addressing him as 'Your excellency Dr Musaddiq', but saying that, according to precedent, this would be done only in those cases 'when the division considers the appellant's presence necessary for the clarification of written or oral objections [to the lower courts' proceedings and/or decisions]'.[27] However, he was to ignore Musaddiq's later letters both to himself and to other judicial authorities; and, instead, went on to reaffirm his position in occasional interviews with the popular press.

The stalling tactics – for example, putting the judges of that apparently overcrowded court on other judicial duties, giving them long leaves, sending the attorney-general (i.e. the chief prosecutor of the Supreme Court) on a journey to Europe, etc. – were used in the hope of wearing the old prisoner out, until he had completed his sentence and was banished to Ahmad-Abad. He understood their strategy, and went on indefinite hunger strike. They had to modify their tactics: feelers were put out and, eventually, press reports were circulated that he was on the royal list of prisoners to be pardoned on the shah's forthcoming birthday on 26 October 1955. His reaction was swift as well as angry, telling Hay'at (in a long letter) that, apart from the fact that his final appeal had not yet been heard:

> As I said in one of the sessions of the military court, if His Majesty the Shah-in-Shah grants me pardon – and as this will be the highest insult to a servant of the country – I will not accept it, and will terminate my own life. Now I wish to inform your excellency as well, that, if the Division does not summon me to the Court, and denies me the right which the law has given to every defendant, and as I have no other means of defending myself, I would rather die than live this life.[28]

The delay and the correspondence from jail – which had to be sent via the military prosecutor, after it had been read by him – continued; and it soon became clear that, contrary to the law, he would not be summoned personally to the court, nor would his counsels be allowed to make an oral presentation of the appeal case. He had to fight with the military prosecutor for permission to meet his three civilian counsels in jail, and was allowed to do so only twice in the course of a year. He wrote more letters to Hay'at (all of which he ignored) quoting various articles of the law, and presenting political and logical reasons why he should be allowed to attend the court – even to the point of offering to conduct research into the precedents as they affected such cases in France, Belgium and Switzerland.

Division 9 of the Supreme Court finally delivered a short judgement, in March 1956, which can be quoted in full:

> Considering all aspects of the case, and in view of the private [or, special] circumstances, the objections cited in the appeal do not seem to be valid, and the [military appeal court's] decision is hereby upheld.[29]

Musaddiq read the news of the judgement in the popular press, since the military prosecutor took six weeks to send him the copy of the decision which, as usual, had to be passed through his department. But the judgement itself caused a public scandal: the grounds for appeal had not been mentioned; no arguments had been offered for dismissing them; no article of the law had been mentioned for reaffirming the jurisdiction of the military courts, and upholding their verdict and sentence. It was a single-sentence judgement which in such an important case – with full regard to '*all aspects of the case*' and '*the private [or special] circumstances*' – ventured the view that the appeal did not '*seem to be*' valid. This is how the wretched judges had decided to succumb to the regime's pressure, while at the same time washing their hands and pointing the finger at the country's rulers. Their embarrassment was so acute that it led Jamal Imami, Musaddiq's old foe, to say in the Senate that it would have been better if the court had upheld the appeal. Jamal Akhavi, the minister of justice, who up till then had enjoyed a good public reputation, offered his resignation in an attempt to dissociate himself from the whole affair, but was put under pressure to stay on for a couple of months. The Supreme Court president's head rolled in a most unprecedented and dishonourable manner – i.e. through dismissal by an address of both houses of parliament – at least in part for his mismanagement of a case which had been the main reason for his appointment.

Musaddiq was incensed, but did not give up the fight. He issued a formal denunciation – direct from jail, since he could not see his counsels – against the judges in the case, to the High Court of Judicial Discipline; and he kept pressing against delaying tactics in the latter case, by writing to the new (acting) Supreme Court president, to the justice minister (Akhavi) who resigned in the meantime, and to his successor, Abbasquli Gulsha'iyan (of 'Gass-Gulsha'iyan' fame). Fortunately for them, the High Court of Judicial Discipline were able to extricate themselves from jurisdiction in the case on a technical point related to a law passed when Musaddiq was in prison. The court's notice of this decision to Musaddiq was held up by the military prosecutor for 50 days before it was sent to its rightful owner. By then there were only two weeks left for the completion of his sentence. But he did not give up, and wanted to see his counsels to be able to pursue his case against the Division 9 judges. He wrote to the prosecutor rebuking him for this (and other) late deliveries of his mail, and demanding the right to see his counsels against which – the acting Supreme Court president had told him in a written reply – there were no '*legal* impediments'. The military prosecutor replied, after showering him with abuse, that he could no longer have legal counsels because he was now a confirmed convict. Musaddiq received this letter a couple of days before his release from jail, in early August 1956. He was sent straight to Ahmad-Abad and put under guard for the rest of his life.[30]

15

The Popular Movement after the coup

Resistance to the coup

In its immediate aftermath, the *coup d'état* left the new regime still frightened and unsettled, and the Popular Movement forces shocked and dismayed. Zahedi and his generals, the conservative politicians and landlords, and the religious establishment all viewed the change essentially as a return to the *status quo ante* in which the 1949 ban on the Tudeh party would be made effective and the Popular Movement would be banished from the Majlis. The shah had his own designs for establishing his personal arbitrary rule much in the style of his father, but these were not obvious to his conservative allies at the time.

Most of the Popular Movement leaders in the Majlis, the cabinet, the bazaar and the political parties were rounded up. They included Shaigan, Nariman, Razavi, Sadiqi, Lutfi, Shamshiri, and Ayatullah Zanjani as well as a large number of activists. Dr Husain Fatemi held out in hiding for a few more months until he was found by accident, and – the officially-inspired attempt on his life while in custody having failed – secretly tried in a military court and executed by firing squad. Khalil Maleki was arrested and banished to Falak al-Aflak (a medieval prison citadel in the west) where a large number of Tudeh leaders and activists were also held.[1]

The bazaar was the first to respond to the new situation. In turn, the regime reacted to these demonstrations and strikes by demolishing the old ceilings of some of the bazaar's arcades, and secretly setting fire to some of its shops. Musaddiq's defiant attitude at his trial provided a rallying point, and this was one of the reasons why the regime was anxious to reach a private settlement with him. But he was aware of the political function and impact of his struggle in the courts; he even once mentioned the official demolition of the bazaar ceilings during his trial.

The idea of organizing a resistance movement to the new regime began to circulate within the first three weeks of the coup. Khalil Maleki drew the analogy with occupied France under Nazi Germany, but he had no direct role in organizing the National Resistance Movement (NRM) which later came into being, since he was arrested shortly afterwards. The initiative was taken by Ayatullah Haj Aqa Reza Zanjani, his brother Ayatullah Sayyed Abulfazl, Mehdi Bazargan, Dr Yadullah Sahabi, Sayyed Mahmud (later Ayatullah) Taliqani, and a few younger activists who mainly belonged to the religious wing of the Popular Movement. The Third Force party and Mohammad Nakhshab's group (now renamed the People of Iran party) were also involved in the formation of the NRM. Shortly afterwards it was joined by the Iran party and Furuhar's youthful Pan-Iranians.[2]

The first organized move by the new coalition came when they called a public demonstration against 'the usurper government of the shah and [General] Zahedi' for 12 November 1953, less than three months after the coup. The immediate issue was the government's intention to restore diplomatic links with Britain prior to a settlement of the oil dispute.[3] The bazaar struck on 12 November, and there were spontaneous demonstrations in various parts of the city. It was a useful show of presence, but not a great show of force: Tehran was still under martial law, and tanks and troops were stationed at sensitive locations.

The University of Tehran and the Alborz College had been restless since the beginning of the academic year, and armed troops were permanently stationed in both. On 7 December, the day of Vice-President Nixon's visit to Tehran, there was a spontaneous demonstration by a group of students shouting slogans against the regime. The troops were under orders to shoot, not only to teach them a lesson in general, but also to forestall a repetition of the event while Nixon was still in Tehran. Three young students were shot dead in a corridor of the engineering faculty.

Until then the greatest source of worry for the new regime (and the US government) had been the fear of a Qashqa'i-led tribal revolt in Fars and the adjacent southern provinces of the country. The Qashqa'is had in fact been threatening to take action for a couple of months. They would not have been able to move on Tehran, but a successful revolt in Fars alone would have been enough to lead to an uprising in the capital and other cities. Both the Iranian and the US governments went out of their way to talk them out of this action. And for reasons which still remain obscure, the Qashqa'i gave up the idea in December when Nasir Khan left his base for Tehran.[4]

The NRM coalition did not last long; there were personality problems as well as differences over tactics. The Iran party soon left the coalition. It was not to engage in organized political activity until 1960, although two of its leading figures – Allahyar Saleh and Dr Karim Sanjaby – took part in a number of protest actions against the regime in the intervening period. The Third Force party's departure had a different cause. Just after Maleki's arrest and imprisonment, two members of the party's executive committee – Dr Mohammad Ali Khunji and Dr Mas'ud Hijazi – began a crusade against him, and demanded his immediate expulsion from the party. Their specific charges were (a) that Maleki had once met the shah (at the latter's request); and (b) that the party had accepted 50,000 rials financial support from the trustee of the shrine in Qum. However, both actions had had the unanimous approval of the party executive, and the meeting with the shah had had the prior approval of Musaddiq as well, to whom, as well as to the party leadership, Maleki had given a report of their exchange of views.[5] In June 1954, Maleki was transferred to the central police jail in Tehran. When, a few weeks later, he was released, there was an internal party investigation into the Khunji-Hijazi affair which led to their departure (together with nine other activists) from the party. Since they had been the party's main representatives in the NRM while Maleki was in prison, their resignation effectively meant that the Third Force was no longer represented in the NRM. By 1955, the NRM consisted almost entirely of the religious personalities and activists of the Popular Movement.

Khunji and Hijazi's action had already resulted in the demoralization of the bulk of the Third Force membership, who were not prepared to take serious risks in fighting the regime while the party itself was being torn apart. Maleki himself was convinced that the whole thing had been organized by General Farhad Dadsitan (head of the regime's internal security at the time) in order to render the Third Force party ineffective from within, and he quoted a published statement by Dadsitan almost admitting to such a plot, though he named no names.[6] It is virtually certain that Khunji could not have known about any plot, and was motived by psychological factors from which he suffered for much of his life.[7]

The campaign against the regime continued, but at a declining rate. The United States and Britain had given full support to the new regime from the start, and in November 1955 they admitted Iran to the

Baghdad Pact, later known – in the wake of Iraq's departure in 1958 – as the Central Treaty Organization, or CENTO. The US began to provide substantial economic grants as well as military aid immediately after the coup, and the 1954 Consortium Oil Agreement brought increasing annual oil revenues. These financial facilities enabled the state to spend unprecedented sums on the army and the security forces which, together with its non-military expenditures, brought a temporary boom for the urban middle classes. Meanwhile, the Tudeh party's back was completely broken, and the Soviet Union had been vying for the new regime's friendship almost from its inception. The Soviet authorities entered an agreement with Zahedi to repay their war debts which they had refused to Musaddiq's government (although the actual payment was made to Husain Ala, Zahedi's successor); and they received the shah with great pomp on a state visit to Moscow.[8] It was not the Soviet Union but the shah who (in 1959) decided to fall out with them, and enter a mutual defence pact with the United States in exchange for still greater American financial assistance.[9]

The shah managed to tighten his grip over the army and government by ridding himself of Zahedi in 1955, and eventually replacing him by Dr Manuchehr Iqbal in 1956. The SAVAK was created in 1957 under the ruthless and self-seeking General Taimur Bakhtiyar who had already been running the secret police in the role of the country's chief martial-law administrator. Small wonder, then, that active resistance declined, although passive discontent was, if anything, on the increase. The NRM was to continue its irregular and semi-clandestine publication, *Rah-i Musaddiq* (Musaddiq's Line) until early 1958. Another occasional publication – *Hashieh-yi bi Hashieh* (Footnote without Footnotes) – also appeared for some time.[10] Maleki and the remaining Third Force activists channelled some of their efforts into writing analytical articles, first for *Nabard-i Zindigi*, which they effectively ran, then in *Ilm va Zindigi* which they themselves began to publish once again, though in the guise of occasional books which did not require an official licence.

Protest against the consortium

Having declared Musaddiq's referendum to close the Seventeenth Majlis unconstitutional, the regime was expected to let it run its course. But this would have meant the return of its deputies, two-thirds of whom had voluntarily resigned their seats in support of the referendum. Worse still, they included the Popular Movement parliamentary group, some of whom were now in jail contrary to the law of immunity for members of parliament. Therefore, all the previous statements about the referendum's alleged irregularity, and even impermissibility by religious law (*tahrim*), were set aside, and general elections were held in 1954 for the Eighteenth Majlis. The ground had first been tested by holding elections for the Second Senate – that is, the selection of thirty Senators through an electoral college, the remaining thirty being appointed by the shah.

In neither case was the Popular Movement allowed to declare a list of candidates, let alone participate in the election campaigns.[11] But their supporters would have known whom to vote for even if a full list of candidates had not been circulated through unauthorized leaflets.[12] Gangs of hirelings were therefore posted at the polling stations to intimidate the voters. In any event, votes cast for the Popular Movement candidates were not counted. Landlords or their candidates were returned from the rural constituencies much as had been the case in the 14th–16th (and, to a lesser extent, 17th) sessions of the Majlis. For the larger towns and cities an official list of deputies was concocted, although many of them were not quite the kind of instrumental 'yes-men' who were to occupy Majlis seats in increasing numbers in the years to come. They even included a couple of independent deputies such as Mohammad Derakhshesh – leader of the country's Teachers Association – who were to cause a few headaches to the regime in that parliamentary session.

The regime's greatest test of strength in the Eighteenth Majlis came when Dr Ali Amini, then minister of finance, submitted the Consortium Oil Agreement Bill for parliamentary approval. It meant the grant of another concession to foreign companies which was precisely what the oil nationalization (and the whole policy of passive balance, with its denial – in the Fourteenth Majlis – of an oil concession to the USSR) had intended to avoid. Apart from that, the terms of the concession were worse for Iran than Stokes's initial proposal of August 1951. The fact that it also brought less comfort to the former Anglo-Iranian Oil Company (now renamed British Petroleum) than they might have wished to bargain for had another cause: the Americans had helped them destroy the Popular Movement and now received their share of the spoils in return.[13]

There was resistance both inside and outside the Majlis. In a Majlis speech, Derakhshesh delivered a long and well-argued attack on the Bill. He had been helped to prepare his speech by Khalil Maleki who, in his turn, had been helped by Kazim Hasibi on technical questions.[14] The NRM, also, issued two long statements which contained cogent arguments against the new oil agreement on legal, political and other grounds. A study of both documents gives a definite impression that their basic sources were the same. But the NRM's statement could emphasize the most fundamental argument against the Bill in a way that (the otherwise more substantial) speech by Derkhshesh could not:

> Following the line of Musaddiq – the lawful prime minister of Iran – the National Resistance Movement places the political aspect of any settlement of the oil dispute, i.e. the liberation of Iran from foreign interference, and the securing of Iran's freedom and independence, above all other considerations.[15]

At the same time, a long letter of protest – addressed to the Senators and Majlis deputies, and signed by Dehkhuda, Zanjani, Mu'azzami, Saleh, Bazargan, Maleki and Shapour Bakhtiyar, among others – was circulated by hand. It emphasized the history of the AIOC's interference in Iran's internal affairs, argued that the proposed oil agreement would once again compromise the country's 'freedom and independence', and pointed out that it violated the Nationalization Act. It also pointed out that there was no chance for a public debate on the issue, because the people's leaders were either in jail or in hiding or under strict police surveillance. It went unacknowledged, and unreported by the press, even though it had been signed by a former Majlis Speaker and head of legislature, a former chairman of the National Iranian Oil Company, a former minister of the interior and of justice, another former minister of justice, and a number of religious leaders, leading scholars and party leaders.[16] The regime reacted by dismissing twelve distinguished university professors – including Mu'azzami, Bazargan, Qarib, Sahabi and Abidi – from their posts.[17] Eleven of them went on to set up the YUD: *Yazdah Ustad-i Danishgah* (Eleven university professors) company to earn their livings.

Qarani's plot

The Nineteenth Majlis elections held in 1956 were rigged with greater ease than those of the Eighteenth. It was not possible for the Popular Movement to announce a list of candidates even – as in the previous case – via private circulation. And the few independent deputies like Derakhshesh whom the regime itself had allowed into the 18th Majlis were excluded. During the Tehran elections, Allahyar Saleh made the symbolic gesture of trying to take *bast* in the Majlis in protest against the regime's election rigging. But the *bast* did not last long: a van-load of soldiers were sent to remove him forcibly, and put him under house arrest. There were other political protests of this kind over the period 1953–60 which led to arrests, banishments, dismissal from public positions, etc.

Once the Popular Movement's threat to the regime had been effectively suppressed, and the shah had reduced the number of loyal but independent conservative politicians, it was inevitable that disagreements and dissent would be shifted to the various trends and pressure groups within the regime itself. From the beginning, the shah had been trying to increase his power at the expense of the conservative politicians, and this led to increasing friction between them. The first casualty was Zahedi himself who was honourably discharged, and exiled to Switzerland for the rest of his life. Dr Ali Amini was first moved from the key position of minister of finance to the justice department, and later sent as Iranian ambassador to Washington. The shah's problem with politicians like Amini, Abdullah Intizam (first, foreign minister, then, chairman of the National Iranian Oil Company) and Abulhasan Ibtihaj (head of the Plan Organization) was not just due to personality differences or even to power politics. These were able and self-regarding politicians and technocrats who were not prepared to take orders blindly; and they were opposed to the growing corruption and inefficiency which the pure 'yes-men' encouraged or tolerated.

The regime's domestic discontent spread to the army. In January 1958, Major-General Qarani, the army chief of intelligence, was arrested and tried *in camera* on charges which were not revealed at the time. In fact, he had been planning a coup to trim the shah's power and establish a reformist regime. He had contacted a wide range of politicians (including some among the Popular Movement leaders),[18] talking vaguely about the need for social and political reforms, and criticizing the inefficiency, corruption and dictatorship. These politicians knew little or nothing about Qarani's plans for a coup, but Hasan Arsanjani – Amini's close collaborator, and agriculture minister in his future government – had been deeply involved in the affair. He was therefore put under arrest for a short time, and Amini was summarily dismissed from his post in Washington. Whether or not the US government had been behind the plot, the fate of those involved in it (and of Qarani in particular, who was eventually given a light sentence by a military court) would have been different without its direct or indirect protection.[19]

Richard Cottam, then a young American diplomat in Tehran, witnessed the affair at close quarters. He reaffirmed to the author (in a conversation in London) Arsanjani's central role in it, and described the cunning cover which Qarani had provided for his dangerous contacts, by first telling the shah that he was trying to uncover a plot. According to Cottam, the US embassy had learned of the affair, but did not inform the regime about it. It was the British embassy who discovered the plot independently and informed the shah directly. Both in *Political Economy* and in *Khatirat-i Siyasi-yi Khalil Maleki* I postulated that the Soviet embassy was likely to have discovered Qarani's plans, and told the shah. Since my conversation with Cottam, my investigations have led to the following information: a colonel in the army had been a Soviet agent; another had been a confidant of Ayatullah Bihbihani. The Soviet embassy first sought immunity for their informer, and then produced him as a witness to the regime. The British embassy, on the other hand, simply told the shah what they knew without producing their witness(es).

The most popular unperson

Musaddiq was largely undisturbed by these events. He had given the lead for resistance through his conduct at his trials and the battles which he constantly fought with the authorities as long as he was in jail. By the time he finished serving his sentence (in August 1956) and was put under guard at his home in Ahmad-Abad, public resistance had already begun to decline. In any event, he could do even less from Ahmad-Abad than from the military prison in Tehran, partly because of the distance and lack of communications (in addition to being under permanent watch), and partly because his family could more effectively stop him taking risks. He had written Book I of his memoirs (covering the period 1882–1924) in jail. Now he began Book II, which he completed in 1961. This was his personal testimony on the oil nationalization episode, including his replies to the shah's personal attacks on him in his *Mission for My Country*, which was serialized in the semi-official daily newspapers, *Kayhan* and *Ittila'at* in 1960.

By now he had become a living legend, and the most popular unperson in the country. It was not possible to mention his name in print but the public had turned him into a political idol. This, as we have seen, was partly because of his defiant attitude throughout his period in jail. But it was also due to growing public dissent against the regime's dictatorship and corruption, and increasing public knowledge about the coup and its makers. Even the Tudeh were left with little choice but to be converted. Musaddiq read widely, and was keen to read the latest foreign memoirs, historical accounts and newspaper articles about the oil nationalization and himself. He still suffered from chronic ill-health, and was now regularly 'catching cold'. There were many moments when he was subdued, and he sometimes spent these with his *tar*, having been taught to play it well by the master *tarist* Husainquli in his youth.

The formation of the Second National Front and the Socialist League

Immediately after the 1953 coup, Iran's economy began to take off and with restored oil revenues and American aid, Iran experienced an economic boom. But in 1960 the bubble burst, and the boom turned into bust. Much of the growing oil revenues and American grants had gone up in the smoke of corruption and incompetence.[20] The shah and the royal family, the landlords as a class, the army and the higher bureaucracy had been the main beneficiaries of the bonanza, with the modern and traditional middle classes also benefiting indirectly from the expenditure boom. The second (five-year) plan had not managed to fulfil its social and economic targets. There had been little industrial development, and agriculture was still poor, traditional, and under the landlords' control. In 1960 the regime's high domestic expenditure and 'open-door' import policy led to an acute economic crisis with high inflation, a persistent as well as cumulative balance-of-payments deficit, and growing unemployment. It soon became difficult for the Central Bank to meets its foreign-exchange obligations from one week to the next. What followed was almost a dress rehearsal for the revolutionary events of 1977–9, although few drew the necessary lessons from it.

The shah no longer enjoyed the US government's unconditional and uncritical support. In influential American circles there had been criticism of his waste of their generous aid as well as of Iran's oil revenues, the lack of social reform, etc., in addition to the notorious corruption of the political system. They were therefore not ready to come to the shah's rescue by giving him the requisite financial support. This in itself was sufficient to spread rumours across the society that the Americans wished to impose an independent government on the shah, if not to get rid of him altogether. The familiar process of self-fulfilling expectations began: rumours (believed by the shah and others) that a foreign power wished to bring about a major change, followed by the belief that, therefore, a change was inevitable, followed by the mobilization and intervention of the dissidents and critics of the regime, followed by some kind of change at least for a time. This was how Dr Ali Amini became prime minister in 1961, although the Second National Front could well have stolen the show from him had it been better prepared.

A few years earlier, Khalil Maleki had tried to persuade the Popular Movement leaders to begin organized but private and informal contacts, and to prepare for the opportunity which, he predicted, would sooner or later arise. Thus in his long letter of March 1963 to Musaddiq in *Khatirat-i Siyasi* (Appendices) he mentioned that, in the end, Saleh had 'frankly said that his Iran party friends blocked the effort to bring about this unity'. And he went on (pp. 472–3):

> I suggested the minimum to Mr Saleh, saying that there would definitely be an opportunity [for political activity] in the future, and that – during the then period of enforced inactivity – it was the task of the [Popular Movement] leaders to study the various issues and problems so as to be ready to seize the opportunity when it comes. I then asked Mr Saleh whether he knew what to do [i.e. had a clear programme in mind] if the opportunity arose. He said he definitely did not, and that if he was offered a task [i.e. the premiership] at the time he would have to turn it down. At any rate, even those small discussion meetings gradually disappeared, until the warmth of 'free elections' [a reference to the shah's announcement of elections in 1960] suddenly brought many out of their nests.

Thus, before 1960, the Popular Movement leaders lacked both hope and energy, and would not be drawn into the argument. Maleki even went so far as to put forward a formal proposal – to the Popular Movement forces – to think seriously about organizing a Socialist League of Iran. Briefly, his argument was that, given the national and international situation at the time, 'a relevant, precise and clear *doctrine*' was needed. It was also necessary to create an organization which would nurture and promote that doctrine. Given the social base to whom such a 'social ideology' was meant to appeal, 'it could not be anything but democratic socialism (*susialism-i demukratik*)'. A socialist league should be founded by those political leaders who believed that '*the future Iranian society must be based on [personal] work and effort, not on inherited or acquired social privileges*'.

There followed a set of proposals (a) for the broad attitude vis-à-vis domestic and foreign politics which the proposed league should adopt; and (b) a programme for socio-economic reforms. In domestic politics, the league should enter a 'life-and-death struggle' against corruption, and strive for the establishment of the rule of law. However, it would not use illegal means to bring down 'the establishment in its entirety' but peaceful means to move the society – 'gradually, and having regard for the nature of the Iranian society, and its national and religious traditions' – towards socialism. The employment of 'peaceful means should not be confused with unprincipled politicking. The Socialist League would seek revolutionary aims by the use of peaceful tactics.' In foreign policy, the league should accept 'the principle of non-alignment', and establish friendly relations with both East and West without compromising the country's independence.

The league's proposed social programme contained (a) a fairly detailed land reform policy; (b) an industrial policy based on planning and state participation in industrial development which explicitly rejected *étatisme*; and (c) 'constitutional and parliamentary democracy based on a welfare state'.[21] These proposals were by far the most comprehensive, detailed and precise that had ever been put forward in Iran. They could equally well have been presented without any reference to democratic socialism. But they were entirely ignored.

The Second National Front

The opportunity came in 1960 when, amid the problems described above, the Nineteenth Majlis came to its natural end, and the shah declared that the impending general elections would be free. The official political parties, *Melliyun* and *Mardum* – which had been created in recent years, but existed in little but name – were then instructed to indulge in critical debate and competitive electioneering, all in the shah's name. Ali Amini and other independent and reformist conservatives also saw their opportunity and went into action. Allahyar Saleh declared his candidacy for his native Kashan, for which he was the obvious deputy.

Only then did the Popular Movement leaders see a chance for renewed activity, and begin to make informal contacts. Many of the meetings took place in Saleh's house, even while he was electioneering in Kashan. On one such occasion a short statement was issued, declaring the formation of the Second National Front. Its members included Ghulamhusain Sadiqi, Karim Sanjaby, Baqir Kazemi and

Mehdi Bazargan among the first-rank leaders; Dariyush Furuhar, Sayyed Mohammad Ali Kishavarz-i Sadr, Shahpour Bakhtiyar, Yaddullah Sahabi, Sayyed Mahmud (later Ayatullah) Taliqani among the middle rankers; and Razi, Karim-Abadi, Khunji, Hijazi, Bihnam and Ghanizadeh among the lower group. Those who had signed the statement or were later co-opted (thirty-six in all) made up the Front's first High Council, later to be named the Central Council. Saleh did not formally join the Front until his election as deputy for Kashan in 1961, partly because he had been annoyed by the lack of consultation, but mainly because it was wiser for him to stand as an independent candidate in Kashan. But he was in regular informal contact with the Council and many of the bazaar activists.

The remainder of the old National Resistance Movement were automatically brought within the Front when their leaders, such as Bazargan, joined in its formation. They brought with them their past grievances against some Popular Movement – and especially the Iran party – leaders, to which others were to be added within the first few months of renewed activity. These were to lead to their formal separation, and the establishment (in 1961) of their own organization, entitled the Freedom Movement of Iran. On the other hand, Maleki and the old guard of Third Force activists who had not been consulted about the new arrangements decided to form a completely new organization, the Socialist League of the Popular Movement of Iran. The words 'of the Popular Movement' were added to their old proposal for the creation of 'The Socialist League of Iran', because it had been intended originally to encompass the whole of the Popular Movement. They put forward a minimum programme, in the shape of a manifesto, which they hoped would be adopted by the whole of the Movement led by the Front.[22] And, apart from the *Ilm va Zindigi* periodical, they began to publish a weekly political review under the same title until they were all banned late in 1961.[23]

There were several reasons behind Maleki's exclusion from the Front. He had hurt some of the Popular Movement's leaders by his habitual plain speaking. Some were afraid that he would dominate the Front's leadership by virtue of his intellectual and organizational ability as well as his full-time commitment to political activity; others were afraid that Tudeh sympathisers might not support the Front if Maleki was among its leadership. The role of Khunji, Hijazi and (Shahpour) Bakhtiyar was crucial in all of this, though others such as Saleh, Sanjaby and Sadiqi would have liked to include him (see chapter 16).

It was a tactical mistake for the new Socialist League to give up the old name – i.e. Zahmatkishan Niru-yi Sevvum (or Third Force). Third Force was familiar, had a reputable history, and was still remembered as the most important Popular Movement party under Musaddiq, whereas the identity of the new organization was bound to remain obscure even to the wider Popular Movement base (let alone the public at large) for a long time. To some extent, the idea had emanated from younger Iranian activists in Europe who had formed themselves into Friends of Socialism (Havadaran-i Susialism), and published an intellectual political quarterly entitled *Susialism*. They were to organize themselves into the League of Iranian Socialists in Europe shortly after the formation of the Socialist League in Iran, with which they had fraternal relations, though they were otherwise independent from it. The League in Europe was made up of three groups: old Third Force activists, such as Amir Pichdad (their most prominent figure), Nasser Pakdaman, Hamid Mahamedi, and Manuchechr Hezarkhani; ex-Tudeh activists, the leading figure among whom was Hamid Enayat; and some non-partisan Popular Movement supporters.

In the summer of 1960 it looked as if the Second National Front would soon come to power. By the summer of 1965, it had collapsed, and the Third National Front, which had just been formed, was ruthlessly suppressed by the regime. By then those Iran party leaders who, together with Khunji and Hijazi, bore the greatest responsibility for the Front's defeat and decline had left the increasingly dangerous political scene. On the other hand, Bazargan, Maleki, Sahabi, Taliqani, Furuhar, and large numbers of student activists who – led by Musaddiq – had formed the Third National Front, were put behind bars and condemned in military courts. Meanwhile, Amini had formed a government and fallen from grace; the riots of June 1963 had been drowned in a pool of blood; and the shah had – for the first time since his accession to the throne – established his own absolute arbitrary rule over all social classes and institutions.

The Twentieth Majlis elections

Late in August 1960 the shah dismissed Iqbal's government. Pressures had been mounting, and the shah had thought it wise to distance himself from the results of his own policies by blaming one of the few men he ever trusted (although he would reward him for his loyalty and co-operation after the storm had been weathered). He went even further and complained that the elections had not been as free as he had wished them to be. He therefore 'advised' those deputies who had already been elected to resign their seats 'voluntarily', so that freer elections could be held.

The National Front had not been able to put forward a list of candidates and join the election campaign if only because by the time it had begun to organize itself the elections were well under way in many provinces. It now had the opportunity to launch an election campaign at the regime's weakest moment, when Hasan Sharif-Imami's caretaker government was effectively bridging the gap until the outcome of the struggle between the three contending forces: the shah, the National Front, and the conservative reformists led by Amini. On the other hand – and in view of the Front's lack of organizational preparedness, as well as the pressures and discriminations which it still suffered at the regime's hands – it could boycott the elections on the ground that the results were already a foregone conclusion, strengthen its organization, and lead a public campaign against election rigging. This way, it could have demonstrated its vast public support (which was largely owing to the unperson in Ahmad-Abad and the memory of his government) to domestic power centres and foreign powers alike, and prepared for accession to office. A variant of the latter choice was for a few of the top leaders to stand for Tehran and one or two other towns and cities amidst an anti-rigging public campaign in the style of Musaddiq and the First National Front during the Sixteenth Majlis elections. All these options were known and recognized at the time, and were discussed within the whole Movement.[24] In the event, the Front took none of these courses, did nothing apart from occasionally issuing short public statements (which were poorly distributed) against lack of freedom, etc., and let Amini take full advantage of its inertia in imposing his own government on the shah.

From August to October 1960, a number of small public meetings were held in the Front's name. All of them were organized by the remainder of the old NRM, led by Bazargan, and none was attended by any of the other Front leaders, or approved by them. The open-air meeting held in August, in a corner of the Jalaliyeh racecourse (now a central park), was attended by a couple of thousand young activists of the NRM, Third Force and Furuhar's Iranian People's party. Its significance lay in breaking the ban on open-air political meetings, and in mentioning Musaddiq's name. The election meetings (as they were described to the police) held at Lebaschi's house in the Pachinar district, were regularly attended by a few hundred activists, if only because the house could not possibly accommodate more. But here, too, the meetings were addressed only by Bazargan and some of his lieutenants, even though the Lebaschi family themselves belonged to the Front's mainstream.[25] Relations between the two sides' leaders and activists were not entirely fraternal, and were to become strained within a few months (see chapter 16).

When the academic year began, the University of Tehran was ready to resume political activity after seven years of enforced silence. It did so, with great symbolism, on 7 December by holding a silent demonstration on the University campus in commemoration of the fallen when soldiers had opened fire on unarmed students on the day of Vice-President Nixon's visit. Further campus demonstrations followed with increasing frequency, with loud slogans shouted by the student demonstrators and public speeches delivered by their leading activists. The regime lacked the confidence to send in the police or troops to teach the students another lesson. On the other hand, the University president, Dr Ahmad Farhad, would not (and did not) yield to its pressures to invite the police onto the University campus. SAVAK agents would therefore try to identify student activists and arrest them outside the University. Many of them went to jail, at least for a few days, where a few – such as Sirus Tahbaz and Houshang Sayyahpour, both medical students – were savagely beaten. At one stage fifty-eight students were held for a month, and then collectively released in a tactical retreat by the regime.

There was no student union in any sense of this term. The activists of the Front's mainstream (including a few Marxist-Leninists, such as Bijan Jazani, who were critical of the Tudeh leadership), of the remainder of the NRM, and of the Socialist League each had their own separate arrangements – the term 'organization' not being accurate in all cases – and co-operated in organizing the demonstrations. They included Houshang Kishavarz-i Sadr, Hashim Sabbaghiyan, Manuchehr Rassa, Abbas Aqilizadeh, Abbas Shaibani, Abulhasan Bani-Sadr, Siygzar Birilian, Bihruz Burumand, Dariyush Ashuri, Ali-Akbar Akbari, Hasan Zia Zarifi, Parvaneh Iskandari, Parvin Fakhara'i among others.

In December 1960, an attempt was made to set up a student union of sorts, though this would still inevitably be dominated by political activists and political issues. But it was frustrated for two main reasons. First, Dr Shahpour Bakhtiyar, whom the National Front put in charge of student affairs, wanted to run the students' activities as he saw fit, and appoint whoever he wished as student leaders.[26] Secondly, the meeting in November held at Abbas Shaibani's house misfired, because the host opened it with a long speech containing a stinging attack on Saleh, Sanjaby and some other (non-NRM) leaders of the Front. As a result, general policy remained in the hands of Bakhtiyar and his appointees, although the NRM and the Socialist League continued their separate organization and presence. This was to have serious consequences, the first of which was tested in the students' sit-in of February 1961.

The students' sit-in and the Tehran elections

By January 1961, the National Front had done little to organize itself to fight the elections, except putting out occasional leaflets explaining that they were not free,. and this despite the fact that it had fully intended to participate, and had put up two candidates for Isfahan, and six (including Bazargan, and two from the local Socialist League organization) for Tabriz. It had also produced two candidates for Shiraz from the local aspirants; but it could not have known much about them, for Firaidun Tavalluli quickly sent a message via Maleki that the two men had no reputation to lose in that city. Two hundred seats were being contested in the familiarly long-drawn-out elections. Knowing that it would face the stiffest resistance to election rigging in Tehran, the regime had decided to hold the elections late in the capital city. But as the Tehran elections approached, the Front had still not been able to produce a list of fifteen candidates, mainly because of internal disputes (even recriminations) over who should be included. In despair, it boycotted the elections everywhere, but Saleh, who was standing as an independent candidate for Kashan, continued his campaign in his own constituency.

The Tehran elections were shamelessly rigged, and the rigging was publicly exposed by the weekly *Ilm va Zindigi* and the daily *Dad* newspapers. The Front's high council decided to stage a show of public protest by taking *bast* in the Senate building, while the chamber was still in session. At first, Senate president Sayyed Hasan Taqizadeh was sent to persuade them to leave, a mission which he undertook without much enthusiasm, and with no success.[27] Having failed, the regime sealed the building and held the protesters inside as prisoners: when Kazim Hasibi tried to leave the building on hearing that his pregnant wife had gone into labour, he was arrested and put in jail.

The high council had been careful to keep two of its members outside the Senate: Karim Sanjaby for general contacts, and Shahpour Bakhtiyar for university affairs. On 26 January, the Front's student activists received orders that the Popular Movement students were to hold a mass demonstration the next day, and that this time they should march out of the campus and onto the streets. The orders were duly passed on to the other activists, but the Socialist League student leaders thought that the demonstration would inevitably fail, because the police – who were always outside the University gates – would attack the students in full force. They thought up an alternative course of action, but did not put it in advance to the Front activists for fear of its being overruled from above.

The police normally blocked the exit just outside the University gates during student demontrations. The Socialist League's student leaders therefore suggested that, since the National Front orders did not include breaking through the police lines by force, a sit-in should be staged at the University to protest against the rigging of the Tehran elections, and in sympathy with the National Front leaders who were effectively jailed in the Senate building. It was a bitterly cold winter's day, and the students remained on the campus itself until 5 pm, by which time their representatives had managed to obtain the overnight use of the Faculty of Letters from the University president, although he had been under pressure to lock all the buildings and let the students freeze in the cold. There was no question at that time of the students occupying a building without the University authorities' permission, but the student leaders *had* mentioned to the University president that they should not be held responsible for a break-and-entry in the bitter cold of the night, if a building was not put at their disposal. They were not making any demands on the University authorities, they did not intend to disrupt teaching, and did not ask for any rooms – other than the halls and corridors – to be made available to them.

By nightfall the campus was surrounded by armed police, and communications between the strikers and the outside world were cut off. In the meantime, however, food had been brought in and stored inside the University. At 7 pm the SAVAK, which had been caught wholly off guard by the new tactic, sent an informer (in the shape of a psychology lecturer) to the Faculty of Letters, and reassured itself that a few thousand male and female students were spending the night in the building.[28]

At about 11 pm, when most of the lights were out, the students were pleasantly surprised by the arrival of Shahpour Bakhtiyar, shadowed by a yonger luminary of the Iran party. Having been carried shoulder high to the main hall, Bakhtiyar congratulated the students on their brave decision. But the rhetoric was followed by an order which no one could remotely have anticipated: he told the students to leave the University forthwith, and go home. There were loud cries of dissent;

some students even shouted that their homes were in Shimiran, and that there was no means by which they could possibly get home at that time of night. Bakhtiyar left in an atmosphere very different from that in which he had been welcomed. There followed an intense debate in informal groups about the new orders, and the previous spirit of unity and co-operation was seriously impaired.

The Socialist League activists decided to send a delegation to Karim Sanjaby (the other Front leader not shut in the Senate), to persuade him to come to the University, and – as the much more popular and authoritative leader – reverse Bakhtiyar's order. Houshang Sayyah-pour, Husain Sarpulaki and Husain Meftah (of the League itself), and Amir Mas'ud Katouzian and Parviz Sanjaby (Dr Sanjaby's son) – who did not belong to any of the parties – were secretly smuggled out of the campus to report to Dr Sanjaby. Sanjaby then told them that at 9 pm the acting SAVAK chief – since Taimur Bakhtiyar was on a visit to the United States (trying to win support to attain power) – had telephoned to ask him to go to the University to tell the students to leave, and that he had told him that the Front leader responsible for the students' section was Shahpour Bakhtiyar.

Next morning, the argument over what to do led the Front's student activists to negotiate with the police outside to let the students leave and march *silently* in the streets without interference. This was agreed, the students were led out, and the minute they were all in the street they faced water cannon, a baton charge, and – if caught – arrest. The protest strike which had begun so well – and had so frightened the regime – thus ended ingloriously, followed by bitterness and recriminations. Had the students held out for a few days, the National Front would have been able to exact a high price from the regime in the generally troubled situation. Claims made in the late 1970s and early 1980s that Shahpour Bakhtiyar had acted against his own better judgement, and in keeping with the wishes of the Front's executive committee, have no foundation in fact. The Front's five-man executive committee was set up almost three months after this event, and in any case only Sanjaby and Bakhtiyar were at that time free outside the Senate building.[29]

Nevertheless, spontaneous demonstrations in the bazaar and at the University continued unabated, and on one occasion Dr Iqbal's car was set on fire while he was on a personal visit to the dean of the Dental School. This was followed by the arrest of Khalil Maleki, Haj Mahmud Maniyan, Qasim Lebaschi, other bazaar leaders and a number of student activists. But they were all released at the Persian New Year by General Bakhtiyar who had just returned from his American visit to be told by the shah to quit his post as the SAVAK chief. Indeed, Maleki and Maniyan, whom (among other leaders) the general had treated with respect before their release, had been surprised to find him converted to the cause of democracy and freedom.

16

Failure of the Second National Front

Conflict within the Movement

The Second National Front had started off on the wrong foot as regards organization and programme, and the group rivalries and personality problems within the Movement as a whole played an important part both in perpetuating these difficulties and in creating new ones. The Second National Front owed its early popularity and prestige to Musaddiq (who had had no role in founding or directing it), and to the few in its leadership – Sanjaby, Saleh, Sadiqi, Bazargan, etc. – who had been his close associates. Within a few months of its formation, however, it had effectively fallen into the hands of three lesser figures: Shahpour Bakhtiyar, Mohammad Ali Khunji and Mas'ud Hijazi.

Bakhtiyar was his own man, but he personified the strong technocratic element within the Iran party which had caused much friction in the Movement during Musaddiq's government and helped alienate other important leaders such as Kashani and Baqa'i. Since the Iran party was a small (though top-heavy) grouping with limited organizing capabilities, he believed that it should effectively be in control of the new Front, and try to turn it into its own mass base. The dashing, authoritarian streak in his personality, and his excellent personal relations with Saleh, Sanjaby and Hasibi (the most important Iran party leaders, and three of the most popular within the new Front) enabled him to exert a quite disproportionate influence inside the National Front. His appointment as the leader in charge of the students' section was helpful, because he was virtually in control of the Movement's most respected and most energetic organ.

Khunji and Hijazi, on the other hand, had led nine other men out of the Third Force party after the 1953 coup, claiming that Maleki was a 'traitor'. They – and especially Khunji – were well-trained in theoretical and organizational matters in which they were virtually unrivalled within the new Front. But they had no force whatever behind them, and likewise needed to turn the Front into their own organization. In time, Khunji became the Front's official theorist, and was put in charge of its internal political education and external propaganda; and Hijazi was entrusted with organizational matters. The Bakhtiyar-Khunji-Hijazi triumvirate therefore recognized their mutual dependence and coincidence of interest, and effectively dominated the Front until its virtual collapse in 1964.

To achieve their objective, they needed to neutralize the effect of strong organizations and powerful personalities within the Movement. Thus, Maleki and the Socialist League and Bazargan and his NRM followers (in that order) had to be contained. As we saw in chapter 15, the Front had been formed without Maleki's knowledge, and the Socialist League had been set up shortly afterwards. In October 1961 Khunji issued a leaflet – on behalf of a 'Socialist Party' which had never existed – claiming that the most important matter facing the Movement was that all the existing Popular Movement parties and organizations should dissolve and join the Front as individual members. This was both inconsistent with the idea of a popular Front, and precisely the opposite of the premises on which Musaddiq's First National Front had been founded in 1949 (see chapter 6). When the Socialist League formally applied to join the new Front as an organized body, it received no answer from its newly-formed executive committee which was dominated by Bakhtiyar. Four years later, the position was explained to Musaddiq (who had wondered why the League had not been admitted) by saying that, because of differences of opinion, the executive committee had decided 'to pass it over in silence'.[1]

Bazargan and the NRM were another matter, for they could neither be described by Khunji and Hijazi as 'traitors', nor by Bakhtiyar as compulsive 'split-mongers'. To exclude Maleki from the Front's leadership Bakhtiyar described him as a 'compulsive split-monger' (*Inshi'ab-chi*). In his recent interview with the Harvard Oral History Project he offered the same explanation, adding that he would have preferred Nur al-Din Kiyanuri (the Tudeh leader who by then had confessed to being a Soviet agent) to Maleki, because he had always remained in the Tudeh party. On the other hand, Dr Sanjaby presented a highly favourable picture of Maleki (in a similar interview with the HOHP) saying that he had been in favour of including him in the Second National Front's leadership, and lamenting that this had been blocked by others. Both Bazargan and the NRM enjoyed the support of the popular Ayatullahs Zanjani and Firuzabadi, and had a considerable social base within the bazaar and the *melli* religious community. On the other hand, mutual ill-feelings arising from the Iran party's short association with the NRM in the past, and some of the NRM activists' tactless open attacks on Saleh and Sanjaby, were not helpful and played into the triumvirate's hands in their internal campaigns against the NRM: whereas these and many other first-rank Front leaders were personally sympathetic to Maleki and the Socialist League, there was little love lost between them and the NRM. In May 1961, the NRM left the Front to form the Freedom Movement of Iran, led by Bazargan, Sahabi and Taliqani. Thenceforth, until the formation of the Third National Front, the Popular Movement was made up of three main organizations: the National Front, which was still the mass movement, and which the other two organizations continued to support despite their growing criticism of its conduct, until there was a revolt against its leadership from within as well as without; and the Freedom Movement and the Socialist League which were increasingly drawn together over a number of tactical and strategic questions affecting the Movement. The remaining parties within the Front – the Iran party, Furuhar's Iranian People, and Nakhshab's People of Iran – were not disbanded, but they were not much more than formal associations with little independent activity.

The Front's first and only congress was held early in January 1963, two and a half years after its formation, and three weeks before the shah's White Revolution referendum which sealed the fate of all democratic opposition for the next fifteen years. It did nothing to heal the breach within the Movement and little to change itself into an effective political force (see further below).

The Popular Movement and Amini's government

By the time the Front held its congress, the two opportunities for the Movement to impose itself on the regime as an alternative government, had been missed, and – although it still took more time for its own leaders and activists to realize this – the Front's fortunes were fast on the decline. The first opportunity offered itself in the early days of its formation, and during the second run of the Twentieth Majlis elections; that is, between October 1960 and March 1961. The second was in the following period – April 1961 to July 1962 – during Amini's premiership, when the Front had a good chance to turn itself into a powerful shadow government.[2]

The Twentieth Majlis (in which Saleh was the only Popular Movement figure, but which also contained a few men of good will such as Rahmatullah Muqaddam-Maragheh'i) had barely begun its work when the teachers' strike led by Mohammad Derakhshesh erupted into the streets of Tehran, and a young teacher was shot dead by the police in Baharistan, the parliament square. This was the final straw, and the shah was forced to ask Amini to form a government. Whatever the Amini lobby may have been in America – and the subject is still open to a good deal of disagreement – it is virtually certain that the US government did not (tacitly or explicitly) tell the shah to make him prime minister, although it is equally certain that the shah believed that this was what the Americans expected of him. Other things being equal, the shah would have preferred a National Front leader such as Saleh whom he did not dislike personally and – more importantly – did not perceive as an American candidate who could use US power against him. Amini agreed to act on condition that the shah used his power under the constitutional amendment of 1949 to dismiss the parliament. Given his well-publicized intention of carrying out a land reform, he was worried that the shah and the landlords would block his every move in the Majlis, and force him out of office – as Musaddiq would have put it – in a seemingly constitutional manner.

Once again there was dual sovereignty in Iranian politics, with Amini's share of power beginning to decline rapidly after the first couple of months of his government, thanks largely to the Second National Front's policy of putting all its efforts into attacking him (in effect in favour of the shah). He soon had to face the combined opposition of the shah, the landlords, the conservative religious leaders, and operators such as Asadullah Rashidiyan and Fathullah Furud, as well as massive public confrontation by the Second National Front. At first, he tried to woo the Front. The news of its activities suddenly appeared in the regular daily press, and (in June 1961) it was allowed to hold the Popular Movement's first authorized open-air meeting since August 1953 at the Jalaliyeh racecourse.[3] Inevitably, there was a massive turn-out, not least because false rumours had been circulated that Musaddiq himself was planning to attend.[4]

The Socialist League's public analysis of the situation was, briefly, as follows. Amini represented the regime's reformist wing which had come into conflict with the shah. He was serious in his land reform policy, and prepared to grant more freedom to the Popular Movement vis-à-vis the shah and the landlords. On the other hand, he was feared by the shah and had turned the landlords as a class against himself. The National Front should therefore take advantage of the new situation and organize itself into a shadow government by publicizing a much more progressive programme to include a better land reform policy, rectification of Iran's oil interests, a non-aligned foreign policy, and democratic government. The Socialist League's own land reform programme was to transfer the ownership of land in every village collectively to the peasantry by a single law, and extend credit and technical services to the cultivators. This would (a) allow the *nasaq* (traditional rights)-holders to retain the landlord's share for themselves; (b) prevent the breaking-up of estates into very small farms either then or later through inheritance; (c) leave the village as the historical unit of agricultural production, and useful traditional techniques and institutions such as the *qanat* (irrigation channel) and the *boneh* (co-operative production unit) undisturbed; (d) maintain the position of the *khushnishin* (landless) peasantry as before, rather than subjecting them to social and legal dispossession; (e) discourage rapid migration to the towns; (f) and cut out all the legal and bureaucratic problems of dividing up the land.[5]

Within a few months, the Freedom Movement also adopted the view that it was unwise for the Popular Movement forces to beat Amini down only to have him replaced by one of the shah's own men, such as Asadullah Alam who did eventually replace him.

There were two main reasons behind the Second National Front's exclusive and indiscriminate attack on Amini. First, it was an easy option, and avoided the wrath of the shah, the landlords and the conservative religious leaders, and happened to be popular among their grassroots constituents who put a high premium on avenging themselves over Amini's role in concluding the Consortium Oil Agreement.[6] Secondly, the triumvirate and their associates within the Front entertained the hope that they could move quickly and – in league with other disaffected parties, such as General Bakhtiyar, the landlords' representatives, etc. – bring down Amini and replace him with a coalition government.

The first open confrontation came over the Front's proposal to hold a mass open-air meeting at Jalalieh on 21 July 1961 to commemorate the popular uprising which had brought Musaddiq back to power in 1952. Amini explained privately that the shah would not tolerate such an affront to himself, and suggested that the meeting be held before or after that day. In return, he promised not to let the shah hold his own annual rally on 19 August, the day of the coup which was officially described as a national uprising. The Front did not agree, and the meeting was banned and the Front's leaders put behind bars for twenty-four hours for their own protection. With no preparations by the Front to organize the crowd, the Socialist League felt obliged to step in and run the show in order to save the Popular Movement's face (as they privately explained). It was not a glorious event, and it helped considerably to reduce the political freedoms which had been enjoyed for a couple of months.[7]

The events of 21 January 1962 (known in Iran as the *Avval-i Bahman* conspiracy) were, however, of a totally different order. As noted earlier, General Taimur Bakhtiyar, the universally hated SAVAK chief, had fallen from grace on account of his attempts to fish in the shah's troubled waters. But he still wielded considerable power within the SAVAK and the army, and among conservative landlords and politicians, and the shah did not yet have enough confidence to get rid of him. Bakhtiyar was prepared to seize power by any means and at any price, which explains how he eventually lost his life at the hands of two SAVAK under-cover agents in 1970, in Iraq, where he was using (and was being used by) the Iraqi regime against the shah.

Bakhtiyar had been at work among three groups: (a) the army officers, which had led to the formation of his own band under the name of 'Constitutionalist Officers'; (b) among the landlords and conservative politicians who were opposed to Amini's land reform policy; and (c) among the conservative religious leaders, such as Ayatullah Bihbahani, who were likewise opposed to land reform. The latter two groups were still hoping that the shah would rescue them from Amini's reformism, but when the Amini-Arsanjani Land Reform Law of January 1962 came into being, some of them promised support to the general on the understanding that there would be no change of regime. It was also rumoured that the shah himself was involved in these moves for fear of Amini completely stealing the show from him (as he firmly believed) with full American backing.

Bakhtiyar had always enjoyed good personal relations with his cousin Shahpour, who was still effectively in control of the university students' activities. To bring down Amini's government without a full blast against the whole regime needed – among other things – a certain amount of popular involvement. And this, at the time, was the exclusive domain of the Popular Movement, led by the National Front. The Front's total confrontation with Amini's government had therefore to be ensured at all costs. Furthermore, the general made occasional gestures of goodwill towards the Front, a strategy which he had already begun (as we saw above) by releasing its leaders from jail the day before relinquishing office, and telling some Popular Movement leaders that they were right in their criticisms of the regime. At one stage, he even sent a message to the Front's leaders saying that he himself was a *melli* figure, and that if the Front helped him come to power, he would apologize to Musaddiq for his part in the 1953 coup. Saleh, Sanjaby, Sadiqi, Hasibi and other Front leaders like them were not the kind of men who would enter a coalition with someone like General Bakhtiyar under any circumstances. But, despite the fact that their personal popularity was indispensable in attracting mass support for the Front, they lacked the necessary drive in deciding the Front's tactics and strategies.

In January 1962, rumours circulated that a pupil at the Daralfunun secondary school had been dismissed on account of his political activities. On this slender pretext, orders were sent from the Front to the university activists that they should plan a massive campus demonstration in protest, and 21 January (*Avval-i Bahman*) was set as the day of action. The day before rumours about a plot to force the government out of office began to circulate widely both inside the government and in Popular Movement circles. By then the Freedom Movement, the Socialist League, and some of the Movement's forces within the National Front – for example, Furuhar's Iranian People's Party – had become convinced that the students were being used as pawns in a plot of which the Front as a whole was unaware.[8] The most radical and vocal student activists – including Marxist-Leninists like Bijan Jazani – began to counsel caution, and tried to prevent the catastrophe. All the various forces and entities within and outside the Front tried hard to persuade it to postpone the demonstration and conduct an enquiry into the plot allegations. Instead, many of those who were trying to stop the demonstrations – including Abulhasan Bani-Sadr, then a Freedom Movement activist – were arrested the night before.

The plan was to send an armed detachment of regular soldiers to the University campus to shoot at the crowd of demonstrators, in the hope that the government would then resign to show its innocence and in recognition of its impotence in controlling events even in Tehran. Having failed to dissuade the Front from its action, Amini managed to call in the army leaders at the eleventh hour and order the troops to remain in barracks for twenty-four hours. The plotters switched tactics, and sent in an irregular and autonomous 'commando' unit (described as *hava-niru*, and comparable to the British SAS), led by Major Khusrawdad – a leading operational officer in the 1953 coup. For reasons that are not known they stopped short of firing at the unarmed demonstrators. Instead, they used bayonets and rifle-butts against everyone in sight – professors, administrative workers, library and laboratory assistants included – with a savagery never experienced before. Students and others who took refuge inside the Faculty buildings were beaten up indiscriminately, and offices and scientific equipment were smashed and books burned. In their collective letter of resignation, the University president and council said that such atrocities had been unknown 'since the Mongol invasion'.[9]

The government did not resign, and blamed the whole event on a conspiracy. An army committee of investigation was set up which, in its hastily prepared report, concluded that the National Front had not been involved in the plot but did not name any specific individuals or groups as the culprits. This tended to confirm the view that the shah himself had had a hand in the plot, since he and Amini could otherwise have brought the plotters to book without difficulty. In any event, Amini asked the shah to order General Bakhtiyar to leave the country, and he left five days after the incident. On the other hand, anger and indignation erupted within the Popular Movement – both inside and outside the Front – and was specifically directed against the triumvirate of Shahpour Bakhtiyar, Khunji and Hijazi. Allegations were openly made that they had been in league with the plotters, and had even been promised specific posts in a cabinet led by General Bakhtiyar.[10] This was the origin of Musaddiq's later charge against the Front's council that it included some of 'our betters' (*az ma bihtaran*) – i.e. enemies of the Movement (see further below). Predictably, however, no internal inquiry was held by the Front, and its affairs continued to be run much as before.

Amini's government fell abruptly in July 1962 and, within a couple of months, the former prime minister was confined to Tehran by a court order. On the eve of his unexpected fall, the Socialist League published (in an unauthorized leaflet) an analysis of the political situation and a frank evaluation of the National Front's balance sheet which must be ranked as one of the most intelligent documents produced in the Movement's history. In its preamble it pointed out that the country was going through a transitional period 'which will leave its mark on the future history of Iran'. It argued that for political victory the Popular Movement needed a firm social base among workers, peasants, artisans, the national bourgeoisie and progressive educated people, and that the Front had done nothing to ensure such a base. A detailed critique of the Front's tactics and strategies followed, criticizing the Front for directing its campaign exclusively against the government's wish to postpone elections, whereas – because of the land reform issue, and the government's fear of a landlord majority in the Majlis – this was the one issue on which no concession could be obtained.

To declare a general strike without adequate preparation was a grave mistake. To do it again and again in the face of repeated failure (when not a single bus stopped running, and not even the bazaar closed down) was downright folly.

[On] the day that landlords and reactionary elements had designated their own day of victory, and had already appointed their cabinet, we entered a blind adventure, and this led to the catastrophe of 21 January (*Avval-i Bahman*). The amazing fact is that the leaders of the National Front had been warned by some well-informed people who knew about the behind-the-scenes conspiracies ... And yet, the Front's leadership astonishingly insisted on throwing thousands of students over to whips, bayonets and batons, and (in return) gained several hundred injuries, the long-term closure of the university, and greater [political] repression ... During this phase [of Amini's government] we could have turned ourselves into a great force ... But the balance-sheet of our actions reveals a force which is on the verge of bankruptcy.

The analysis concluded with the following accurate prediction about the fate of the Second National Front:

If things go on in the same way, the National Front will disappear as a political force, and – instead of it being the centrepiece of the Popular Movement of Iran – will become a disused temple for its most faithful believers to attend only for each other's funerals, and nod their heads to each other to renew their acquaintance and show their regret.[11]

The Front's Congress and the White Revolution

The fall of Amini had been preceded by a visit by the shah to Washington where he had threatened abdication unless he was given a free hand, and had been told that he was free to take his own decisions.[12] On the other hand, he wished to be known in the West as a reformist ruler, and he recognized that it would be impossible to go back on the land reform as if nothing had happened. While Amini was prime minister, he was in a tactical alliance with the landlords and reactionaries, but he was now free to launch a full-scale 'revolution' whereby he could establish his own arbitrary rule (*istibdad*) over all social classes and institutions.[13] The National Front still maintained total silence on the land reform and other social issues except when (in October of 1962) it published a small pamphlet,[14] the gist of which was that since European-style feudalism had never existed in Iran, the question of a land reform was irrelevant. Meanwhile, the regime was conducting intensive and extensive propaganda about a social reform programme, including a comprehensive land reform, women's suffrage and workers' shares in their firm's profits.

The shah's six-point programme – described as the Revolution of the Shah and the People, or the White Revolution – was put to a referendum (though this was a mere formality) on 26 January 1963. Only two weeks before, the Second National Front concluded its first and only congress, attended by 170 delegates from the various sections and provincial bodies, including three *official* delegates from the Iran, People of Iran and Iranian People parties, though there were others from these parties in other capacities. The Freedom Movement was not formally represented, but its leaders attended at first, as did some of its other members as sectional delegates. The Socialist League was not invited or represented in the congress, but a leader of its provincial organization in Azerbaijan (where it was particularly strong) was sent as a provincial delegate.

The congress started off on the wrong foot with charges being made (especially by students) of favouritism and 'election rigging' in deciding on sectional delegates. When a delegate tried to raise the question of the *Avval-i Bahman* fiasco, he was physically removed from the conference room, and Furuhar's protest was shouted down.[15] It soon became clear that the triumvirate's policy of disbanding the parties had the support of Saleh and Sanjaby and (therefore) of the majority of the delegates, and the Freedom Movement delegates withdrew amid recriminations. The congress elected a 39-man central council and, with the shah's referendum on the White Revolution imminent, approved a political programme covering a wide range of issues, but offering no concrete and specific policies – a clear indication of the indecisiveness and lack of commitment of the top leadership. For example, it talked about 'women's progress, and the affirmation of their rights' while the shah was proposing to give them the right to vote and be elected.[16] And as regards agriculture:

The Iranian National Front believes that the reform of the agricultural system should take place in such a way that farmers (*kishavarzan*) would be freed from bondage and benefit from the result of their labour ... In order to fulfil these objectives, it would be necessary to remove the ownership of those individuals who have obtained their ownership of land by illegitimate means. The landlord-peasant system, and all kinds of landownership which involve the exploitation of farmers must be abolished.

A supreme example of this deliberate vagueness occurred in the outline of the Front's foreign policy. No clear policy, 'neutrality or otherwise, alignment or non-alignment, is acceptable as a long-term foreign policy'. Instead, it recommended an 'independent national Iranian [foreign] policy' which (in its brief description) contained nothing about CENTO, the Iranian-American mutual defence pact, or any other concrete issue in Iran's foreign relations. It thus repudiated a hallmark of the Popular Movement's doctrine – namely, non-alignment – in a seemingly feeble attempt to reassure the Americans that the Front would be a safe horse to back. Two years before, it had not been prepared to so much as issue a short statement that it had no contact (as it did not) with the Tudeh party, for fear of offending the (unorganized) Tudeh sympathisers among the educated middle class. Now it gave up the Popular Movement's historical attitude towards foreign policy, without even bargaining for something in return. Thenceforth, the shah himself described Iran's foreign policy as 'an independent national Iranian policy'.

The organizers had sought a message from Musaddiq which was read out at the beginning of the congress, after he had been elected president (*in absentia*). By then, Musaddiq had been well informed of the conflict within the Movement and the reasons behind it. He devoted almost half his message to the importance of parties in a democratic movement, and pointed out that 'in the early days of Constitutionalism when no parties had yet been founded in this country' the triumph of the Constitutional Revolution had, in large measure, depended on the societies (*Anjumanha*) which had organized the people behind it. He therefore emphasized the need for 'the Front's gates to be opened to all individuals, groups, and parties which are ready for struggle and self-sacrifice to overthrow the colonial apparatus, and every effort to be made so that those who seek the freedom and independence of Iran are brought into the circle of activists'.[17] However, as he was to complain more than a year later,[18] the congress leaders completely ignored the message; it was not published either in Iran or in Europe, until it was put out by Tehran University students who by then were virtually leading the opposition from within the Front itself.

Two weeks later, when the shah put his six-point 'revolution' to the vote, the same indecisiveness was revealed again. A couple of days before the event, the Front issued an *ilamiyeh* (communiqué) containing the usual rhetoric about freedom, etc., and ending by saying 'land reform; yes, I agree; dictatorship; no, I disagree'. This was neither a boycott nor did it make clear which way the voters were advised to vote.

The people's grievances against the regime's corruption and dictatorship had not dissipated, however, but increased. Not only were Amini and his circle (apart from Arsanjani who had been won over by the shah) in opposition and under surveillance, but the landlords and conservative politicians were also extremely angry with the shah, and their leaders – such as Husain Ala, the court minister, Ayatullah Bihbahani, Sardar Fakhir Hikmat (the longest running Majlis Speaker since 1941), etc. – had received a harsh reply to their private representations to him.

The religious community and leaders were also agitated for a combination of different reasons. Some, for example Ayatullahs Milani and Zanjani, were pro-Popular Movement; others like Ayatullahs Khansari and Shari'atmadari were moderate conservatives who (though they were concerned about the fate of religious endowments) were not necessarily opposed to a land reform, and were more worried about the rising tide of dictatorship; still others like Ayatullahs Bihbahani and Khomaini were opposed to land reform and the proposed women's suffrage, as well as angry about the growing exclusion of the religious leadership from major public affairs. Qum was restless and, for the first time, the Theological College students there were attacked and beaten up by the police. The university students in Tehran were also restless, and this time bus-loads of hirelings – described as 'workers and peasants, angry with the students' opposition to their liberation' – were sent in by the regime to beat them up with sticks and clubs. Khomaini's daring public speeches against the regime quickly turned him into the most distinguished leader of an anti-despotic movement which finally erupted in June 1963, and led to the famous riots which were savagely put down by the army.[19]

It was in many ways a dress rehearsal for the revolution of 1977/9, not least because almost every urban social class and every ideology was represented. All the Popular Movement forces supported the movement, including the bazaar, the university students, and the Freedom Movement and Socialist League. The fact that the National Front did not openly back the demonstrations was partly because some of its leaders had been in jail since February, and partly because of its usual inertia and fear of taking decisions. But it did not discourage its sections and grassroots from becoming fully involved. Khalil Maleki's analysis of events at the time is still basically sound. He described the riots as a response to the regime's total insensitivity towards the public, whose leadership had fallen into non-Popular Movement hands because of the National Front's long incapacity to organize and give a lead. He was fully aware of the conservative forces and ideas which were also involved in the process, and lamented the fact that the people's anger against the regime had been allowed to be used for reactionary aims and objectives as well.

> Unfortunately a comparison of the intensity of the people's resistance ... during the recent events with the more-or-less similar events of the past two years, reveals that the self-styled leaders of the people [i.e. the second National Front] were incapable of providing effective leadership to mobilize the people ... behind progressive aims and objectives, and that landlords, reactionaries and their allies among those who pretend to be spiritual leaders (but who are not real spiritual leaders) were technically better equipped ... to misuse the religious and revolutionary sentiments of the selfless and self-sacrificing people of the cities for their devilish aims.[20]

He was writing from Vienna where he had been since March 1963 having treatment for his chronic heart disease and easing his son into the Austrian university system. Before leaving Tehran, he had sent a long report (in the shape of a personal letter) to Musaddiq which made an important contribution to Musaddiq's direct intervention in the ongoing conflict, and the formation of the Third National Front under the old man's own leadership (see chapter 17).

17

Musaddiq and the Third National Front

Musaddiq's intervention

In February 1963, shortly after the shah's referendum, many of the National Front leaders (in addition to large numbers of students and other activists) were put in jail. In March, Maleki sent his now famous letter to Musaddiq. In the postscript he said that he had begun to write the letter five months earlier when he had first applied for a passport, but had run into difficulties, and meanwhile the Front's leaders had been imprisoned. He felt bad about sending the letter (together with its critique of the Front's leadership) now that they were in jail, but he thought the matter too important politically to be dropped for sentimental reasons.

He began the letter by saying that, now that he was leaving the country for a few months, he was impelled by 'a heart-felt need to give you a short report on what has happened to the Popular Movement of Iran since the *coup d'etat* of 19 August 1953'.[1] Much of the letter concerned the activities of the Third Force (after the coup) and the Socialist League, but it also contained a critique of the Second National Front's record:

> The result of all these amazing mistakes of the heads of the National Front [is] that, at this stage, it lost the struggle, and the establishment succeeded in deceiving the peasantry (at least for some time), improving its relations with the Soviet government, and persuading President Kennedy to congratulate the position of the ruling regime, and acknowledging the shah's undisputed leadership [of the country].[2]

In 1960 'when the ruling regime was weak vis-à-vis both the

domestic situation and its external relations', the shah had sent Asadullah Alam three times to see Maleki and – during several hours of conversation – had tried to persuade him to have a private meeting with the shah. The meeting took place 'after the approval of the Socialist League's executive committee, and direct consultations with Messrs Sadiqi and Sanjaby'.[3] The shah had said that he would not mind if Saleh or another Front leader became prime minister, so long as the Front made clear its position towards the Constitution and the Tudeh party. Maleki had reported the matter to them but they took no steps at all:

At that time when the establishment was shaken and all sorts of concessions could have been extracted from it in favour of the Popular Movement, the announcement of a couple of words about the constitution and the Tudeh party could have clarified the Movement's position from both the domestic and foreign standpoints. But the [Front's] leaders remained silent over these two questions until they themselves became defenders of the constitution and constitutional monarchy, and – in response to the charges which the SAVAK was making against them – were forced to issue many public statements against the Tudeh party and radio broadcasts in Persian from the Soviet Union. Whereas, had they first clarified the position, they would not have been compelled to react to such charges.[4]

Thus, if the Front had acted wisely it could have come to power instead of Amini, and even during Amini's government it could have taken advantage of the rift within the establishment, and become its successor. 'But the Front's leaders also missed this opportunity with their amazing mistakes.' Yet he went on to add that even though the regime was now confident and satisfied with its successes, all was not lost, and the Popular Movement could still prepare itself for effective action:

A serious struggle lies ahead for which the Popular Movement of Iran should prepare itself. And since in this period the question of the relations between various social classes may become an important issue, the Popular Movement must have an appreciably more sophisticated social doctrine than before, and offer progressive solutions to the various socio-economic problems.[5]

Having written at some length about Khunji's and Hijazi's role in demoralizing the Third Force party after the coup when he himself was in jail, he explained:

> The reason why I have discussed this matter here is, to some extent, because these two traitors later went to the National Front, and no matter how much we warned the Front's leaders to be careful with them, they not only ignored our warnings but, instead, gave them the most important responsibilities regarding the Front's organizational and educational affairs . . . And now that their betrayals . . . have been exposed, the Front's activists and students are loudly protesting against this situation.[6]

In fact, Musaddiq had already been concerned about the tactics of the Front's leadership, and the conflict within the Movement, and had tried to help indirectly. His most effective intervention to date had been through the inscriptions underneath a photograph which he had issued some time in October or November (*Aban*) 1962. This put an end to the National Front's negotiations with Asadullah Alam, then prime minister, for forming a coalition government, or one that was acceptable to both sides. The episode was as follows.

After dismissing Amini in July 1962, and putting his own loyal servant in his place as a caretaker, the shah began to prepare for his newly-conceived White Revolution. The National Front was still strong, and he knew that he had to reckon with the opposition of the landlords and other forces who were opposed to land reform as well as his arbitrary rule. He decided to try and enlist the co-operation of the National Front, or at least to neutralize them over the crucial months ahead. The plan was first to isolate the Front's leaders, and then try to negotiate with them. The top leaders were arrested for a few weeks, and an agent was sent to talk to Saleh in prison. After consulting his colleagues, Saleh told the agent (Homayam San'atizadeh, a former Tudeh activist) that any settlement ('*qarar va madar*') should be left until the Front's leaders were released. Alam invited them for lunch at his home, Saleh invited him back, and the luncheon parties continued.[7] The shah's first proposal was that they nominate two established figures for the premiership, and he would give one of them the post. They suggested Abulqasim Najm (Najm al-Mulk) and Mohammad Sururi. Najm was not acceptable to the shah; he offered the post to Sururi (then, as under Musaddiq, President of the Supreme Court), but the latter declined the offer.[8] They then began to explore the possibility of forming a coalition government.

At this stage, Musaddiq got wind of what was afoot, and issued a photograph with the following inscription:

> To all those who, when there is a question of public interest, would put aside their private interests and personal views, to those who do not wheel-and-deal (*sazish*) in politics, and would bravely carry on and show persistence until victory, and to those who would sacrifice all they have for the freedom and independence of dear Iran, this unworthy picture is dedicated.[9]

As soon as Saleh saw the photograph (which was handed to him by Hasan Enayat, Musaddiq's notary public, who sometimes acted as a courier for him) he turned pale and said: 'What is the meaning of this; who's been wheeling-and-dealing?'[10] Other Popular Movement forces also received copies of the photograph, and the Freedom Movement reproduced and circulated them widely within the Popular Movement. The negotiations with Alam were stopped forthwith. Negotiations, as such, could not (and should not) have given cause for concern. The fact was, however, that the Front had done everything in its power to bring down Amini's government, in effect to the shah's (and *not* their own) advantage. And it now looked as if they were prepared to do a deal with the shah, without gaining anything for the Movement's aims and objectives.

As we saw above, the Front's leaders had again been interned late in February 1963, after their congress and the shah's referendum. At about the same time as Maleki wrote his letter to Musaddiq, the Students' Committee at the University of Tehran also wrote to him, sending him a whole file about the points of conflict arising from the congress. He wrote back saying that since the Front's leaders were then in jail there was 'no point in studying the record of the congress', and that he was returning the file for them 'to keep, because it might somehow be lost here'.[11]

While the Front's top leaders were still in jail, the regime announced in the summer that the 21st Majlis elections would be held in September. As we saw in chapter 15, while Amini was prime minister the National Front had spent almost all its energies demanding that he should hold elections for the Majlis. Students and other activists sent word to the leaders in jail, urging that the Front should fight the elections with all its force. The same indecisiveness prevailed; the leaders replied that 'prisoners should not express any views', and referred the students to the leaders who were free. The latter were of the opinion that the executive committee should give the lead, but they declined to commit themselves, and implied that the students were free to make their own decisions.[12] This they did, and planned a public meeting for 6 September in Baharistan Square. Two days before, the regime released all the Front's leaders, who issued a written order to the students not to hold the meeting.[13] The meeting was held, nevertheless, and was attacked by the police. In the event, the National Front took no part in the elections, and issued a directive to the students and other activists to go on 'vacation' (*murrakhasi*) for a month.

The Front's executive committee having resigned, the central council then held a series of meetings in the autumn of 1963 to reappraise the situation, in view of the fact that 'the regime's position has been strengthened'. They voted to give Saleh full executive powers, and he suggested that the Front should 'pass this period in patience and forbearance (*sabr va mitanat*), and refrain from any action which would lead to reactions [by the regime]'.[14] All members except Bakhtiyar, Furuhar and Kishavarz-i Sadr agreed to Saleh's full powers as well as his strategy of inaction; Bakhtiyar said that he was 'in agreement with the strategy of silence and quiet, but opposed to the granting of full powers to Mr Saleh'.[15] In the end, the council reaffirmed the powers and endorsed the 'wait and see' strategy. Two months later, when (on 20 March, 1964) the Students' Committee sent Musaddiq a letter of greetings for Oil Nationalization Day and the Persian New Year (which also included a report of their activities), he wrote back a short letter saying that he was 'extremely pleased that that worthy Committee are still concerned about the problems which face the people of Iran, and have not closed down [their activities]'.[16] By then, he had made up his mind to intervene directly in the Movement's troubled affairs.

Two days later, he wrote a lengthy letter in reply to the executive committee of the National Front Organizations in Europe which was to explode like a bombshell throughout the whole Movement. In their letter of 5 March, 1964, the committee had sent Musaddiq a report on their activities, emphasizing that they had disbanded the European outposts of the Popular Movement parties within the European organizations of the National Front. Musaddiq wrote in reply:

> I should be very grateful that that worthy Committee have
> informed me about the activities of the Front's European
> organizations . . . and that despite the fact that you have been
> aware of my message of 24 December 1961 to the first congress
> of the National Front via a recorded tape, you have decided to

disband the [Popular Movement] parties ... In my view, the action has not been right ... The National Front should be regarded as the central organization of all those parties which believe in a common principle, namely the freedom and independence of the country. If parties and groups are not to join the Front, the Front will become exactly what it now is ... and [they] are incapable of taking one step in defending [the rights of the people] ... They asked me to send them [i.e. the congress] a message, but paid no attention to it, and brought the Front into a state whereby it is unable to do anything ...[17]

The recipients decided to suppress the letter, thereby proving Musaddiq's point when – in reply to their request to name a leader – he had written with some sarcasm that if he did so 'no one would pay any attention to it'.[18] But he had sent copies to other Popular Movement parties and organs, and it was reproduced and circulated in Iran and published by the League of Iranian Socialists in Europe.

Almost exactly a week later, the Front's central council and new executive committee in Tehran wrote a letter to 'the exalted leader' explicitly in response to this letter which – as they said – 'has been reproduced and distributed by some people in Tehran'. It was a long letter and contained much unnecessary detail.[19] It claimed that parties had not been excluded from the Front, and that the Freedom Movement had been told that it could remain a member on condition that it purged its 'unreliable (*na-saleh*) elements' and sent a report on it to the Front's central council:

The Tudeh party is the only party which has repeatedly applied for membership of the National Front, and whose request has not been granted on account of its unacceptability [*adam-i salahiyat*) ... Because of this party's nature and policies, the Popular Movement has never wanted and will never want to admit it into its own ranks.[20]

The letter (which, with its references to 'the principle of centralization and democracy',[21] must have been drafted by Khunji) contained a long argument to the effect that the 1953 coup would have been avoided had the First National Front been organized along the lines of the Second. They then implicitly accused their Popular Movement critics of a plot to destroy the Front from within:

Since the beginning of the [Front's] activities these elements have analysed every decision of the Front — be it political or organizational — under the magnifying glass, in the hope of finding a point for attacking, provoking and falsifying [its activities], thus creating confusion and preventing the correct course of action. Right now, such elements are using your letter [to the Front's European organizations] for a propaganda drive against the organization of the National Front of Iran, so as to present us with an organizational and political crisis, and disappoint and disperse the activists.[22]

The letter concluded by saying that the Front's leadership now faced an even bigger dilemma because, on the one hand, to oppose Musaddiq's views 'is not in the interest of the country, the people or the Movement', and, on the other hand, it 'could not act against its own beliefs, and the decisions of the congress which has created this council':

If, despite the above explanations, his excellency still retains the views which he has expressed in that letter [to the European organizations], it may result in the destruction of the National Front's organization. And, given the great wave of opposition [to the regime] which has swept all classes [of people] there can be no doubt that the ruling establishment would be much happier to see the destruction of the only organization which can occupy its position in the interest of the people.

But the old man was not impressed either by the threat or the empty boast. His reply hit harder than ever. Alluding with sarcasm to the long lecture he had been given about parties and organizations, he said that they obviously had more experience of these matters, and that what little he had known about them he had forgotten during his eleven years of imprisonment and enforced isolation:

Yet when you were about to hold the congress you asked me to send a message which I obeyed, and I mentioned that the Front's gates should be opened to parties and groups . . . And I certainly did not have in mind the Tudeh party which you have named in your letter, and used as a stick (*pirahan-i Osman*). The Tudeh party is the same party which in the first year of the nationalization of oil vehemently opposed it, but — since society did not buy and approve of its views — it gave up its opposition to the oil nationalization policy, but in any case remained in opposition. [My reference was] to those parties and groups which were ready to sacrifice everything they had on the path to freedom.[23]

Why had the Socialist League not been invited to attend the Front's congress, he asked. They had asked the parties affiliated to the Front to supply the full list of their members and a brief description of their past activities to the Front's secretariat, and here he dealt a mortal blow to the leaders:

I am bound to say that, given the presence of a few of our betters (*az ma bihtaran*, i.e. agents of the regime) in the [Front's central] council, these people would be very naive to give their dossiers to the National Front ... and end up with the same fate as that of the poor his excellency.[24]

Immediately on receiving this letter, the central council called an emergency meeting. They wrote back explaining that they had had no intention of 'arguing with the esteemed leader', but had tried to show that the information which others had sent him was 'not in accord with the truth'. Once again, they went on to give unimportant details about the composition of their congress. However, they explained that since the Socialist League's application (of May 1961) for membership in the Front had been opposed by 'some of the gentlemen in the then executive committee of the Front', it had been decided not to take a decision on it, and their application 'has not been discussed in the central council to this day'. They concluded by saying that since he was 'the leader of the Popular Movement' they did not wish to confront him. On the other hand, they were not prepared to change their rules; therefore, unless he accepted the content of this and their previous letter 'this council would be unable to continue its work'.[25]

Musaddiq sent a copy of their letter to the Students' Committee, who wrote back answering it point by point. The Freedom Movement had not been admitted to the congress as a political party, only as individuals. The Socialist League's membership had not been considered (by their own admission) for three [though they said 'four'] years. The opposition within the Front itself consisted not of a few individuals and groups, but of all the affiliated parties other than the Iran party but including its youth and activists, as well as the bazaar and the university.[26] Musaddiq wrote a short reply congratulating them which concluded 'now that I am unable to do anything, and am living in jail, I pray God for your ever increasing success with a heavy heart and tearful eyes'.[27]

He still refused to give up, and wrote again to the council, enclosing the replies and reactions of the Students' Committee, the Freedom Movement, the Socialist League and the other dissident parties.[28] He once again told them to put aside their opposition to the full representation of all the Popular Movement parties and organs, and ended by saying that if they did not accept his suggestion, this would be his last letter to them.[29] They did not even bother to reply. Six weeks later (on 2 June 1964) he wrote an extremely polite and friendly (even humble) letter to Saleh, pleading with him to do something. Saleh wrote back saying that he himself was unwell, and that regarding the question of 'the Front's constitution, to which you have – once again – referred, the answer is the same as has been given to you in the formal letters of the Front's council and executive committee'.[30]

The regime was daily getting stronger, the Freedom Movement's top leaders had already been put on military trial, and the Front had been unable to do anything at the best of times. It was convenient (even if inglorious) to quit the stage quietly, and blame everything on Musaddiq's 'interference'. The leaders of the National Front Organizations in Europe who had been the keenest partisans of the Front's leadership in Tehran therefore wrote him a long letter accusing him of wishing to 'interfere in the affairs of the National Front after many years of inactivity'. He replied that – being incarcerated in Ahmad-Abad – he had no such intention, and had merely suggested a few changes in the Front's membership rules.[31] Having dealt so contemptuously with the man to whose immense prestige and popularity they owed almost all their public support, and whom they had otherwise turned into a useful idol, a single word from whom on any subject could be questioned by anyone (but themselves) at the cost of being described as a SAVAK agent, the Second National Front withered away, and most of its members in Europe (and some in Iran) soon turned to Maoism and other brands of Marxism-Leninism.

The Third National Front

Musaddiq continued his contact with the Popular Movement parties and forces, and decided to help them found a new front under his own guidance. Since 1960 he had been receiving an increasing number of messages from various party and student conferences in Iran and abroad, as well as reports and personal letters regarding the

Movement's activities. All of these were delivered to him by hand, usually by members of his family who were allowed occasional visits to Ahmad-Abad. Also, he was regularly asked by parties, groups and individuals to send them signed photographs, which they then reproduced and circulated within the Movement.

A permanent military guard was stationed in Ahmad-Abad, which kept all his visitors and other contacts under surveillance. When he began his direct intervention in the Movement's affairs, the SAVAK learned about it and informed the shah, who ordered them to intensify their surveillance and put pressure on the old man. The chief of the Tehran SAVAK himself began to turn up in Ahmad-Abad without prior notice, and behave 'as if he was trying to frighten a baby.[32] He asked the colonel in charge of the guard why they did not put a stop to Musaddiq's correspondence (although it is difficult to see how this could have been done without stopping members of his family from seeing him).[33] The colonel had said they had no specific orders on the matter, but later asked Musaddiq not to answer his letters. Musaddiq replied that they should either handcuff him, or put him on trial and keep him incommunicado as had been done after the coup, or at least write a letter telling him to stop his correspondence. Life was made more difficult for him by further restrictions. In September 1964, two months after these visits and contacts, he asked permission for a specialist physician to examine him, but this was denied.[34]

The Freedom Movement leaders – Bazargan, Sahabi, Taliqani – as well as some of their activists were still in jail. Two members of the Socialist League's executive committee – Manuchehr Safa and Abbas Aqilizadeh – were likewise put on military trial and condemned to three years' imprisonment. Many students and other activists were also in custody. But Maleki and other Socialist League leaders and many leaders of the other Popular Movement parties and the Students' Committee were still free, though their movements and contacts were under strict surveillance. The circumstances were extremely difficult even for holding small private meetings to continue the task of organizing the Third National Front.

But efforts continued on both sides – i.e. Musaddiq's as well as the Popular Movement forces – although it was a slow and painful process. The composition of the new Front and its constitution, rules and procedures had to be determined. The Iran party refused to co-operate or take part in it. Having become weary of 'the old and retired people whose sole purpose in sitting in the [Front's] council meetings is to pass the time',[35] Musaddiq was keen that no self-appointed leader should again find his way into the Third National Front. The new

Front's constitution was drafted early in 1965, and was personally approved by Musaddiq. The style and composition of its Article (1) gives the distinct impression that the final draft was written by the old man himself:

> The Third National Front is the centre of parties, political groups, religious societies, student societies, trade unions, professional bodies and local associations each of which have their own programme, but all of which share a single principle within the Third National Front, namely [a firm commitment to] the freedom and independence of Iran. Therefore, no one who is not a member of one of its affiliated bodies can sit on the National Front's council.[36]

On 29 July, Khalil Maleki wrote to Amir Pichdad (secretary of the League of Iranian Socialists in Europe) that there had been a lot of 'provocation' (by the Iran party leaders) against the new Front 'but it had not got, and would not get, anywhere':

> The Third National Front's first *ilamiyeh* was greeted with much enthusiasm. The eminent father [i.e. Musaddiq] fully approved of it, and said that nothing could be added to or subtracted from it.[37]

Commenting on the regime's increasingly harsh treatment of the activists, he added:

> This state of [political] strangulation has greatly weakened the subjective conditions for the struggle, although, in my view, the objective conditions are very good . . . Efforts are being made to overcome the weaknesses.

Here, though, he made an incorrect prediction:

> Although the regime had threatened the [Third National] Front's leaders, and especially our [Socialist League] friends [within its leadership] that the Third National Front should not be founded or else they would take strong measures against it, they have — nevertheless — not done anything. Perhaps because they now have confidence in themselves and their success.

Three weeks later, he and the remaining members of the Socialist

League's leadership – Alijan Shansi, Reza Shayan and Husain Sarshar – were arrested on the shah's personal orders, and were later tried and convicted in a military court.[38] Furuhar, Kazim Sami (of the People of Iran party) and others were also put behind bars. The Third National Front was thus bombed out of existence before it could get off the ground. The regime thus opened the gates for mass conversion to Maoism, other non-Tudeh Marxism-Leninism and Islamicism, and paid the price for it during and after the revolution of 1977–9 when the Popular Movement forces were too unfashionable and too battered to be able to lead events, although they still conducted themselves with greater wisdom and foresight than any other political force except the Islamic purists.[39]

The death of Musaddiq

A month before the regime's assault on the Third National Front, Musaddiq's wife died, and the loss of so close a life-long companion at the eclipse of his own life caused him insufferable grief. He wrote, in a brief reply to the condolences of a well-wisher:

> I am deeply in pain from this tragedy. Because for more than 64 years, my dear wife put up with everything I did, and – after my mother – she was my only hope for living. I longed to depart from this world before her. And now I pray God to take me soon, too, and relieve me of this pathetic existence.[40]

He had been abandoned by some of his closest former associates, the Movement had once more been defeated, its leaders and activists were in jail or on trial, his political contacts had been lost, the regime's pressures and restrictions had increased, and there was no hope for the future. On 26 March 1966 (during the Persian New Year) he wrote in reply to a well-wisher's greetings:

> After spending more than twelve years in two jails – that is, in the Second Armoured Division's prison, and now in Ahmad-Abad – I have been left with no spirit, and I constantly pray God for death so as to be relieved from this pathetic existence. I will not add any more to make you unhappy.[41]

In the autumn of 1966 his health deteriorated, and in December he was moved to a private house in Tehran, albeit under escort and constant watch, for regular treatment at the Najmiyyeh, the hospital endowed by his mother, where his son, Dr Gholam-Hossein, had been director for decades. He was suffering from cancer of the throat. The shah declined his family's request for permission to take him to Europe for treatment. In his last letter which is publicly available, he thanked the executive committee of the League of Iranian Socialists in Europe for their letter and enquiries after his health, and said that his electro-therapy treatment 'has made my condition worse than before'.[42] While under treatment for cancer, his old, chronic nervous illness led to an active bleeding of the stomach which could not be stopped. He died on 5 March 1967, at the age of 85.

He was deeply mourned by the public everywhere in the country, but a public funeral, mourning and memorial services were forbidden. His family's request to bury him, at his own express wish, by the side of the fallen of the uprising of 21 July 1952, was refused. Other public cemeteries were also declared out of bounds. In the end he was buried in his own home at Ahmad-Abad – where he had lived for a total of 24 years in exile – in the dining room on the ground floor of the house.

On the first anniversary of his death – which, in Iran, formally marks the end of the mourning period and is always observed by visiting the deceased's grave – the regime did its best to top thousands of visitors from Tehran. A month later, Maleki wrote to Pichdad (in Paris):

> Almost a month ago when, on the occasion of the anniversary of dear Musaddiq's martyrdom, we tried to go to Ahmad-Abad, they did not let us [at first]. In the end, the students told me that we should go with Dr Musaddiq's son. This we did, and took a wreath of flowers on behalf of the [Socialist] League. A group of people had assembled there, and thousands of others had been stopped [or arrested: *tawqif*] on the way. Our comrades [who, unlike myself, were not accompanying Musaddiq's son] were not allowed to come. But the students who were with us carried the wreaths of flowers with them with pomp and ceremony. The Iranian People's party (Furuhar) and the [Socialist] League were the only parties to present a wreath.[43]

On 5 March, 1979, less than a month after the fall of the shah's regime, over a million people travelled by every means of transport, as well as on foot, to gather at Musaddiq's graveside. But the occasion was not silent, and the noise camouflaged the political contracts which were quietly in the making.

The Popular Movement during the revolution:
a brief note

The revolution of 1977–9 caught the old Popular Movement forces unprepared. The collapse of the Second, and the quick suppression of the Third, National Front in the 1960s had exhausted and demoralized many of their leaders and activists. The change in the nature of the regime, from dictatorship to absolute and arbitrary rule, was devastating for an open movement in pursuit of democratic goals by peaceful means. Other developments both inside and outside the country led to the spread of Marxist and Islamic ideas, and the use of clandestine and violent tactics in fighting the regime.

The regime's strategy of economic development – if this is the appropriate term to use – enriched a small minority, frustrated an increasing majority, resulted in a massive and uncontrolled migration from village to town, and – in short – widened the gap between what actually existed and what the shah claimed there to be. In time, even those who obviously benefited from the oil bounty became dissatisfied with the regime, partly because they took these benefits for granted, and partly because they were angered and humiliated by a regime which, for example, forced them to join a 'political' party created overnight on the shah's orders.

The official imposition of cultural Americanism (which went much further than the Europeanism of the 1930s) became offensive now to a growing number of the modern middle class as well. The United States' uncritical involvement with the regime made matters worse: the public regarded the shah as literally the puppet of the United States; and they began to hold America directly responsible for all the country's ills – moral, cultural, political, economic and social.

World developments helped the tendency away from democratic goals, and towards romantic and millenarian solutions. Maoism – with its rejection of both the United States and the Soviet Union, its apparent Marxist-Leninist purity, and its revolutionary fervour – claimed large numbers of converts among Iranians at home and abroad, including many younger members of the Second National Front. The United States' folly in Vietnam added to its unpopularity, and helped popularize both revolutionary Marxism and guerrilla warfare in Iran. This was reinforced by America's total and uncritical commitment to the state of Israel, and by the Palestinian armed struggle, especially in view of the estrangement of the religious community from the Iranian regime after 1963, and the reaction against the regime's anti-traditionalism in society at large.

Put in a few words, the oil bounty became counterproductive, the US was believed to be destroying the country by means of the shah's regime, the suppression of all criticism and dissent both prevented and discredited peaceful movements for change, and revolutionary ideas and tactics – both Marxist and Islamic – became dominant. Yet, the movement which began early in 1977 and brought the regime down in February 1979 was launched by writers, lawyers and judges, and civil servants as well as old Popular Movement leaders such as Bazargan and Sanjaby. The Popular Movement forces were divided among the Freedom Movement, the Fourth National Front (which was hastily set up), and others who acted through human rights organizations and similar channels. There can be little doubt, however, that, had the shah been prepared to come to a genuine settlement with them – especially before, but even, to a lesser extent, after September 1978 – things would have turned out differently. For neither the bazaar, nor the civil service, nor the oil company (forces which both financed and led the general strike) would have supported a life-and-death struggle against an independent government led by Sanjaby or Bazargan. Indeed, such a government would have had the sympathy of senior religious leaders such as Ayatullah Shari'atmadari, and of Ayatullah Taliqani whose prestige as a national leader was then second only to that of Ayatullah Khomaini himself.

Even as late as November and December 1978, when the shah offered the premiership to Ghulamhusain Sadiqi, the subsequent history would have been different had he agreed to Sadiqi's condition that he should hand over all executive power to his proposed cabinet. Sadiqi was acting in his personal capacity, and did not join the National Front until after the revolution. But he was an able as well as highly-respected figure, and would have had a good chance had the shah agreed to his terms.

On the other hand, Shahpour Bakhtiyar's acceptance of the shah's offer, a few weeks later, was a different matter. He was not well known, let alone a popular figure, and his conduct during the Second National Front was remembered with bitterness and suspicion by Popular Movement activists. He was formally expelled from the National Front (of whose executive he was a member) for refusing to discuss the matter with them before accepting office. The result was that his action was seen as one of changing sides rather than leading a major tendency within the revolution itself towards an alternative solution. A couple of months before (in October 1978) Sanjaby had issued a public statement in Paris after seeing Khomaini, which effectively recognized Khomaini as the undisputed leader of the revolution. Sanjaby has subsequently been criticized for this decision, but the critics often overlook the fact that he had acted under great pressure from the Popular Movement activists and supporters as well as the rest of the revolutionary forces. Indeed, many, if not most, of the critics themselves had welcomed Sanjaby's statement with much enthusiasm at the time.[44]

Bazargan's short-lived provisional government after the revolution was isolated and powerless. From the start, it was confronted by the Islamic party as well as all the Marxist-Leninist parties. Its tenure of office can hardly be described as glorious. But the Freedom Movement, the National Front and other *melli* groups and individuals were almost the only people opposed to romantic zeal and revolutionary justice. Indeed, Bazargan's government resigned in November 1979 when Khomaini backed the hostage-taking of American diplomats in Tehran, though it had offered its resignation several times before.

Of the old Popular Movement figures, Maleki had died in July 1969 in poverty and destitution. Saleh and Shaigan both died in 1981, the former in Tehran, the latter in the United States. Taliqani and Zanjani died after the revolution. Bazargan lives in Tehran and is still leader of the Freedom Movement party. Sadiqi and Hasibi are also in Tehran, and Sanjaby lives in the United States.

Musaddiq's legend still survives, and the failure of both Marxist and Islamic romanticism has again begun to attract the politically active – old as well as new – to the principles and traditions of the Popular Movement of Iran.

18

The Movement and the man

The Movement and its origins

The Popular Movement of Iran is at least a century old. Its first important public manifestation occurred during the Tobacco-Régie struggle, although its social and intellectual origins go further back in history. At the time, the Movement's social composition included merchants, landlords, the religious leadership and community, the modernized elite and other urban classes, and its principal aim was to abolish arbitrary rule (*istibdad*) and foreign domination. The Constitutional Revolution itself was a product of the Movement. It went beyond the initial demand for an end to arbitrary rule, and aimed at establishing a democratic system of government. This was the Revolution's open and dominant trend, but it contained other forces which – at least with hindsight – can be seen as not belonging to the Popular Movement as it developed later in the century. First, the landlords and conservative religious leaders (e.g. Farmanfarma, Sipahsalar-i Tunukabuni, Bihbahani, Mukhbir al-Saltaneh Hedayat) who were opposed to arbitrary rule, but were not too keen about democracy or a serious struggle against foreign domination. Secondly, the dynamic, but still covert, intellectual trend (set by Akhunduf, Malkam Khan, Mirza Aqa Khan Kirmani, etc., and continued by Taqizadeh, Haidar Khan, Arif and others) who, while they vehemently opposed foreign (especially Russian) domination, were hoping to change Iranian society into one which almost exactly resembled a European country. The dominant trend was still opposed to foreign domination, but it was not pseudo-modernist: it was in favour of social and economic change, and the gradual adaptation of useful and relevant European techniques and ideas within the context of Iranian culture and history. In their different ways, Asad-Abadi (Afghani), Sur-i Israfil, Naini, Tabataba'i, Ashraf al-Din Husaini, Kuchik Khan, Sattar Khan, Khiyabani, Mudarris, Dehkhuda, Musaddiq and many others, represented this trend which, as mentioned above, dominated the Revolution in terms of its aims and slogans.[1]

The continuing fact of foreign intervention, the First World War, the Bolshevik Revolution, the centrifugal forces which had been unleashed throughout the land, the obvious economic backwardness, the conservatism of the landlord-dominated system which had inherited the ruling power, etc., helped to spread the ideas and aspirations of the Europeanist trend of the Constitutional Revolution among the modern educated classes, the bureaucratic and military elites, and the younger and lesser religious figures. This became the main nationalist force in the country, a force which was acutely and uncritically conscious of real and imagined ancient Iranian glories, which saw little use in the existing Iranian culture, regarded religion (and the Arabs) as almost the sole cause of the country's decline, and aimed at *replacing* what there was with a European model. At first, its political model was exclusively derived from the Kaiser's Germany, the successful and powerful Aryan country, the enemy of Britain and Russia, and the hot-bed of modern theories of nationalism in general, and Aryanism in particular. The Bolshevik Revolution supplied another model which captured the imagination of a minority of the nationalists. Both nationalist trends co-operated in bringing down the Constitutional regime, and replacing it with Reza Shah's dictatorship. The landlords and conservative religious leaders were unhappy about these developments, but they bowed to 'the inevitable' in the hope of mellowing the process. The democratic trend of the Constitutional Revolution – the Popular Movement – fought against, but was defeated by, it. Mudarris, Musaddiq, Mustawfi, Mushir, Mu'tamin, etc. were its political leaders and spokesmen at the time (see chapter 3).[2]

Reza Shah's dictatorship quickly turned into arbitrary rule, and alienated landlords, merchants and the whole of the religious leadership, apart from individual religious leaders who accepted the new model and moved into other professions. It also alienated the pro-Bolshevik nationalists (who, by then, had formed small Socialist and Communist groups and parties), partly by its very nature, but perhaps mainly as a result of the deteriorating relations with Stalin's Russia.

Reza Shah's enforced abdication in 1941 brought a completely new political atmosphere. The new shah still symbolized Pahlavi nationalism, especially within the army, but had to depend heavily on landlords, conservative politicians and (later) the British government for his survival. The Tudeh party at first represented a coalition of Communist as well as popular forces, but soon became an instrument of Soviet diplomacy, and lost its broad popular base after the Azerbaijan adventure. During the Fourteenth Majlis, Musaddiq emerged as the leading figure and spokesman of the Popular Movement, with his clear and unequivocal opposition both to British and Soviet influence in Iran, and to dictatorship and corruption. Many had sought to follow the aims of the Movement through the Tudeh party at first. It was therefore no coincidence that that party's quick abdication of this role led to the swift rise of the Popular Movement independently from it, as soon as the proposed Gass-Gulsha'iyan agreement offered itself as an appropriate issue. As has been shown throughout this book, the binding factor in the whole of the Movement was the twin (and inseparable) objectives of independence and democracy.

The shah and the conservatives wanted dictatorship and an inevitably subservient alliance with the West. The Tudeh wanted their own brand of dictatorship, and an inevitably subservient alliance with the Soviet Union. The Popular Movement wanted independence, non-alignment, and a democratic system which was firmly rooted in Iranian culture and society, including the traditions of the Constitutional Revolution. Nothing is quite inevitable, but it is perhaps not surprising that the Movement was finally defeated by the opposition of the other two forces, and their foreign patrons and allies.

Melli and nationalism

In its classical use the word *mellat* referred to peoples of given religions, hence *mellat-i Islam*, *mellat-i Masih*, etc. Hence, also, a famous reference by Hafiz to 'the seventy-two *mellats*'. There are literally countless examples of this in Persian history and literature. In the nineteenth century, while still retaining its classical sense, the term began to be used to mean 'the people' as opposed to 'the state'. For example, in the meetings where the leaders of the Tobacco-Régie rebellion negotiated with representatives of the state, the former were described as representatives of *mellat*, and the latter, of *dawlat*.[3] *Mellat* did not therefore have the same socio-historical meaning as the European 'nation', although later in the twentieth century this European term and concept was translated as *mellat* at least in part because no equivalent for it existed in Persian language or society.

Mellat is separate from *dawlat* and is contrasted with it, whereas the European 'nation' includes the state.

The term *melli* was almost certainly coined around the turn of the century as an adjective: *mellat* meant the people; *melli*, popular. 'Democracy' was then translated into '*hukumat-i melli*', or popular (though not *populist*) government, and has retained this sense ever since. However, later in the century when *mellat* began to be used in translation for 'nation', *melli* was likewise used for the European 'national' as opposed to 'international'. Yet, in the division of firms and industries into private and state-owned, *melli* persisted as meaning non-state, as in the case of private schools, and *dawlati* as meaning state-owned, as in the case of 'the state radio', or 'the state railways'. The major exceptions to this rule occurred in the names of Bank Melli and the National Iranian Oil Company, in which case it meant that they were non-foreign as opposed to the Imperial Bank and the Anglo-Iranian Oil Company which they replaced. It is only since the 1960s that the term *melli* has also been used to describe a few other state monopolies.

However, although *melli has* been used to mean 'national' as opposed to 'foreign' or 'international', it *has not* been used to mean 'nationalist'. In this case, the Franco-Persian 'nasionalist' was invariably used, for example, by the shah in the 1950s, when he was fond of describing himself as a '*nasionalist-i musbat*' (positive nationalist). The term was never used by Musaddiq, nor by any other leading figure in the Movement as a description of the Popular Movement, or of its aims and aspirations.[4]

The above argument is not simply linguistic but, in particular, cultural and sociological as well. Yet we can put all that aside and look at the question from a completely different angle. The question is whether or not the Popular Movement can be legitimately described as a nationalist movement?

Nationalism – much like many other social and political concepts and categories – is all things to all men: it sometimes means the ideology of the bourgeoisie in its earlier developments, and sometimes that of the petty bourgeoisie in the later stages of industrial capitalism. To some, it is the ideological weapon of militarist and expansionist dictatorships; to others, the political instrument of movements for freedom from colonialism. It is a domain in which Cromwell, Napoleon, Garibaldi, Bismarck, Ataturk, Hitler, Mussolini, Franco, Reza Shah, Gandhi, Musaddiq, Nasser – perhaps even Stalin and Mao Tse-tung, as well as Chiang Kai Shek – are deemed, in the annals of history, to have held important tenancies. The subject becomes further complicated when an Abu-Muslim Khurasani, a Joan of Arc or an Alexander Nevsky is also included in the illustrious list. Yet, there are important differences – and sometimes palpable contradictions – in the thoughts, deeds, aspirations and achievements of these figures, and the movements which they led and symbolized. Are we not in danger, then, of reducing the concept of nationalism from an analytical, if not scientific, category to a mere tautology?

For the purpose of this short discussion, let us propose two separate concepts of 'nationalism': *Romantic nationalism*, or the hysterical passion to prove the superiority of the Great Nation, often through the denigration, humiliation and subjugation of other peoples; and *democratic patriotism*; that is, the social and psychological urge to defend one's home, culture, social existence, political sovereignty and economic independence from the aggressive designs of powerful states. Romantic nationalism is a holistic and organic vision, in theory, and a chauvinistic, if not racist, attitude in practice. By contrast, democratic patriotism, though like any other concept it has its abstract and idealized counterparts, is, in essence, an open and realistic conception both in theory and application. Its principal aim is to liberate, not subjugate; to free, not enslave; to generate constructive energies, not release destructive forces. Within a given nation state, romantic nationalism has been often – though not always – the ideology of rulers, while democratic patriotism has tended to represent the hopes and aspirations of the ruled.

When we speak of nationalism in modern Iran, and perhaps other Third World countries, we face yet another dimension of the problem. For like Liberalism, Marxism, the motor-car and micro-electronic chips, modern nationalism is a product of *European* history. And, like some of these other ideas and techniques, it has been either uncritically copied and adopted or, less often, critically adapted and applied to Iranian society from its European source.

The application of romantic nationalism would almost inevitably involve aping and emulation as opposed to learning and adaptation. For all it requires is to take the basic slogans about the glories of, not the Great Nation, but the once-great nation which has now sunk to its knees because of metaphysical misfortunes, demonological conspiracies, or real and imagined injustices at the hands of the less glorious but more powerful nations – to take such slogans, sentiments, passions and professions from their European sources, and dress them in local garb.

Democratic patriotism, on the other hand, would involve adaptation, assimilation, and integration into the local culture and tradition.

For if it is to be realistic and open to criticism, it has to be understood
and accepted within the cultural framework of the wider political
public. That is to say, although modern patriotic, anti-colonial and
democratic sentiments do not stem from cultural or political
traditionalism, they still have to be based on the country's history and
experience in order to make social and political sense. The Indian
freedom movement was an example of democratic patriotism in a
modern colonial and developing country.

Regarding nationalist movements in modern Iran, the Popular
Movement represented democratic patriotism, while the Pahlavi state
was the official manifestation of romantic nationalism. Here, though,
we run into an apparently serious difficulty. Until a few years ago, not
only the opposition but also many of those who collaborated with the
Pahlavi state were convinced that it was no more than a product and
puppet of the Western powers. Reza Shah was a British agent, pure
and simple, and his successor was first a British, then an American
puppet. How can foreign agents and puppets be described as
nationalists of *any* type? There is no need to become entangled in a
web of 'pros' and 'cons' on this subject, for both reason and the
evidence strongly suggest that these men were not paid agents of
foreign powers. In their attempts to impose and maintain their absolute
and arbitrary rule over a weak and dependent country, they took care
not to provoke the wrath of the great powers against themselves; and,
at the same time, they tried to use these powers to their own
advantage, even, when necessary, at the expense of their country.
Theirs was the nationalism of all-powerful rulers in an otherwise weak
and vulnerable society. It is perhaps of more significance, however, that
the rise of romantic nationalism in Iran was neither due to a foreign
conspiracy, nor even the product of one or two powerful arbiters. On
the contrary, Reza Khan himself was largely a product of the romantic
nationalist and pseudo-Europeanist sentiments and values which swept
Iran after the First World War.[5]

The Popular Movement could be described as 'nationalist' only in the
democratic-patriotic sense described above, although if the application
of the concept of nationalism is legitimate in such a case, then it would
mean that any and every political force and party anywhere in the
world which does not sell its country short to outside powers must be
described as nationalist. In any event, within the broad confines of its
fundamental principles, the Popular Movement had its own right- and
left-wing parties, trends and supporters. Hence Khalil Maleki's
distinction between what he called 'the Third Force in general' and 'the
Third Force in particular' (see chapter 8).

The man and his make-up

Musaddiq's political attitude and practice were entirely consistent with these fundamental principles. He opposed the 1919 Agreement and the granting of an oil concession to the Soviet Union, and nationalized Iranian oil expressly in order to guarantee Iran's 'freedom and independence'. He opposed Reza Shah's dictatorship and his successor's attempts to do the same whenever he could, fought against election rigging and other encroachments on the rights of the people, and against financial privilege and bureaucratic corruption, and defended democracy and extended it further through progressive legislation in the brief period when he was prime minister. He supported the adaptation of modern ideas and techniques, but opposed romantic emulations which went against what he himself described as Iran's cultural identity (*iraniyat*). He wanted 'freedom and independence', the rule of law, democracy, and modernization based on cultural realism and the people's consent.

Most of his life he suffered from a nervous illness which was apparently never diagnosed as a chronic problem. But he himself was aware of it at least on certain occasions. In his *Memoirs* and elsewhere he mentioned a debilitating disease while he was a student in Paris, which was apparently cured after he returned home and spent some time with his family. He put it down to the pressure of academic work, and this was not inconsistent with general nervous frailty (see chapter 1).[6] Returning to Iran from Switzerland in 1914, he reported that he took to his bed with a fever on account of some false rumours which a newspaper had spread about him, and that his mother had told him: 'The weight of individuals in society is determined by the amount of hardship they endure for the sake of the people'.[7]

As governor of Azerbaijan – after he fell foul of the local magnates – he began to fear for his life, began to bleed in the mouth, and felt so exhausted that his doctor advised him to isolate himself, and talk as little as possible, a recommendation which is normally made in cases of hypertension (see chapter 2).[8] The bleeding in his throat in 1935, for the treatment of which he eventually travelled to Germany in 1936, was described as 'nothing' by the two German specialists who examined him. When he was in jail after the 1953 coup, blood began to appear in his urine, and he connected it with the old haemorrhage in his mouth and throat, though he said nothing about a possible neurological basis in either case (see chapter 3).[9] In 1964, when he complained to the SAVAK against their decision to stop a physician from examining him, he opened his letter by saying: 'For many years now I catch cold and have a temperature at the slightest wind, antibiotics have been of little help, and so far none of my doctors has been able to diagnose my illness'.[10] Apparently, he did not suspect that these mysterious colds which he caught regularly might be related to his old nervous problems. He died in the end because of a stomach haemorrhage while he was receiving electro-therapy treatment for cancer.

He was quick to quit the stage in anger and frustration. He went to Switzerland during the negotiatons for the 1919 Agreement, and led a desperate campaign against it in Europe when, on scanty evidence, he felt that he was being watched by British agents (see chapter 2).[11] On receipt of the news from Tehran that the Agreement had been concluded, he was so acutely unhappy that he decided to become a Swiss citizen and stay in Europe for the rest of his life.[12] In 1921 he became finance minister and made so many enemies by his frontal attacks on some of the country's most powerful people – including the Prince Regent – that the whole cabinet fell, and some of his personal friends – such as Samsam al-Saltaneh (Bakhtiyari) – refused to speak to him. He felt ostracized in Tehran, and this was one reason why he agreed to go to Tabriz as governor of Azerbaijan. But the minute he felt that Reza Khan was trying to restrict his hold over the security forces in the province, he resigned and returned to Tehran despite prime minister Qavam's express wishes that he should remain at his post (see chapter 2).[13]

In the Fifth and Sixth Majlis he made a persistent stand against growing dictatorship and encroachments on the public's rights and freedoms. But when (predictably) he was not allowed to be elected by a free vote in the Seventh, he quickly withdrew from the political scene and Tehran itself, long before the regime could openly or indirectly confine him to Ahmad-Abad. He remained there even after his official exile was lifted in 1941, and re-entered politics only when he was elected the first deputy for Tehran, virtually *in absentia*. After his energetic one-man opposition in the Fourteenth Majlis, he vigorously campaigned against Qavam's rigging of the Fifteenth Majis elections. Having failed to arouse sufficient public support, he went back to Ahmad-Abad openly protesting that he was quitting politics for good. Yet, as soon as the small opposition in that Majlis began its noisy campaign against the proposed Gas-Gulsha'iyan Supplemental Oil Agreement, and directly asked him to come and lead the Movement, he returned with his familiar zeal and vigour (see chapters 4, 5 and 6).

In July 1952, he resigned as prime minister without the slightest fuss, apparently because of the shah's insistence on appointing the war minister himself. He would, in any case, not have agreed to this, but we now know that the real reason why he resigned in the manner he did was because he was certain that the International Court would decide in favour of Britain's case against Iran. Indeed, he had planned to live permanently abroad if this happened (see chapter 9). Several times he left parliamentary meetings in frustration, threatening never to return; the most famous occasion was when he described the Fourteenth Majlis as a 'den of thieves', and returned to it only after his supporters gathered outside his house and carried him back to the Majlis (see chapter 5).

He was frequently unwell, and this must have been a reason for his interest in herbal and traditional medicines.[14] He was easily moved, and often had a lump in his throat when he spoke in public. On a few occasions he broke down and wept while delivering a formal speech; a couple of times he even fainted in public, although the frequency of these public faints and weepings has been greatly exaggerated by his detractors. He was frequently in a state of extreme nervous tension. Once, after a difficult meeting with the shah, Karim Sanjaby found him shivering though it was midsummer, and he explained that there were times when he shivered in the summer heat and other times when he sweated in the winter cold.[15]

Most of his life he was formally dressed in public, and the image which his foreign detractors made of him as a prime minister who wore pyjamas was much exaggerated. But he increasingly tended to work in bed during the latter part of his premiership, and receive official visitors in bed while wearing domestic clothes made of a cheap Iranian-made material which ordinary people wore at the time. He told Jalil Buzurgmehr (his defence counsel in the military court) that the reason why he frequently worked in bed when he was prime minister was because this would excuse him from attending official parties and banquets which he did not enjoy.[16] It is well known that people with his kind of sensitivity and personality are wary of formal and impersonal contacts, especially in large gatherings. The reason why he virtually stopped going to the Majlis (which was normally expected, but not legally required) after Baqa'i and the others went over to the opposition must have been due to the same psychological inhibitions.

He was angry and defiant in 1940 when he was arrested without charge, and fearful that he might suffer the fate of Mudarris and many others who had been murdered in jail with indignity. He swallowed a fistful of tranquillizers, which he carried in his pocket, with the express purpose of committing suicide, and was only saved by the weakness of his stomach and the roughness of the road to Mashad. The prison governor in Birjand was worried that he might try it again, and the Mashad police chief informed the General Police HQ in Tehran that the prisoner suffered from 'chronic hysteria (*bimari-yi ghash*)'. Musaddiq himself had used the European term *hysteria* in talking to Makki when the latter was his disciple, and he used it in his book on Musaddiq at the same time (see chapter 3).[17] It is clear therefore that Musaddiq himself was well aware of his nervous problems, although, apparently, he did not think that his chronic ailments and frailties might be related to them.

He was an extremely polite, kind, modest (even, at times, humble) man. But he did not suffer fools gladly, and would not succumb to aggressive pressures. He might well have given Kashani and Baqa'i what they wanted if he had been asked nicely. But perhaps their personalities were similar to his in this respect, and this may have been the source of the problem between them. His treatment of the Second National Front leaders, though hardly unmerited, was not sufficiently diplomatic. They owed almost all their popular support to their public idolization of him, and yet they were not prepared to pay the slightest attention to his advice which was reasonable, realistic and essential for the survival of the Movement. Nevertheless, he might have been more sensitive to their personality traits, in the hope of getting a more positive response. This, incidentally, is also true of Khalil Maleki's open and direct, though accurate, criticisms of their political feebleness and incapacity (see chapters 16 and 17).

Musaddiq was not a demagogue, and was far from being a rabble-rouser. Throughout his long public career, he seldom addressed public meetings or attended demonstrations. The openness and directness which were characteristic of his parliamentary speeches (especially when he was in opposition) reflected both his personality and his firm commitment to his principles. He was extremely good at making personal enemies on account of the same openness and directness, and the refusal to give in to aggressive pressures which his critics perceived as stubbornness, inflexibility and 'negativism' (*manfi-bafi*). There certainly was an idealistic streak in his public and private conduct, but he did understand political processes and – unlike many of his colleagues – had the courage to take difficult and unpopular decisions. He was not afraid of the mighty, whether powerful individuals or 'the masses'. His frailties were of an altogether different kind.

Objectively, he did everything he could to settle the oil dispute honourably, except when he rejected the World Bank's intervention (which was no more than an interim measure), although we know that he himself had been inclined to accept it (see chapter 11). Yet, his

openness and honesty wounded British pride, and turned the oil
company and the British establishment into his personal enemies even
before he had become prime minister. True, he would have had to go
against his own nature, and bend the Movement's principles somewhat
to make a deal which countries like Holland and Sweden would never
have been expected nor prepared to make had they had a similar
dispute with Britain. Yet, had he done so, the country would have had
a much better fate than it has suffered since his violent downfall. For
he had managed to achieve his most basic programme, and cut back
Britain's improper influence in Iran, as he himself realized later and
argued both at his trials and in his *Memoirs*.

Indeed, the shah was the beneficiary of this historic achievement of
Musaddiq and the Popular Movement. Iran's later troubles were
largely due to dictatorship (later, arbitrary rule), corruption and feeble
political leadership rather than sinister interferences in its domestic
affairs by foreign powers. And to the extent that some of these
interferences survived, they were mainly the product of the domestic
political system. Had the Popular Movement not been violently
suppressed, the country would have been able to use its newly-won
'freedom and independence' for genuine political, social and economic
development, even in the absence of an absolutely just settlement of the
oil dispute. In time this, too, would have been put right, perhaps even
sooner than the 1970s when the shah and his system benefited from
massive oil revenues and left the country to pay for their follies.

Khalil Maleki saw the truth of this, analysed it, and wrote many
tracts and articles on it (see chapter 8). Like Musaddiq, he, too, was an
outsider in his own context, and believed that open, direct and rational
arguments would suffice to convince all. Maleki did not work in bed,
but otherwise he ignored the use of instrumental political and personal
contacts, and played into the hands of his enemies by making 'friends'
feel jealous, offended, confused and suspicious. On the other hand, it is
perhaps only outsiders, like these two men, with their extraordinary
capacity to suffer isolation and persecution, who can break important
new ground and make historic achievements, in both science and
society. There are always others like them with intelligence and
intellectual potential who become important leaders in their own fields.
Their worldly success is much more than that of the great outsiders;
their historical achievements, far less. The former are men of their own
times; the latter, men for all times.[18]

For all these reasons, Musaddiq should never have become prime
minister. He did not want the office and would not have captured it
except for an outside chance. Like all outsiders, like Blum, like

Churchill, like De Gaulle, Musaddiq was swept to power by extraordinary circumstances. Normal politics require lesser men. Yet, for the circumstances in which he and the country were caught, Musaddiq produced the best government that Iran has had this century. Even if we set aside the questions of freedom, democracy, rule of law, independence, etc., the achievements of his cabinets were not unimpressive, given the great economic and political constraints within which they worked: his ministers were honest, qualified and responsible to the public; his management of the economy was realistic; and his legal, administrative and social reforms were extensive but restrained (see chapter 10). He is sometimes criticized for not having organized the Popular Movement into an effective political force when he was in power. But he lacked the personal and political attributes for this; he was not an executive organizer and he left this to others who had already begun the task and would have taken it much further had the Movement not been defeated so quickly. The greatest shortcoming of his government was its tolerance of overt and covert violations of the law by the shah, the conservatives and the Tudeh party. Had it not done so, it is unlikely that he and the Movement would have suffered the fate they did. At least he should have backed the Third Force party's readiness to organize 'Popular-Movement district committees' and a 'Popular-Movement guard', which they desperately argued were necessary to defend the Movement from illegal blows against it which they likewise predicted long before they happened (see chapters 8 and 12).[19]

Flaubert once said of Renan, 'If a man is *someone*, why should he want to be *something*?' The same could have been said about Musaddiq. His greatness made him behave with modesty; his pride enabled him to be humble; his self-assuredness made him feel ill at ease with lesser mortals (except when he was sure of their approval); his personality was better suited for leading the Movement with a free hand rather than coping with the enormous administrative problems which he faced as prime minister. In thought as well as in action, he could rise well above ordinary mortals, and be ready to pay the price for it. His achievements and his failures combined to make him one of the outstanding men of this century: the personification of his people's aspirations for independence and dignity outside, and for recognition as citizens within, their own country.

Notes

1 From Mirza Mohammad to Dr Musaddiq

1 See Afzal al-Mulk, *Afzal al-Tavarikh* (ed. Mansureh Ittihadiyyeh and Sirus Sa'dvandiyan), (Tehran: Nashr-i Tarikh-i Irran, 1982), p.83.

2 i.e. belonging to the Iranian bureaucracy, selection for which involved a relatively high degree of social mobility.

3 For example, Mirza Yusif Mustawfi al-Mamalik and his son, Mirza Hasan of the same name; Mu'tamid al-Saltaneh and his sons, Vusuq al-Dawleh and Qavam al-Saltaneh; Vazir Daftar, and his son Musaddiq.

4 See his Fourteenth Majlis speech in Husain Kay-Ustuvan, *Siyasat-i Muvazineh-yi Manfi*, vol. 2 (Tehran, 1950).

5 See *Musaddiq's Memoirs* (London: Jebhe, 1988), chapter 5.

6 Quoted by Musaddiq himself on many occasions, including *ibid.*, and Jalil Buzurgmehr (ed.) *Taqrirat-i Musaddiq dar Zindan* (Tehran: Sazman-i Kitab, 1980).

7 First Mirza Fazlullah Vakil al-Mulk, the father of Hishmat al-Dawleh (Vala-tabar), and later Siqat al-Mulk (Diba).

8 He himself explained this youthful appointment, by pointing out, with some embarrassment, that such appointments were quite usual at the time. See *Musaddiq's Memoirs*, chapter 5.

9 See Mohammad Reza Shah Pahlavi, *Mission for My Country* (London: Heinemann, 1960), chapter 5.

10 i.e. Abdulmajid Mirza Ain al-Dawleh, then chief minister.

11 See, for details, Nazim al-Islam Kirmani, *Tarikh-i Bidari-yi Iranian* (ed. Sa'idi Sirjani) (Tehran: Agah-Nuvin, 1982), and Ahmad Kasravi, *Tarikh-i Mashruteh-yi Iran* (Tehran: Amir Kabir, 1947).

12 See *ibid.*

13 See, for example, Denis Wright, *The Persians Amongst the English* (London: I.B. Tauris, 1985).

14 For an almost literal version of this view, see Hasan Ayat, *Chehreh-yi Haqiqi-yi Musaddiq al-Saltaneh* (Tehran: Intisharat-i Islami, 1984).

15 See, for example, Buzurgmehr, *Taqrirat*, and *Musaddiq's Memoirs*.

16   See, for example, Buzurgmehr, *Taqrirat*.

17   For well-documented examples, see Kirmani, *Tarihk-i Bidari*, vol. 2.

18   These letters have recently been discovered by Abbas Amanat who has kindly put copies of all of them at this author's disposal. Five of them were written by Musaddiq in his own handwriting and the remaining four (two of which are quite long) are in another hand but with insertions or additions by Musaddiq. Those written by Musaddiq are undated, while the others are dated 13, 18, 20 and 25 Safar. No year is mentioned, but they include many references to the First Majlis. In Safar 1325 (A.H., lunar) Farmanfarma was in Tehran (cf. Kirmani, *Tarikh-i Bidari*, vol. 2), and in Safar 1327, he was no longer governor of Azerbaijan. Therefore, the letters must have been written in 1326, i.e. 1907. The other correspondent may have beem Musaddiq's elder brother (Mirza Husain Khan Vazir Daftar) though there is no proof of this.

19   See, for example, Buzurgmehr, *Taqrirat*.

20   His stepfather's son, Hishmat al-Dawleh, happened to be the shah's private secretary at the time, and helped him in many ways on account of his known Constitutionalism, though Musaddiq says he generally did what he could for those who were persecuted by *dawlati-ha* (i.e. those on the side of the state) – a highly significant use of language for understanding Iran's historical sociology. See *Memoirs*, chapter 7.

21   Though he mentioned, or alluded to, the illness itself on many occasions. See, for example, *Memoirs*, and Buzurgmehr, *Taqrirat*.

22   It led to internal bleeding and at least one suicide attempt, and was the immediate cause of his death in the end.

23   See Musaddiq's Fourteenth Majlis speech in which he attacked Reza Shah's arbitrary method of removing women's *hijab* in Kay-Ustuvan, *Siyasat-i Muvazeneh*, vol. 2, p. 79.

24   Musaddiq was to remember Shaikh Mohammad Ali with great admiration in a Fourteenth Majlis speech, because he had refused to remove his turban and wear a 'Pahlavi hat' instead, when this had been made compulsory under Reza Shah: he had not left his house until his death. See *ibid.*, p. 79, and Buzurgmehr, *Taqrirat*, p. 150.

2   Academic, administrator and politician

1   For a detailed pro-German account of events, see Abulqasim Kahhalzadeh, *Dideh-ha va Shinideh-ha*, (ed. Murtiza Kamaran) (Tehran: Nashr-i Farhang, 1983). For pro-German poets and poetry, see Yahya Arianpur, *Az Saba ta Nima* (Tehran: Jibi, 1978), vol. 2. For an eye-witness account of some of the events, especially in the Fars province, see Ahmad Akhgar, *Zindigi-yi Man . . .* (Tehran: Akhgar, 1987).

2   The young Jamalzadeh crossed the European battlefields into Egypt, and finally managed to reach Baghdad via the Red Sea and the Arabian desert to become the provisional government's consul in that city – a post which did not last for long, but which inspired his moving, anti-Russian short story, 'The Friendship of Auntie Bear'.

3 *Memoirs*, Book I, chapter 14.
4 See 'Isqat-i D'avi', *Majalleh-yi Ilmi*, no. 1, 1293 (1914), reprinted in Iraj Afshar (ed.), *Musaddiq va masa'il-i Huquq va Siyasat* (Tehran: Zamineh, 1979).
5 The Persian terms have been translated here into their French originals.
6 See Afshar, *Musaddiq va Masa'il*, p. 19–24. Emphasis added.
7 See *ibid.*, pp. 39–48.
8 'Al-Dharuryat-i Tabiyh al-mahzurat' (a *Shari'a* tradition).
9 Afshar, *Musaddiq va Masa'il*, pp. 49–55.
10 *Ibid.*, p. 53.
11 However, given the trouble his nerves had caused and were to cause him in the future, the diagnosis may have been wrong, and he could have been suffering from acute stomach cramps instead.
12 He was declared an infidel by an obscure divine after his opponents twisted a single sentence in his thesis. Decades later, the military prosecutor was to bring the matter up again and again in Musaddiq's trials after the 1953 coup, accusing him of abandoning Islam. See *Memoirs*, chapters 14 and 17.
13 The member in question was Mirza Ahmad Khan Ashtari. See further, *Memoirs*, chapter 17.
14 See Buzurgmehr, *Taqrirat*, p. 49.
15 *Memoirs*, chapter 19; also Buzurgmehr, *Taqrirat*.
16 *Memoirs*, Book I, chapter 20, and Buzurgmehr, *Taqrirat*, chapter 11. Throughout the Constitutional era (i.e. after 1909) Musaddiq never drew his salary as minister, Majlis deputy or prime minister.
17 See *inter alia*, *Memoirs*, Buzurgmehr, *Taqrirat*, and Musaddiq, *Nutqha va Maktubat*, vol. 8 (Paris: Intisharat-i Musaddiq, 1971) p. 9.
18 For a comprehensive history of the SPR see Floreeda Safiri, *Pulis-i Junub-i Iran* (Tehran: Nashr-i Tarikh-i Iran, 1986). For a personal account of some of the events involving the SPR, see Akhgar, *Zindigi-yi Man*.
19 *Memoirs*, chapter 20, and Kay-Ustuvan, *Siyasat-i Muvazeneh*, vol. I.
20 Cited in Donald N. Wilber, *Riza Shah Pahlavi: The Resurrection and Reconstruction of Iran* (New York: Exposition Press, 1975).
21 See further Husain Makki, *Tarikh-i bist Saleh-yi Iran*, vol. 1 (Tehran, 1943); M T. Bahar, *Tarikh-i Mukhtasar-i Ahzab-i Siyasi dar Iran* (Tehran, 1944); and Ibrahim Khajeh-Nuri, *Bazigaran-i Asr-i Tala'i* (Tehran, 1942–5).
22 Bahar himself had been contacted by Smart only three days before the coup. But, for reasons which are not clear, he had decided not to commit himself then, or immediately after the coup when Sayyed Zia asked for his co-operation. See further, Bahar, *Tarikh-i Mukhtasar*.
23 Cited in R. H. Ullman, *The Anglo-Soviet Accord: Anglo-Soviet Relations, 1917–1921* (Princeton NJ: Princeton University Press, 1921) p. 387. For a study of Reza Khan (and Reza Shah), see H. Katouzian, 'Reza Shah Pahlavi: The Making of an Arbitrary Ruler', paper presented to Centre for Middle Eastern Studies, Harvard University, April 1988, and forthcoming in Reza Shaikoleslami (ed.).
24 See H. Katouzian, 'Nationalist Trends in Iran, 1921–1926', *The International Journal of Middle East Studies*, November 1979); and 'Iranianism and

Romantic Nationalism', in Paul Luft (ed.), *Literature and Society in Iran Between the Two World Wars*, forthcoming.

25 He did the same decades later when he was prime minister with similar reactions (see chapter 14 below). In this case the combination of vested interests and the extraordinary powers of the Majlis would not have allowed any reform to proceed without such a temporary delegation of power. Indeed, they aborted the reforms even after granting him the powers he had asked for.

26 See for example, Abdullah Mutawfi, *Sharh-i Zindigani-yi Man*, vol. 3 (Tehran, 1962) for a full (and sympathetic) contemporary account of the whole event by someone other than Musaddiq himself. See also *Memoirs*, Buzurgmehr, *Taqrirat*, and Afshar. *Musaddiq va Masa'il*.

27 See *Memoirs* and Buzurgmehr, *Taqrirat* for his own detailed and somewhat entertaining account of various events and episodes.

28 *Memoirs*, Book I, chapter 22.

29 See further Katouzian, 'Nationalist Trends'.

30 See Buzurgmehr, *Taqrirat* (especially for the quotation) and *Memoirs*, Book I, chapter 24.

31 Musaddiq's memoirs stop at this point. But there is much direct and indirect evidence about the rest of the earlier period from his speeches, memories, etc., as well as the Majlis minutes and other people's witness.

3 Opposition and isolation

1 As if to apologise after the event, Musaddiq on many occasions described the line he took at the time as an 'unconstitutional expediency'. However, it is not clear why he should have so interpreted the matter, because this was indeed consistent with democracy and the constitution. See Dawlat-Abadi, *Hayat-i Yahya*, vol. 4, Musaddiq, *Memoirs*, and Buzurgmehr, *Taqrirat*. In the latter source (chapter 16) Musaddiq says that Mudarris had already agreed to co-operate on the matter.

2 See Homa Katouzian, *Political Economy of Modern Iran* (London: Macmillan, and New York: New York University Press, 1981) and 'Nationalist Trends in Iran'. See further, the long poem 'Jumhuri-nameh' wrtitten by Bahar, but believed to have been by Ishqi, which directly contributed to Ishqi's assassination (on Reza's orders) within a couple of weeks.

3 See Bahar's *qasideh*, in the first volume, and his *masnavi* in the second volume of his *Divan* on this incident.

4 See his *Hayat-i Yahya*, vol. 4 (Tehran, 1950).

5 See Khajeh-Nuri, *Bazigaran*; Makki, *Tarikh-i Bist Saleh*; Bahar, *Tarikh-i Mukhtasar*; and Afshar, *Musaddiq va Masa'il*.

6 See further, Husain Makki, *Duktur Musaddiq va Nutqha-yi Tarikhi-yi U* (Dr Musaddiq and his Historic Speeches) (Tehran: Ilmi, 1945) (especially for the full text of the speeches); Dawlat-Abadi, *Hayat-i Yahya*, vol. 4; and Khajeh-Nuri, *Bazigaran*.

7 Musaddiq explained that this procedure had been previously agreed among themselves. See Afshar, *Musaddiq va Masa'il*.

8 See further, Katouzian, *Political Economy*, chapter 5.
9 See 'Tasvib-i Budjeh dar Parlimanha-yi Mukhtalif', *Ayandeh*, vol. 1, 1925, reprinted in *Musaddiq va Masa'il*.
10 The Iranian Constitution had provided for a second chamber, but it was not convened until the late 1940s.
11 'Tabi'iyat dar Iran', *Ayandeh*, vol. 2,. 1926, reprinted in *Musaddiq va Masa'il*.
12 'Usual-i Muhimmeh-yi Huquq-i Madani va Huquq-i Tijarati dar Iran', *Ayandeh*, vol. 2, 1926, reprinted in *Musaddiq va Masa'il*.
13 'Intikhabat dar Urupa va Iran', *Ayandeh*, vol. 2, 1926, reprinted in *Musaddiq va Masa'il*.
14 *Ibid.*, p. 73.
15 For the full text of the speech, see Makki, *Duktur Musaddiq*. His attitude towards Furughi might seem inconsistent in view of the fact that, in 1920, he had agreed to keep him as the head of the Supreme Court when he himself had been named as minister of justice (see chapter 2 above). That, however, had been done to allay Furughi's fears that Musaddiq might dismiss him for a personal disfavour which Furughi had done him in 1918. See *Memoirs*, chapter 19.
16 For the full text of the speech see *ibid*. See also his later remarks on the subject when he was responding to the shah's attacks on him (in the latter's *Mission for My Country*) in *Memoirs*, Book II.
17 See Makki, *Duktur Musaddiq*, for the full text of the speech.
18 *Ibid*.
19 See Kay-Ustuvan, *Siyasat-i Muvazeneh*, vol. 2.
20 Scarves were also forbidden, but European hats were allowed. See further, Katouzian, *Political Economy*.
21 See further, Buzurgmehr, *Taqrirat, Musaddiq's Memoirs*, and Afshar, *Musaddiq va Masa'il*.
22 See the full text of his speech in Makki, *Duktur Musaddiq*.
23 See Kay-Ustuvan, *Siyasat-i Muvazeneh*, vol. 1, p. 22, and Afshar, *Musaddiq va Masa'il*, pp. 115–16.
24 This episode was recalled by Musaddiq in the Fourteenth Majlis. See Kay-Ustuvan, *Siyasat-i Muvazeneh*, vol. 1, p. 22, and Afshar, *Musaddiq va Masa'il*, p. 116.
25 He was first poisoned, then strangled while he was saying his last prayers. The full account of his murder in jail was given by Shaikh al-Islam Malayeri in October 1941 in a Majlis speech specifically on this subject. See Khajeh-Nuri, *Bazigaran*.
26 *Memoirs*, Book I, chapter 22.
27 See further, Makki, *Duktur Musaddiq*.
28 See, for the document in question, *ibid.*, p. 18, n. 1.
29 Cited in Gordon Waterfield, *Professional Diplomat: Sir Percy Loraine* (London: John Murray, 1973), p. 75.
30 See, for example, Dawlat-Abadi, *Hayat-i Yahya*, vol. 4, p. 343. See further, *Musaddiq's Memoirs*, and Buzurgmehr, *Taqrirat*.

31 See, for example, Musaddiq's own long and explicit version of this story in his *Memoirs*, Book II, part III.
32 See further, Mustafa Fateh, *Panjah Sal Naft-i Iran* (Tehran: Chehr, 1956); Fu'ad Ruhani, *Tarikh-i Melli Shudan-i Naft-i Iran* (Tehran: Jibi, 1971); R. W. Ferrier, *History of the British Petroleum Company*, vol. 1, *The Developing Years 1901–1932* (Cambridge: Cambridge University Press, 1982) and L. P. Elwell-Sutton, *Persian Oil* (London: Lawrence & Wishart, 1955).
33 See Fateh, *Panjah Sal*, Fu'ad Ruhani, *Zindigi-yi Siyasi-i Musaddiq* (London: 1987), and Katouzian, *Political Economy*.
34 To Iranians themselves the country's name had always been Iran. *Persis* was the name by which the Greeks called the country after the formation of the Achaemenid Empire, and this was later passed on to other European countries. Cf. 'Germany', 'Allemagne', etc., for Deutschland.
35 See, for example, William Shirer, *The Rise and Fall of the Third Reich* (London: Pan Books, 1964).
36 See further, on Reza Shah's abdication, 'Yaddashthay-yi Abbasquli Gul-sha'iyan', in Cyrus Ghani (ed.), *Yaddashthayi, Duktus Qasim Ghani*, vol. 11 (London: Cyrus Ghani, 1984), 'Suhaili', in Khajeh-Nuri, *Bazigaran*, and Katouzian, 'Reza Shah'.

4 Occupation and interregnum

1 See Gulsha'iyan's diary in Ghani, *Yaddashtha*, vol. 11.
2 See Wright, *The Persians Amongst the English*.
3 For a theory of the historical sociology of Iran as well as its application to social change, past and present, see Homa Katouzian, 'The Aridisolatic Society: A Model of Long Term Social and Economic Development in Iran', *The International Journal of Middle East Studies*, July 1983, and further, *Political Economy*.
4 This was not quite true of the Constitutional Revolution which attempted consciously to replace the arbitrary state with one which was contained within a constitutional framework. None the less, many of its elements were also present in that episode.
5 See Katouzian, *Political Economy*, chapter 8.
6 The full text of the speech is highly instructive in many ways. See 'Dashti' in Khajeh-Nuri, *Bazigaran*, first edition (1942), pp. 285–93, for the full text. These parts have been omitted from the much shorter editions published in the 1960s and 1970s.
7 The first occasion is well known and has been well documented. For the second occasion, see *Ayandeh*, April–June 1985.
8 See the full text in Ghani, *Yaddashtha*, vol. 9 1982, pp. 675–86.
9 See Ghani, *Yaddashtha*, especially vols 2, 3 and 7–10.
10 A group of Marxist and socialist individuals with considerably different personal temperaments and political persuasions whom 'fate' brought together in Reza Shah's jails, and – apparently – turned into a solid and uniform Marxist group. See further, Homa Katouzian, *Khatirat-i Siyasi-yi Khalil*

Maleki (second edition, Tehran: Intishar, 1990); Anvar Khameh'i, *Panjah Nafar va Seh Nafar* (Tehran: Intisharat-i Hafteh, 1982); Buzurg Alavi, *Panjah va Seh Nafar* (Tehran: Ulduz, 1978).

11 See *Siyasat* and *Rahbar* (successive official party organs) various issues, 1941–44. For example: 'The Tudeh party represents the real majority of the Iranian people. Whatever its members do is for the sake of organizing the masses, preventing conflict and insanity [among them] and preserving constitutional government and the principles of democracy.' See further, *Siyasat* (the party organ), 22 February 1942. For a detailed history of the Tudeh party, with a somewhat different approach from that of this book, see Ervand Abrahamian, *Iran Between Two Revolutions* (Princeton, NJ: Princeton University Press, 1982).

5 The first deputy

1 See, for example, the article entitled 'The Conflict between Democracy and Dictatorship' in *Rahbar* (The Tudeh party official organ), 8 March 1944.

2 See Kay-Ustuvan, *Siyasat-i Muvazeneh*, vol. 1, p. 35.

3 See H. Katouzian, '*Khalil Maleki va Mas'leh-yi Adam-i Ghair-i Adi*' in H. Katouzian and A. Pichdad (eds) *Yadnameh-yi Khalil Maleki* (Tehran: Intishar, 1990).

4 See Kay-Ustuvan, *Siyasat-i Muvazeneh*, vol. 1, pp. 26 and 34.

5 *Ibid.*, pp. 147–8.

6 See *Rahbar*, 7 June 1945.

7 For the relevant parliamentary speeches and press reports, see Kay-Ustuvan, *Siyasat-i Muvazeneh*, vol. 1. See also Parsa Yumgani, *Karnameh-yi Musaddiq* (Tehran: Ravaq, 1979).

8 '*Duzdgah*'; See Kay-Ustuvan, *Siyasat-i Muvazeneh*, vol. 1.

9 Yumgani, *Karnameh-yi Musaddiq*.

10 *Manfi* generally means 'negative'; but in this context the term 'passive' is more appropriate (cf. *muqavimat-i manfi* for 'passive resistance'). Also, 'balance' is the proper word for *muvazeneh*, while 'equilibrium' is the equivalent for *ta'adul*.

11 See 'Mudarris' in Khajeh-Nuri, *Bazigaran*.

12 See Kay-Ustuvan, *Siyasat-i Muvazeneh*; Khameh'i, *Fursat-i Buzurg*; Yumgani, *Karnameh*; Katouzian, *Khatirat-i Siyasi-yi Khalil Maleki*; Firaidun Kishavarz, *Man Muttaham Mikunam* (Tehran: Ravaq, 1979).

13 See the above references. Jalal Al-i Ahmad, then a young Tudeh intellectual, tells of his emotional agony when he ran away from the demonstration and threw off his party badge, in his *Dar Khidmat va Khiyanat-i Rushanfikran* (Tehran: Ravaq, 1978).

14 See the newspaper, *Mardum, Bara-yi Rushanfikran*, 3 November 1944.

15 See Ghani, *Yaddashtha*, vol. 10 1983. For further evidence on the general Tudeh reaction, see Katouzian, *Khatirat-i Siyasi-yi Khalil Maleki*; Khameh'i, *Fursat-i Buzurg*; and Yumgani, *Karnameh*.

16 See Rahimiyan's recollections in *Umid-i Iran* magazine, new series, no. 11, 16 April 1979.
17 See Kay-Ustuvan, *Siyasat-i Muvazeneh*, vol. 2, for his parliamentary speeches on this issue.
18 See *ibid.* for the quotation, and his various schemes for avoiding a long recess.
19 See Katouzian, *Khatirat-i Siyasi-yi Khalil Maleki* and *Political Economy*; Khameh'i, *Fursat-i Buzurg*; Khalil Maleki and Anvar Khameh'i, *Pas az Dah Sal Inshi'abiyyun-i Hizb-i Tudeh Sukhan Miguyand* (Tehran, 1957); and Louise L'Estrange Fawcett, 'The Struggle for Persia: The Azerbaijan Crisis of 1946', unpublished D.Phil. Thesis, University of Oxford, 1988. See further the latest evidence of Colonel (later Professor) Ahmad Shafa'i in his memoirs *Qiyam-i Afsaran-i Khurasan va Si-u-haft Sal Zindigi dar Shuravi* (Tehran: Kitab-Sara, 1987). Shafa'i was a member of 'the Khurasan officers' (who failed to organize a revolt in 1944) and had fled to the Soviet Union before being sent back to become an important officer in the Azerbaijan Democrats' army. He crossed the Soviet border, once again, after the Azerbaijan fiasco and spent almost forty years in the Soviet Union before returning to Iran at the age of seventy.
20 See, however, Qavam's later defence (though not complete denial) of this practice in his long and important 'open letter' aimed at the shah (which was widely, but privately, circulated) in Ghani, *Yaddashtha*, vol. 9, 1982.
21 See Kishavarz, *Man Muttaham Mikunam*; Anvar Khameh'i, *Az Inshi'ab ta Kudita* (Tehran: Intisharat-i Hafteh, 1984); Katouzian, *Khatirat-i Siyasi-yi Khalil Maleki*.

6 Supplemental Agreement and National Front

1 'Lackeys of the state' has been translated from the Persian original, *nawkar-i dawlat*.
2 See further, Ghani, *Yaddasht-ha*, vol. 8, pp. 392–410.
3 See Francis Williams, *A Prime Minister Remembers* (Attlee's Memoirs) (London: Heinemann, 1961) pp. 249–54.
4 Fateh, *Panjah Sal*, p. 436.
5 *Ibid.*, p. 431, emphasis added.
6 See *ibid.*, p. 447. See further, Khameh'i, *Fursat-i Buzurg*, pp. 314–18.
7 In some sources the date is given as 22 October.
8 Letter of 17 July 1949 to Dr Qasim Ghani, in his *Yaddashtha*, vol. 9.
9 See, for example, Yumgani, *Karnameh*, p. 125, emphasis added.
10 *Ibid.*, p. 128. However, when Mohammad Husain Khan Qashqa'i intervened to say that 'there is therefore no legal basis for the agreement', Taqizadeh added that he had 'no comment on this matter'. See further, Khameh'i, *Az Inshi'ab*; Husain Makki, *Kitab-i Siyah* (Tehran: Intisharat-i Naw, 1977); and Musaddiq, *Nutqha va Maktubat*, various volumes.
11 See Kishavarz, *Man Muttaham Mikunam*, and Khameh'i, *Az Inshi'ab ta Kudita*.

12 See Sa'id's interview with the newspaper *Iradeh-yi Azerbaijan*, quoted verbatim in Khameh'i, *ibid.*, pp. 128–9.
13 See Ali Akbar Siyasi, *Guzarish-i Yek Zindigi* (London: Siyasi, 1988), pp. 214–15.
14 See *Az Inshi'ab ta Kudita*, pp. 123–47. See further Husain Ala's indirect hint at Razmara's involvement in the affair in his letter of 12 February 1949 to Dr Qasim Ghani, *Yaddashtha*, vol. 9, pp. 564–5.
15 Ayatullah Burujirdi sent a telegram of support to the shah, but said nothing about the rough treatment of Kashani (who was in fact innocent of the charge). Almost at the same time a conference of religious leaders in Qum resolved to ban political activity by the *ulama*. See further, chapter 12 below.
16 For full details, see Ghani, *Yaddashtha*, vol. 8.
17 For the full text of Qavam's letters, see Ali Vusuq, *Chahar Fasl* (Tehran: Vusuq, 1982), pp. 33–43; and Ghani, *Yaddashtha*, vol. 9, pp. 610–17.
18 *Bakhtar-i Imruz*, 18 October 1949. See Husain Makki's eye-witness account of the *bast* in his *Khal'-i Yad* (Tehran: Bungah-i Tarjumeh va Nashr-i Kitab, 1981). See further, Khameh'i, *Az Inshi'ab*, and Yumgani, *Karnameh*.
19 On the meaning and significance of *mellat, melli* and *melliun*, see Katouzian, 'The Aridisolatic Society', *Political Economy*, and *Khatirat-ir Siyasi*, and chapter 18 below.
20 See *Mardum*, 23 October 1949.
21 *Bakhtar-i Imruz*, 10 November 1949.
22 *Ibid.*, 7 December 1949.
23 See Ghani, *Yaddashtha*, vol. 9, p. 561.
24 R. W. Ferrier, 'The British Government, The Anglo-Iranian Oil Company, and Iranian Oil' in J. Bill and R. Louis (eds), *Musaddiq, Iranian Nationalism and Oil* (London: I.B. Tauris and Austin: University of Texas Press, 1988).
25 For details of the Majlis proceedings on that day (27 June 1950), see Musaddiq, *Nutqha na Maktubat*, vol. 1.
26 *Ibid.*, for the full text of his public statement (27 June 1950).
27 For a full account of the incident, see Baqa'i's defiant speech in the Majlis in Baqa'i, *Dar Pishgah-i Tarikh* (Kirman: Parm, n.d.) (preface signed in June 1979).

7   The Popular Movement and oil nationalization

1 For some graphic descriptions of Razmara as an army leader, see Colonel G. Musavvar-Rahmani, *Khatirat-i Siyasi: Bist-va-panj Sal dar Niru-yi Hava'i-yi Iran* (Tehran: Ravaq, 1984).
2 Even as late as the day before the 21 July 1952 uprising (when Qavam was briefly prime minister), the Tudeh party described Razmara as a British, and Musaddiq as an American, 'agent'. See *Bisu-yi Ayandeh*, 20 July 1952.
3 The British document in question has been fully quoted in Khameh'i in *Az Inshi'ab ta Kudita*, pp. 283–6. For American support of Razmara see Ghani's account of his conversation with John Wiley (the US Ambassador) in Ghani, *Yaddashtha*, vol. 11.

4 Quoted in *Kayhan*, 19 March 1951 (the day before the oil nationalization). See further George McGhee, *Envoy to the Middle World: Adventures in Diplomacy* (New York: Harper and Row, 1983).

5 *Bisu-yi Ayandeh*, 19 April 1951. The phrase 'a few shots were fired' is meant to imply that Tahmasibi was not his only assailant. See further below.

6 See Baqa'i's defence speech in Ja'fari's trial, *Shahed*, 12 September 1950. According to Ghani (*Yaddashtha*, vol. 8, p. 395) Dihqan had been a member of Princess Ashraf's inner circle. See further, Khameh'i, *Az Inshi'ab ta Kudita*, who puts forward a detailed argument for the co-operation of Razmara and Kiyanuri in the affair.

7 See the full direct quotation from the official records in H. Makki, *Kitab-i Siyah* (first edn 1951) (Tehran: Intisharat-i Naw, 1978).

8 See *ibid.*, p. 297, though here Imami was reacting to the recent Irano-Soviet trade agreement concluded by Razmara. See further below.

9 For extensive contemporary documentation on the antagonism between the shah and Zahedi, on the one hand, and Razmara on the other, see Qashqa'i, *Salha-yi Buhran* and Ghani, *Yaddashtha*, vol. 11.

10 Razmara's and Zahedi's conflict and quarrel went so far that they broke off relations in 1950. See further Qashqa'i, *Salha-yi Buhran*.

11 This was the real reason for his dismissal by the shah after a short period of premiership, following the 1953 coup, despite his important role in saving the shah's throne for him.

12 See Musaddiq's and Razmara's public revelations about their meetings etc., in *Nutqha va Maktubat*, various volumes. For the shah's proposal of the premiership through Imami, see Musaddiq, *Nutqha* and *Memoirs*.

13 See JAMI, *Guzashteh Chiraq-i Rah-i Ayandeh* (Paris: JAMI, 1977), p. 511; Katouzian, *Political Economy*, chapter 8; Ali Akbar Siyasi, *Guzarish-i Yek Zindiqi* (London: Siyasi, 1988), p. 215.

14 Nasir Qashqa'i, *Salha-yi Buhran*, ed. Nasrullah Haddadi (Tehran: Rassa, 1987), p. 146.

15 Musavvar-Rahmani, *Khatirat-i Siyasi*, pp. 272–3.

16 *Ibid.*, p. 275.

17 Khameh'i, *Az Inshi'ab ta Kudita*, p. 292.

18 See the text of Bahrami's recantation letter after the coup, in Khalil Maleki and Anvar Khameh'i, *Pas az Dah Sal Inshi'abiyun-i Hizb-i Tudeh Sukhan Miguyand* (Tehran: Pedram, January 1958). See further Khameh'i, *Az Inshi'ab*.

19 See, for example, Musavvar-Rahmani, *Khatirat-i Siyasi*.

20 See further, Katouzian, *Musaddiq's Memoirs*, Introduction, and Book II; Khameh'i, *Az Inshi'ab ta Kudita*.

21 The NF members of the committee were Musaddiq, Makki, Hayerizadeh, Shaigan and Saleh. Its other members were: Jamal Imami, Hasan Alavi, Nasir Zulfaqari, Khusraw Qashqa'i, Sayyed Ali Bihbahani, Javad Ganjeh'i, Javad Ameri, Faramarzi, Kasimi, Faqihzadeh, Palizi, Hedayati and Sartip-zadeh.

22 In what follows the historical facts are based on Husain Makki's bulky *Kitab-i Siyah*, about 700 pages of which contain the minutes of the oil committee.

23   Two months later, the AIOC offered him a 50–50 agreement which he did not disclose. See further below.
24   Makki, *Kitab-i Siyah*, p. 297.
25   See, for example, the arrogant and indignant letter of 23 February 1951 to Razmara from the British ambassador, Sir Francis Shepherd, asking why he had not made the matter public. See Fateh, *Panjah Sal*.
26   Makki, *Kitab-i Siyah*, p. 356.
27   *Ibid.*, p. 225.
28   *Ibid.*, p. 752.
29   *Ibid.*, p. 737.
30   This is the date given by Musaddiq in his memoirs. It is given as 27 April in some other sources.
31   Musaddiq had earlier rejected the shah's repeated offers through Imami. But even after Razmara's assassination he did not want the premiership, because his chief aim was to put all his efforts into the full implementation of the Nationalization Act with public backing. He saw no further use for his own premiership which would (and did) tie him up with countless other problems.
32   See Musaddiq, *Nutqha va Maktubat*, as well as other sources, but the fullest and most explicit account of the episode is given in *Musaddiq's Memoirs*.

8   Maleki and the Popular Movement

1   See further, Katouzian, *Khatirat-i Siyasi-yi Khalil Maleki* (second edition, Tehran: Intisharat 1990); Khameh'i, *Panjah Nafar, Fursat-i Buzurg*, and *Az Inshi'ab*; Jalal Al-i Ahmad, *Dar Khidmat va Khiyanat* (especially 'Qaziyeh Inshi'ab va Khalil Maleki'); Alavi, *Panjah va Seh Nafar*; Katouzian and Pichdad, *Yadnameh-yi Khalil Maleki*.
2   Al-i Ahmad was at the time working for *Shahed* (apparently without pay) in the evenings, and it was he who brought Maleki and Baqa'i together. See his *Dar Khidmat va Khiyanat*.
3   See further H. Katouzian and A. Pichdad (eds), *Barkhurd-i Aqayed va Ara* (Tehran: Intishar, 1990) (forthcoming).
4   The literal meaning of *Ilm va Zindigi*; its intellectual meaning is: Theory and Praxis.
5   See further, Katouzian, *Khatirat-i Siyasi-yi Khalil Maleki*; Al-i Ahmad, *Dar Khidmat va Khiyanat*.
6   See Middleton's testimony in Brian Lapping, *End of Empire* (London: Grafton Books, 1985).
7   Here Maleki is playing with the Perso-Arabic word *negib* (Persian pronunciation: *najib*) which literally means 'noble and dignified'.
8   *Niru-yi Sevvum* (daily), no. 1, 14 October 1952 (emphasis added). Four days later, Al-i Ahmad wrote a sardonic open letter to Baqa'i, 'my leader'. *Ibid.*, no. 4, 18 October 1952.
9   See Baqa'i in *Shahed*, 15 October 1952: 'From the very beginning, a small number of people, led by Mr Khalil Maleki, had deviationist ideas . . . Many a time they discussed communism in the party cells . . . They were planning to

turn Zahmatkishan into a communist party, but one which was not connected to Moscow.' Still, Baqa'i says in the same speech that his original 'resignation' was because he had been told that 99 per cent of the party members were behind Maleki.

10 He suffered great mental torture in jail, and he believed that the regime had deliberately put him in prison with his bitterest enemies. See, for example, *Nameh-yi Sargushadehi-yi Khalil Maleki*, 20 February 1961, reprinted in Katouzian, *Khatirat-i Siyasi-yi Khalil Maleki*, Appendices.

11 They did, and went on doing, the same to Maleki until the fall of the Tudeh party in 1983. In his memoirs, published almost forty years after the event, Ihsan Tabari still claims that Maleki had become a British agent and been instructed by Morgan Phillips, the then General Secretary of the Labour Party, to split the Tudeh party. See his *Kazhraheh: Khatirati az Tarikh-i Hizb-i Tudeh* (Tehran: Amir Kabir, 1987). For a single specimen of the language used by the Tudeh party against Maleki, see *Niru-yi Sevvum, Paigah-i Ijtima'i-yi Ampirialism*, 1952. This pamphlet was written by Zakharian under direct instructions from Kiyanuri.

12 *Niru-yi Sevvum Piruz Mishavad* (Tehran: Zahmatkishan Party Publications, 1951) p. 3 (emphasis added).

13 *Ibid.*, pp. 4–5.

14 *Ibid.*, p. 21.

15 *Ibid.*, p. 26.

16 *Niru-yi Sevvum Chist* (Tehran: The Zahmatkishan Party Publications, 1951).

17 'Nihzatha-yi Melli-yi Urupa va Asiya', *Ilm va Zindigi*, 1 December 1951–January 1952.

18 *Niru-yi Sevvum Chist*, pp. 11–12.

19 *Ibid.*, pp. 2 and 4.

20 *Ibid.*, p. 8.

21 *Ibid*, p. 9 (emphasis in the original).

22 *Niru-yi Muharrikeh-yi Tarikh* (The Motive Force of History) (Tehran: Zahmatkishan Party Publications, 1952).

23 See *Niru-yi Sevvum*, April–July 1953, several issues.

24 Here, he was explicitly referring to St-Beuve's question: What would have happened if Robespierre had died and Mirabeau had lived instead? See 'Siyasatmadar-i Nuvin' ('The Modern Politician'), *Ilm va Zindigi*, 2, January–February 1952.

25 *Niru-yi Muharrikeh*, p. 5.

26 *Ibid.*, pp. 6–7.

27 See 'Dar Pishgah-i Sarnivisht ya dar Muqabil-i Tarikh', *Ilm va Zindigi*, 3, March 1952.

28 *Niru-yi Muharrikeh*, pp. 33–4.

29 See *Dar Barabar-i Buzurgtarin Azmayesh-i Tarikh* (Tehran: Zahmatkishan Party Publications, 1951).

30 See 'Susiyalism va Kapitalism-i Dawlati', *Ilm va Zindigi*, April 1952.

31 See 'Mubarehzeh ba Buzurgtarin Khatari keh Nihzat-i Melli ra Tahdid Mikunad', *Ilm va Zindigi*, vol. 2, no. 2, June 1953. See also, the same

journal, vol. 1, no. 8, November 1952, for the third article on 'socialism and state capitalism'. These articles were later expanded and published as a book entitled *Susiyalism va Kapitalism-i Dawlati* (Tehran: *Niru-yi Sevvum*, 1953, reprinted by Ravaq, 1978).

9 Musaddiq's first government

1 See Sadr al-Ashraf (Muhsin Sadr)'s letter of 14 January 1952 to Dr Ghani, where he said that, after his earlier dismissal from the governorship of Khurasan, 'in an audience with His Majesty, I complained of this manner of dismissal through a [coded] telegram'. He expressed his regrets, adding, 'they have also dismissed Dr Iqbal, the governor of Azerbaijan, and Sa'id, the ambassador to Turkey'. See Ghani, *Yaddashtha*, vol. 9.

2 See Musaddiq, *Nutqha va Maktubat*, various volumes, and *Memoirs*, Book II.

3 Decades later, the same view, only in reverse, impelled the Tudeh party to support the Islamic Republic, and become wholly committed to it after the hostage-taking of American diplomats in November 1979. The consistently anti-American stance of the Islamic Republic was the most important (if not the only) reason for its Tudeh support, to the exclusion of all other considerations.

4 See Ismail Ra'in (ed.), *Asrar-i Khaneh-yi Sidan (Seddon)* (Tehran: Amir Kabir, 1979), Seddon enjoyed diplomatic status. Other AIOC officials were also implicated in the secret campaigns, including Sir Eric Drake, the general manager in Abadan. According to official reports, 56 suitcases containing documents were removed before discovery, and some of those discovered were half-burnt. Nevertheless, what was seized (and is now public) was sufficient to indicate the depth and breadth of their activities against the government.

5 FO371/91459/EP1015/201, cited in W. Roger Louis, *The British Empire in the Middle East, 1945–51* (Oxford: Clarendon Press, 1984).

6 See Jalil Buzurgmehr (ed.), *Duktur Mohammad Musaddiq dar Dadgah-i Tajdid-i Nazar-i Nizami* (Tehran: Shirkat-i Sahami-yi Intishar, 1986).

7 *The New Statesman* was the exception that proved the rule, although there was some variation in the tone and views of the others as well. The *Daily Express* concluded one of its articles on the subject by saying: 'The Persians are trying to grab something which does not belong to Persia at all'. See Hamid Enayat's careful survey of the British press in his 'British Public Opinion and the Persian Oil Crisis' (M.Sc.(Econ.) thesis, University of London, 1958).

8 See Sir Eric Drake's recollections of his report to a full meeting of the British cabinet at the time, in Lapping, *End of Empire*.

9 See Williams, *A Prime Minister Remembers*, pp. 249–54.

10 Documented in 'Timewatch', BBC 2, September 1984.

11 This was eventually admitted by the Court itself in July 1952.

12 For the reasons behind this false impression, see McGhee, *Envoy*, and 'Recollections of Dr Mohammad Musaddiq' in Bill and Louis, *Musaddiq, Iranian Nationalism and Oil*.

13 75,000 rials were then roughly equal to $1,800. See further, *Memoirs*, Book II.
14 See McGhee, 'Recollections', and Katouzian, 'Oil Boycott and the Political Economy' in Bill and Louis, *Musaddiq, Iranian Nationalism and Oil*.
15 See *Musaddiq's Memoirs*, Book II.
16 Since the Majlis elections used to take months to complete, it was a convention that the shah would open the new Majlis as soon as a majority of the deputies had been elected.
17 Baqa'i had known about Musaddiq's desire to quit the stage at this time, though he did not know the real reason for it. See chapter 12.
18 FO248/1514, quoted in W. Roger Louis, 'Musaddiq, Oil and the Dilemmas of British Imperialism' in Bill and Louis, *Musaddiq, Iranian Nationalism and Oil*.
19 Lapping, *End of Empire*.
20 See, for example, *Musaddiq's Memoirs*, Book II, although his report of the incident occurred in several of his speeches and broadcasts while he was prime minister.
21 See *Musaddiq's Memoirs*, Book II, chapter 8 (chapter 5, in the Persian edition).
22 In his secret circular of 12 July to the senior leaders of his own party, Baqa'i had openly said that Musaddiq was looking 'for some excuse to shirk his responsibility, and be relieved of the problems which it has created'. But he cannot have known the real reason behind it. See *Niru-yi Sevvum* (daily), 5 December 1952. In his letter of 18 August 1953 to Musaddiq, Kashani made a critical reference to this quiet – almost secret – departure the year before, although (like Baqa'i) he could not have known the reason for it. See chapter 12.
23 See Baqa'i, *Cheh Kasi Munharif Shud*.
24 See Katouzian, *Political Economy*, chapter 9.
25 Only three years before, Kashani had been an honoured guest at Qavam's house, when he was arrested on suspicion of involvement in the attempt on the shah's life, and banished to Lebanon. Qavam mentioned the incident with bitterness, and great deference to Kashani in his 'open letter' of June 1950 aimed at the shah. See Vusuq, *Chahar Fasl*, p. 42, and Ghani, *Yaddashtha*, vol. 9, p. 615 (and, incidentally, note the peculiar vicissitudes of Iranian politics).
26 See, for the relevant documents, *Ruhaniyat va Asrar*. The claim made later by Hasan Arsanjani (then Qavam's Assistant for Political Affairs) that they were about to arrest Kashani may be safely discarded if only because it flies in the face of the above documents. Arsanjani was also keen to attribute the uprising to the Tudeh party which was, once again, contrary to well-establishd facts. See his *Yaddashtha-yi Siyasi, Siyum Tir 1331* (Tehran, 1956), reprinted in Baqa'i, *Cheh Kasi Munharif Shud*, and Ayat, *Chehreh-yi Haqiqi*.
27 *Bakhtar-i Imruz*, 17, 19 and 20 July 1952.
28 See Musavvar-Rahmani, *Khatirat-i Siyasi*.
29 For example: 'Whatever the result of the conflict between *the two wings of the political establishment* ... they are, all of them, enemies of the people, and

defenders of the exploitative machine of the ruling establishment' (*Bisu-yi Ayandeh*, 18 July 1982, emphasis added). And further: 'In the first instance, Dr Musaddiq wanted to put the agents of the American policy in Majlis seats ... But in practice, and in order to prevent any victories by real popular (*melli*) candidates [i.e. Tudeh candidates] he entered a deal with the royal court and the agents of British imperialism' (*Ibid*, 20 July 1952, the day before the public uprising.)

10   Musaddiq's second government

1   See Maleki, *Niru-yi Sevvum Chist*.
2   See *Niru-yi Sevvum* (daily), 27 December 1952, but the campaign ran through several issues of both the daily and weekly *Niru-yi Sevvum* in late December and early January.
3   For the texts of Musaddiq's economic and social legislation see Hasan Tavanayan-Fard, *Duktur Musaddiq va Iqtisad* (Tehran: Alavi, 1983). For a comprehensive description and appraisal of the reforms see Habib Ladjevardi, 'Constitutional Government and Reform under Musaddiq' in Bill and Louis, *Musaddiq, Iranian Nationalism and Oil*.
4   See Katouzian, 'Reza Shah Pahlavi'.
5   See Musavvar-Rahmani, *Khatirat-i Siyasi*.
6   *Ibid*., pp. 106–7.
7   See *Musaddiq's Memoirs*, Book II.
8   This was the origin of the later charge against Musaddiq by his foreign and domestic detractors that he had 'dissolved the Supreme Court'. See, for example, the shah's *Mission for My Country*.
9   Hence Musaddiq's argument later in his military trial that the Department of Military Prosecutions' indictment against himself was legally void of meaning. See Jalil Buzurgmehr (ed.), *Musaddiq dar Mahkameh-yi Nizami* (Tehran: Nashr-i Tarikh-i Iran, 1985) and chapter 14.
10   See the full text of his speech in Makki, *Musaddiq va Nutqha*; see also *Musaddiq's Memoirs*, Book I.
11   *Memoirs*, Book II.

11   The oil dispute and non-oil economics

1   See Makki, *Kitab-i Siyah*, p. 737.
2   Cf. Musaddiq's argument for his opposition to the Soviet oil demand in the 1940s (see chapter 5).
3   See Anthony Eden, *Full Circle, The Memoirs of Sir Anthony Eden* (London: Cassell, 1960) chapter IX, for a general summary of this view. For detailed documentation, see Enayat, 'British Public Opinion and the Persian Oil Crisis'; James Bill, 'America, Iran, and the Politics of Intervention' in Bill and Louis, *Musaddiq, Iranian Nationalism and Oil*.

4 See Anthony Nutting, *No End of a Lesson* (London: Constable, 1967).

5 They even denied such access to Richard Stokes, Lord Privy Seal and Britain's chief negotiator with Iran in August 1951.

6 See Katouzian, *Political Economy*, chapter 9, appendix.

7 See Enayat, 'British Public Opinion', p. 91.

8 For details, see Musaddiq, *Nutqha va Maktubat*, vol. V, pp. 51–71; Katouzian, *Political Economy*, chapter 9.

9 See McGhee, *Envoy*, chapter 31, and 'Recollections' and chapter 9 above.

10 Cf. the increasing public campaign by the British press and government that Iran was about to go communist under Musaddiq.

11 See Eden, *Full Circle*; McGhee, *Envoy*, and 'Recollections'.

12 Eden, *Full Circle*, p. 201.

13 See Katouzian, *Political Economy*, chapter 9.

14 Cf. George McGhee's formula, above.

15 For a full documentation, see *Nutqha va Maktubat*, vols 5, 6, and 8.

16 I am grateful to Mr Hasibi for his detailed replies to this and other important points.

17 See the Tudeh party, *Nashriyeh-yi Ta'limati*, no. 13, Tehran, 1952.

18 It was at this point that Richard Stokes – now out of office, and well aware of the Conservatives' real strategy towards Musaddiq – followed up his moral dilemma of the year before and, in his long letter of 6 September to *The Times*, criticized the British government for refusing to negotiate directly with Iran.

19 Cf. McGhee's and World Bank's proposals.

20 See *Ruznameh-yi Rasmi-yi Kishvar*, 1952–3, various issues; Musaddiq, *Nutqha va Maktubat*, various volumes; *Musaddiq's Memoirs*, Book II; Fu'ad Ruhani, *Tarikh-i Melli Shudan-i San'at-i Naft-i Iran* (Tehran: Jibi, 1971), and *Zindigi-yi Siyasi-yi Musaddiq* (London: 1987); and Fateh, *Panjah Sal*.

21 See Musaddiq, *Nutqha va Maktubat*, vol. V, pp. 101–5.

22 See Buzurgmehr, *Musaddiq dar Mahkameh-yi Nizami*, vol. 2, p. 777.

23 See H. Motamen, 'Development planning in Iran', *Middle East Economic Papers* (1956); also N. S. Roberts, *Musaddiq: Economic and Commercial Conditions* (Overseas Economic Surveys, Board of Trade, London, 1948); G. B. Baldwin, *Planning and Development in Iran* (Baltimore: Johns Hopkins University Press, 1967); B. Olsen and P. N. Rasmussen, 'An Attempt at Planning in a Traditional State: Iran' in E. E. Hagen (ed.), *Planning Economic Development* (Homewood, Ill., Richard D. Irwin Inc., 1963).

24 See further, J. Bharier, *Economic Development in Iran, 1900–1970* (London: Oxford University Press, 1971).

25 For more details, see Katouzian, 'Oil Boycott and the Political Economy'.

26 For the full text of the relevant legislation, see Tavanayan-Fard, *Duktur Mohammad Musaddiq*.

27 For example, compare Fateh, *Panjah Sal* and Ruhani, *Tarikh* on this question.

28 This is documented in various places; for example, in Musaddiq's letter to President Eisenhower (in May 1953). See, *Nutqha va Maktubat*, vol. VIII, pp. 159–61.

29 See, for example, *Ittila'at*, September 1951.

30   See *Ruznameh-yi Rasmi-yi Kishvar*, no. 2820, 16 October 1954.
31   See Buzurgmehr, *Duktur Mohammad Musaddiq dar Dadgah-i Tajdid-i Nazar-i Nizami* for the exact details.
32   See further, Katouzian, 'Oil Boycott and the Political Economy'.
33   Based on the economic estimates of GNP in K. Afshar, 'Monetary Estimates of Iran's GNP 1900–1975', unpublished Ph.D. thesis, Florida State University, 1977.
34   See *Chilingar*, 10 March 1952.
35   For a more detailed discussion of the government economic strategy, see Katouzian, 'Oil Boycott and the Political Economy'.

12   Religion and rift in the movement

1   See, anon., *Ruhaniat va Asrar-i Fash-nushudeh* . . . (Qum: Dar al-Fikr, n.d.) (preface signed: Paris 1979). This source should be treated with caution since it occasionally contradicts certain facts. See further, M. H. Faghfoory, 'The Role of the Ulama in Twentieth Century Iran with Particular Reference to Ayatullah Haj Sayyed Abulqasim Kashani', Ph.D. dissertation, University of Wisconsin, 1978.
2   Sources on Kashani in Tehran during the years 1920–25 are mainly of an oral nature. See, however, M. Dihnavi, *Majmu'eh-yi Maktubat . . . Ayatullah Kashani* (Tehran: Chapakhsh, 1982), .ol. 1.
3   See further, Katouzian, *Political Economy*, and Willem Floor, 'The Revolutionary Character of the Ulama: Wishful Thinking or Reality' in Nikki Keddie (ed.), *Religion and Politics in Iran* (New Haven and London: Yale University Press, 1983).
4   See further, Dihnavi, *Majmu'eh-yi Maktubat*; Musaddiq, *Nutqha va Maktubat*, vol. 1; Khameh'i, *Az Inshiab*; Shahrough Akhavi, *Religion and Politics in Contemporary Iran* (Albany: State University of New York Press, 1980), and 'The Role of the Clergy in Iranian Politics, 1949–54' in Bill and Louis, *Musaddiq, Iranian Nationalism and Oil*; Faghfoory, 'The Role of the Ulama'; Yann Richard, 'Ayatullah Kashani: Precursor of the Islamic Republic' in Keddie, *Religion and Politics*.
5   See anon., *Rihaniyat va Asrar*.
6   Although some of them (and notably Karim-Abadi) defected to the other side after a period.
7   *Ruhaniyat va Asrar*, p. 132. See further Khalil Maleki's open letter to Kashani (14 October 1952) in Katouzian, *Khatirat-i Siyasi-yi Khalil Maleki*.
8   See *Tarraqi* (weekly magazine), 13 May 1951.
9   *Niru-yi Sevvum* (daily), 5 May 1953 (see the issue of 4 May as well).
10   Katouzian, *Political Economy*, pp. 160–2.
11   Dihnavi, *Majmu'eh-yi Maktubat*, p. 253.
12   *Ruhaniyat va Asrar*, p. 122.
13   See *Musaddiq's Memoirs*, Book II.
14   For the full text of the documents in question see Isma'il Ra'in, *Asrar-i Khaneh-yi Seddon* (Tehran: Amir Kabir, 1979), pp. 250–5, especially p. 255.

15 See Amir-Ala'i, *Khal'i Yad az Shirkat-i Naft-i Inglis va Iran* (Tehran: Dehkuda, 1979) and *Naqdi bar Kitab-i Siyah* (Tehran: Dehkuda, 1981), who (as a star witness) confirmed Makki's and Baqa'i's charge against Matin-Daftary despite his serious differences with them over other issues. See further Makki, *Khal'i Yad*; Baqa'i, *Cheh Kasi Munharif Shud* (Tehran: Sinubar, 1984), *Dar Pishgah-i Tarikh* (Kirman: Parm, 1979); Ayat, *Chehreh-yi Haqiqi*.

16 See further Baqa'i, *Dar Pishgar, Cheh Kasi*, and *An Keh Guft Nah* (New Jersey: Rafizadeh, 1984). Kazim Hasibi was witness to Makki's openly calling Musaddiq 'that old dog' after he had heard that he was not on the delegation list (Hasibi's communication to the author, January 1988).

17 See parts of Fatemi's defence in his military trial which have been recently published in Nijati, *Junbish-i Melli Shudan* (second edition, 1987).

18 *Niru-yi Sevvum* (daily), 5 December 1952. Baqa'i had the habit of using the title 'His Excellency' for all important public figures, especially if he happened to dislike them.

19 See Baqa'i's curious (almost amusing) arguments for this charge in his *An Keh Guft Nah*.

20 See further, Katouzian, *Khatirat-i Siyasi*, and Baqa'i, *Cheh Kasi Munharif Shud*.

21 See *Ruhaniyat va Asrar*, pp. 156–7.

22 See Baqa'i's Majlis attack on Musaddiq for these appointments in his *Dar Pishgah*.

23 In an attack on Musaddiq's government in the Majlis Baqa'i openly accused Daftary of sending the police to attack the premises of *Shahed*, Baqa'i's newspaper, when he had been police chief under Razmara. See Baqa'i, *Dar Pishgah*. See further chapter 7.

24 See Musavvar-Rahmani, *Khatirat-i Siyasi*.

25 Yet, he claims that, while in the hospital, he had been summoned by the shah to his palace and offered the premiership, which he did not accept. This is extremely unlikely, especially as it was only two weeks after the July uprising. See Baqa'i, *An Keh Guft Nah*.

26 See, for example, the leading article of *Niru-yi Sevvum* (weekly), 3 October 1952.

27 See *Shahed*, 14, 15 and 16 October 1952. See further, Al-i Ahmad's account of the incident in *Dar Khidmat va Khiyant*, and Maleki's (in his 'Open Letter to Kashani') in Katouzian, *Khatirat-i Siyasi-yi Khalil Maleki*.

28 He said that he himself was a socialist, whereas Maleki was a 'non-Moscow' communist. See *Shahed*, *ibid*.

29 Baqa'i, *An Keh Guft Nah*.

30 See the full text of his Majlis speech on 31 July 1952, in *Dar Pishgah* (the first part of the speech, on land reform, had been written by Khalil Maleki). Also, the Majlis speech on 26 May 1953, in *Tuti'eh bara-yi Tagh'ir-i Rizhim*, a *Shahed* publication, June 1953.

31 A law was eventually passed for the confiscation of Qavam's property, but it was not implemented before the coup, and was abolished afterwards.

32 See e.g. Baqa'i's Majlis speech on 15 January 1953, in *Dar Pishgah*.

33 For the text of these letters, see *Ruhaniyat va Asrar*, pp. 158–65.

34 See *Kayhan* and *Niru-yi Sevvum* (daily), various issues, November 1952. In its issue of 29 November *Niru-yi Sevvum* reported that the reinstatement of Tawliyat had been obtained against 'the payment of a considerable amount of money to a number of the supporters of the National Front'.

35 See Dihnavi, *Majmu'eh-yi Mukatibat*, vol. 3, p. 192 for Kashani's comments on the subject.

36 See the full text in Abdulhusain Meftah, *Rasti Birang Ast* (Paris: Parang, 1983). For one of his letters to the shah, see Katouzian, *Khatirat-i Siyasi*. For the other public statement, see *Kayhan*, 28 February 1953. The remaining letter has not been published, although Kashani mentions it in the existing one.

37 See, for example, numerous issues of *Niru-yi Sevvum* (daily), May–August 1953. See chapter 13.

38 See M. Gasiriowski, 'The 1953 Coup d'Etat in Iran', *International Journal of Middle East Studies*, August 1987. See also chapter 13.

39 See, for example, *Ruhaniyat va Asrar*, pp. 185–7. Kashani said in his letter that if Musaddiq was agreeable, he would send Nasir Khan Qashqa'i to negotiate on his behalf. The posthumously-published diaries of Nasir Khan make it plain that he was not in Tehran at that time. This would seem to lend support to the view that the letter was a forgery. But I still remain convinced of its authenticity. The reference to Nasir Khan could well have been a slip of the pen and his brother Khusraw (who was much more active in politics) might have been intended.

40 As for how the Kashani family still held the original copy of his letter to Musaddiq, a distinct possibility is that it had been recovered by his friends and contacts among the *putschists* (e.g. General Nadir Batmanqilich) after they took, and blew open, Musaddiq's famous Russian-made safe when his house was sacked and looted the next day.

41 See further, *Nabard-i Mellat*, 20 August 1953.

42 See *Kayhan*, 14 September 1953.

43 He used the metaphorical '*sag-i Naziabad*' (a dog of the Naziabad district of Tehran) which is supposed to have the characteristic described above. See, *Tauti'eh bara-yi Tagh'ir-i Rizhime* (the text of Baqa'i's long speech in the Majlis on 26 May 1953), p. 9.

44 *Cheh Kasi Munharif Shud.*

13 Ways of overthrowing Musaddiq

1 See Eden, *Full Circle*; McGhee, *Envoy* and 'Recollections'; Louis, *British Empire*; and chapters 9 and 11 above.

2 See, for example, Richard Cottam's first-hand witness in Lapping, *End of Empire*.

3 See C. M. Woodhouse, *Something Ventured* (London: Granada, 1982); K. Roosevelt, *Countercoup: The Struggle for Control of Iran* (New York: McGraw-Hill, 1979); and Lapping, *End of Empire*, among many other books and publications on this subject. See further Gasiriowski, 'The 1953 Coup'.

4 See Musaddiq, *Musaddiq's Memoirs*, and *Nutqha va Maktubat*, various issues.
5 See Nijati, *Junbish-i Melli Shudan*; Baqa'i, *Cheh Kasi Munharif Shud*; Musaddiq's 'Statement of 6 April, 1953' (address to the Iranian people), reprinted in *Memoirs*, Book II.
6 See *Musaddiq's Memoirs*, Book II, chapter 7 (part II, chapter 4 in the Persian edition).
7 See Musaddiq, 'Statement of 6 April, 1953', and *Memoirs* Book II, chapters 2 and 7.
8 I am grateful to Dr Karim Sanjaby for letting me see the relevant parts of his recollections in the Oral History of Iran project conducted by Harvard University, and his further replies to my inquiries concerning the differences in detail between his version of events and that of Musaddiq.
9 See Mu'azzami's full account in the Majlis meeting of 26 May, 1953, reprinted in Baqa'i, *Cheh Kasi Munharif Shud*.
10 Documented in *ibid*.
11 See, *Niru-yi Sevvum* (daily), 26 February 1953.
12 His reasoning is quite persuasive. See *Musaddiq's Memoirs*, Book II, chapters 2 and 7.
13 See, further, *Musaddiq's Memoirs*, Book II, and Katouzian, 'Introduction'.
14 *Musaddiq's Memoirs*, Book II.
15 For the full text of the report, see *Ittila'at*, 13 March 1953, reprinted in Nijati, *Junbish-i Melli Shudan*, Appendix 2. See further, Baqa'i, *Cheh Kasi Munharif Shud*, and *Dar Pishgah*.
16 Musavvar-Rahmani, *Khatirat-i Siyasi*.
17 See the full text of the confessions in Mohammad Turkaman, *Tuti'eh-yi Rubudan va Qatl-i Sarlashgar Afshar-Tus* (Tehran: Turkaman, 1984). The police chief was kidnapped late at night on 19 April 1953. The government learned of his disappearance next day. The day after, Khatibi fell under suspicion, his house was searched, and a few arrests were made. On the same day, Afshartus was killed in the cave outside Tehran. Within the following few days Khatibi and all the others involved (except for Baqa'i) were interned, and the police chief's body was discovered in a shallow grave near where he had been killed. See *Kayhan* and *Niru-yi Sevvum* (daily), 20–7 April 1953.
18 Baqa'i, *An Keh Guft Nah*.
19 See Turkaman, *Tuti'eh-yi Rubudan*.
20 See Baqa'i, *An Keh Guft Nah*.
21 See, for example, Lapping, *End of Empire*.
22 See, both for the facts and the above reasoning in the case, *Musaddiq's Memoirs*, Book II.
23 I am grateful for Dr Sadiqi's detailed replies (in writing) to my inquiries regarding this matter.
24 See Katouzian, *Khatirat-i Siyasi-yi Khalil Maleki*.
25 *Ibid*., and Sanjaby's interview in the Oral History Project of Harvard University.
26 See, however, Musaddiq's own defence of this decision in his *Memoirs*, Book II.

27 Lapping, *End of Empire*.
28 See Nijati, *Junbish-i Melli Shudan*, 1987 edition, which contains important new details, especially on the military side of the operations.
29 His name appears in a footnote in Buzurgmehr (ed.) *Dr Musaddiq dar Dadgah-i Tajdid-i Nazar* as *Hashim* Ashtiyani, but I have checked the matter with Colonel Buzurgmehr himself, and it is now certain that it was Mohammad Husain.
30 See *Musaddiq's Memoirs*, Book II.
31 See Katouzian, *Khatirat-i Siyasi-yi Khalil Maleki*.
32 See Major Ilmiyyeh's 'Testament' (written a few days later, which came to light recently), and Dr Sadiqi's 'Notes' (regarding the events of 19 and 20 August) in Nijati, *Junbish-i Melli Shudan*, 1987 edition.
33 See his extensive interview with Nijati, *ibid.* (Appendix 4).
34 See Turkaman, *Tuti'eh-yi Rubudan*.
35 Sadiqi's 'Notes', in Nijati, *Junbish-i Melli Shudan*.
36 *Ibid.*
37 *Ibid.*, and Buzurgmehr, *Musaddiq dar Mahkameh*.
38 See Colonel Mumtaz's reminiscences in *Parkhash*, 19 August 1979.
39 *Ibid.* and Nijati, *Junbish-i Melli Shudan*.
40 See Sadiqi's 'Notes'; and Buzurgmehr, *Musaddiq dar Mahkameh*.
41 Sadiqi confirms the account of how they had sent Zahedi a message through Hasan Sharif-Imami, but reveals (for the first time) that they were discovered by chance, nevertheless. See *ibid.*, and Sadiqi's 'Notes'.
42 See Nur al-Din Kiyanuri, *Darbareh-yi Bist va Hasht-i Murdad* (Tehran, 1979); Kishavarz, *Man Muttaham Mikunam*.

14 Musaddiq's trials

1 See Buzurgmehr, *Musaddiq dar Mahkameh*,
2 See Buzurgmehr, *Musaddiq dar Dadgah*.
3 Buzurgmehr, *Musaddiq dar Mahkameh*, vol. 1, p. 6.
4 However, General Azmudeh has continued, and is still continuing (in the royalist press abroad) his case against Musaddiq, although his more recent statements seem to be by way of self-justification.
5 See further, *Musaddiq's Memoirs* and Buzurgmehr, *Musaddiq dar Mahkameh*.
6 Buzurgmehr, *ibid.*, p. 47.
7 See Buzurgmehr's long introduction to *Musaddiq dar Mahkameh*, vol. 1. I am grateful to Colonel Buzurgmehr for his written replies to my inquiries regarding a number of important points.
8 *Ibid.*, vol. 1, p. 264.
9 For the prosecutor's repeated attack on Musaddiq on religious grounds see *ibid.*, for example, vol. 1, pp. 378–85, and vol. 2, pp. 413 and 649–54.
10 For example, a letter from General Farhad Dadsitan (martial-law administrator) to General Zahedi, recommending an army colonel who, he said, had been active in the *coup* of 19 August. but there were several other important documents as well. See *ibid.*

11   Buzurgmehr, *ibid.*, vol. 2, pp. 778–9.
12   See Buzurgmehr, *Musaddiq dar Dadgah*, pp. 27–39.
13   Buzurgmehr, *Musaddiq dar Mahkameh*, vol. 2, p. 801.
14   Buzurgmehr, *Musaddiq dar Dadgah*, pp. 52–4.
15   *Ibid.*, p. 58.
16   *Musaddiq's Memoirs*, Book II.
17   Buzurgmehr, *Musaddiq dar Mahkameh*, vol. 2, pp. 17–19.
18   Buzurgmehr, *Musaddiq dar Dadgah*, pp. 58–62.
19   *Ibid.*, p. 523.
20   Although by the 1960s they too had been reduced to mere instruments of the state.
21   They later paid for the assertion of their judicial independence by being made redundant as a result of the closing down of their division.
22   '[Which states] The appellants shall be summoned to the court of cassation [i.e. any division of the Supreme Court] for the hearings, but, unless they can offer a good reason for it, their absence shall not result in the postponement of the hearings and the decision [by the court]'.
23   '[Which states] On the day of the proceedings, the cassant (cassation judge) shall present the report of his investigations [to the court]. The appellants or their counsels shall then be called upon by the presiding judge to present their case.'
24   A sports club founded and run by Major [later, General] Khusruvani which organized regular street demonstrations and similar activities in favour of the shah (note: *taj* is Persian for crown). Some of its members had been planted in the courts as observers to shout abuse and invective at Musaddiq occasionally when he spoke.
25   Classical Arabic expression, '*ma la yudriku kull-ih, la yutriku kull'ih*', which means, verbatim, 'Do not leave it all [unsaid even] if not all of it can be understood'.
26   *Musaddiq's Memoirs*, p. 385.
27   *Ibid.*, p. 387.
28   *Ibid.*, p. 392.
29   *Ibid.*, p. 402.
30   For a full documentation of Musaddiq's long-drawn-out battle with the judicial authorities, see *Musaddiq's Memoirs*, Book II, chapter 10; and J. Buzurgmehr, *Duktur Musaddiq va Risidigi-yi Farjami dar Divan-i Kishvar* (Tehran: Shirkat-i Sahami-yi Intishar, 1988).

15   The Popular Movement after the coup

1   See Katouzian, *Khatirat-i Siyasi-yi Khalil Maleki*. See also Khalil Maleki, *Khatirat-i Zindan-i Falak al-Aflak*, *Firdowsi*, various issues, 1956.
2   For an extensive description of how the NRM came into being, see Houshang Esfandiar Chehabi, *Iranian Politics and Religious Modernism* (London: Tauris, 1990), vol. 1, chapter 4.
3   Even Kashani, who had supported the coup, read a statement from Tehran

Radio warning the government against making a shabby deal over the oil dispute, although he ended his statement by saying that Zahedi 'himself has been a member of the National Front'. See *Kayhan*, 2 November 1953.

4 For extensive documentation, see Qashqa'i, *Salha-yi Buhran*. For an analysis, see H. Katouzian, 'Barkhi az Salha-yi Buhran dar Yeki as Qarnha-yi Burhran' (review article), *Fasl-i Kitab*, vol. 4, 1989.

5 See further, Katouzian, *Khatirat-i Siyasi-yi Khalil Maleki*, Introduction.

6 See Maleki's long letter to Musaddiq in *ibid.* Appendices.

7 *Ibid.*, Introduction.

8 In one of its last issues, the newspaper *Mardum* (the official organ of the central committee of the Tudeh Party which still circulated secretly in Tehran) welcomed the Soviet invitation to the shah, and described it as necessary for the cause of peace. See *Asnad-i Nihzat-i Muqavimat-i Melli-yi Iran* (Tehran: Nihzat-i Azadi-yi Iran, 1984), vol. 2, pp. 201–2.

9 See Katouzian, *Political Economy*, chapter 10, and *Khatirat-i Siyasi-yi Khalil Maleki*, second edition.

10 See *Asnad-i Nihzat*, various volumes.

11 See the leaflets signed by Dehkhuda, Mu'azzami, Saleh, Zanjani and others which demanded the restoration of the people's 'democratic right (*haqq-i melli*)' to vote freely in the elections, in *Asnad-i Nihzat*, vol. 2, pp. 707–13.

12 A list for Tehran was circulated by hand. The candidates were Razavi, Mu'azzami, Saleh, Shaigan, Hasibi, Angaji, Nariman, Sanjaby, Jalali-Musavi, Parsa, Akhgar, and Zirakzadeh. See *ibid.*, p. 713.

13 40 per cent of the shares of the new company went to American oil companies, 40 per cent to BP, 14 per cent to Shell, and 6 per cent to the French Oil Company.

14 See Katouzian, *Khatirat-i Siyasi Khalil Maleki*.

15 *Asnad-i Nihzat*, vol. 2, pp. 466 and 471.

16 See Nijati, *Junbish-i Melli Shudan*, pp. 463–7.

17 See Mehdi Bazargan, *Mudafi'at* (containing the text of his defence speech in the military court, 1964) (Paris: Intisharat-i Mudarris, 1971), pp. 106–7.

18 See Qarani's interview with *Umid-i Iran*, 30 April 1979.

19 See Katouzian, *Khatirat-i Siyasi-yi Khalil Maleki* and *Political Economy*.

20 For a detailed account and statistical analysis of the state's receipts and expenditures during this period, see Katouzian, *Political Economy*, chapter 10.

21 See 'Tashkil-i Jameh'eh-yi Susialistha-yi Iran ra Mitavan Murid-i Mutali'eh va Iqdam Qarar Dad', *Nabard-i Zindigi*, vol. 1, no. 10, May 1956, pp. 1–15.

22 See *Manshur-i Jami'eh-yi Susialistha-yi Nihzat-i Melli-yi Iran*, Tehran, September 1961.

23 For a lengthy analysis and appraisal of the political situation and the tasks of the opposition, see Khalil Maleki's (unsigned) article, 'Imruz Cheh Bayad Kard', *Ilm va Zindigi*, new series, no. 9, July 1960.

24 See, for example, the public statement and analysis on these very questions issued by the Socialist League (and signed by all individual members of its executive committee) in October 1960.

25 For an extensive account of these activities, see Chehabi, *Iranian Politics and Religious Modernism*, vol. 2.

26 In the end, there was a general revolt of student leaders (including most of the Front's own activists), and the Committee of the Students of the University of Tehran turned its guns against the Front's leadership. See chapter 16.

27 See further Bazargan, *Mudafi'at*.

28 The campus was entirely deserted and normal access to it was not possible except with permission from SAVAK.

29 This account of the 1961 students' sit-in is based on my own personal experience of the events. Other witnesses whom I have consulted include Manuchehr Rassa (now a consultant radiologist in England), Houshang Sayyahpour (now a consultant anaesthetist in Austria), and Abbas Aqilizadeh (now a businessman in Germany). Parviz Sanjaby is a specialist doctor of medicine in Illinois, USA.

16   Failure of the Second National Front

1 See Musaddiq's letter of 30 April 1964 to the central council of the National Front and their reply of 2 May, in Musaddiq, *Mukatibat-i Musaddiq*, vol. 10 (Paris: Intisharat-i Musaddiq, 1965).

2 See Katouzian, *Political Economy*, chapter 11, and *Khatirat-i Siyasti-yi Khalil Maleki*, Introduction.

3 Earlier, the Front had been allowed to rent a large derelict house (141 Fakhr-abad Street) for occasional public meetings. But thugs and hirelings sent by Fathullah Furud (the Mayor of Tehran appointed by the shah) had broken up its third and last meeting about three months before.

4 The day before the meeting, Musaddiq's wife had indignantly told a hapless Sanjaby on the telephone that they should 'leave this old man in peace', although he had had no role at all in spreading the rumours.

5 See H. Katouzian, 'The Agrarian Question in Iran', in A. K. Ghose (ed.), *Agrarian Reform in Contemporary Developing Countries* (London: Croom Helm, 1983).
   In a personal conversation (in June 1961) with a Socialist League member over the land reform issue. Saleh finally threw up his hands and said that if they offered a land reform programme 'the religious leaders (*akhundha*) would turn against us'. See Katouzian, *Khatirat-i Siyasi-yi Khalil Maleki*.

6 But the same grassroots were to regret their attitude immediately after the fall of Amini's government.

7 See Katouzian, *Khatirat-i Siyasi-yi Khalil Maleki*.

8 See Bazargan, *Mudafi'at*, p. 169, and Maleki's letter of March 1963 to Musaddiq in *Khatirat-i Siyasi Khalil Maleki*.

9 See *Kayhan*, 22 January 1962, Bazargan, *Mudafi'at* (p. 167), and Ali Akbar Siyasi, *Guzarish-i Yek Zindigi* (London: Siyasi, 1988), pp. 285–6.

10 This claim appeared in *Ba-tafsir va Bi-tafsir* (a Freedom Movement publication) a couple of months after the event, and has also been cited by Chehabi in *Iranian Politics and Religious Modernism*. The Socialist League made the

same allegations in an analysis of the incident sent to the League of Iranian Socialists in Europe immediately after the catastrophe.

11 For the full text, see *Susialism* (published by the League of Iranian Socialists in Europe), November 1962. For extensive extracts see Katouzian, *Khatirat-i Siyasi-yi Khalil Maleki*, pp. 137–49.

12 Information supplied by Richard Cottam.

13 See Katouzian, *Political Economy*, chapter 11.

14 *Khatt-i Asli-yi Jebheh-yi Melli*, Tehran, October 1962.

15 This was reported in a long assessment of the Front's record sent by the Socialist League (and signed by Manuchehr Safa) to the League of Iranian Socialists in Europe in August 1963.

16 I am grateful to Houshang Kishavarz-i Sadr (himself a delegate at the congress) for putting a copy of this programme at my disposal.

17 *Mukatibat-i Musaddiq*, vol. 10, pp. 1–3.

18 See Musaddiq's letter to the Organizations of the National Front in Europe, 23 March 1964, *ibid.*, p. 12.

19 For a full documentation of these developments, see Ali Davani, *Nihzat-i Ruhaniyun-i Iran*, vol. 2 (Tehran: Bunyad-i Farhangi-yi Imam Reza, 1982).

20 The article – entitled 'Who Bears the Responsibility for the Bloodbath of June 1963' – was written a few days after the riots and was circulated by hand in Europe and Iran. I hold a copy of the handwritten material.

17   Musaddiq and the Third National Front

1 Katouzian, *Khatirat-i Siyasi-yi Khalil Maleki*, p. 464.

2 *Ibid.*, p. 465.

3 *Ibid.*, p. 474.

4 *Ibid.*, p. 476.

5 *Ibid.*

6 *Ibid.*, pp. 468–9. 'Their betrayals' is an allusion to the 21 January 1962 plot.

7 See the recollections of Dr Mehdi Azar in *Iran-i Azad*, no. 54, July 1988.

8 Information supplied by Sururi, and Najm (who was in regular contact with the Front's leaders at the time).

9 The photograph, together with the inscription, has been reproduced in Bazargan, *Mudafi'at*.

10 Enayat told the story of his delivery of the photograph (though he knew nothing about the background to it) in a conversation in London with Hamid Enayat, Parviz Nikkhah and the present author in July 1963.

11 See *Mukatibat-i Musaddiq*, vol. 10.

12 *Ibid.*, pp. 4–5.

13 For the documents, see *ibid.*, pp. 124–5.

14 See the report of these meetings sent to Shaigan and the National Front organizations abroad, in *ibid.*, pp. 128–9. In fact, Saleh's words were '*sabr va intizar*' – 'wait and see'.

15 *Ibid.*, p. 131.

16 *Ibid.*, p. 8.

17 See *ibid.*, pp. 10–13.
18 *Ibid.*, p. 12.
19 *Ibid.*, pp. 20–35.
20 *Ibid.*, p. 26.
21 Cf. the Leninist principle of 'democratic centralism'.
22 *Mukatibat*, vol. 10, pp. 34–5.
23 *Ibid.*, pp. 37–8.
24 *Ibid.*, p. 41. He was ridiculing the super-polite style of the council's way of addressing himself in their letters, not just as 'your excellency' but as 'his excellency'.
25 *Ibid.*, pp. 43–9. The letter's date is 2 April 1964.
26 *Ibid.*, pp. 43–63.
27 *Ibid.*, p. 64.
28 The latter documents are not publicly available, though they have been cited as part of the enclosures. Musaddiq's letter was dated 19 May 1964.
29 *Mukatibat*, vol. 10, pp. 69–73.
30 *Ibid.*, p. 68.
31 *Ibid*, pp. 74–6.
32 See Musaddiq's letter of 19 July 1964, *ibid.*, p. 84.
33 See his letter of 23 June 1964, *ibid.*
34 See the text of the handwritten letter reproduced in *Jebheh*, no. 83, July 1985.
35 See his letter of 21 July 1964 to the National Front's European Organizations, *Mukatibat*, vol. 10, p. 76.
36 See his letter of 3 January 1965, to the Front's Organizations in Europe, *ibid.*, p. 88.
37 I hold a copy of this letter, and it has been published in parts in *Khatirat-i Siyasi-yi Khalil Maleki* (second edition), Appendix.
38 See *ibid.*, Introduction.
39 See Katouzian, *Political Economy*, chapters 17 and 18.
40 See *Parkhash*, 20 June 1979, for the full handwritten copy.
41 See *Mukatibat*, vol. 10, p. 195.
42 The letter is dated 10 January 1967. See *ibid.*, p. 196.
43 I hold a copy of this letter, and it has been published in part in *Khatirat-i Siyasi-yi Khalil Maleki* (second edition), Appendix.
44 For a more detailed discussion of the causes as well as the process of the revolution, see Katouzian, *Political Economy*.

18   The Movement and the Man

1 See further, Katouzian, *Political Economy*, chapters 4 and 5.
2 See *ibid*, chapter 5.
3 See, for example, Kirmani, *Tarikh-i Bidari*, vol. 1.
4 For a detailed and documented discussion of these terms and concepts, see H. Katouzian, 'Yad-dashti darbareh-yi Mellat, Melli, Melli-gara, va nasion-alism', *Fasl-i Kitab*, 2 and 3, summer and autumn 1988, and *Khatirat-i Siyasi-yi Khalil Melleki*, second edition, Appendix to Introduction.

5 See H. Katouzian, 'Iranianism v Romantic Nationalism in Iran: Problems of Politics and Literature under Reza Shah' in Paul Luft (ed.), *Literature and Society in Iran between the Two World Wars* (forthcoming).

6 See his *Memoirs*.

7 See *Memoirs* and Buzurgmehr, *Taqrirat*.

8 *Memoirs*.

9 *Memoirs*.

10 The handwritten letter has been reproduced in *Jebheh*, 83, 21 July 1985.

11 See *Memoirs*, and Buzurgmehr, *Taqrirat*.

12 *Ibid*.

13 In fact it had been the Prince Regent, trying to avenge himself on Musaddiq for having cut his state salary by a half when he was finance minister. See *Memoirs*.

14 See his letter in *Mukatibat*, vol. 10, pp. 113–14; and Roy Mottahedeh, *The Mantle of the Prophet* (London: Chatto & Windus, 1986).

15 See Buzurgmehr, *Taqrirat*.

16 Sanjaby, Harvard Oral History interview.

17 See Makki, *Musaddiq va Nutqha*.

18 See 'Khalil Maleki va Mas'aleh-yi Adam-i Ghair-i Adi', in Katouzian and Pichdad, *Yadnamehyi Khalil Maleki*.

19 See *Niru-yi Sevvum* and *Ilm va Zindigi*, various issues.

Index

Munazzah, Brigadier, 183–4
Munshizadeh, Dr Davud, 89
Muqaddam-Maragheh'i, Rahmatullah, 230
Musaddiq, Ahmad (son), 2
  Dr Gholam-Hossein (son), 2, 34, 183, 252
  Khadijeh (daughter), 2, 34
Musaddiq, Dr Mohammad, 1–38, 51–61, 69, 72–4, 76–7, 88, 91–4, 113–207, 215–16, 237, 239–52, 262–7
  and Azerbaijan crisis, 58–9
  and Baqa'i, 98–9, 162–70, 175, 176, 178
  and corruption, 12–13, 55–6
  and economy, 145–55
  and electoral reform, 26–7, 129–30
  and Freemasonry, 4
  and Islam, 10–11, 12, 25, 28, 199, 270n12
  and Kashani, 157, 160, 165–71 *passim*, 173–5, 178, 183
  and Maleki, 98, 105–8, 240–2
  and modernization, 10–12, 27–9, 262
  and Mohammad Reza Shah, 54, 82–3, 113–15, 119, 122–3, 125, 172, 178–83 *passim*, 195, 198, 200, 202, 262, 264
  and National Front, 240–51
  and oil, 69, 90, 93–4, 106, 116–19, 137–45, 155, 215, 262, 263, 265–6
  and religious establishment, 156–7, 161–2, 170–3 *passim*
  and Reza Shah, 21, 23–5 *passim*, 27, 30, 262, 263
  early days, 1–3
  Governorships, Azerbaijan, 19–21, 262, 263; Fars, 15–16, 18
  health, 7, 20, 33, 251–2, 262–5 *passim*
  legal training, 6–7, 9–11, 13–14; writings, 9–11, 26–8
  Majlis deputy, 4–6, 20–5, 27–30, 51–61, 127, 263
  Minister, Finance, 12–13, 19, 263; Foreign, 20–1, 28; Justice, 14

passive balance policy, 56–61
political objectives, 51–5
premierships, 93–4, 106–8, 112–55, 177–93, 263–4, 266–7
relations with Britain, 20, 90, 93–4, 106, 116–19, 137–45, 265–6 *see also* oil; with Soviet Union, 20, 56–60, 262
trials, 146, 194–208
Musavat, Sayyed Mohammad Reza, 9
Musavvar-Rahmani, Ghulamreza, ix, 84, 131
Mushar, Yusif, 73, 120, 127, 201
Mushir al-Dawleh, 14, 19–21 *passim*, 23, 28, 30, 32, 33, 46, 257
Muslim Brotherhood, 160
Mustashar al-Dawleh, 5
Mustawfi al-Mamalik, Mirza Hasan, 8, 12, 20, 23, 24, 27, 28, 30, 33, 43, 56, 257
Mustawfi al-Mamalik, Mirza Yusif, 1
Mu'tamin al-Mulk, 23, 30, 33, 46, 257
Muvarrikh al-Dawleh, 124
Muzaffar al-Din Shah, 4
Muzayyeni, Brigadier, 183–4

Nabard-i Zindigi, 211
Nadirpur, Nadir, 98
Nashriyeh Ta'limati, 85
Najm al-Mulk, Abulqasim, 47, 242
Najm al-Saltaneh (mother), 1–2, 7, 12
Nakhshab, Mohammad, 87, 209, 229
Naqdi, General, 197
Nariman, Mahmud, 72–4 *passim*, 76, 77, 113, 120, 192, 208
Nasir Khan, 210
Nasiri, Colonel, 189, 196
Nasir al-Din Shah, 2, 3
Nasser, President Gamal Abdul, 138
National Front, 43, 50, 61, 71–7, 80, 81, 85, 88–92 *passim*, 105, 113, 120, 160, 165, 228
  Second, 218–42, 253, 254
  Third, 220, 249–51, 253
  Fourth, 254
  Organizations in Europe, 244, 248
National Iranian Oil Co., 116, 140, 150, 153, 164, 213, 259